MICROSOFT®
SHAREPOINT® 2010
QuickSteps®

MARTY MATTHEWS

NANCY BUCHANAN

New York Chicago San Francisco
Lisbon London Madrid Mexico City
Milan New Delhi San Juan
Seoul Singapore Sydney Toronto

The McGraw·Hill Companies

Library of Congress Cataloging-in-Publication Data

Matthews, Martin S.
  Microsoft Sharepoint 2010 Quicksteps / Marty Matthews,
Nancy Buchanan.
      p. cm.
  Includes index.
  ISBN 978-0-07-174193-4 (alk. paper)
1. Microsoft SharePoint (Electronic resource)   2. Intranets
(Computer networks)   3. Web servers.   I. Buchanan, Nancy.   II. Title.
TK5105.875.16M38 2010
006.7—dc22
                                                              2010027633

McGraw-Hill books are available at special quantity discounts to use
as premiums and sales promotions, or for use in corporate training
programs. To contact a representative, please e-mail us at bulksales@
mcgraw-hill.com.

All trademarks or copyrights mentioned herein are the
possession of their respective owners and McGraw-Hill makes
no claim of ownership by the mention of products that contain
these marks.

Information has been obtained by McGraw-Hill from sources
believed to be reliable. However, because of the possibility of
human or mechanical error by our sources, McGraw-Hill, or
others, McGraw-Hill does not guarantee the accuracy, adequacy,
or completeness of any information and is not responsible for any
errors or omissions or the results obtained from the use of such
information.

MICROSOFT® SHAREPOINT® 2010 QUICKSTEPS®

234567890   QVS   109876543

ISBN   978-0-07-174193-4
MHID   0-07-174193-3

SPONSORING EDITOR / Roger Stewart

EDITORIAL SUPERVISOR / Patty Mon

PROJECT MANAGER / Rajni Pisharody, Glyph International

ACQUISITIONS COORDINATOR / Joya Anthony

TECHNICAL EDITOR / Nancy Buchanan

COPY EDITOR / Lisa McCoy

PROOFREADER / Carol Shields

INDEXER / Karin Arrigoni

PRODUCTION SUPERVISOR / Jean Bodeaux

COMPOSITION / Glyph International

ILLUSTRATION / Glyph International

ART DIRECTOR, COVER / Jeff Weeks

COVER DESIGNER / Pattie Lee

SERIES CREATORS / Marty and Carole Matthews

SERIES DESIGN / Bailey Cunningham

To the New SharePoint User:

When you see SharePoint and are told you should use it, the learning task may look insurmountable, yet the tool you have in front of you is extremely powerful and can be highly valuable to you when you learn to harness it. Whether you plan to read this book cover to cover or to look up tasks as you face them, it is our hope and intention that this book goes a long way to help you get the most from SharePoint every day.

—Marty and Nancy

Contents at a Glance

Contents

7

8

Acknowledgments

This book is a team effort of truly talented people. Among them are:

Joya Anthony, acquisitions coordinator, tracked all the parts of the book, making sure they all went where they were supposed to go. Thanks, Joya!

Lisa McCoy, copy editor, added greatly to the readability and understandability of the book while always being a joy to work with. Thanks, Lisa!

Patty Mon and **Rajni Pisharody**, project editors, greased the wheels and straightened the track to make a very smooth production process. Thanks, Patty and Rajni!

Roger Stewart, sponsoring editor, believed in us enough to sell the series, and continues to stand behind us as we exceed 40 titles. Thanks, Roger!

Introduction

Microsoft SharePoint 2010 QuickSteps is aimed at new or inexperienced SharePoint users with the objective of helping them turn SharePoint into a powerful tool for accomplishing their and their group's work. The book does not assume any knowledge of SharePoint and takes the reader from this novice position to one of a comfortable journeyman user able to successfully use SharePoint on a day-to-day basis.

QuickSteps books are recipe books for computer users. They answer the question "How do I…" by providing a quick set of steps to accomplish the most common tasks with particular software.

The sets of steps are the central focus of the book. QuickSteps sidebars show how to quickly perform many small functions or tasks that support the primary functions. QuickFacts sidebars supply information that you need to know about a subject. Notes, Tips, and Cautions augment the steps and are presented in a separate column so as not to interrupt the flow of the steps. The introductions are minimal, and numerous illustrations and figures, many with callouts, support the steps.

This book is organized by elements within SharePoint, like lists and libraries, or components of the system, like Designer and Workspace. These divisions are further segmented into the tasks needed to use an element or component. The elements or components form chapters. Each task, or "How To," contains the steps needed for utilizing the element or component, along with the relevant Notes, Tips, Cautions, and screenshots. You can easily find the tasks you need through:

- The table of contents, which lists the elements or components (chapters) and tasks in the order they are presented

- A How To list of tasks on the opening page of each chapter

- The index, which provides an alphabetical list of the terms that are used to describe the elements, components, and tasks

- Color-coded tabs for each chapter, with an index to the tabs in the Contents at a Glance section (just before the table of contents)

Conventions Used in this Book

Microsoft SharePoint 2010 QuickSteps uses several conventions designed to make the book easier for you to follow:

- A ⊙ in the table of contents and in the How To list in each chapter references a QuickSteps sidebar in a chapter, and a ⊘ references a QuickFacts sidebar.

- **Bold type** is used for words or objects on the screen that you are to do something with—for example, "click **Start** and click **Computer**."

- *Italic type* is used for a word or phrase that is being defined or otherwise deserves special emphasis.

- <u>Underlined type</u> is used for text that you are to type from the keyboard.

- SMALL CAPITAL LETTERS are used for keys on the keyboard, such as **ENTER** and **SHIFT**.

- When you are expected to enter a command, you are told to press the key(s). If you are to enter text or numbers, you are told to type them.

How to...

- *Review What SharePoint Provides*
- *Managing Information with SharePoint*
- *Consider the Benefits of SharePoint*
- *Understand the SharePoint Suite of Services*
- *Understanding SharePoint Foundation and SharePoint Server*
- *Examine the SharePoint Parts*

Chapter 1
Exploring SharePoint 2010

Quite possibly you are like a lot of other people today who, upon joining an organization, are shown SharePoint running on a monitor and told to "use it!" Or an edict comes down that your organization has installed SharePoint and you are expected to use it. The purpose of this book is to help you do that. If you have some choice in the matter, your first question might be, "Why should I?" In any case, you may well ask, "What is SharePoint and what can it do for me and for my organization?" In this chapter we'll answer both of those questions, as well as look at what makes up a SharePoint 2010 Web site, and SharePoint itself.

What Is SharePoint?

SharePoint is a suite of services that enables a team of information workers to easily collaborate and work together better by facilitating the development,

NOTE

This book applies equally to SharePoint users accessing a SharePoint site running on their organization's servers, as well as those users of Hosted SharePoint accessing a site running on servers belonging to an Internet hosting company. With Hosted SharePoint, the terms used here "SharePoint Administrator" and "IT professional" may require translation to different terms, but the functions should be clear.

TIP

There is an important difference between an Internet or intranet Web site and a SharePoint site. A Web site has a Web master who is responsible for all the content (although it may be created by others). In a SharePoint site, all organization members are responsible for updating the site's content, often without a single person in charge of it.

sharing, and management of information, and the tracking and management of business processes.

The potential benefits of SharePoint include improved team effectiveness, rapid response to changing situations, better content management, enhanced control of tasks, broader dissemination of information, reduction in costs, and faster accomplishment of objectives.

Review What SharePoint Provides

SharePoint's central focus is *collaboration*, people working together to achieve a common objective. SharePoint's objective is to improve the effectiveness and performance of those people by providing:

- An easy and familiar environment
- An easy-to-use, customizable platform
- A central repository for information
- Tools for collaboratively creating information
- Controls for protecting information
- Means for exchanging information
- Tools for managing workflows

AN EASY AND FAMILIAR ENVIRONMENT

SharePoint uses a Web browser, such as Internet Explorer, to look at its sites and pages, the same Web browser that is used with the Internet or an intranet. A SharePoint site and page look similar to an Internet Web page, but in most cases is only viewable by people on your organization's network. It has many of the same elements and tools, including links, menus, and content. At this point, very few people have not used the Internet or are unfamiliar with navigating by clicking a link or using a menu. Figure 1-1 shows the Home page for a new SharePoint team site as displayed with Internet Explorer. You'll see many common elements that are also used on a Web page, including the ability to click a link, such as "Discussions" shown in the figure.

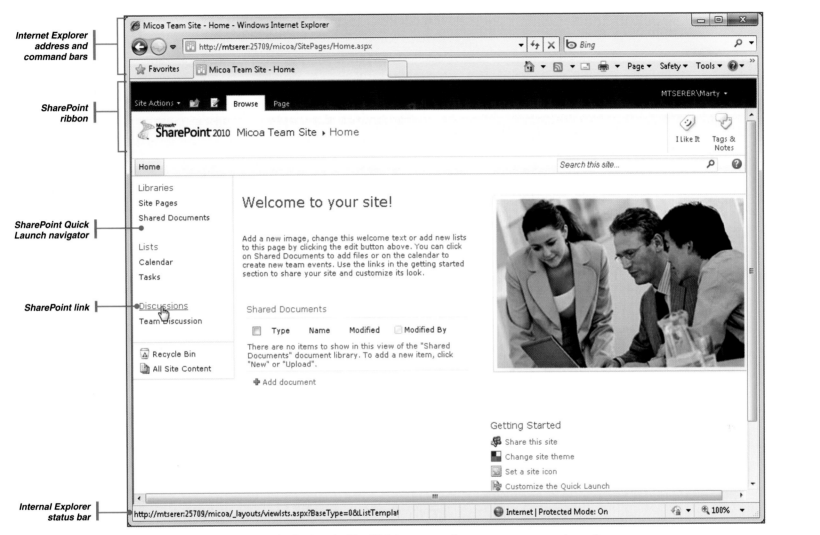

Internet Explorer
address and
command bars

SharePoint
ribbon

SharePoint Quick
Launch navigator

SharePoint link

Internal Explorer
status bar

Figure 1-1: *A SharePoint page is displayed with a Web browser and uses many common elements.*

A CENTRAL REPOSITORY FOR INFORMATION

A SharePoint site for a team, project, or other organization can be the single location where all information related to the organization and its work is stored. If that is done, then:

- All members of the organization with the appropriate permission can access the information
- The information will be easier to search and locate
- It will be easier to find information on the same topic because it is all in the same place
- It will be easier to control both the access and the currency of the information
- Outdated or no longer useful information can be more easily discarded

All types of information should be considered for storing in SharePoint, including:

- Electronic documents, such as manuals, proposals, white papers, letters, plans, budgets, financial reports, scripts, presentations, contracts, legal pleadings and decisions, bills and invoices, designs, and bills of materials
- Pictures, including photographs, drawings, diagrams, logos, icons, and other digital images
- E-mail messages
- Contact lists
- Calendar schedules, appointments, events, and meetings
- Presentations and spreadsheets

A READY-TO-USE, CUSTOMIZABLE PLATFORM

SharePoint, as it is initially installed, is immediately ready for you to use with little more than naming the site. In the site shown in Figure 1-1, it was only given a name, yet in that site, right out of the box, you can immediately add shared documents, site assets, site pages, announcements, calendar events, links, tasks, discussions, and surveys, as you see in Figure 1-2, which shows all site content.

SharePoint also allows for and provides the means to make many levels of changes, such as:

- Changing the title, introductory paragraph, and other text
- Adding new libraries, lists, and discussions
- Changing themes and colors

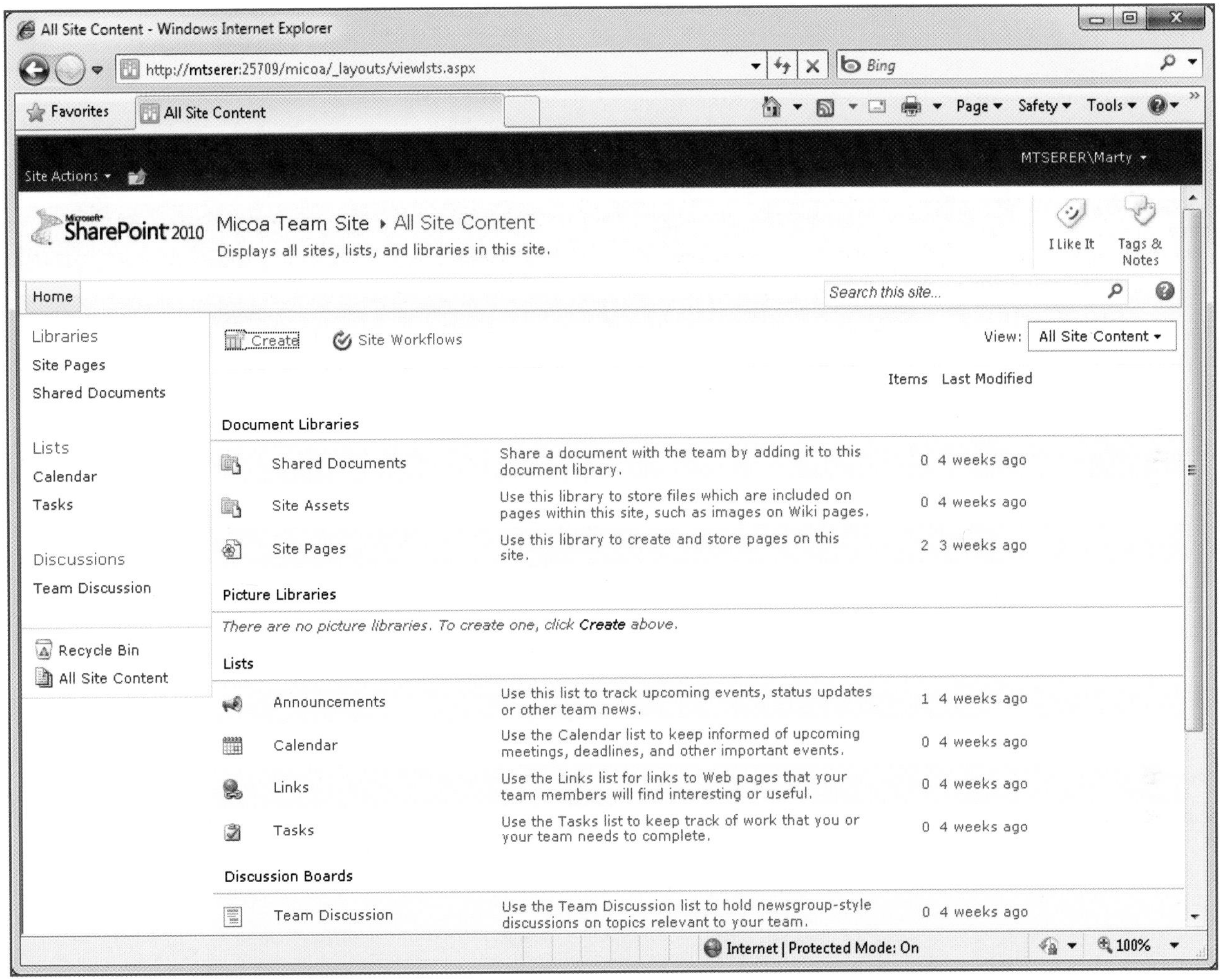

Figure 1-2: *Without any changes, SharePoint immediately allows you to add a number of documents and list items to a site.*

- Adding pictures and other artistic elements
- Building or modifying the site in SharePoint Designer

Figure 1-3 shows the same SharePoint site as Figure 1-1, but with a number of easy changes and additions, listed on the figure.

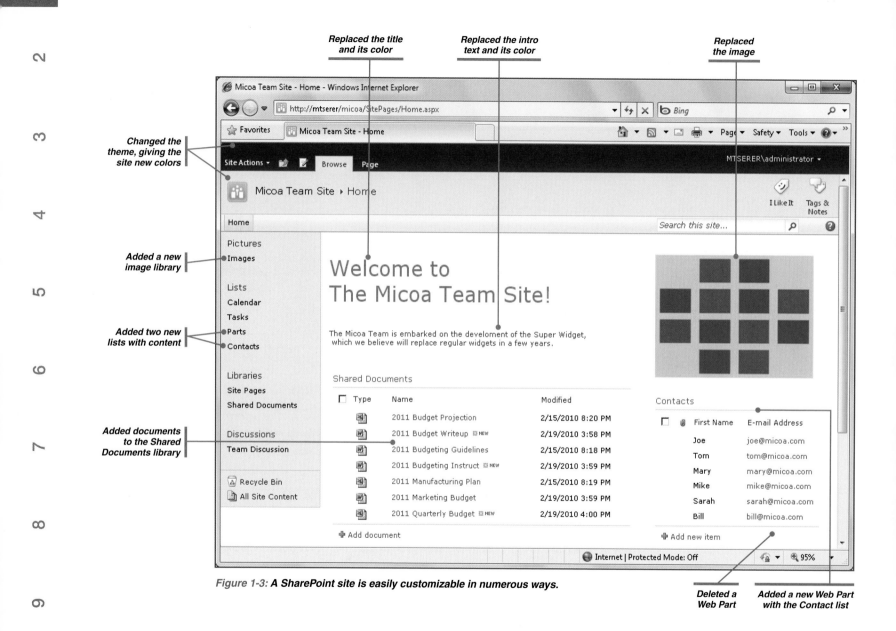

Replaced the title and its color

Replaced the intro text and its color

Replaced the image

Changed the theme, giving the site new colors

Added a new image library

Added two new lists with content

Added documents to the Shared Documents library

Deleted a Web Part

Added a new Web Part with the Contact list

Figure 1-3: *A SharePoint site is easily customizable in numerous ways.*

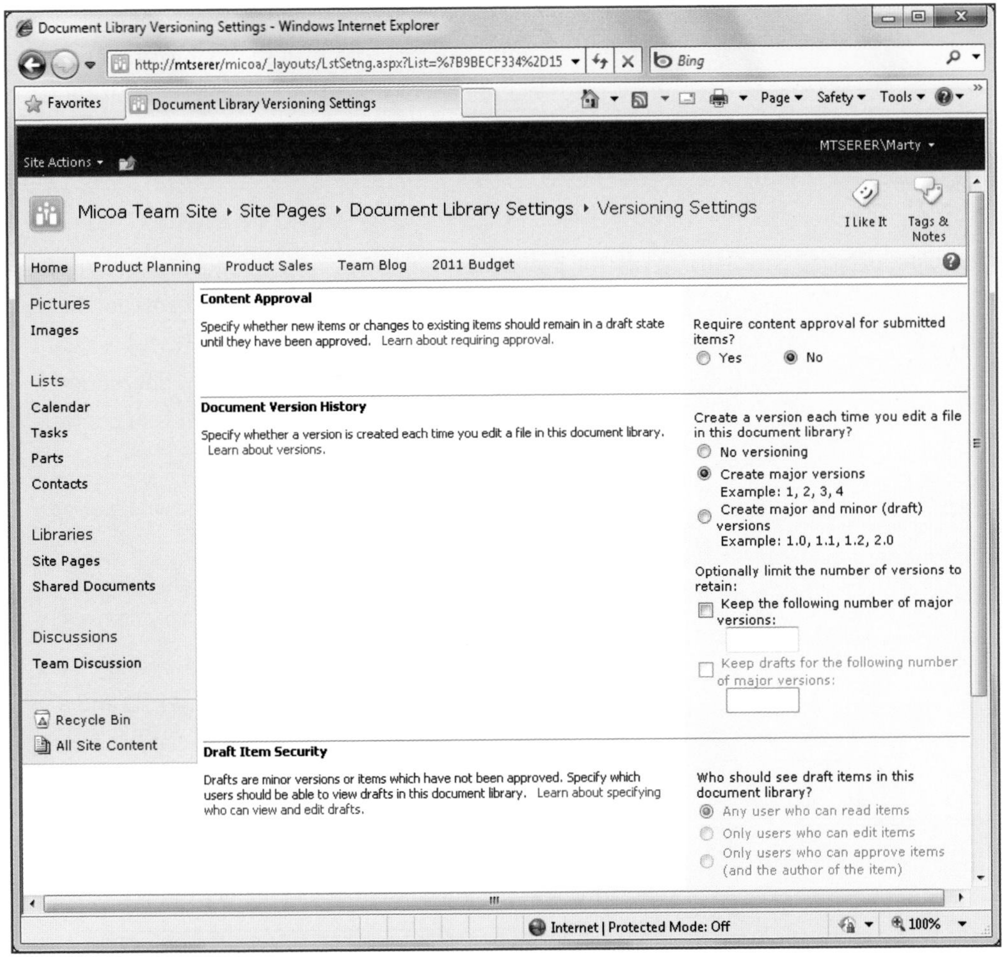

Figure 1-4: *SharePoint provides several ways of controlling the creating and changing of documents.*

TOOLS FOR COLLABORATIVELY WORKING WITH INFORMATION

Collaboration occurs in SharePoint in at least two ways. Simply sharing information and making it easily available is in itself a collaborative process. The other way, of course, is to have multiple people working on the same item. Once you have added documents to your SharePoint site, anybody with the appropriate permissions may open it and work on it. This includes creators, contributors, reviewers, and approvers. With a number of people working on a document, it may be become important to manage the evolution of the document. In Word, you can turn on Track Changes to see the changes made by everybody, but SharePoint also provides several additional versioning controls (see Figure 1-4), including content approval and version history.

A good example of SharePoint collaboration that points out its benefits is the situation where several people need to review a document, as shown in Figure 1-5. Without SharePoint, you would e-mail a copy of the document to each of the reviewers; they, in turn, would send you back their comments, and you would incorporate the comments you wanted in the master document. With SharePoint, you write or post the Microsoft Word document on SharePoint, notifying your reviewers it is there. The reviewers make their comments and changes directly in the document using Word's Track Changes as they normally would, but because the document is stored on SharePoint,

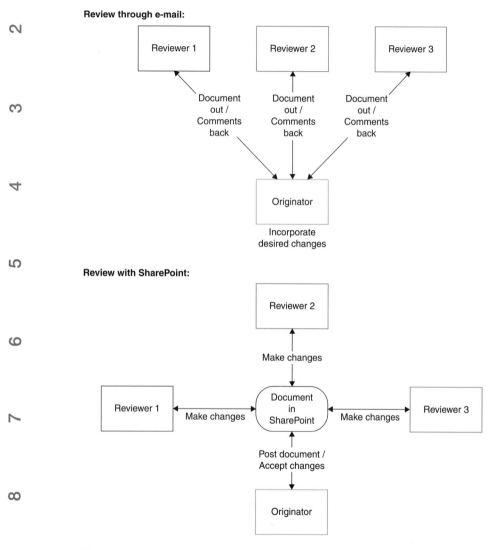

Review through e-mail:

Reviewer 1 → Document out / Comments back

Reviewer 2 → Document out / Comments back

Reviewer 3 → Document out / Comments back

Originator

Incorporate desired changes

Review with SharePoint:

Reviewer 2 — Make changes

Reviewer 1 — Make changes — Document in SharePoint — Make changes — Reviewer 3

Post document / Accept changes

Originator

Figure 1-5: **With a Word document stored on a SharePoint site, reviewers see each other's changes without additional e-mail and the originator has less work.**

all reviewers can see each other's work. When the review process is completed, you look over the changes that have been made and accept or reject them. During this process, you can enable versioning and keep track of who changed what at every step.

CONTROLS FOR PROTECTING INFORMATION

With the potential for many people to use a SharePoint site, and with the possibility of very sensitive information being stored on the site, very good controls on who sees what information and how it is used are necessary. SharePoint, combined with Windows, provides those kinds of controls through two structures (see Figure 1-6):

- The *authentication* **in Windows** of people who will be using SharePoint

- The *authorization* **in SharePoint** of authenticated people, granting them permission to work with SharePoint information

When a user signs on to a computer or a network, they are authenticated, usually by Windows with a user ID and a password, and then assigned to groups that can later be referenced by SharePoint. Examples of groups are Users, Contributors, Approvers, Administrators, and so on. The groups refer to the types of activities that the user normally performs and the permission level they warrant.

Windows Security ✕

Connecting to MTSerer.

User name
Password
Domain: WIN7
☐ Remember my credentials

OK   Cancel

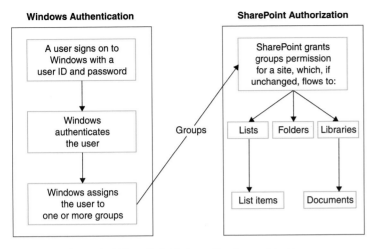

Windows Authentication

A user signs on to Windows with a user ID and password

↓

Windows authenticates the user

↓

Windows assigns the user to one or more groups

Groups →

SharePoint Authorization

SharePoint grants groups permission for a site, which, if unchanged, flows to:

Lists · Folders · Libraries

List items · Documents

Figure 1-6: Control of SharePoint information is provided by a combination of Windows authentication and SharePoint authorization.

NOTE

Many organizations use Microsoft Active Directory to grant users rights to their organization's corporate network. Instead of using a separate user name and password to access your SharePoint site, you can use your corporate network user name and password to access your SharePoint site, as long as your account is added to one of the groups on your SharePoint site.

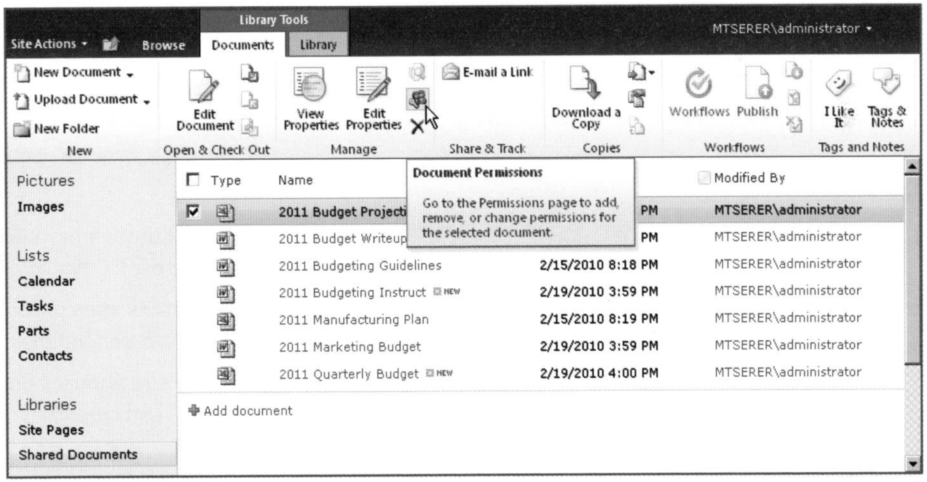

Within SharePoint, permissions are granted to groups specifying what they can do. Permissions apply to the use of:

- Sites
- Lists
- Libraries
- Folders
- List items
- Documents

Initially, the same level of permission is propagated through all elements by *inheritance*, but changes can be made for each element. For example, if a group has permission to enter and read information on a site, they initially also have permission to read all lists, list items, libraries, documents, and folders on the site. A SharePoint site administrator, however, can change the permissions for any element (see Figure 1-7), but if a change is made to, say, a library, then that change will be inherited by all the documents in the library, unless individual documents are changed.

Figure 1-7: Permissions can be set or changed for sites, lists, libraries, list items, documents, and folders.

MEANS FOR EXCHANGING INFORMATION

Simply having a single place to put all the information that relates to an organization where it can be easily searched and found is a good start at exchanging information, but SharePoint doesn't stop there. It also provides several ways to collect, update, comment on, and exchange current information in the form of specialized sites, lists, and libraries. In addition to the standard team sites, task lists, and document libraries, some of the specialized elements include (see "Know the SharePoint Parts" toward the end of this chapter for a full discussion of sites, lists, and libraries):

- **Sites**
  - **Blog sites** are dedicated to one or more people providing their thoughts, comments, explanation, or direction on a single given subject.
  - **Meeting workspace sites** provide a place to hold all the information related to a meeting or series of meetings, including agendas, attendees, presentations, minutes, comments, and reviews.
- **Lists**
  - **Announcements** list news, status, and other information to be disseminated to everybody in the organization.
  - **Calendars** provide the means to track and update group schedules, deadlines, meetings, and events.
  - **Discussion boards** provide for linked discussions a given topic, similar to newsgroups.
  - **Surveys** allow the quick collection and graphical summation of status and opinion.
- **Libraries**
  - **Form libraries** provide easy access to and management of company forms (such as Microsoft Office InfoPath forms).
  - **Report libraries** provide a place where organizational, corporate, and competitive goals and performance can be tracked.
  - **Wiki Page libraries** provide a place where articles on subjects can be added, edited, and organized.

Most of these elements provide for information to be not only exchanged from the creator to the reader, but also to be contributed to and edited, making it a higher level of collaboration.

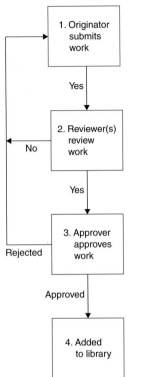

Add to Library Process

Figure 1-8: Workflows provide for the management of processes.

TOOLS FOR MANAGING WORKFLOWS

A *workflow* divides a process into steps that can be measured and reported upon to better manage the process. An example is the process of adding a new document to the library, where the originator submits their work first for review and then for approval. This can be broken into these steps (see Figure 1-8):

1. Originator submits work—Status is Yes or No

2. Reviewer(s) review work—Status is Yes or No

3. Approver approves work—Status is Approved or Rejected

4. If approved, work added to library

5. If rejected, work sent back to originator

By default, SharePoint has eight workflows that can be made available for association with a list, library, list item, or document. You can also create your own workflow with SharePoint Designer (see Chapter 8). The primary workflows available in SharePoint are:

- **Approval** workflow routes a document for approval, which can be approved, rejected, reassigned, or changes requested.

- **Collect Feedback** workflow routes a document for reviewers' comments, which are sent to the originator.

- **Collect Signatures** workflow accumulates signatures for final completion of a document.

- **Disposition Approval** workflow tracks the retention and expiration of a document to determine when to delete it.

- **Three State** workflow tracks the status of an item as being in one of three states, such as assigned, completed, and accepted.

A workflow is based upon a template that you fill out and add to a list or library, as shown in Figure 1-9. When a workflow has been associated with a list or a library, you can add its information to an element by simply clicking **Workflows** in the ribbon. That will add columns to elements containing such things as who is assigned to approve it and the due date. Workflows are discussed further in several places in this book, but particularly in Chapter 6.

TIP

Workflows make a static list into a management reporting tool by allowing the status of items to be tracked.

NOTE

Your SharePoint administrator may have to activate the workflows before you are able to associate them with a list, library, item, or document.

QUICK**FACTS**

MANAGING INFORMATION WITH SHAREPOINT

It is easy to get caught up in SharePoint's ability to produce, collect, and easily share information and not pay equal attention to its ability to both manage information and use that information to better manage an organization, yet a lot of the bottom-line value of SharePoint is in these areas.

IMPROVED INFORMATION MANAGEMENT

Information is only as good as its validity, so simply collecting information is of little value unless you can assure that it is both current and accurate. SharePoint gives an organization the ability to handle both of these through the use of permissions and workflows.

- Controlling permissions for information creators, reviewers, and approvers assures that the information is coming from the right people
- Using both review and approval workflows, the validity of information can be significantly improved.
- Using retention workflows, the "currentcy" of the information can be improved.

IMPROVED ORGANIZATION MANAGEMENT

The quality of organization management depends on many factors, but two major ones are the ability to quickly and effectively communicate within the organization, and the quality and timeliness of information with which to make decisions. In both of these areas, SharePoint provides strong support. The quality and timeliness of information are reflected in points supporting the previous section, "Improved Information Management."

Continued . . .

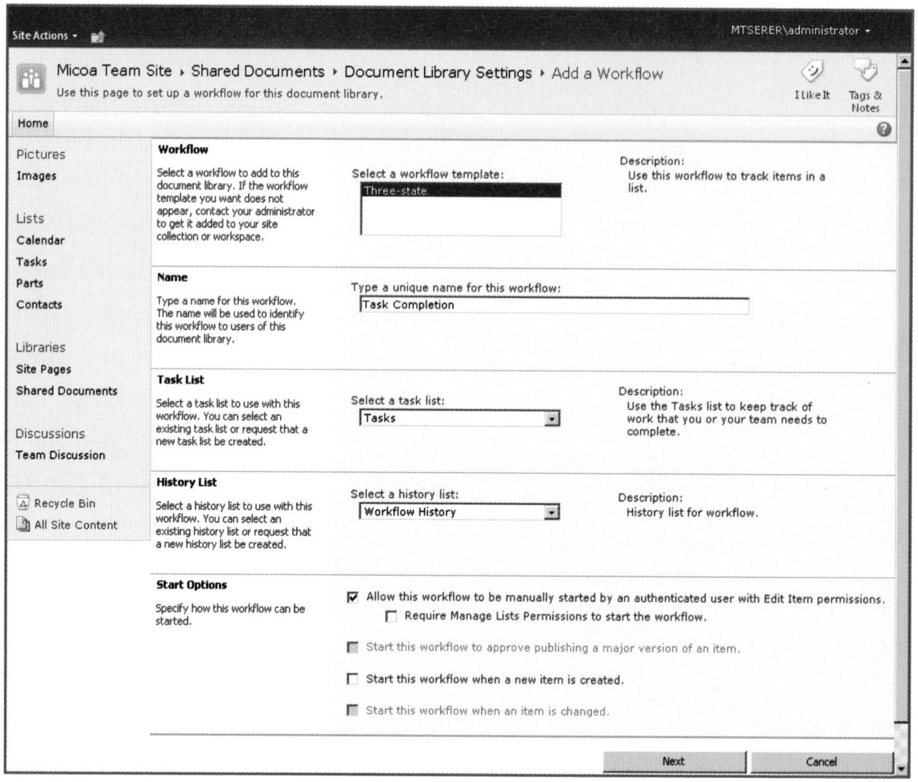

Figure 1-9: *Workflows are built using templates in which information for the workflow can be collected.*

Consider the Benefits of SharePoint

SharePoint has a number of interesting tools, but what are the potential benefits of its implementation? Here are some of the more common benefits that organizations realize:

- **Increased productivity and effectiveness** through collaboration by reducing the steps that have to be performed for a given task and the duplication of effort that would otherwise occur

- **Faster response** to a situation through improved availability of information, sophisticated search tools, shorter lines of communication, and a more efficient working environment

MANAGING INFORMATION WITH SHAREPOINT *(Continued)*

Quick and effective communications are enhanced in SharePoint by:

- Having one place that all organization members look to for information

- Having the information source be both familiar and easy to use

- Providing a wide range of communication tools in one information source, including alerts, announcements, blogs, forums, and wikis.

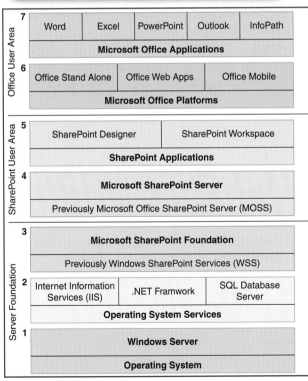

Figure 1-10: *SharePoint can be thought of as a stack of integrated services.*

- **Better use of information** through central storage, improved tagging, indexing, and comprehensive searchability, allowing easier locating and improved reusing and repurposing

- **Improved security** of information by being able to set and easily maintain policies and permissions for accessing, updating, approving, and disposing of information

- **Faster learning and lower support costs** through a common Internet browser interface and links in addition to a common command ribbon similar to Office

- **Better management** of an organization, and particularly its information, through using workflows to track status, require approval, provide alerts, identify responsibility, and comprehensive setting of permissions

- **Easier growth** through a scalable system that can go from moderate organization, such as a single team, to a large enterprise

- **Reduced costs and improved profits** through all of the previously noted benefits, making it easy for content owners to upload information to the SharePoint site themselves instead of having to rely on a Web master

It is the objective of this book to help you and your organization achieve these benefits.

What Makes Up SharePoint?

SharePoint is a suite of services produced by several programs working together to promote collaboration, improve information dissemination, and foster management within an organization. It does this with a rather simple set of components or parts that function together to provide a very powerful capability.

Understand the SharePoint Suite of Services

The initial SharePoint screen you see, and the many capabilities available from it, are the result of an integrated suite of services shown in Figure 1-10, sometimes called the "SharePoint stack." While your work and the focus of this book is contained in the top four layers, you will hear people talk about all the layers, and it is worthwhile knowing what they are even if you won't directly work with all them.

The seven layers in the SharePoint suite of services can be divided into three sections:

- **Server Foundation**, which is the bottom three layers and contains the foundation elements that are needed to support SharePoint. These include:
  - **Windows Server**, currently Windows Server 2008 SP2 or R2, is the recommended operating system for SharePoint 2010.
  - **Internet Information Services** is the web server that hosts SharePoint so it can function on an intranet, the Internet, or an extranet.
  - **.NET Framework** is a programming technology on which SharePoint is built and allows the creation within SharePoint of "Web Parts," which contain document libraries or lists, the elements that make up much of a SharePoint site. .NET Framework has a large library of ready-made elements that can simply be installed in a SharePoint site without programming.
  - **SQL Database Server** provides all the information storage and retrieval functions that are a vital part of what SharePoint does.
  - **Microsoft SharePoint Foundation**, which prior to SharePoint 2010 was called Windows SharePoint Services (WSS), provides the foundation services for SharePoint and is its interface with the operating system and the operating system services needed by SharePoint.
- **SharePoint User Area**, which is layers 4 and 5, provides the user experience with SharePoint. Only Microsoft SharePoint Server is required. The SharePoint applications are needed only if you want their services.
  - **Microsoft SharePoint Server**, which prior to SharePoint 2010 was called Microsoft Office SharePoint Server (MOSS), builds upon and enhances SharePoint Foundation to give you the fullest experience with SharePoint.
  - **Microsoft SharePoint Designer**, which in an early incarnation was Microsoft FrontPage, is a WYSIWYG (what you see is what you get) Web page creation tool that is now used to customize SharePoint sites. You can create SharePoint pages using the templates that are available in SharePoint Server, but if you want to go beyond that, you will need SharePoint Designer.
  - **Microsoft SharePoint Workspace**, which prior to SharePoint 2010 was called Microsoft Office Groove, allows the creation of shared workspaces for collaboration and access to SharePoint resources on a variety of devices, both online and offline.
- **Office User Area**, which is the top two layers, provides the Microsoft Office applications on any of three platforms, available for use from within SharePoint.

UNDERSTANDING SHAREPOINT FOUNDATION AND SHAREPOINT SERVER

The differentiation between SharePoint Foundation and SharePoint Server is not very clear, even in Microsoft literature. SharePoint Foundation is a free add-on included with or available for download to Windows Server. As mentioned elsewhere in this chapter, it serves as the interface to the operating system and operating system services, and provides a basic set of SharePoint services, including some site and list templates (see "Know the SharePoint Parts" in this chapter). SharePoint Server is a fee-based product requiring volume licensing (it is not available at retail). It requires and enhances SharePoint Foundation and passes through all of its features. SharePoint Server also extends SharePoint Foundation with additional features and capabilities, including a number of additional templates, such as a social computing site, and the ability to search data in other applications, such as SAP (business management software).

SharePoint Foundation can provide a basic SharePoint experience on its own with limited templates and capabilities. You do not have to have SharePoint Server unless you want the added features it provides. You can think of SharePoint Foundation as the free getting-started product, while SharePoint Server fills out the product. Most installations of any substance will have both Foundation and Server, and this book assumes that is what you have.

SharePoint runs on and requires that Internet Information Services (IIS), .NET Framework, and SQL Server be installed and running on the server prior to installing SharePoint.

Examine the SharePoint Parts

SharePoint, the bottom four layers in Figure 1-10, uses five major parts as the primary building blocks of all that is done in SharePoint. You add and customize these parts to create the facilities you need to conduct business, handle information, and display performance. These parts, which can be used in a number of different ways, are:

- **Sites**
- **Web Parts**
- **Lists**
- **Libraries**
- **Views**

SITES

Sites are collections of Web pages and are the medium through which everything in SharePoint is created, controlled, and viewed. You start with a site to which you add pages, and to the pages you add Web Parts, which can contain either lists or libraries. Finally, you can choose how to view the lists and libraries. The easiest way to create sites and pages is with the many templates that are available in SharePoint, as shown in Figure 1-11. Some of the site templates that are available include:

- **Blog Site** for a team or individual to post their thoughts
- **Document Workspace Site** for a team to collaborate on the creation and handling of documents
- **Group Work Site** to provide for the basic functions of a group, such as contacts, calendars, phone memos, general documents, and other lists
- **Meeting Workspace Site** available in several varieties to set up and document a meeting
- **Team Site** for a team to collaborate on projects and documents with the necessary lists and libraries.

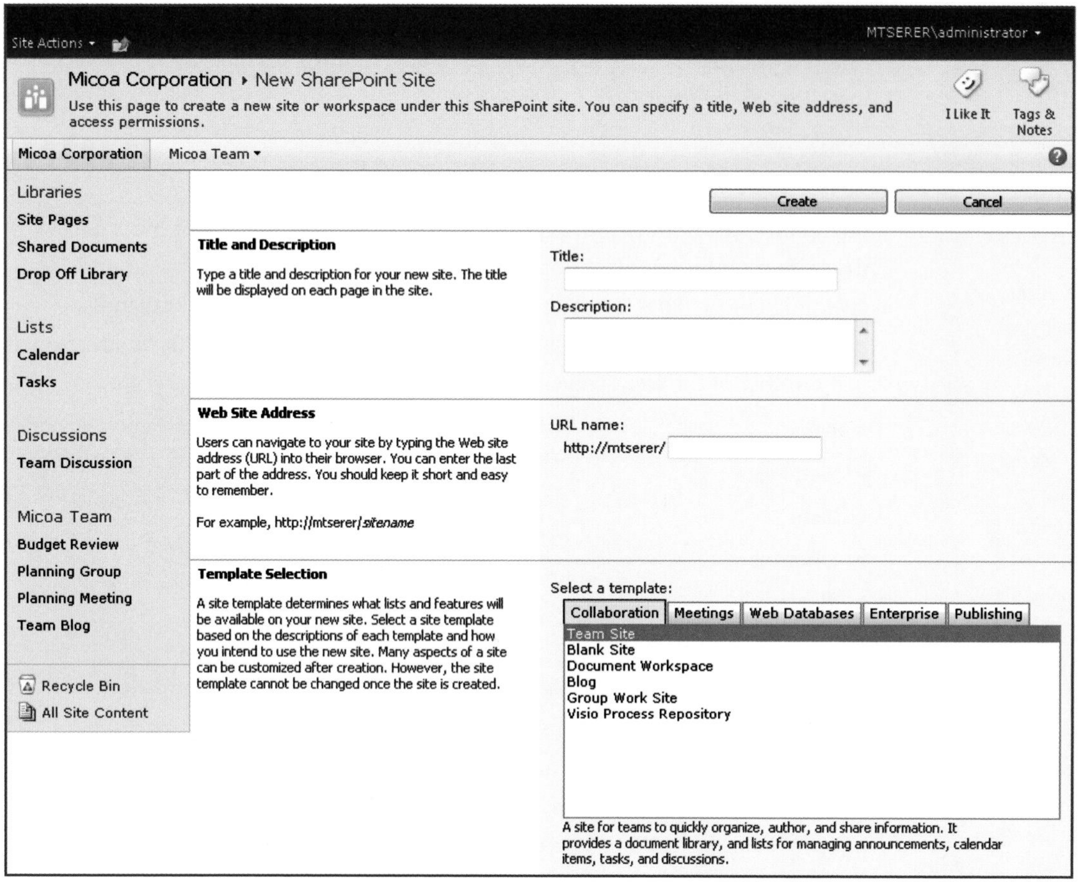

Figure 1-11: **SharePoint provides a wide variety of site templates, as well as the ability to do a lot of customization.**

Sites are discussed throughout this book, but primarily in Chapters 2 and 3.

LISTS

Lists provide for the storage, management, and sharing of information, and are the central connecting thread throughout SharePoint. A new site may automatically have one or more lists. For example, the team site template creates five lists: Announcements, Calendar, Links, Tasks, and Discussions, as shown in Figure 1-12. A SharePoint list is similar to an Excel worksheet, with rows and columns and the ability to do math in the intersecting cells (see Figure 1-13, where the Value column is the product of the cost times the quantity). Lists are created from a list template, but can be customized to your needs, most importantly by adding columns and math functions. List templates in SharePoint include:

- **Announcements** to post messages on the Home page
- **Calendar** for meetings and other events
- **Contacts** for shared names, e-mail addresses, and phone numbers
- **Custom** for a blank list to which you can add columns
- **Discussions** for threaded comments on a subject, as used in a newsgroup

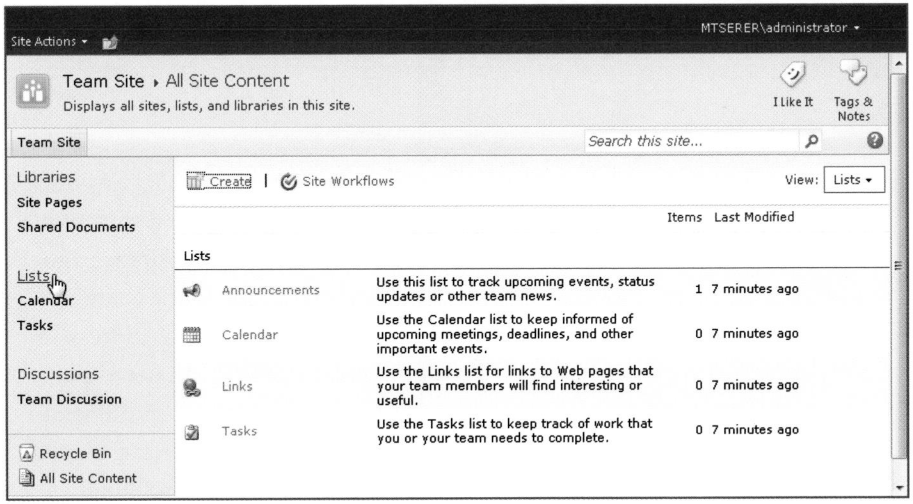

Figure 1-12: *Many site templates automatically create several lists.*

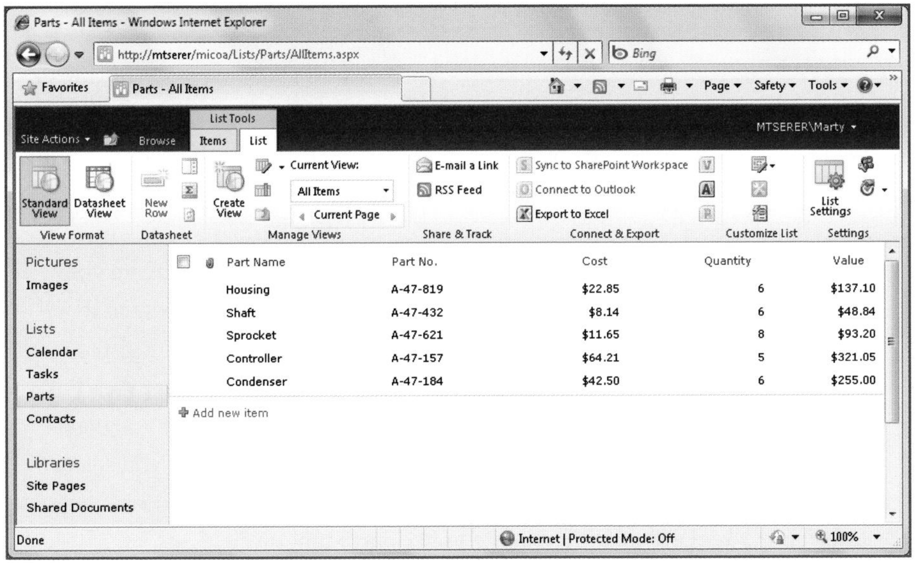

Figure 1-13: *Lists closely resemble worksheets where you can do math in selected columns.*

- **Issue Tracking** for issues that need to be resolved
- **Links** to link pages to the site
- **Reports** for an index and repository for reports
- **Status** to track the accomplishment of goals
- **Tasks** for what needs to be done.

Lists are further discussed in Chapter 4.

LIBRARIES

Libraries store documents of all types, including writings, drawings, diagrams, forms, photos, spreadsheets, notes, videos, and presentations. Libraries are, in essence, a list with attached documents. Libraries can contain a hierarchical structure of folders, track versions of documents, and provide for checking out and checking in documents. You add views of libraries to sites and pages, specifying an application template for creating and changing their content.

Libraries are discussed in Chapter 5.

VIEWS

Views allow you to display the items in a list or the contents of a document in a way that is most beneficial for its use. You can have several views of the same list or library and allow users to choose which they want to use. SharePoint provides a number of controls of views in the ribbon of a page, as shown previously in Figure 1-13. When you create a new view, SharePoint presents six initial formats that you can use for your view, as shown in Figure 1-14. For the selected view, you can choose from several display alternatives,

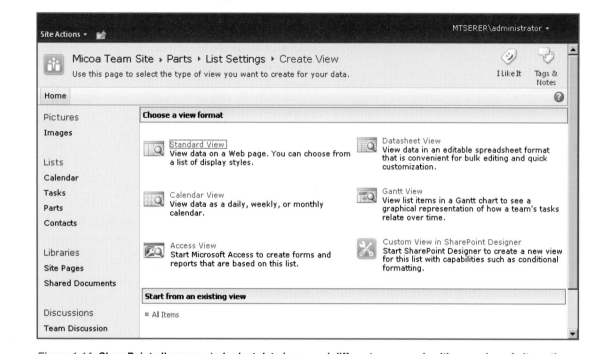

Figure 1-14: *SharePoint allows you to look at data in several different ways, each with a number of alternatives.*

including the columns to be included, the desired sorting, and the filtering and selection needed for the view.

For example, if you have a contact list, you can display a view of the contact list on your Home page that only displays the Name, Job Title, and E-mail Address fields, and on the Contacts page the view could display all fields. Views allow you to reuse displays of SharePoint lists and libraries throughout your site.

WEB PARTS

Web Parts provide the means for you to add your own custom elements to a page, most importantly lists and libraries.

Web Parts can be added to any page, and you can create a Web Part page with a layout that is structured around several Web Parts, as shown in Figure 1-15. SharePoint comes with a number of ready-made Web Parts, you can buy others from third-parties, and, with programming knowledge, you can create your own Web Parts. (Note that many organizations tightly control access to the server. If you do not have access to the server, you cannot install third-party Web Parts on it.) When you edit a page, you can insert a SharePoint Web Part you choose from an expanded ribbon, as you see in Figure 1-16. If you create a Web Parts page, you get the same expanded ribbon from which you select a Web Part, and you get a layout you selected, in which you can choose where to place your Web Part, as shown in the lower part of Figure 1-16.

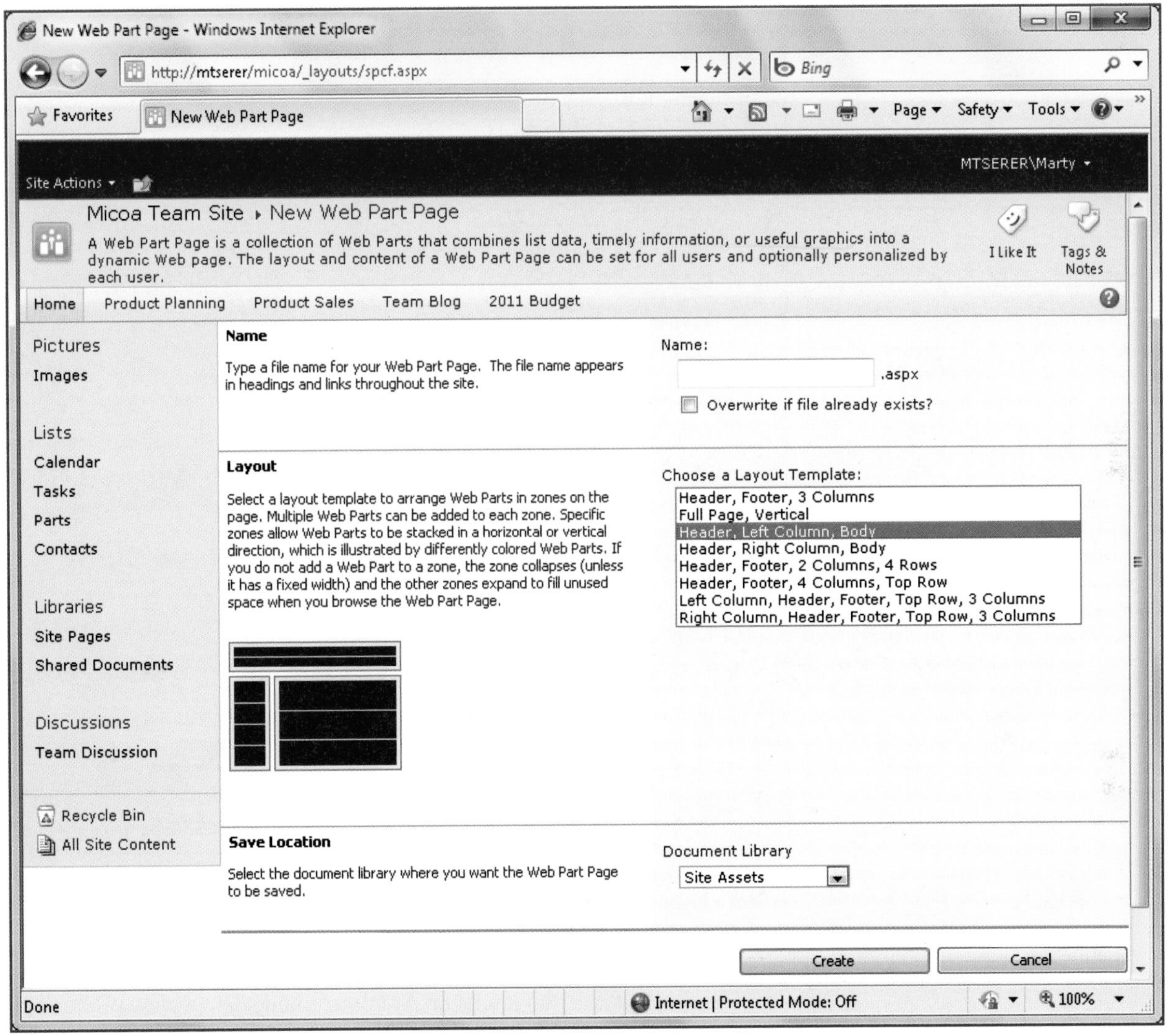

Figure 1-15: *With a Web Part page, you can create your own layout of Web Parts.*

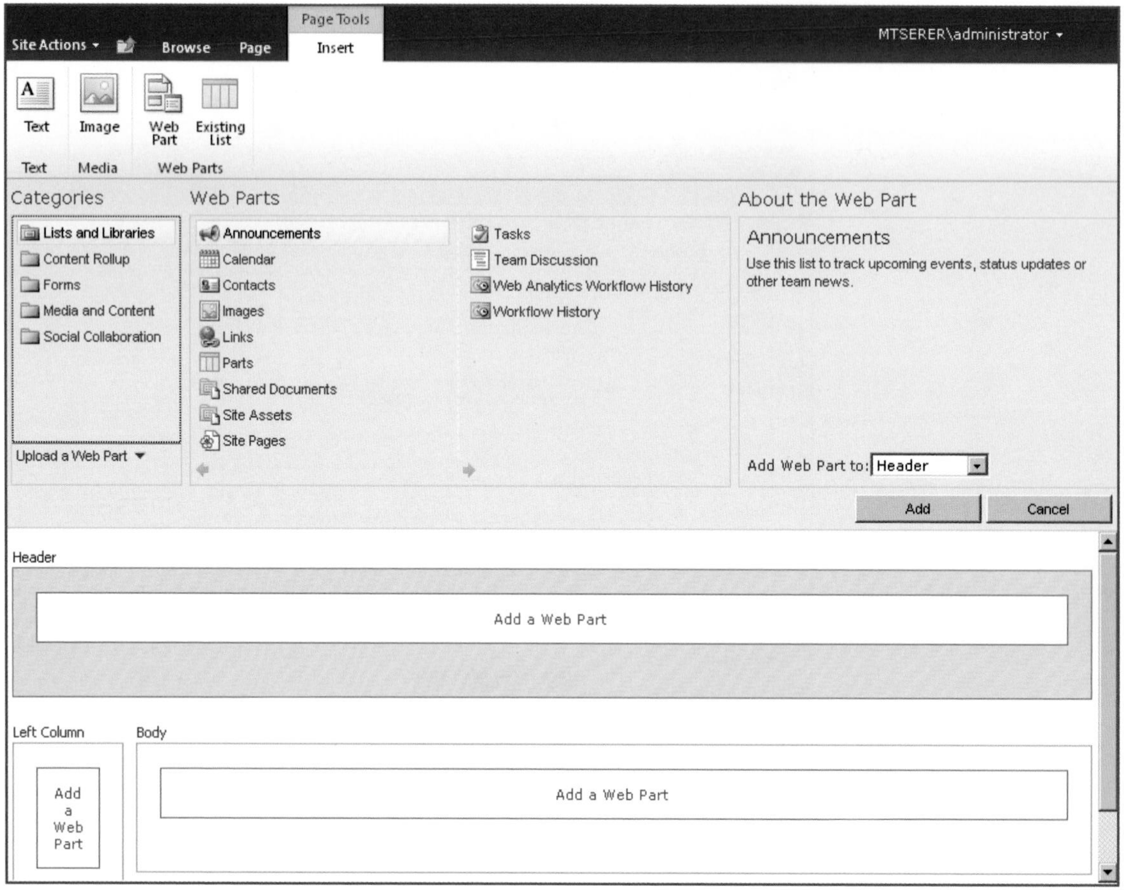

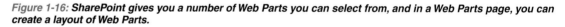

Figure 1-16: SharePoint gives you a number of Web Parts you can select from, and in a Web Parts page, you can create a layout of Web Parts.

For example, you could create a Web Part page from a template and then insert a view of an Announcements list, a view of the Shared Documents document library, and a view of the Calendar list. Web Part pages make it easy to add and remove Web Parts from the browser and without any programming expertise or additional Web development tools.

In Chapter 2 you'll see how to use an existing SharePoint site without modification.

Chapter 2

Using SharePoint

To provide all of the capabilities described in Chapter 1, SharePoint has to be a reasonably sophisticated system. It is also very easy to use, as you'll see. In this chapter we'll look first at a SharePoint site and how to navigate around it. Then we'll see how to use a SharePoint site by adding, changing, and removing information from lists, libraries, tasks, a calendar, a survey, and a discussion. In future chapters we'll look at changing the elements themselves.

Explore SharePoint

A SharePoint site is a Web site that is used with a browser, such as Internet Explorer. To bring up your SharePoint site, you need to know the web address or URL (Uniform Resource Locator) of your site. Most likely, whoever told you to use SharePoint also told you the URL. With that information:

1. Start your browser (Internet Explorer) in your normal way.

NOTE

While SharePoint will work with both Mozilla Firefox and Google Chrome browsers, I believe that it is best to use Internet Explorer for this work. SharePoint is a Microsoft product, so it is most likely that it will work closest to what was intended with the Microsoft browser. Throughout this book I will be using Internet Explorer 8 (which, as this was written, is the most recent version) and assume you will be also.

2. In the address bar, drag over the current address and type the URL for your SharePoint site. This will be something like http://*[your server]/[your site]*/SitePages/Home.aspx. For example, mine is http://mtserer/micoa/SitePages/Home.aspx, as you'll see in several figures in this chapter.

3. You may be asked to enter your user name and password, as shown next. If so, do that, and click **OK**.

4. You will probably want to add your site to your favorites list and/or make it your Home page. To do both of those, with the Home page of your site open in Internet Explorer:

a. Click **Favorites** in the upper-left corner of the browser window.

b. Click **Add To Favorites**. Change the name and folder as desired, and click **Add**.

c. Click the **Home** page icon down arrow and click **Add Or Change Home Page**. If you don't see a Home button, right-click the Internet Explorer toolbar and make sure that the **Command Bar** option is selected.

d. Click the option that makes sense for you:

- Have your SharePoint site as your only Home page

- Add your SharePoint site to your current Home page tabs

- If you have multiple sites open and therefore multiple tabs, you will have a third choice to have your SharePoint site along with the other tabs you have open be your Home page tab set.

e. Click **Yes** when you are ready.

Examine the Parts of a SharePoint Home Page

The SharePoint Home page that you see when you first bring up your site was created for your team or organization and can take many forms, with as much variety as there is in Internet Web sites. The configuration of the Home page is determined by the site template someone chose when they created your site. For example, the Team Site template produces a site with a different Home page than the Blog Site template does. Here we will look at a Home page, shown in Figure 2-1, that has only a few simple changes from the default SharePoint page, as described in Chapter 1. While they may physically look different, you should see a number of similarities between the page shown here and your Home page.

Explore a SharePoint Page

The SharePoint page occupies the body of a Web browser window, between the browser's address and command bars at the top, and its status bar at the bottom (see Figure 1-1 in Chapter 1). A SharePoint page is divided into four major elements:

- **The ribbon** at the top of the page is a primary means of controlling what you want to do in SharePoint. At its top is the tab bar where you can select the major tasks you want to perform. Below the tab bar is the ribbon body, which changes depending on the tab that has been selected. In Figure 2-1 the Browse tab is selected. Later in this chapter you'll see other examples of the ribbon body.

- **The horizontal navigation bar** underneath the ribbon provides links to the site's Home page, to its subsites, and to other pages and other links on or off the current site.

- **Quick Launch**, the vertical navigation bar on the left, provides links to the site's pages, documents, lists, and discussions, as well as the Recycle Bin. Both the Quick Launch and the horizontal navigation bar can be customized to have just the links you want them to have (see Chapter 3).

- **The page body** represents the balance of the page and contains all the information that is displayed on the page. Anything that can be put on a webpage can be on a SharePoint page, including text, photos, graphics, and links to other sites, pages, and information. In addition, SharePoint pages use Web Parts to display views of lists, libraries, discussions, and other items.

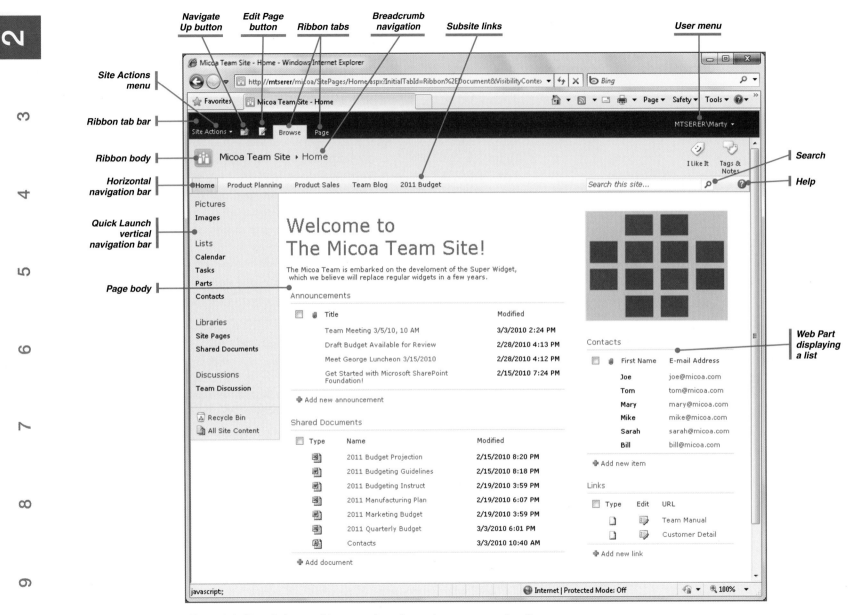

Figure 2-1: *SharePoint provides a number of ways to move around a site.*

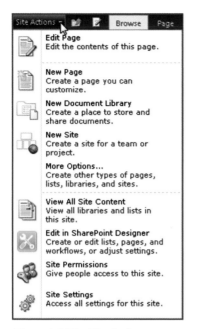

Figure 2-2: The Site Actions menu provides the "heavy lifting" in creating new pages and sites.

USE THE RIBBON TAB BAR

The ribbon tab bar at the top of the SharePoint page contains two menus, two command buttons, and, initially, only two tabs in the default configuration (yours, which we assume has been tailored to your organization, may contain more). These, from left to right, are:

- **Site Actions menu**, shown in Figure 2-2, provides for the creation and editing of major elements of the site, such as new subsites and pages. Site actions are discussed beginning in Chapter 3.

- **Navigate Up button** provides the means to navigate up in the site hierarchy, possibly to a parent site. You'll see this used later in this chapter. The Navigate Up button is also useful when you are viewing the contents in a folder in a document library and want to go back up a level.

- **Edit page button** opens the Editing Tools contextual tabs and puts the page into editing mode, where you can add and delete content using the editing tools, as shown in Figure 2-3. The editing tools are more fully discussed beginning in Chapter 3.

- **Browse tab** is the default view of a SharePoint page. You return here when you are done working in other ways on or with a SharePoint site. Most importantly, the Browse tab gives you access to the Home page on the horizontal navigation bar.

- **Page tab** opens a number of page, list, and library options in the ribbon. This tab is discussed in Chapters 3, 4, and 5.

- **User menu** opens a menu of personal options and settings. Some of these are discussed later in this chapter.

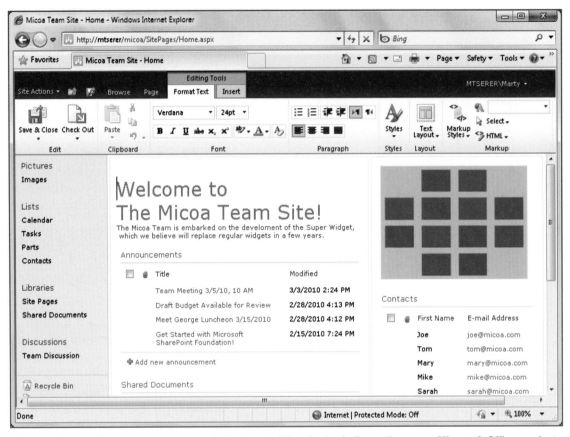

Figure 2-3: The Editing Tools tabs open a full-featured ribbon body similar to the recent Microsoft Office products.

CAUTION

The Edit page button becomes a Save & Close button when the page is in edit mode. It is very important to click this button, or the Save & Close button on the left of the ribbon body, when you are done editing a page or you will lose all the changes you have made.

USE THE HORIZONTAL NAVIGATION BAR

The contents of horizontal navigation bar can be determined by the person creating your SharePoint site or, with the appropriate permissions, by members of your team, including you. By default, however, it contains links to the site and related subsites' Home pages. The Home option is heavily used to return to the site's Home page. The horizontal navigation bar also contains a text box in which you can enter a word or phrase and click the Search icon to search

QUICKFACTS

UNDERSTANDING THE WIKI CONCEPT

A SharePoint site is, by its nature, a *wiki* site, which means that it can be collaboratively added to and changed by anyone who has access to it and the permission to do it. The most common wiki site is Wikipedia, a huge online encyclopedia that has been built by a myriad of people coming to the site and adding and changing articles. In the case of SharePoint sites, most start with some basic framework, but major parts of the site are added and changed by the team or organization members who have access to it. In SharePoint, with the appropriate permission, you can add and change subsites, pages, lists and list items, libraries and documents, discussions, surveys, and text, all in an effort to share knowledge and collaborate with your fellow team members.

Wikipedia says that the term "wiki" was coined by Ward Cunningham, the developer of the first wiki software, and originally came from the Hawaiian word for "fast."

your SharePoint site for that word or phrase. Finally, the horizontal navigation bar contains the Help icon, which you can click to open SharePoint Help. Search and Help will be further discussed later in this chapter.

USE QUICK LAUNCH

Quick Launch, the vertical navigation bar on the left of the default SharePoint Home page, can have links to the important lists, libraries, and discussions in the site. The Quick Launch shown here, which has been modified from the initial default (compare with Figure 1-1 in Chapter 1), contains links to various elements and pages in the site. Clicking **Lists**, for example, opens a list of the lists that are active in the site, as you see in Figure 2-4.

Although an element, such as a list or a library, may be displayed on the Home page where normally it is an abbreviated view, it can also be displayed on its own page more fully (see Figure 2-5). You can open this page by clicking either the link in the Quick Launch or by clicking the element title on the Home page.

Two special links on the Quick Launch are the Recycle Bin and All Site Content.

- **The Recycle Bin** holds items from the site that have been deleted and allows you to restore or permanently delete the items.

| Pictures |
| Images |
| |
| Lists |
| Calendar |
| Tasks |
| Parts |
| Contacts |
| |
| Libraries |
| Site Pages |
| Shared Documents |
| |
| Discussions |
| Team Discussion |
| |
| ▲ Recycle Bin |
| ▣ All Site Content |

Site Actions ▾   📑   MTSERER\Marty ▾

Micoa Team Site ▸ Recycle Bin   😊 I Like It   🏷 Tags & Notes
Use this page to restore items that you have deleted from this site or to empty deleted items. Items that were deleted more than 30 day(s) ago will be automatically emptied.

Home   Product Planning   Product Sales   Team Blog   2011 Budget | Search this site... 🔍 ❓

Pictures
Images   ◻ Restore Selection | ✖ Delete Selection

	Type	Name	Original Location	Created By	Deleted↓	Size
Lists
Calendar
◻	📄	2011 Budget Writeup.doc	/micoa/Shared Documents	MTSERER\Administrator	3/6/2010 1:18 PM	23.5 KB

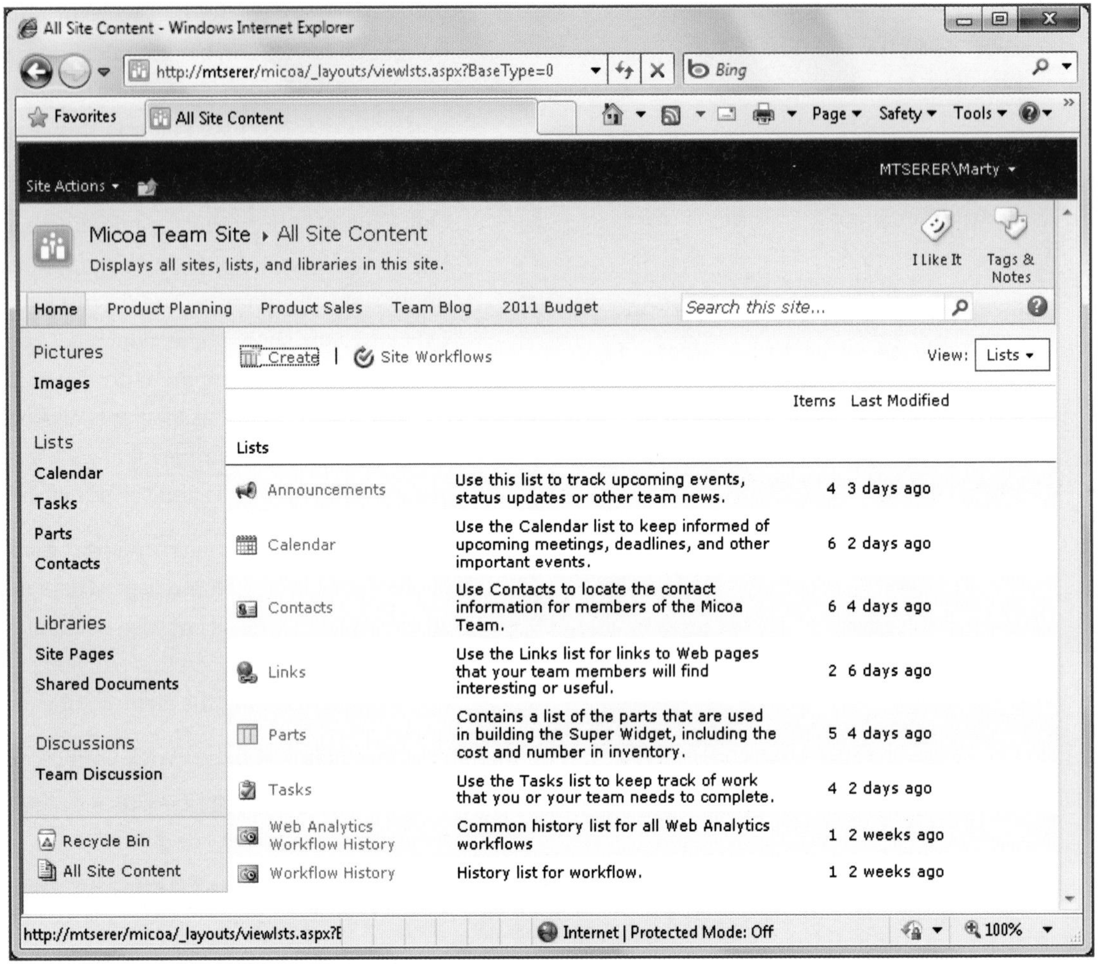

Figure 2-4: The Quick Launch provides links to both lists of other elements, as well as individual elements, such as the team calendar.

- **All Site Content**, as the name implies, displays all of the subsites, libraries, lists, discussions, and surveys in the site, as shown in Figure 2-6.

Navigate a SharePoint Site

Navigating, or getting around, a SharePoint site is simply a matter of clicking the link you want. Sometimes, however, it is not obvious which link you need to

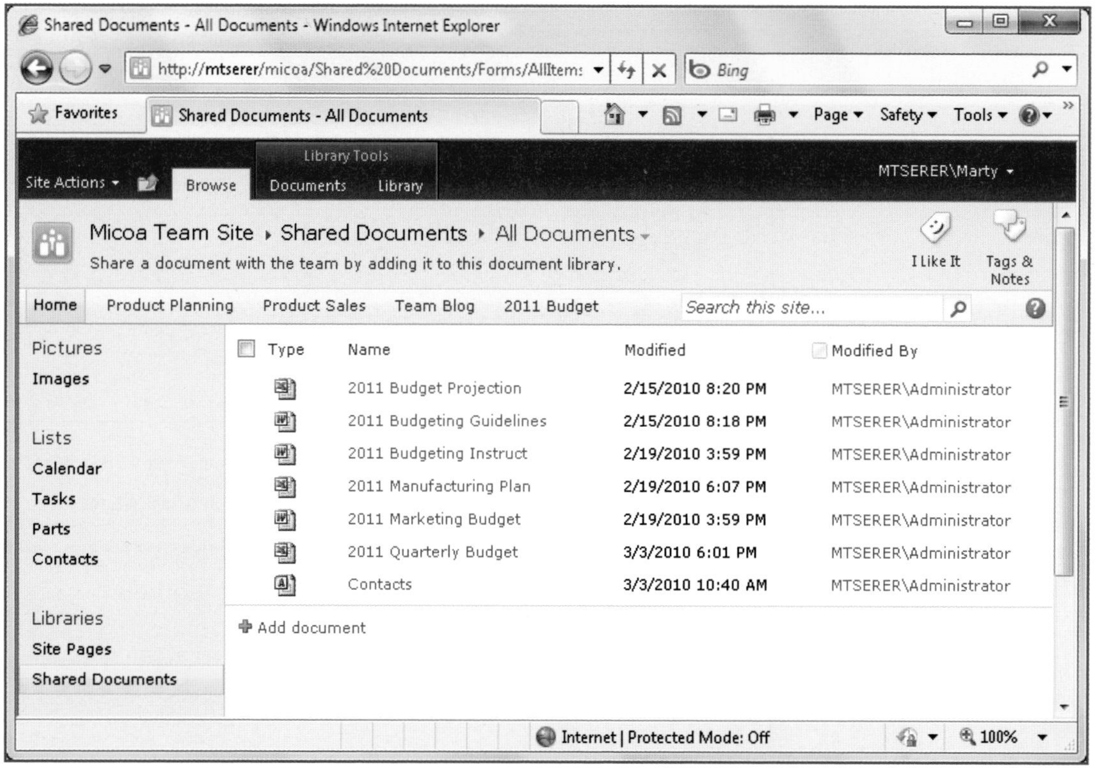

Figure 2-5: *Lists, libraries, and discussions can be opened in their own page, displaying a fuller view of their contents.*

use to get where you want, although SharePoint tries hard to give you clues as to where you are going and where you have been. This section will lead you on several excursions through a SharePoint site, but first look at the SharePoint site hierarchy.

UNDERSTAND SITE HIERARCHY

SharePoint has three layers that can be intermixed to create a hierarchy through which you navigate to fully use a SharePoint site. These layers are:

- **Elements** including lists, libraries, discussions, and surveys

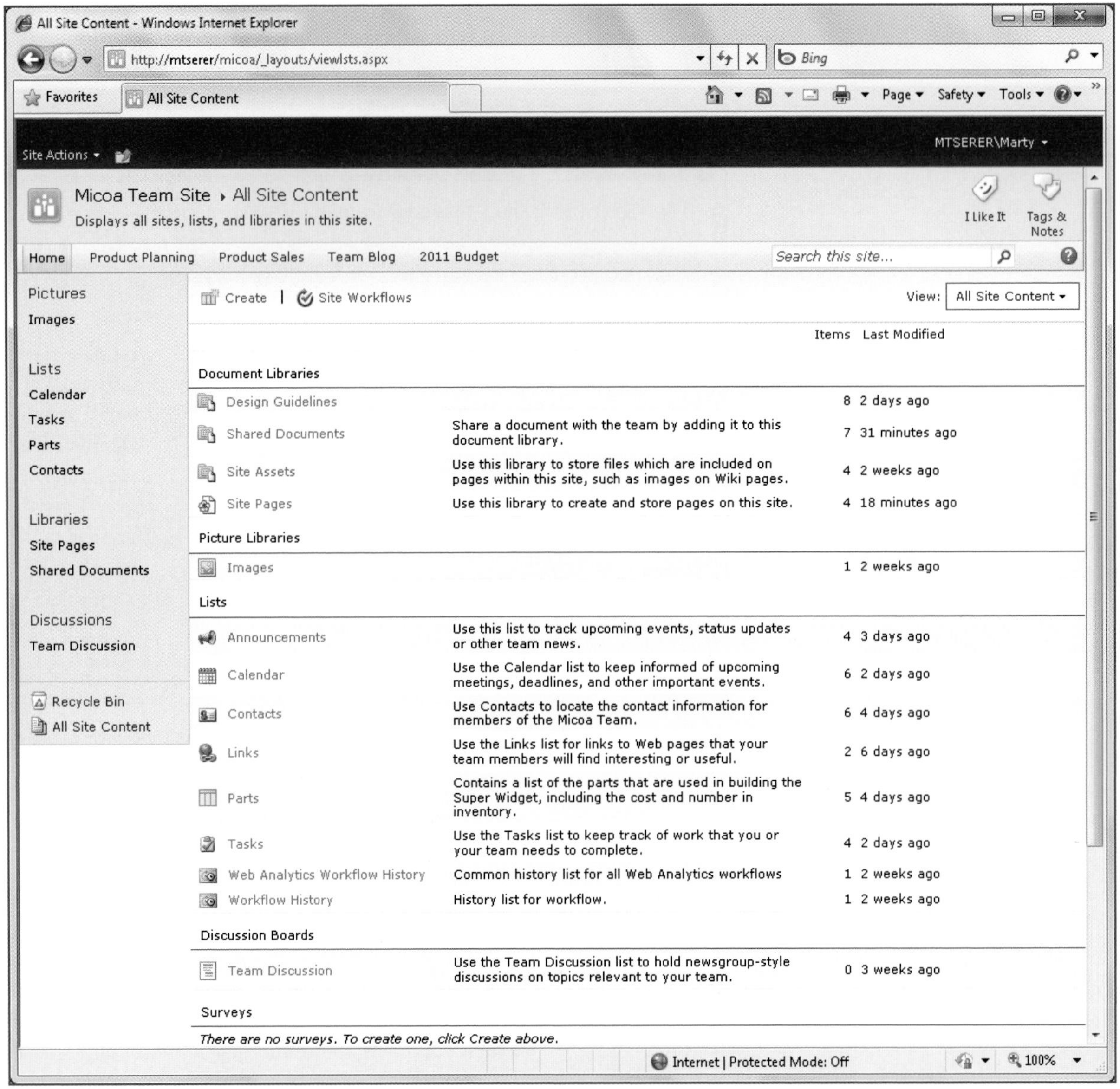

Figure 2-6: *All Site Content is a good place to go to find a site element that you know exists but you cannot find.*

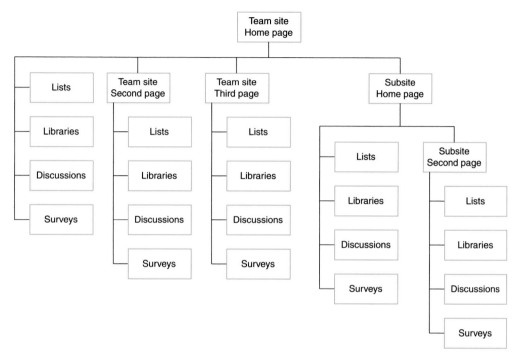

Figure 2-7: *As you move through a SharePoint site, you may need to traverse elements, pages, and subsites.*

- **Pages** in addition to the Home page, which can contain other pages and any of the elements

- **Subsites**, which can contain other subsites and additional pages, which in turn can contain elements

So a site, in its simplest form, can be a Home page with several elements on it, or there can be several additional pages with elements on them, or finally there can be subsites with additional pages, and elements on everything, as you can see in Figure 2-7.

To efficiently use such a site as the one in Figure 2-7, you need to be able to quickly go from one place to another without having to laboriously go up and down the hierarchical steps. Fortunately, SharePoint has a number of tools to help you do this. One of the most valuable of these is breadcrumb navigation, which is described in the "Using Breadcrumb Navigation" QuickFacts. Other tools for speedy navigation include:

- The browser's **Back** and **Forward** buttons in the upper-left corner of the browser window, which, along with their shortcut keys **ALT+LEFT ARROW** and **ALT+RIGHT ARROW**, respectively, take you back and forth through the recent series of pages you have viewed.

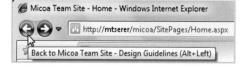

- The browser's **Recent Pages** button, which, when clicked, lists and lets you select a page from the recent pages you have visited.

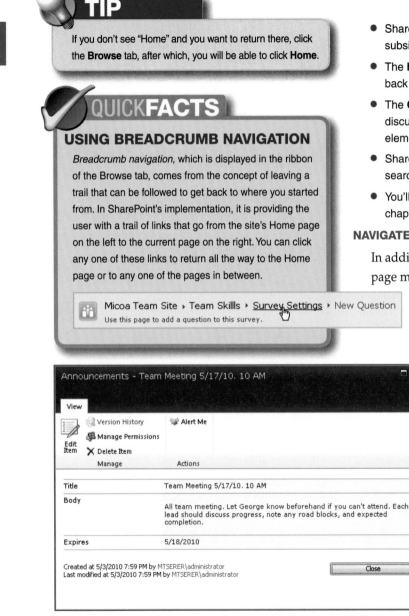

QUICKFACTS

USING BREADCRUMB NAVIGATION

Breadcrumb navigation, which is displayed in the ribbon of the Browse tab, comes from the concept of leaving a trail that can be followed to get back to where you started from. In SharePoint's implementation, it is providing the user with a trail of links that go from the site's Home page on the left to the current page on the right. You can click any one of these links to return all the way to the Home page or to any one of the pages in between.

Micoa Team Site ▸ Team Skillls ▸ Survey Settings ▸ New Question
Use this page to add a question to this survey.

Announcements - Team Meeting 5/17/10. 10 AM

View

Edit Item ⊘ Version History   ⚙ Manage Permissions   ✕ Delete Item   ✉ Alert Me

Manage   Actions

Title   Team Meeting 5/17/10. 10 AM

Body   All team meeting. Let George know beforehand if you can't attend. Each lead should discuss progress, note any road blocks, and expected completion.

Expires   5/18/2010

Created at 5/3/2010 7:59 PM by MTSERER\administrator
Last modified at 5/3/2010 7:59 PM by MTSERER\administrator   Close

Figure 2-8: List items, when clicked, open to provide detail about the item, and allow editing with the appropriate permission.

- SharePoint's **Navigate Up** button easily moves you from a sub-subsite up to a parent subsite and the primary site.

- The **horizontal navigation bar** can take you to any of the subsites shown there or back to the site's Home page.

- The **Quick Launch** vertical navigation bar can take you to any of the lists, libraries, discussions, or pages listed there, or through the All Site Content option to any element in the site.

- SharePoint's **Site Search** on the right of the horizontal navigation bar allows you to search for any content in the site.

- You'll see examples of using these navigation tools in the rest of this and subsequent chapters.

NAVIGATE THE HOME PAGE

In addition to the various navigation elements discussed earlier, your Home page most likely has a number of links that open various elements, similar to what is shown in the Home page in Figure 2-1. Explore how several of these work next.

1. With the Home page open as described at the beginning of this chapter, click a list item such as an announcement or a task. For example, I might click the Team Meeting announcement shown in Figure 2-1.

2. The item will open, displaying detail for it, as shown in Figure 2-8. Read and handle the item as needed. Note that the item has its own ribbon and View tab.

3. When you are ready, click **Close** to return to the Home page.

4. Click a library document; for example, I might click the 2011 Quarterly Budget in my Shared Documents.

5. This will open the document either in the browser or in the program that created it, depending on the default option your network administrator has chosen for your SharePoint site. In my case, Microsoft Excel opens and displays the worksheet shown in Figure 2-9.

6. When you are ready, click **Close** to close the program and return to the Home page if the file opened in a program, or click **Back** on your browser if it opened in the browser.

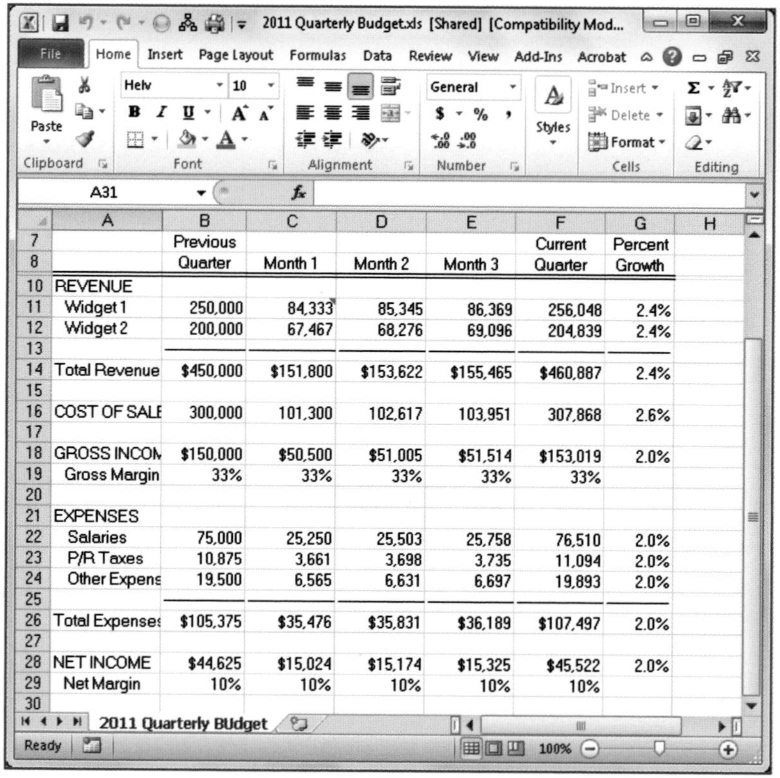

Figure 2-9: *Opening a document from SharePoint allows you to read and, with permission, edit the document as you otherwise would in its program.*

NOTE

Depending on how permissions are set up, when you initially open a document, you may be in read-only mode and not be able to edit the document. To get edit permission, you may need to talk to an administrator. In addition, Office 2010 programs like Word 2010 and Excel 2010 open files from network locations in protected mode by default. You may need to click **Enable Editing** to edit the document you opened.

NAVIGATE WITH QUICK LAUNCH

Your Quick Launch contents are dependent on what the creator of your site and your team members have put there. The initial installation of SharePoint contains a default set of links in Quick Launch, as shown in Figure 1-1. These can be easily added to and changed, as you see in comparing Figures 1-1 and 2-1. In the steps that follow, we'll explore the default Calendar and Tasks links as examples of Quick Launch links. If you do not have those links, use any links you do have.

1. From the Home page, click **Calendar** in the Quick Launch. The calendar will open, as shown in Figure 2-10.

2. Review the calendar and click one of the meetings or events on the calendar. For example, I might click "Meet with George." The individual calendar item will open like this:

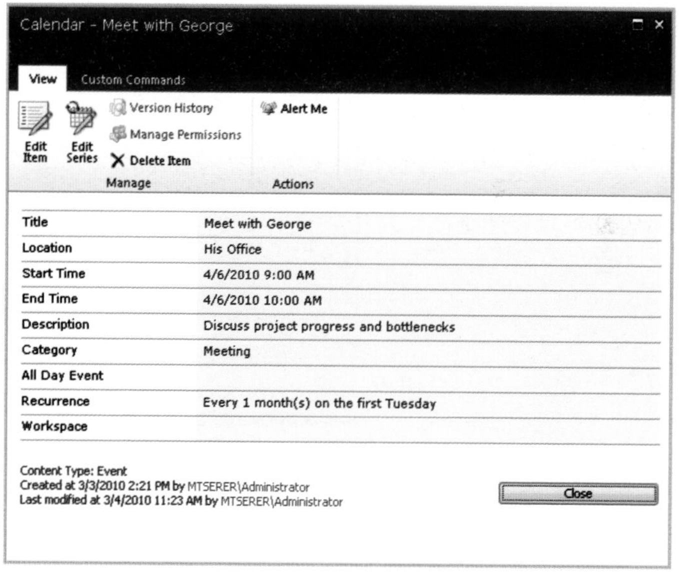

3. Review the item. Note how you can make an item recur on a periodic basis. When you are ready, click **Close** to return to the initial Calendar view.

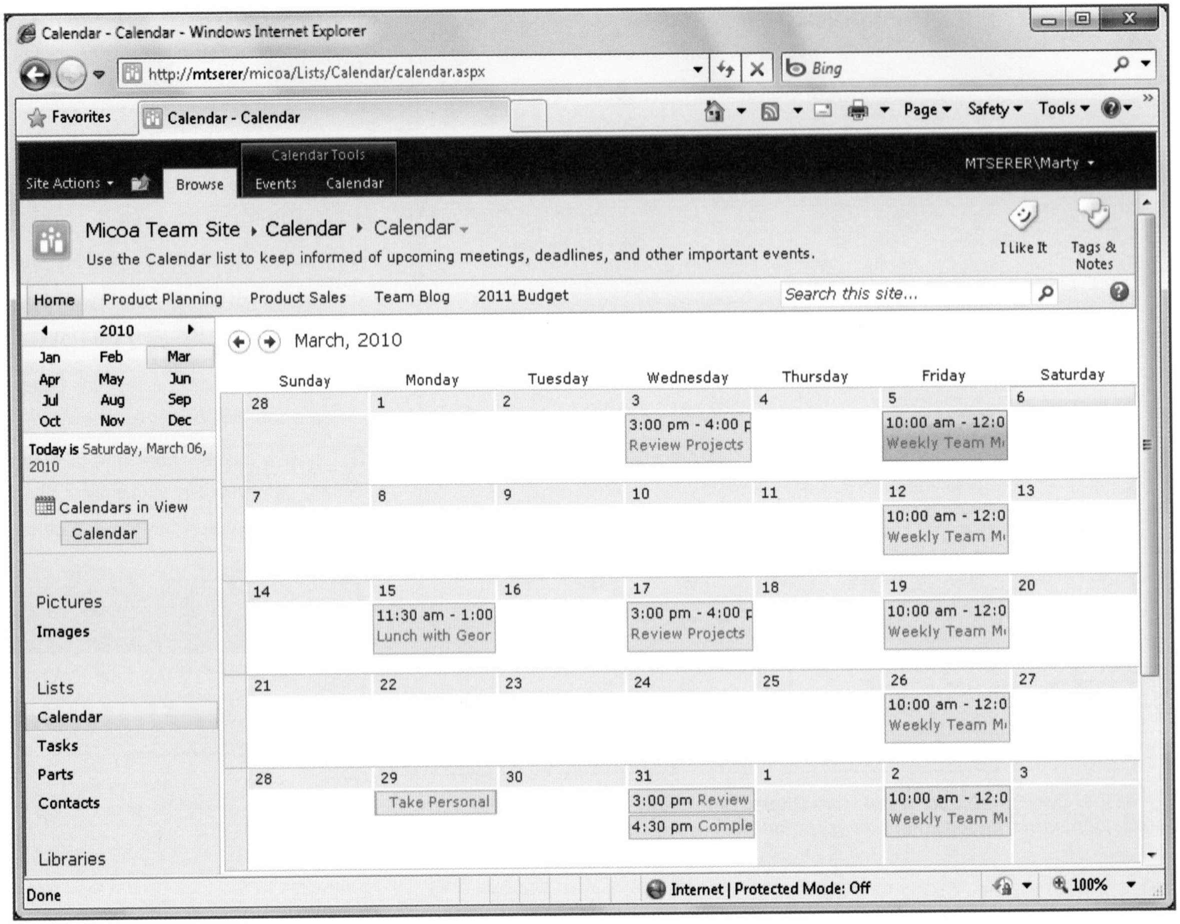

Figure 2-10: *SharePoint has only one calendar template, but it can be used to create a team calendar, a project calendar, and a personal calendar.*

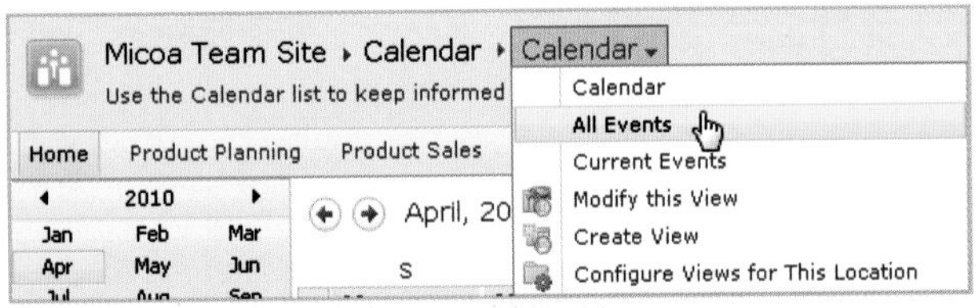

4. Click **Calendar** on the far-right side of the breadcrumbs navigation bar to open its drop-down menu, and click **All Events**. A list view of the calendar appears, similar to Figure 2-11.

5. Note the contextual tabs and ribbon that also appear with the Items tab displayed. Click the **List** tab to display its ribbon options.

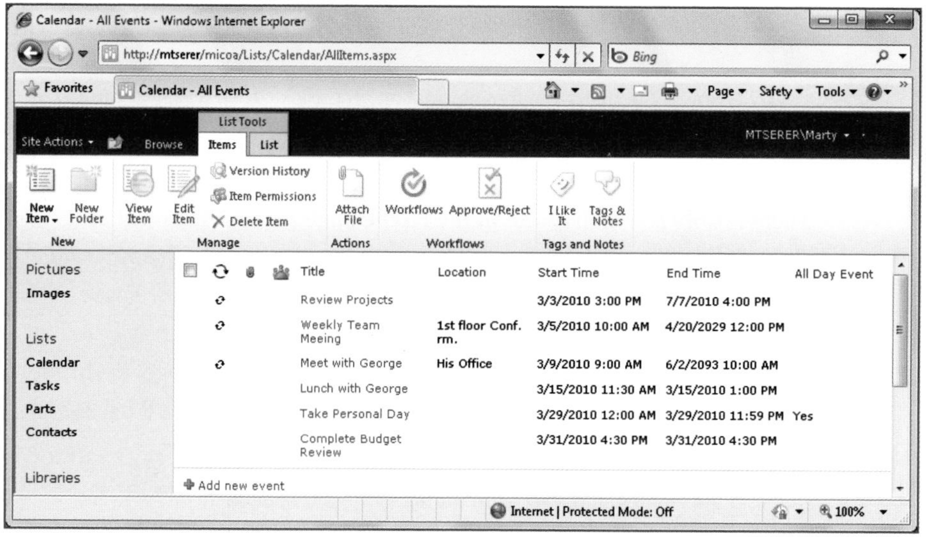

Figure 2-11: *SharePoint often offers multiple views of the same element.*

6. When you're ready, click **Browse** and click **Home** to return to your Home page.

7. Click **Tasks** to open the Tasks list in All Item view, as shown in Figure 2-12.

8. Review the Tasks list, note the contextual tabs, and click **All Tasks** on the far-right side of the breadcrumbs navigation bat to view the six predefined views of the Tasks list.

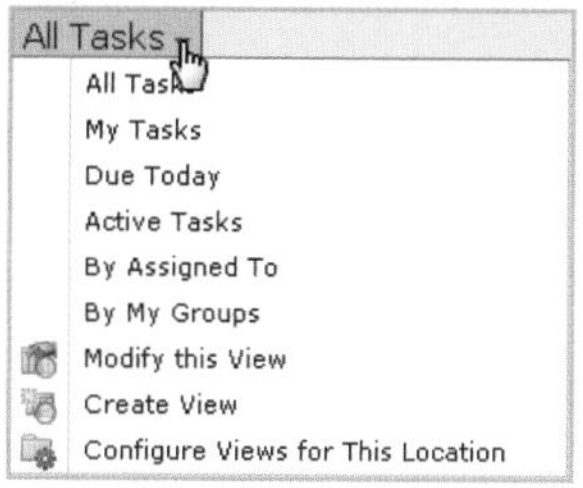

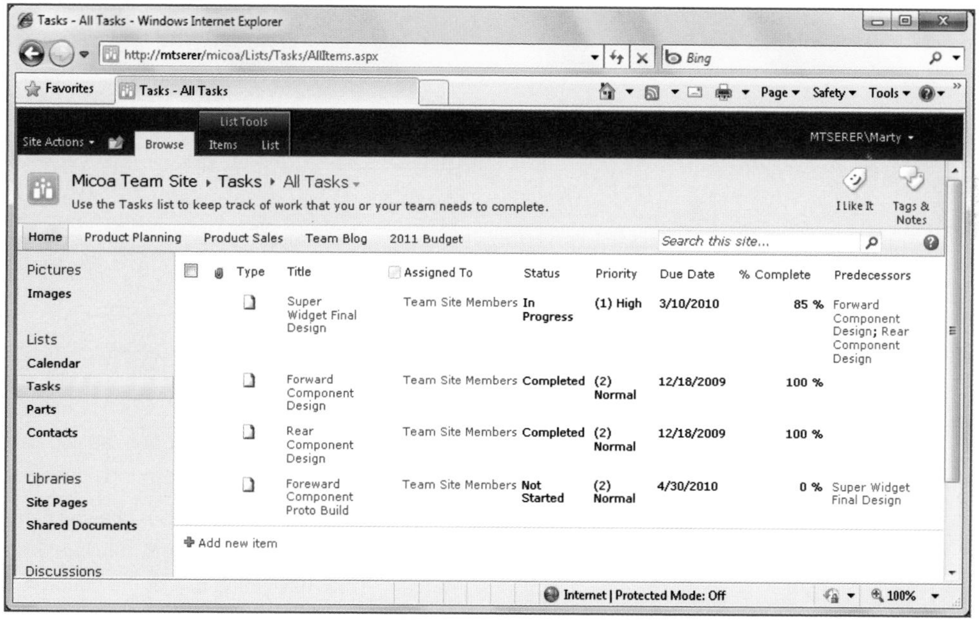

Figure 2-12: *The Tasks list provides a comprehensive means for tracking what needs to be done.*

Tasks - Super Widget Final Design

View

Edit Item | Version History | Alert Me
Manage Permissions | Claim Release
Delete Item

Manage | Actions

Title	Super Widget Final Design
Predecessors	Forward Component Design; Rear Component Design
Priority	(1) High
Status	In Progress
% Complete	85%
Assigned To	Team Site Members
Description	Detail design that draws together all the component designs.
Start Date	1/4/2010
Due Date	3/10/2010

Content Type: Task
Created at 3/4/2010 1:18 PM by MTSERER\Administrator
Last modified at 3/4/2010 1:23 PM by MTSERER\Administrator

Close

9. When ready, click a task title to open it. The detail information about a task is displayed.

10. Scroll to the bottom of the information, and click **Close**. Click **Home** to return to the Home page.

NAVIGATE TO OTHER SITE PAGES

There is only so much room on the Home page, and so in almost all SharePoint sites there are a number of additional pages with a full range of content, including lists, libraries, discussions, and surveys. These additional pages are accessed in several ways: by being directly listed on the Quick Launch, by having their own list on the Home page, or through the default Site Pages feature on the Quick Launch. Here we'll use the latter, but other options will be explored later in this book.

Libraries
Site Pages
Shared Documents

1. From the Home page, click **Site Pages** in the Quick Launch.

2. In the Site Pages list that opens, click the name of a page you want to see. For example, I will click **Design Guidelines**.

Library Tools

Site Actions ▼ | Browse | Documents | Library

Micoa Team Site ▸ Site Pages ▸ All Pages ▾
Use this library to create and store pages on this site.

Home | Product Planning | Product Sales | Team Blog | 2011 Budget

Recently Modified		Type	Name	Modified By	Modified
Home			Home	MTSERER\Marty	3/6/2010 1:31 PM
Design Guidelines	☐		Design Guidelines ▾	MTSERER\Administrator	3/4/2010 10:25 PM
Team Skills and Assignments			Team Skills and Assignments	MTSERER\Administrator	3/4/2010 4:18 PM
Parts Suppliers			Parts Suppliers	MTSERER\Administrator	3/4/2010 4:16 PM
Pictures		✚ Add new page			

3. Your page will open, as you can see mine has in Figure 2-13. Note the list of recently modified pages in the upper-right area, just above the Quick Launch.

4. On a page in your site you can do anything you can do on the Home page, including opening list items and library documents, or using the Quick Launch, the horizontal navigation bar, or the ribbon.

5. When you are ready, click **Home** to return there.

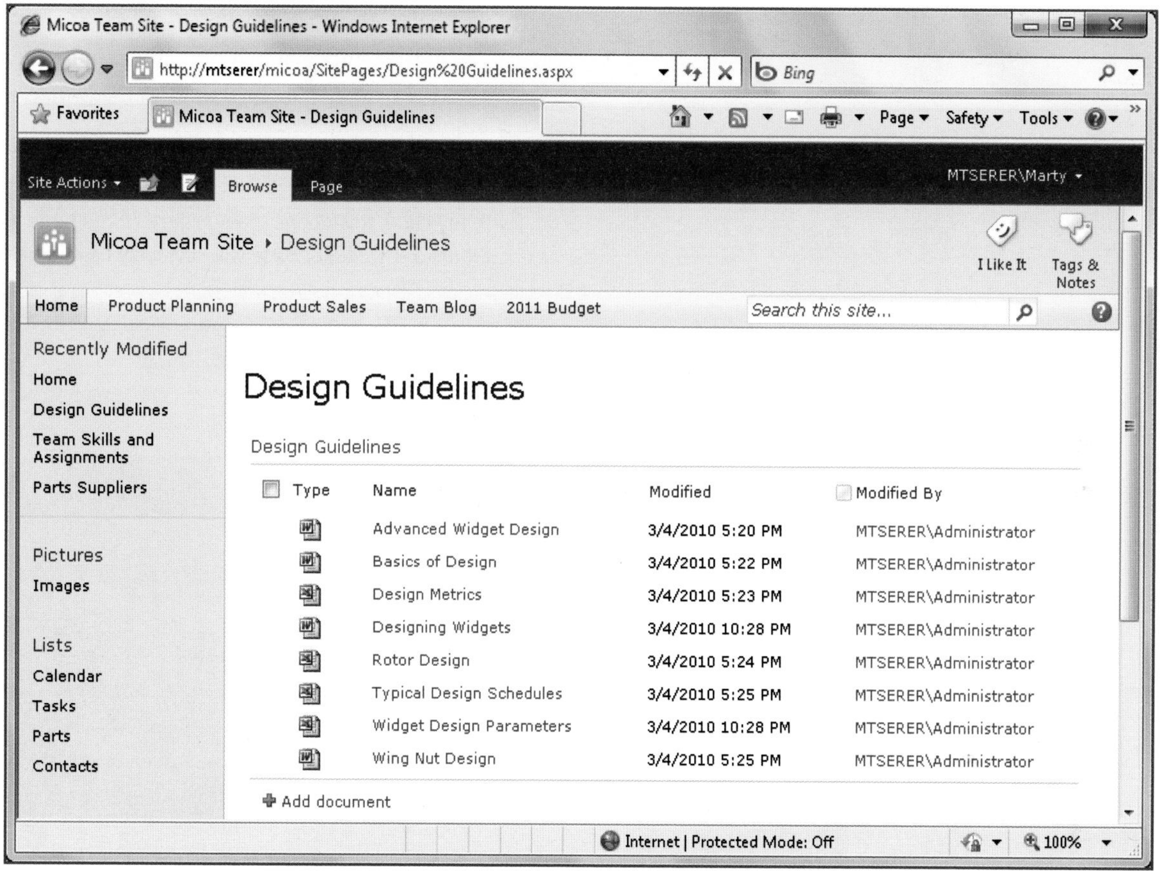

Figure 2-13: *Additional site pages allow you do anything you can do on the Home page and add more elements to your site.*

NAVIGATE TO SUBSITES

Often, SharePoint site creators want to organize content better instead of having an endless string of site pages in a site. In place of this, subsites can be used to create a hierarchical structure that is both more intuitive and easier to get around. Within a subsite you have a Home page and you can have additional pages, and even additional subsites, so the site hierarchy can become quite complex.

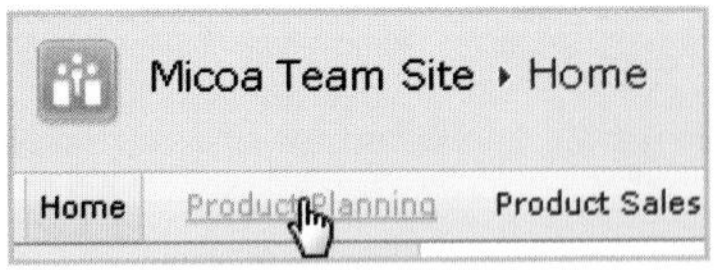

In most sites, the links to subsites are on the horizontal navigation bar, but they can be in the Quick Launch or on the page itself. Here we'll keep it simple and work with a single subsite that is on the horizontal navigation bar.

1. From the Home page, click a subsite in the horizontal navigation bar. I'll click the Product Planning subsite.

2. In my case, this opens the subsite's Home page with the group calendar shown in Figure 2-14. Your subsite will obviously have a different Home page.

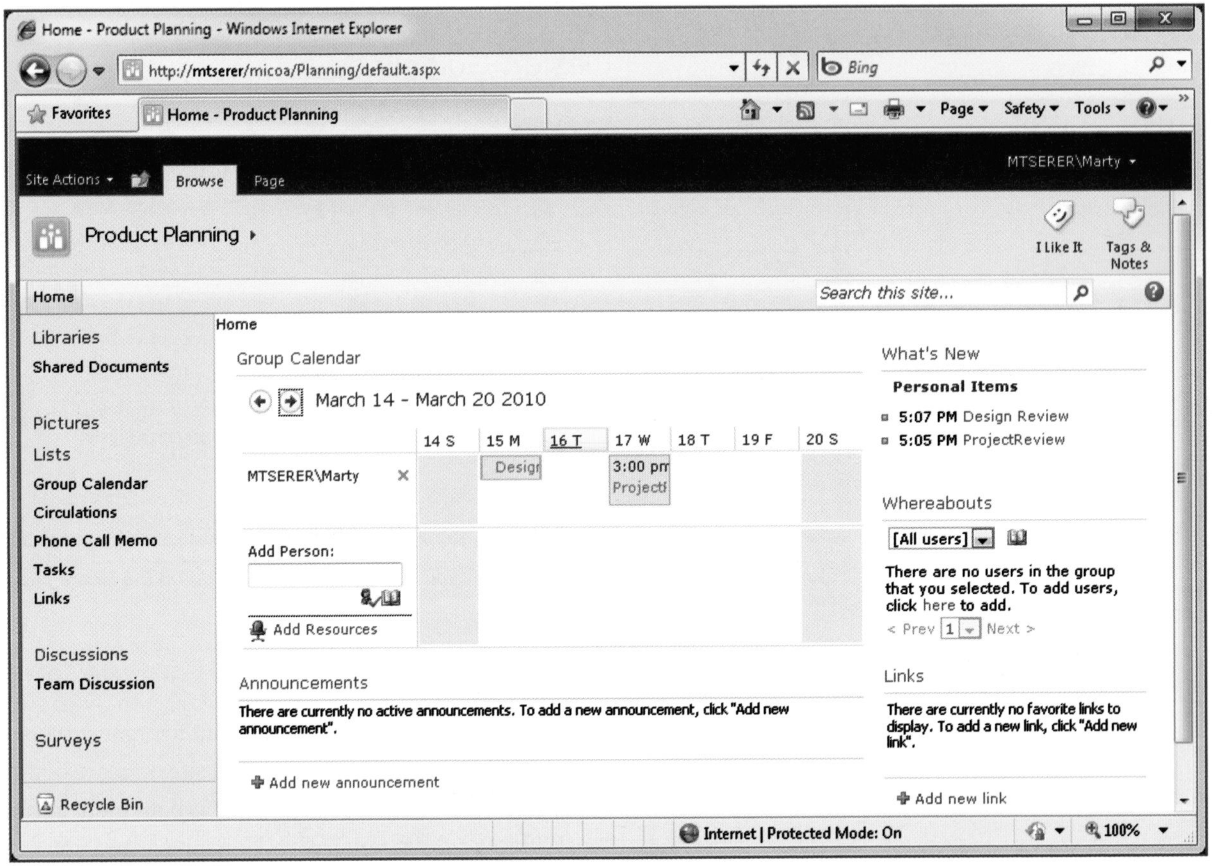

Figure 2-14: *Subsite pages are often for a special purpose, like group calendars, blogs, and surveys.*

3. In a subsite you can do everything that you can in the primary site you have explored already in this chapter, including using the Quick Launch and the horizontal navigation bar, links in the body of the page, the ribbon tabs and menus, and the browser controls.

4. When you are ready to return to the primary site, click the **Navigate Up** button in the ribbon tab row, and click your primary site.

Use SharePoint

A SharePoint site is most often a place for collaboration, where you are expected to add content, as well as look at the content added by others. This is the concept of a wiki site, where the people who are using it are also creating it (see the "Understanding the Wiki Concept" QuickFacts earlier in this chapter).

In this section we'll look at adding, changing, and deleting items in lists and documents in libraries, as well as how to work with calendars, surveys, discussions, workspaces, and the Recycle Bin.

Use Lists

Lists are a foundational element in SharePoint. Much of the system is based upon lists, including libraries (see the "Understanding Lists and Libraries" QuickFacts later in this chapter). There are a number of different types of lists, and you can make your own, as you'll see in Chapter 4. Here, we'll look at adding to, changing, and deleting items in two existing lists: Tasks and the Calendar.

ADD TASKS

A task list is a set of items with assignments and due dates, as you saw in Figure 2-12 earlier in this chapter. To add a task, you simply have to fill out a form with the information.

1. From the Home page, click **Tasks** in the Quick Launch. The Tasks list opens.

2. If needed, scroll down to the bottom of the list and click **Add New Item**. The Tasks – New Item dialog box will appear, as shown in Figure 2-15, with a blinking cursor in the Title text box.

NOTE

If, for some reason, you don't have Tasks on your Quick Launch, use another list other than Calendar for the following exercises.

Tasks - New Item

Edit

Save | Cancel | Paste | Cut | Copy | Attach File | Spelling
Commit | Clipboard | Actions | Spelling

Title *	
Predecessors	Foreward Component Pr Forward Component Des Rear Component Design Super Widget Final Desi **Add >** **< Remove**
Priority	(2) Normal
Status	Not Started
% Complete	%
Assigned To	
Description	A A¹ B I U | ≡ ≡ ≡ | ≣ ≣ ≣ ≣ | A ✍ ▸¶ ¶◂
Start Date	3/6/2010
Due Date	

Figure 2-15: SharePoint provides a ready-made form for adding new tasks.

3. Type the title of the task. It can be quite long if desired.

4. Review the list of predecessors, tasks that need to be completed before the task you are adding. Click a task that is a predecessor, and click **Add**. Repeat this as needed to add all predecessors.

5. Click the **Priority** down arrow, and then click the priority you want to assign to this task.

Priority	(2) Normal
Status	(1) High (2) Normal (3) Low

6. Click the **Status** down arrow, and then click the status that is correct for your task.

7. If applicable, enter a percentage complete number.

8. Enter the persons or group the task is assigned to. You can select these from the Select People And Groups dialog box, opened by clicking the **Browse** icon on the far right of the Assigned To area. If you type a name or group, to can check its accuracy by clicking **Check Names**, the other icon on the right.

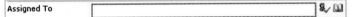

9. If you wish, enter a description using any of the formatting tools located above the description text box.

10. Enter or select from a calendar, which is opened by clicking the icon on the right, the start and due dates for the task.

Start Date	3/29/2010	
Due Date		

◄		March, 2010				►
S	M	T	W	T	F	S
28	1	2	3	4	5	6
7	8	9	10	11	12	13
14	15	16	17	18	19	20
21	22	23	24	25	26	27
28	29	30	31	1	2	3

Today is Saturday, March 06, 2010

11. When you are done creating the task and you are satisfied with it, click **Save**. When you have entered all the tasks you want, click **Home**.

CHANGE TASKS

Given human nature, there is often a need to change what has been done. For example, in the task list shown in Figure 2-12, the word "foreward" in the bottom task is misspelled. To change that:

1. From the Home page, click **Tasks** in the Quick Launch. The Tasks list will open.

2. If needed, scroll down so you can see the item that you want to change. Move the mouse over the item so a check box appears on the left.

3. Click the check box. The List Tools Items tab will open in the ribbon, as you can see in Figure 2-16.

4. In the List Tools I Items tab, click **Edit Item**. The Task item form will open, as shown in Figure 2-15, just as it did for entering a new task.

5. Go down through each of the fields and make the changes that you need to make.

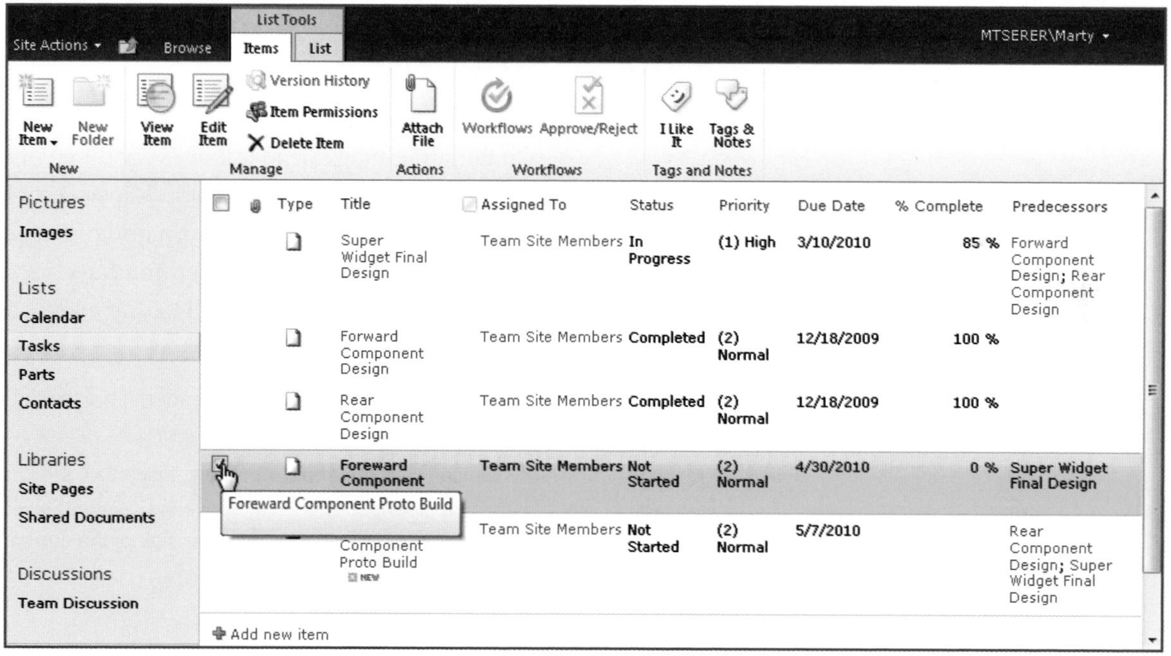

Figure 2-16: Changing a list item, such as a task, lets you edit the same form fields used to create the form.

6. When you are satisfied with your changes, click **Save**. Select any other task you want to change, make those changes following steps 3 through 5, and then when you have entered all the changes you want, click **Home**.

DELETE TASKS

Deleting tasks is similar and straightforward.

1. From the Home page, click **Tasks** in the Quick Launch. The Tasks list will open.

2. If needed, scroll down so you can see the item that you want to delete. Move the mouse over the item so a check box appears on the left.

3. Click the check box. The List Tools Items tab will open in the ribbon.

4. In the List Tools | Items tab, click **Delete Item** ✕ Delete Item . A message box appears asking if you are sure you want to delete this item to the Recycle Bin (see "Use the Recycle Bin" later in this chapter).

5. Click **OK** to complete the deletion, or click **Cancel** if you change your mind.

6. Make any other changes to the task list, and when you are ready, click **Browse** and then click **Home**.

WORK WITH A CALENDAR

On the surface the calendar looks very different from the task list or other standard lists. In reality, a calendar is just a list of calendar events that are displayed in a special view using a grid of days and weeks, which you saw in Figure 2-10 earlier in this chapter. You can also see a more conventional list of events in Figure 2-11. Here we'll look at adding an event to the calendar, making changes to it, and deleting an event.

Home	Product Plannin
◄	2010	►
Jan	Feb	Mar
Apr	May	Jun
Jul	Aug	Sep
Oct	Nov	Dec

Today is Sunday, March 07, 2010

▦ Calendars In View
Calendar

1. From the Home page, click **Calendar** in the Quick Launch. The calendar will open as you saw in Figure 2-10.

2. You can click **Calendars In View**, just above the Quick Launch, to select a different or new calendar. Next, just above the calendar choice, click the month if in the current year, or click the arrows on either side of the current year to change the year, and then click the month.

Calendar - New Item

Edit

Save   Cancel   Paste   ✂ Cut   📋 Copy   Attach File   ABC Spelling

Commit | Clipboard | Actions | Spelling

Title *

Location

Start Time *   3/24/2010   📅 10 PM ▼ 00 ▼

End Time *   3/24/2010   📅 11 PM ▼ 00 ▼

Description   A A¹ | B I U | ≡ ≡ ≡ | ≡ ≡ | 輝 輝 | A 例 | ▸¶ ¶◂

Category   ⊙ [▼]
⊙ Specify your own value:
[   ]

All Day Event   ☐ Make this an all-day activity that doesn't start or end at a specific hour.

Recurrence   ☐ Make this a repeating event.

Workspace   ☐ Use a Meeting Workspace to organize attendees, agendas, documents, minutes, and other details for this event.

Save   Cancel

Figure 2-17: A calendar event can be as simple as a title with a start and end time, or you can add as much detail as you wish.

NOTE

A SharePoint calendar can be viewed in Outlook by transferring calendar events to an Outlook calendar from one in SharePoint. The calendar, however, can only be updated in SharePoint. This is discussed in Chapter 7.

3. With the correct month displayed, move the mouse over the day of the month in which you want to add an event, and click **Add** to open the Calendar – New Item dialog box shown in Figure 2-17.

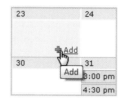

4. Enter, at a minimum, a title, start time, and end time. You may optionally enter a location, description, and category, and indicate if it is an all-day event, is a recurring item, and if you want to use a meeting workspace.

5. If you choose for the event to be a recurring one, the dialog box expands to let you specify how it will recur.

Recurrence   ☑ Make this a repeating event.

⊙ Daily   Pattern
⊙ Weekly   ⊙ Every [1] day(s)
⊙ Monthly   ⊙ Every weekday
⊙ Yearly

Date Range

Start Date   ⊙ No end date
3/24/2010   ⊙ End after: [10] occurrence(s)
                ⊙ End by:
                [   ]

6. When you have completed entering the event, click **Save**, either in the ribbon or at the bottom of the dialog box.

7. To change or delete a calendar event, click the name of the event to open its dialog box.

8. To change the event, click **Edit Item** in the ribbon to open the dialog box shown in Figure 2-17, make any desired changes, and click **Save**.

9. To delete the event, click **Delete Item** in the ribbon, and click **OK** to confirm it.

10. Make any other changes to the calendar, and when you are ready, click **Browse** and then click **Home**.

UNDERSTANDING LISTS AND LIBRARIES

Lists and libraries are interrelated, but have an important difference. A library stores a file along with additional information called *metadata* (such as the name of the person who uploaded the file and the date of upload, essentially data that defines other data). Files stored in document libraries could be Word, Excel, or PowerPoint files, or even a picture or graphics file. Lists, on the other hand, store data (such as a hyperlink or text, as well as metadata such as the name of the person who made the entry and the date they made the entry). So you upload files to libraries, and information to lists.

If you are adding information to a SharePoint site that is simply bits of data that fit into an ordered sequence, then it should be in a SharePoint list. If you have a block of information or a picture that exists as a file outside of SharePoint, then it should be added to a SharePoint site as a library document.

Use Libraries

A major objective of SharePoint is the sharing of information, with a corollary of making information readily available. While lists play a role in this, libraries play the dominant role of storing documents of all types, including those from all the Microsoft Office products, as well as pictures, graphics, and video and audio files.

ADD AND DELETE DOCUMENTS

Adding a document to a library is little more than telling SharePoint where it is on your computer or network, and deleting a document is simply removing it.

1. Click the library, such as Shared Documents, in the Quick Launch to which you want to add a document.

2. Scroll to the bottom of the library, and click **Add Document**. The Upload Document dialog box appears.

Shared Documents		▼ ☐
☐ Type	Name	Modified
📄	2011 Budget Projection	2/15/2010 8:20 PM
📄	2011 Budgeting Guidelines	2/15/2010 8:18 PM
📄	2011 Budgeting Instruct	2/19/2010 3:59 PM
📄	2011 Manufacturing Plan	2/19/2010 6:07 PM
📄	2011 Marketing Budget	2/19/2010 3:59 PM
📄	2011 Quarterly Budget	3/3/2010 6:01 PM
📄	Contacts	3/3/2010 10:40 AM

➕ Add document

3. Click **Browse** and navigate to and select the file on your computer or network that you want to upload. If the file being uploaded possibly has the same name as another file in the library, determine if you want to overwrite the existing file, select (or check) the check box accordingly, and then click **OK**.

4. To delete an existing document in a library, move the mouse over the document, and click the check box that appears on the left of the document. In the Library Tools | Documents tab, click **Delete Document** ✖ and then click **OK** to confirm that is what you want to do.

Upload Document

Upload Document

Browse to the document you intend to upload.

Name:

[_____] Browse...

☑ Overwrite existing files

[OK] [Cancel]

CHANGE DOCUMENTS

Library documents are changed by editing them in the program that created them or in the browser with the new Office 2010 Web Apps. For example, if you want to change a document that was created in Microsoft Word, you would open it in Word or the browser Web App. While SharePoint has a particular affinity for Microsoft Office products, the files of virtually any program can be opened if you have the program available to open them. In this book we'll talk about Office files, but much of that commentary also applies to files belonging to other programs, provided you have the programs on your computer.

To change a library document:

1. Click the library, such as Shared Documents, in the Quick Launch that contains the document you want to change.

2. If needed, scroll down, and then click the name of the document. If you are asked, choose if the file should be opened for reading only or if you want to edit it by selecting one of those options, and then click **OK**.

3. The Office program or Web App will open and display the file as you saw in Figure 2-9 earlier in this chapter. Depending on where the files are stored and the settings and permissions established, you may see a message that the program has opened in Protected view. If you trust the file and want to edit it, click **Enable Editing**, either in the ribbon, if it is displayed there, or in the Info area of the Backstage view.

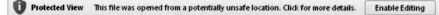

4. Edit the document as you otherwise would in the program that opened it using all the tools available to you.

5. When you are done editing, be sure to save the file without changing the path and folder name where the program is stored so it remains available in your SharePoint library.

6. Finally, close the program that you were using to change the document and reopen your SharePoint site, which may be already open on your desktop, or be an icon you can click on in the taskbar at the bottom of the screen.

NOTE

After saving a document back to the SharePoint library, you can save it a second time to a different location if you wish and have the appropriate permission, but make sure you first save it back to the library.

QUICK**FACTS**

EDITING OFFICE DOCUMENTS

A unique and recent development relating to Office files—in particular, Word, Excel, and PowerPoint files—is that they can be opened with either a copy of the Office program running on your computer, or with the Office Web App running on the SharePoint server or server farm you are connected to (see Figure 2-18). While some of the features in the stand-alone programs are not available with the Web Apps, most of the commonly used features are in both. If you have Web Apps available to you, it may open automatically when you go to edit an Office document. If you want to use the stand-alone program, there is an option on the right of the ribbon to open it.

In the majority of circumstances, either the stand-alone Office program or the Web Apps can be used with the exercises in this book that talk about using Office. When it is important that you use one or the other, we'll specifically state that. Otherwise, it's your choice.

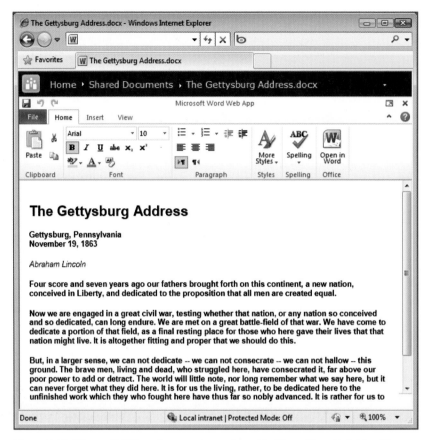

Figure 2-18: *Microsoft Office documents can be edited from SharePoint in either the stand-alone program or in your browser with Office Web Apps, as shown here.*

Use Surveys

Surveys are a way of collecting information. SharePoint provides a way of doing that along with some simple analysis of the information that is collected. SharePoint surveys are created in SharePoint, as described in Chapter 6, and then filled out and the data collected and analyzed on the site. Here we will look at how to fill out a simple survey on skills, and then look the data

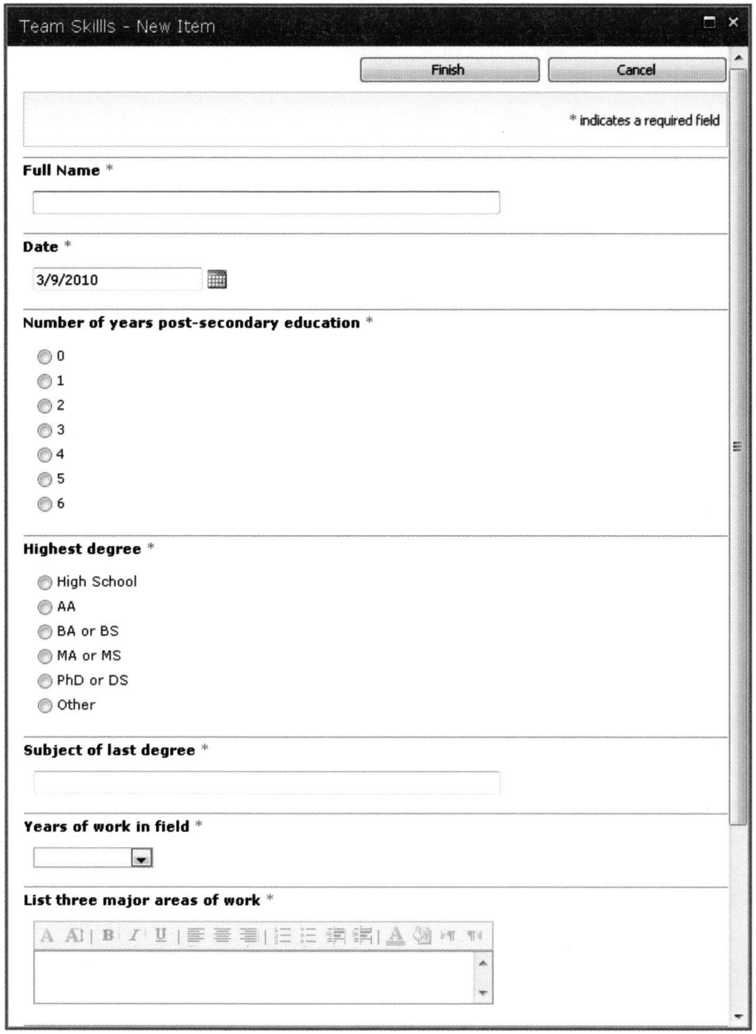

Figure 2-19: Surveys are a quick, low-cost way of getting information from a small or large group of people.

analysis that results. The link to a survey can be in many places. For simplicity, we'll assume that it is on the Home page's Quick Launch. You may have to go through several other links to locate yours. See "Use All Site Content" later in this chapter to locate a survey on your site.

1. Navigate to the location of your survey, and click its link. The survey overview will open.

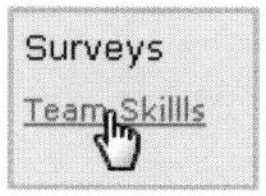

2. Confirm that this is the survey that you want to take, and then click **Respond To This Survey**. The survey will open, similar to what is shown in Figure 2-19.

3. Fill out the survey, entering the information it requests, making the appropriate choices, and when you are done, click **Finish**. The types of fields you may encounter include single and multiline text fields, number and date fields, sets of option or radio buttons, check boxes, and rating scales. All are straightforward to use.

4. Given that you have the appropriate permission, you can look at all responses by clicking **Show All Responses** and then look at individual responses by clicking one in the list. The individual response will open, as shown next, where you can edit or delete it with the links at the top of the response.

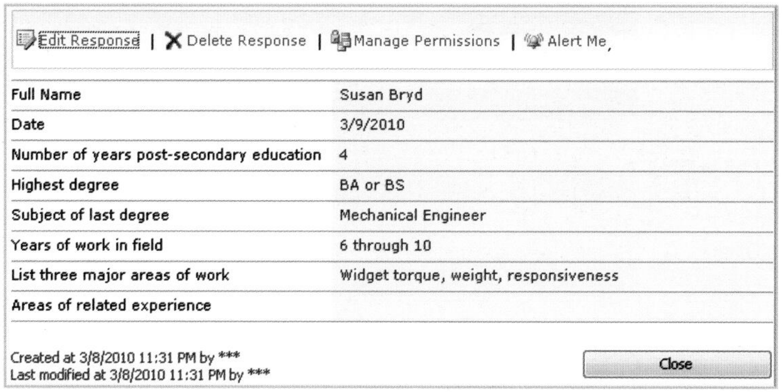

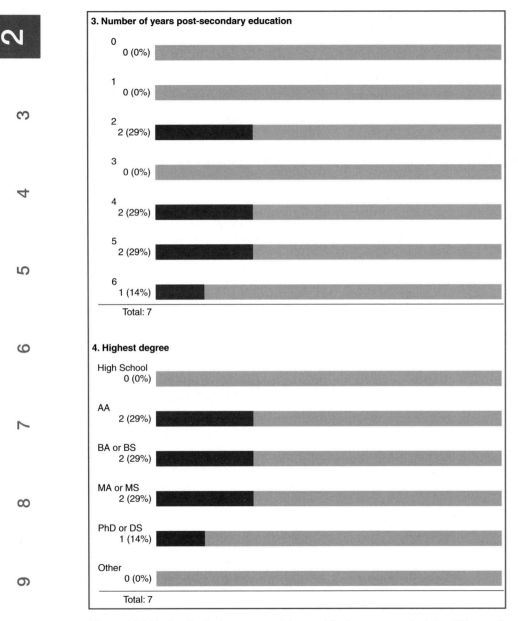

3. Number of years post-secondary education

0	0 (0%)
1	0 (0%)
2	2 (29%)
3	0 (0%)
4	2 (29%)
5	2 (29%)
6	1 (14%)

Total: 7

4. Highest degree

High School	0 (0%)
AA	2 (29%)
BA or BS	2 (29%)
MA or MS	2 (29%)
PhD or DS	1 (14%)
Other	0 (0%)

Total: 7

Figure 2-20: *During its design, you need to consider how a survey's data will be used.*

5. When you are ready, click **Close** and then click **Team Skills** or your equivalent next level up in the breadcrumb navigation.

6. From the survey overview, you can also click **Show A Graphical Summary Of Responses** and have the results of the survey graphically summarized and displayed, as shown in Figure 2-20.

7. When you are finished with the survey, click **Home** to return there.

Use Discussions

SharePoint discussions provide a threaded discourse that allows someone to start a discussion and others to reply to it, as shown in Figure 2-21. Look at how to both add to an existing discussion and start a new one.

ADD TO A DISCUSSION

Discussions can be anywhere in a site, but, by default, SharePoint puts a team discussion on the Home page of a new site. If you do not see a discussion on your Home page, click **All Site Content** and look under Discussion Boards.

1. Navigate to and then click the discussion you want to add comments to. In the list of subjects that appears, click the one that interests you. That should open a discussion thread similar to what you see in Figure 2-21.

2. Read through the discussion and determine if you want your reply to be to the original comment or to one of the respondents. In the one you choose, click **Reply** to open the New Item dialog box.

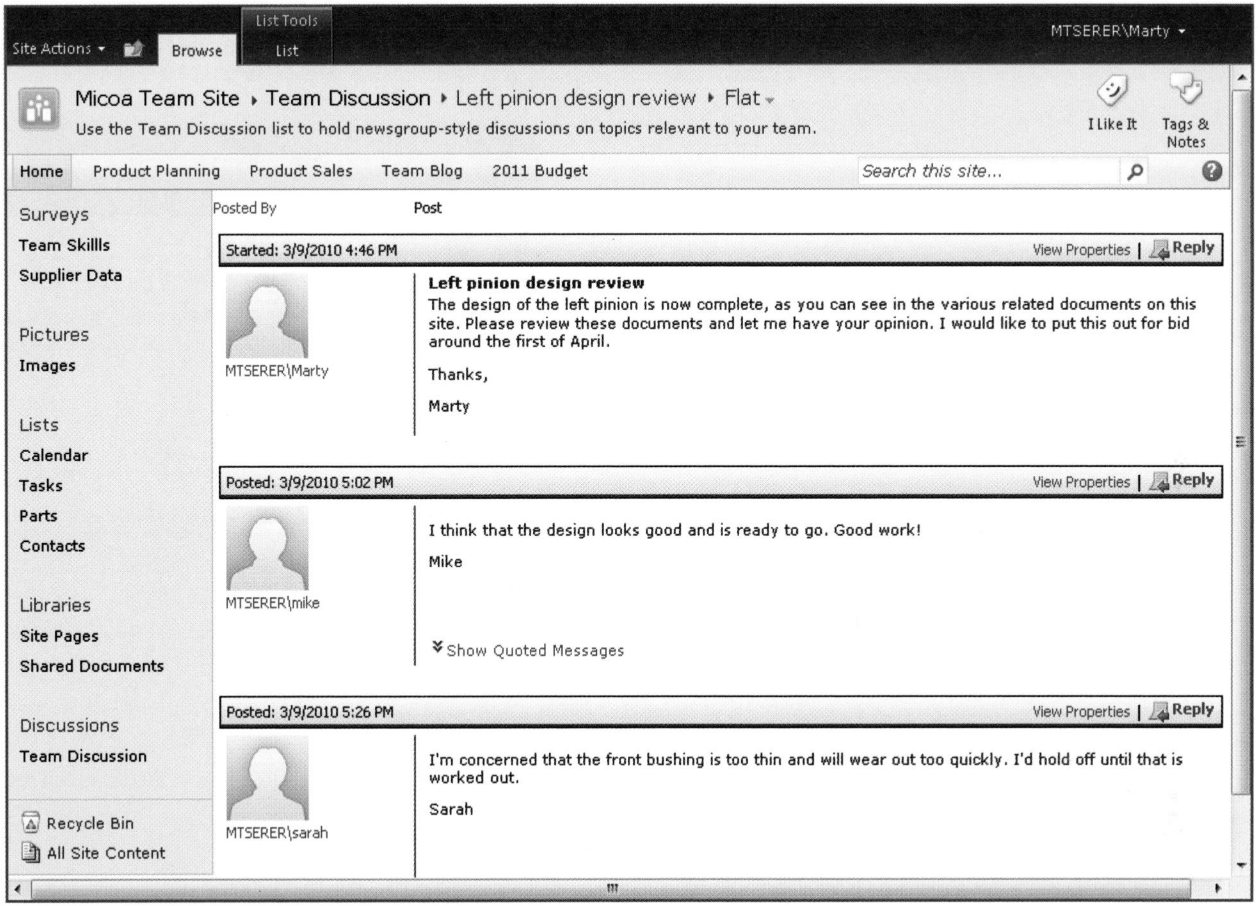

Figure 2-21: *Discussions provide an easy way to gather comments on a particular topic.*

TIP

SharePoint provides a quick analysis of a survey, but it can also be exported to Excel for further analysis. Click **Actions** from the survey overview, and then click **Export To Spreadsheet**.

3. In the top text field, type your entry, as you see next. You may attach a file, check spelling, and format the text using the tools in the ribbon (these are further discussed in Chapter 3).

4. When you are done, click **Save** to return to the threaded discussion. If you are ready, click **Home** to return there.

START A DISCUSSION

If you wish to discuss a new subject that is not currently under discussion:

1. Navigate to and then click the discussion to which you want to add a new subject.

2. At the bottom of the list of subjects, click **Add New Discussion**. The New Item dialog box appears.

3. Type a subject and then the body of the discussion you want to start, as you see in Figure 2-22. You can open the Edit tab to attach files and check spelling. The Editing Tools Format Text tab provides formatting assistance, while the Insert tab allows you to add tables, pictures, and links to files.

4. When you have completed your new discussion, click **Save** and then click **Home** to return there.

TIP

Depending on the practice in your organization, if you want a timely response to your discussion, you might drop an e-mail to the people you most want to respond, telling them you have put a new discussion on your group's SharePoint site. And the reason not to just use e-mail for the discussion is that SharePoint allows everybody to see what everybody else is saying, making it a much more open process. You could also have the team subscribe to alerts, where they would automatically receive an e-mail message when an item in a list or library they are interested in changes. See Chapter 6 for a discussion of alerts.

NOTE

You can include graphics in discussions and blog entries, but you have to make sure that they are posted in a location everyone has access to. If you link to a graphic file on your computer, only you will be able to see it. Therefore, to display graphics, first upload them to a library on the site, and then use the Insert tab to tell SharePoint to display a view of the pictures from the library.

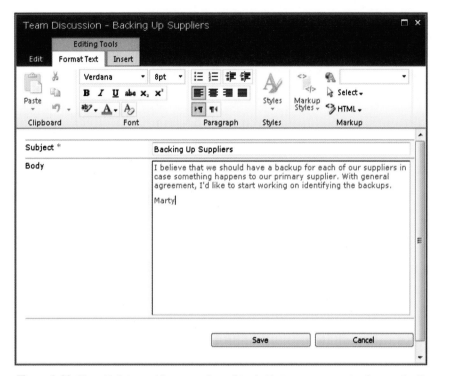

*Figure 2-22: **SharePoint provides a number of tools that you can use to do practically anything you want in the body text box.***

Use All Site Content

All Site Content, which you saw in Figure 2-6, is the central place to find anything on your site. It lists all of the libraries, pages (the list of site pages is a library, with the pages being individual files), pictures, lists, discussions, surveys, sites, and workspaces. The individual elements (libraries, lists, discussions) are listed alphabetically within their categories. You can open All Site Content by clicking that title at the bottom of any page in the site that has a Quick Launch.

You can open any element by clicking its name, and you can create any element by clicking **Create** at the top of the All Site Content. When you click **Create**, a dialog box appears listing all of the templates that are available by default in SharePoint for libraries, lists, pages, and sites, as shown in Figure 2-23. In Chapter 3 we'll discuss creating sites, pages, and Web Parts. In Chapter 4 we'll discuss creating and managing lists; Chapter 5 will cover libraries; and Chapter 6 will cover creating surveys, discussions, and forms.

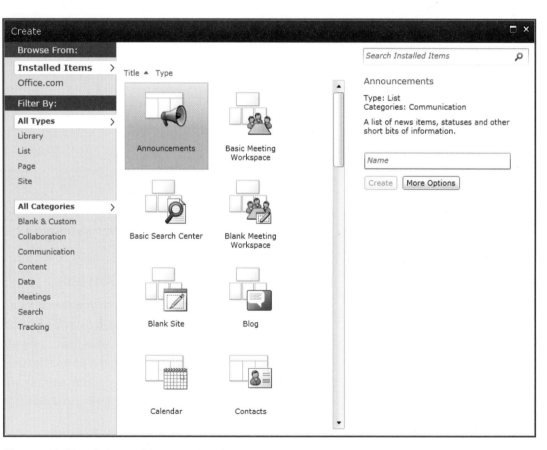

*Figure 2-23: **SharePoint provides a number of templates for creating several variations of each of its elements.***

Use the Recycle Bin

The concept of a Recycle Bin has been in Microsoft Windows for at least 15 years, so you probably know that when you delete something, it goes into the Recycle Bin, where you can retrieve it should you change your mind. The Recycle Bin in SharePoint works in the same way. Anything that you delete in SharePoint goes into the Recycle Bin. At a later time you can open the Recycle Bin and choose to restore the item or permanently delete it. To open and use the Recycle Bin:

1. On any site page with a Quick Launch, click **Recycle Bin**, the second-to-last item in the Quick Launch. The Recycle Bin opens similar to what you see in Figure 2-24.

2. To either restore an item to its original location or permanently delete it, click the check box on the left of the item.

3. To restore the item, click **Restore Selection** above the list of items. A message box opens and asks if you are sure you want to restore the item. If so, click **OK**; otherwise, click **Cancel**.

4. To permanently delete the selected item, click **Delete Selection**. Again a message box opens and asks if you are sure. If so, click **OK**; otherwise, click **Cancel**.

5. If you want to either restore or permanently delete all the items in the Recycle Bin, click the check box in the title bar to the left of Type, and then click the action you want to take.

6. When you are done with the Recycle Bin, click **Home** to return there.

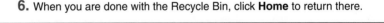

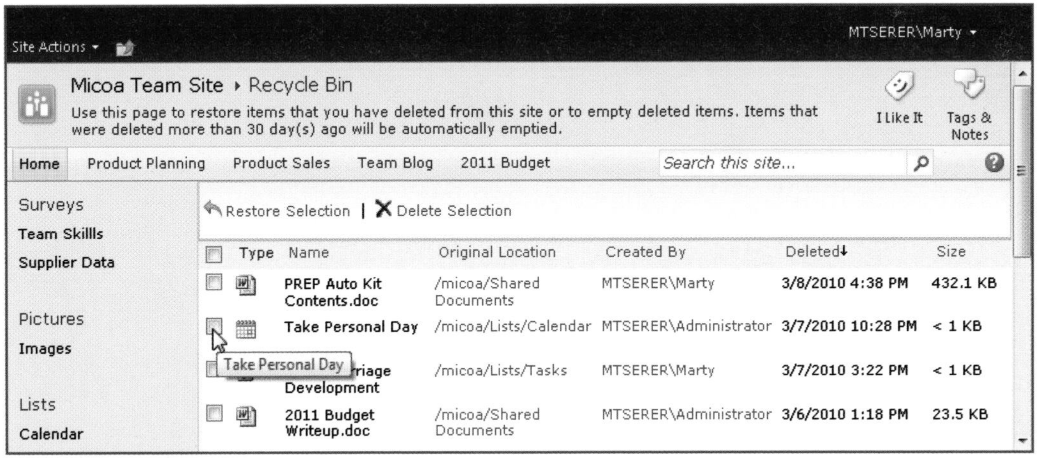

Figure 2-24: The Recycle Bin is a good safety valve to prevent accidently deleting something.

Chapter 3
Adding Sites, Pages, and Web Parts

A SharePoint site is meant to be modified by its users, such as you. There are a large number of ways to modify a SharePoint site, and the rest of this book will be spent explaining how to do that. In this chapter we'll look at adding and working with the foundation elements of a site, subsites, workspaces, pages, and Web Parts.

Create and Configure Subsites

Subsites, as discussed here, are sites within or subsidiary to the primary site for your organization, which itself may be a subsite of your parent organization's site (as the Micoa Team Site, shown in the examples in this book, is of the Micoa Corporate site). A *subsite* is a discrete web entity with its own Home page and subsidiary pages, as well as its own permissions, settings, views, and features. It has both a hierarchically higher and more independent structure than does a webpage, which is part of and dependent on a site. (See the "Understanding Subsites versus Pages" QuickFacts later in this chapter.)

Plan a New Site

To create a SharePoint site, you first need the permission to do that. Different organizations have different philosophies about this permission. Here we assume that you have or can get it, possibly with some restrictions about what you can do with the site.

With this permission, you then need to determine what the major purpose and content of the site will be. This is a mandatory first step because it provides the means of determining many other facets of the site—most importantly, you next need to determine where within the primary site you want the new site to be and what is the best template to use for the site.

SET THE SITE LOCATION

Your new site's location, where it can be found and accessed, is an important factor in its usability. If it supports a major topic or area of focus for your organization and is of broad interest for all the organization's members, you probably want the site to be accessed from the Home page where all site users can easily find it. If the new site has a smaller area of focus and interest and fits well within the scope of another site, you probably want to put your site in the secondary site.

To know where your site belongs, look at the existing structure and sites in the current system and see where your site logically fits. Then talk to other site users who may use your site and see what parts of the primary site they currently use and what would be easiest for them to get to your site.

CHOOSE A TEMPLATE

Although you can build a site from scratch, it is a considerable task and not recommended without a lot of experience. To get you up and running quickly, SharePoint provides 14 site and workspace templates (see the "Understanding Workspaces" QuickFacts in this chapter). These templates provide a complete site that is ready to use with lists, libraries, and discussions appropriate for the type of site, as shown in Table 3-1. You can, of course, customize the site in any way you choose, but you start out with a lot of work already done for you.

Your organization may have additional site templates that you may be directed to use, and there are a number of third-party SharePoint templates that are available for purchase. Start out with a template that looks to be a good starting place for the site you want to create. The Team Site is a common starting template. In this and the following several chapters, you'll see how to make many changes and additions to the site so that it becomes the final product you want.

SITE TEMPLATE	DESCRIPTION	LISTS	LIBRARIES
Basic Meeting Workspace	To plan, organize, and capture the results of a meeting	Agenda, Attendees, Objectives	Documents
Basic Search Center	To facilitate searching a site	Search results, which can be filtered	None
Blank Meeting Workspace	To create a custom meeting site	Attendees	None
Blank Site	To create a custom site	None	None
Blog	For posting comments by a person or team	Categories, Comments, Links, Posts	Photos
Decision Meeting Workspace	For decision-making and status-checking meetings	Agenda, Attendees, Decisions, Objectives, Tasks	Documents
Document Center	To create, update, store, and manage documents	Tasks	Documents
Document Workspace	To collaboratively work on a document	Announcements, Calendar, Links, Tasks	Documents, Discussions
Group Work Site	Enables teams to create, organize, and share information	Announcements, Circulations, Group Calendar, Links, Phone Calls, Resources, Tasks	Documents, Discussions
Multipage Meeting Workspace	To plan, organize, and capture the results of a meeting	Agenda, Attendees, Objectives,	None, but two blank pages
Personalization Site	To direct information to a specific user going to their My Site	Current Contact	None
Records Center	To store, protect, and manage records	None	Drop Off Library
Social Meeting Workspace	To organize a social gathering	Attendees, Directions, Things to Bring	Pages, Discussion, Photos
Team Site	To facilitate the creation, review, sharing, and organization of information	Announcements, Calendar, Links, Tasks	Shared Documents, Site Assets, Site Pages, Team Discussion

Table 3-1: SharePoint Templates That Are Available for Creating a Site

TIP

Throughout this book you will see the phrase "navigate to…" If you are not familiar with that, it means to use the links, buttons, and menus to change what you are looking at on the screen to whatever you are supposed to navigate to. Another way to say this is to "change what is on your screen to…."

Create a Site

With the location in mind of where you want to base your site and the template you want to use, you are ready to create the site.

1. From the Home page of your organization's primary site, navigate to the page that will contain the link to your new site (see the Tip about the phrase "navigate to"). Initially, this link will be in the horizontal navigation bar, but later in this book, you'll see how you can put that link anywhere.

2. Either on the Quick Launch or in the Site Actions menu, click **View All Site Content**, and then, at the top of the All Site Content page, click **Create**. The Create dialog box appears.

3. Click **Site** in the middle-left area to show only the site templates, shown in Figure 3-1. You can click the various templates and read about them in the column on the right.

4. Click the site template you want to use, and click in the **Title** text box. Type the official name of the site. This is the name that will appear in the subsite's parent's horizontal navigation bar.

5. Press **TAB** to move to the URL text box. The URL name is the part of URL that will reference your new site. See the "Naming Sites and Pages" QuickFacts in this chapter for what you should consider when creating a URL name.

6. Type the URL name you want, and click **Create**. You new site will open, as you can see in Figure 3-2.

If you do not have Microsoft Silverlight installed on your computer, your list of new sites, pages, lists, and libraries will look different than what you see in Figure 3-1. Your options, though, will be the same.

I chose the Group Work Site template. I gave the site the name of "Planning Group" and the URL name of "group." The new site is a subsite to the Planning site, which is in turn a subsite to the primary site "Micoa." The site is hosted on the server MTSerer. You can see all this in the URL displayed in the address box of Internet Explorer.

NAMING SITES AND PAGES

The title of a new site can be anything within reason that you might want. The only consideration is that it, at least initially, has to go in the title area of the subsite's SharePoint ribbon and in the parent's horizontal navigation bar. The URL name, however, is a different story. As has already been discussed, the URL name you provide when you create a new site or page is only part of the full URL. Therefore, you should follow several rules when creating a URL name:

- Keep it short and concise.

- Do not include spaces, because a space translates into "%20," three characters in place of one.

- Make it easy to remember, clearly relating to the site or page.

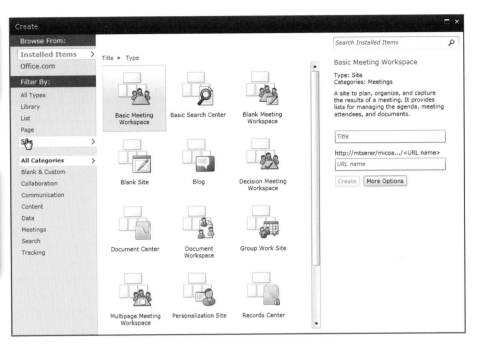

Figure 3-1: SharePoint templates give you a significant starting place when building a site.

Configure a Site

Having created a new site, you now need to consider its settings, most importantly, the site permissions. SharePoint provides a large number of settings you can configure, but all of them come with a default that you can leave set if you want. A site is configured through the Site Settings page, shown in Figure 3-3. To open Site Settings:

1. With the new site's Home page displayed on your screen, click **Site Actions** in the ribbon's tab bar.

Site Actions ▾

Edit Page
Modify the web parts on this page.

New Document Library
Create a place to store and share documents.

New Site
Create a site for a team or project.

More Options...
Create other types of pages, lists, libraries, and sites.

View All Site Content
View all libraries and lists in this site.

Edit in SharePoint Designer
Create or edit lists, pages, and workflows, or adjust settings.

Site Permissions
Give people access to this site.

Site Settings
Access all settings for this site.

2. Click **Site Settings** to open the page with that name, as you see in Figure 3-3.

3. Slowly run your mouse down each of the options and look at the screen tip that is displayed with each. You'll see the large amount of flexibility that you have in configuring your new page to look and behave in the way you want.

In this chapter we'll talk about some of these options, and in later chapters we will talk about other options. There are some settings, including Master Pages, Related Links Scope Settings, and Term Store Management, that are beyond the scope of this book because of the advanced nature of the settings and their infrequent use.

SET SITE USERS AND GROUPS

Setting users and groups determines who can use your new site. The settings are made through the first option in the upper-left area of Site Settings. Explore what you can do with this to control who has access to your site.

Figure 3-2: The template creates a new site for you with all the necessary elements.

TIP

The most frequent technique used with permissions is to create groups to which you give permissions and then add individual users to the groups. This makes it easier to manage permissions.

Figure 3-3: *Site Settings provide a number of options for configuring a site.*

1. With Site Settings open on your screen, click **People And Groups**. The People And Groups page opens to display the members of the primary group inherited by your site (for me, this is the Team Site Members group), as shown in Figure 3-4.

2. Click the other groups in the Group list on the left above the Quick Launch. By default, SharePoint creates three groups for a primary site (Team Site in my case):

   ● **Owners:** People who have full control of all aspects of the site

   ● **Members:** People who can read and contribute content to the site, but who cannot add elements such as lists and libraries

   ● **Visitors:** People who can only read the content of the site and cannot make changes

NOTE

Remember the discussion in Chapter 1 about authentication and authorization, where the Windows operating system performs the authentication and SharePoint performs the authorization. Windows controls who the users and groups are and authenticates them when they sign in. SharePoint controls what those users and groups can do.

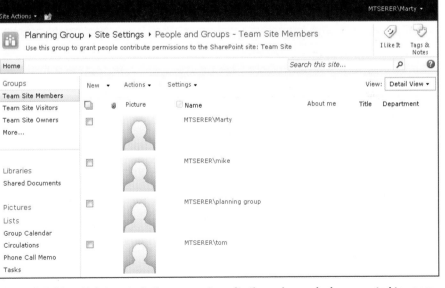

Figure 3-4: *SharePoint controls the access to a site through permissions granted to users and groups.*

CAUTION

Initially, your site has inherited the users, groups, and permissions that have been established by the sites that are hierarchically above it. They were probably originally established by the primary site for your organization or its parent and, unless they were changed by an intermediate site, they remain the same for your site. If you want different permissions from those that were inherited, you must set them yourself.

NOTE

Distribution lists in your e-mail system are not necessarily Windows security groups. If a group name cannot be found, it is probably because it is an e-mail distribution list you are looking for, not a Windows security group. Contact your network administrator or help desk for assistance in finding out what security groups are available for you to use to grant permissions to your site.

CAUTION

The only way to fully customize the permissions for your site is to stop using the inherited permissions from the parent site. The biggest problem with this is that any changes in the parent permissions, such as people leaving or joining the team, will not automatically flow down to your site; you will have to manually update them.

3. To **add users and groups** to the currently selected group, click **New** above the Group list to open the Grant Permissions dialog box. Enter user names, group names, or e-mail addresses, separated by semicolons. Then, click **Check Names** (the second from the right icon beneath the text box) or press **ENTER**. The names will be checked against those that have been set up in Windows. If they are found, the full name will replace your entry and be underlined; otherwise, you will be told of the error. When all the names are the way you want them, click **OK**.

4. To **remove users or groups** from the selected group, click in the check box on the left of the user or group, click **Actions** above the list, click **Remove Users From Group**, and click **OK** to confirm this action.

5. To **make changes to the group** that is currently selected, click **Settings** above the list, and then click **Group Settings**. Change Group Settings will appear. The primary item here is the name of the group, although you can also use this page to delete a group. When you are ready, click **OK**.

6. To **view more group options**, click **More** below the list of groups on the left. A list of the groups will appear on the right. You can click **New** above the list to add a group, but you will be reminded that your site is inheriting its groups from the parent site and you should create a new group at that level (you'll see how to stop inheriting permissions in the next section).

7. To **change the members of the list of groups** in the upper-left area, click **Settings** and click **Edit Group Quick Launch**. Add or delete groups in the text box that appears, then click **Check Names** to do that, and then click **OK**.

8. Click **Site Settings** in the breadcrumb navigation to return to Site Settings.

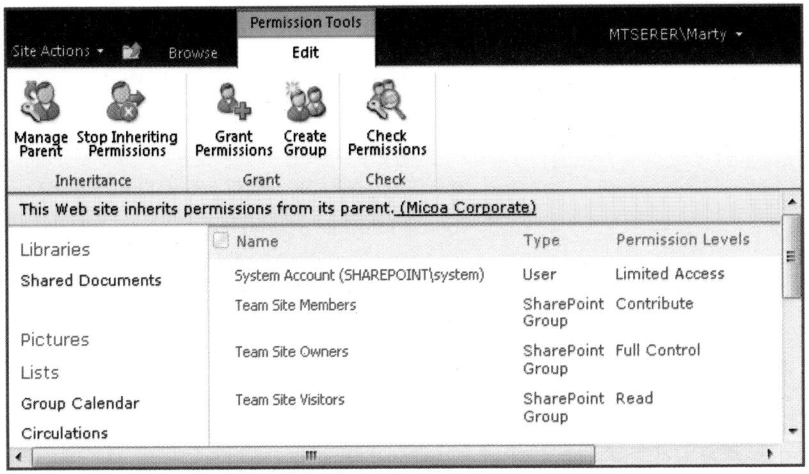

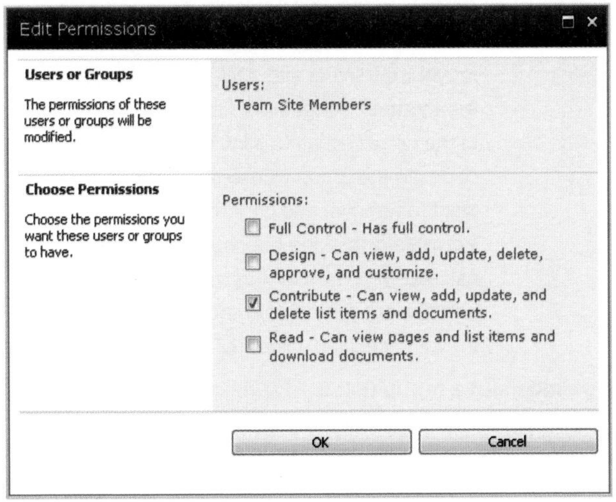

SET SITE PERMISSIONS

Settings permissions determine what the users and groups on the site can do. This is handled through the second option in the upper-left of Site Settings.

1. With Site Settings open on your screen, click **Site Permissions**. The Permissions page opens displaying the groups inherited by your site, as shown in Figure 3-5.

2. The first step is to decide if you want to **use inherited permissions**. If you use them, you are limited in what you can do on this page. You can still add users to the existing groups by clicking **Grant Permissions**, and you can check a user's or group's permissions by clicking **Check Permissions.**

3. If you decide you want to **not use inherited permissions**, you can set up your own groups and users, and give them the permissions you feel are appropriate for your site. Start by clicking **Stop Inheriting Permissions**. A message box appears reminding you what this means. If you want to go ahead, click **OK**.

4. The next decision is whether you want to **use the groups that came from the parent site** or create your own groups. The benefit of using the parent's groups is you don't have to re-create them and add all the users to them. On the other hand, a different makeup of groups could be your major motivation.

5. If you **use the parent's groups**, you can still change a group's permissions by selecting the group (click its check box) and clicking **Edit User Permissions**. The Edit Permissions dialog box appears, and you see the set of four permission levels that have been inherited from the parent site. You may select a different permission level from the set of four, but if you want a different level, you must change the permission levels that are available on the parent.

6. Select the desired permission level for the group, and click **OK**.

7. If you want **a new group**, click **Create Group** to open the Create Group page. Enter a group name, description, accept or replace the group owner (see Figure 3-6), and answer the questions about viewing and editing membership, as well as what to do about requests to join the group.

Figure 3-5: Site permissions start with inherited groups and permissions from the parent site. You can live with that, turn it off, or try to change the parent.

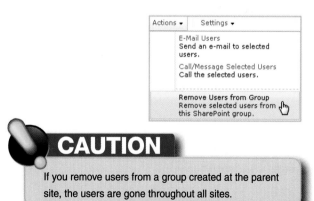

Figure 3-6: *You create your own group and give it the users and permissions that are correct for your site.*

CAUTION

If you remove users from a group created at the parent site, the users are gone throughout all sites.

8. At the bottom of the page, choose the level of permission that you want to apply to the group, and click **Create**. The People And Groups page opens similar to what you saw in the previous section, except that it is now displaying your new group with the owner as its only member.

9. To **add another user** to the group, click **New** in the Grant Permissions dialog box that appears, enter the names that you want in the group, and click the **Check Names** icon. When you have the correct set of users, click **OK**.

10. If you want to **remove a group** other than one you inherited (which can't be removed), click the group in the left column, click **Settings** above the list, click **Group Settings**, scroll down to the bottom of the page, and click **Delete**. A message will appear and ask if you are sure. If so, click **OK**.

11. If you want to **remove a group's permissions** for your particular site, click **Site Settings** in the breadcrumb navigation, click **Site Permissions** in the upper-left area, click the check box opposite the group whose permissions you want to remove, and click **Remove User Permissions** in the ribbon. A message appears asking if you want to remove the permissions for the selected group for your site. If so, click **OK**.

12. If you want to **remove the members of a group** (this is NOT recommended; see the accompanying Caution), click **Back** on the top-left area of the browser window, click **People And Groups** in the upper-left area of Site Settings, click the group in the left column, click the check box at the top of the list to select all the members (or just select the individual members you want to remove), click **Actions** above the list, and click **Remove Users From Group**. A message will appear and ask if you are sure. If so, click **OK**.

13. When you are ready, click **Site Settings** in the breadcrumb navigation to return to Site Settings.

CONFIGURE OTHER SITE SETTINGS

In this section we'll discuss several of the most commonly used options that appear on the Site Settings page. Other options are discussed elsewhere in this book. You can use the index to determine where. For example, Site Libraries And Lists is discussed in Chapters 4 and 5 on lists and libraries.

Start by going to the Site Settings of your new site. From the Home page of the new site, click **Site Actions** and then click **Site Settings**. Click each of the options discussed, and see the features available. When you are done with each option, click **Site Settings** in the breadcrumb navigation to return there.

- **Site Administration:**

  - **Sites And Workspaces:** See the current sites and workspaces beneath the current site, go to those sites, and create new ones, as you can see in Figure 3-7.

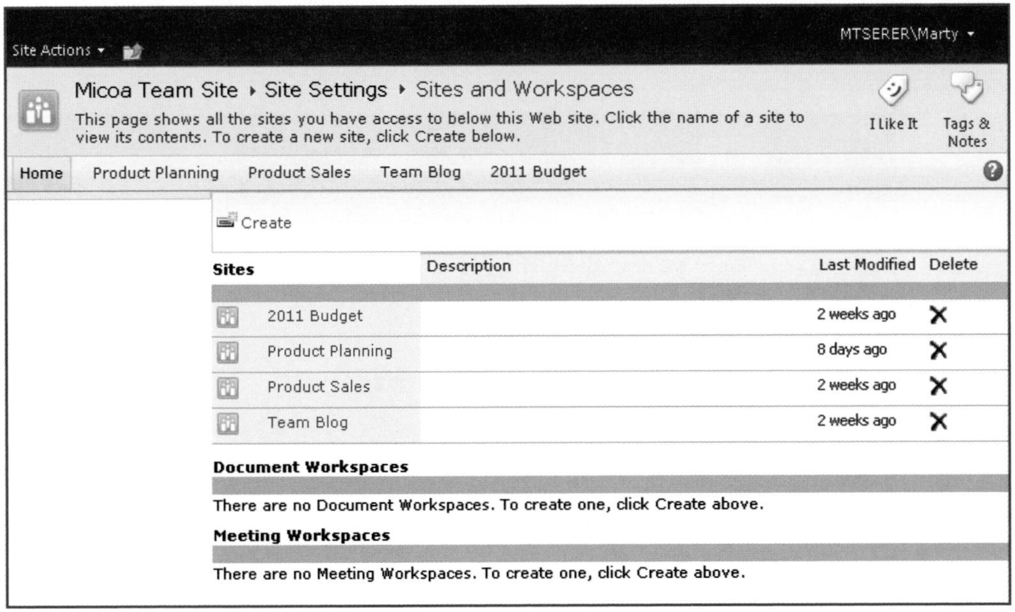

Figure 3-7: The Site Settings Sites And Workspaces provides an alternative way to go to, add, and delete sites and workspaces.

- **Look And Feel:**

  - **Title, Description, And Icon:** Change or add the current site title, description, logo, and web address.

  - **Quick Launch:** Add, delete, and change links, headings, and descriptions, as well as reorder the links and their headings, as shown in Figure 3-8. See "Customizing the Quick Launch" QuickSteps later in this chapter.

  - **Top Link Bar:** Add, change, and delete links, and add the links from the parent.

  - **Tree View:** Turn the Quick Launch and/ or the Tree View on or off. Tree View lists all the elements in the site without headings, like looking down from directly above a tree. Figure 3-9 shows the Planning Group site with the Quick Launch turned off and Tree View turned on.

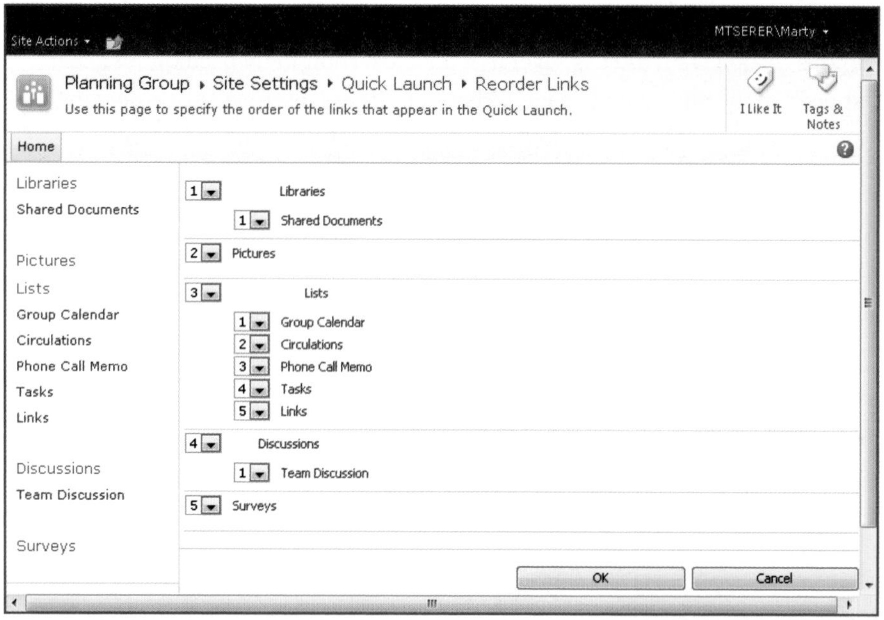

Figure 3-8: The Quick Launch can contain any links you want, with any headings, and be in any order; or it can be turned off.

Site Theme: To turn on or change the theme used to apply color and fonts to a site. The default is No Theme. The Micoa Team site shown in the first two chapters of this book used the Classic theme. The Planning Group site shown so far in this chapter has the default (no theme). Click several of the themes in the column on the right to see the effects in the middle column. If you see a theme you would like to use, select it and click **Apply** at the bottom of the page. Try one—you can always come back and change it. From here on in this chapter, you'll see the Planning Group in the Classic theme, as you can see in Figure 3-10.

● **Site Actions:**

● **Manage Site Features:** Access to ten major features that you can turn on or off to add or remove features from your site. Scroll through each of the items so you can see what is active in your current site and what options you have that might be turned on.

CAUTION

Both Reset Site Definition and Delete This Site are final and cannot be reversed. In the first case, all changes made to the site are lost. In the second, both changes and site content are permanently lost.

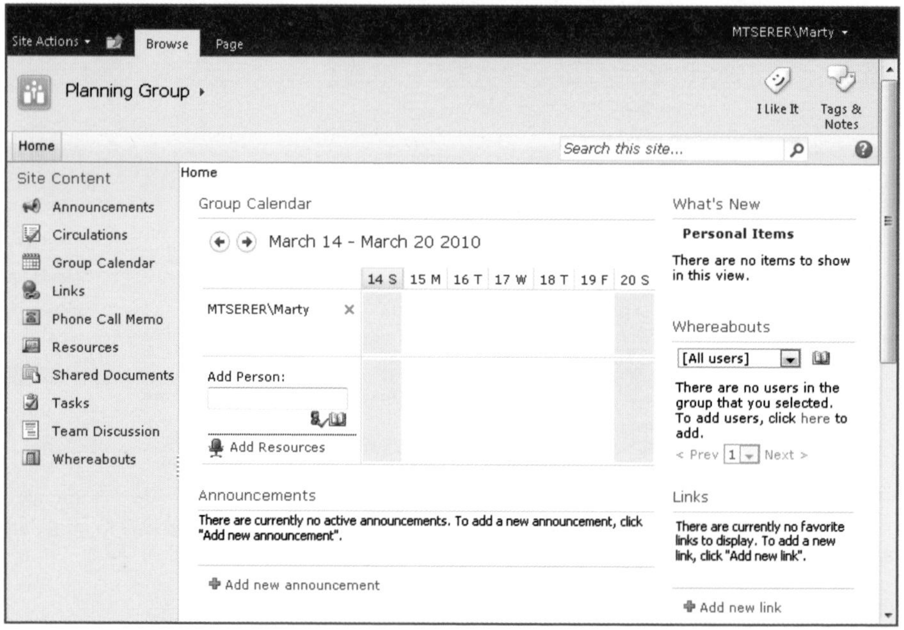

Figure 3-9: Tree View of all the site elements can replace the Quick Launch on the left of a page.

QUICKSTEPS

CUSTOMIZING THE QUICK LAUNCH

The Quick Launch navigation bar on the left of most SharePoint pages is an important navigation tool. As such, it should contain the most important links on the site and no extraneous information. To do this, you may need to add links to the Quick Launch, add headings, delete links, and change the order.

ADD LINKS TO THE QUICK LAUNCH

1. From the site's Home page, click **Site Actions**, click **Site Settings**, and click **Quick Launch**.
2. Click **New Navigation Link** at the top of the page.
3. Enter the URL for the new link. (You can do this by going to the objective of the link—for example, opening a new page you want the link to access, dragging across the URL in the address bar of Internet Explorer, and copying it by pressing **CTRL+C**. Then, in the New Navigation Link Form, dragging across **http://** and pressing **CTRL+V**.)
4. Enter a description for the link, select the heading the link will be under, and click **OK**.

ADD HEADINGS TO THE QUICK LAUNCH

1. From Site Settings Quick Launch, click **New Heading** at the top of the page.
2. Enter the URL for the link to be associated with the heading, if there is one.
3. Enter a description for the heading, and click **OK**.

DELETE LINKS FROM THE QUICK LAUNCH

1. From Site Settings Quick Launch, click the icon on the left of the heading or link that you want to delete.
2. At the bottom of the page that opens, click **Delete**. A message box opens warning you that deleting this link will delete any links under it. Click **OK**.

Continued . . .

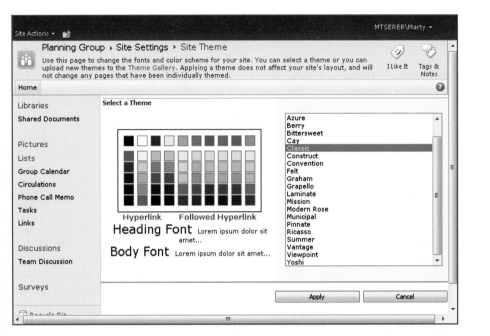

Figure 3-10: SharePoint provides a number of themes that you can use to make your site colorful.

- **Save Site As Template:** To save the current site as a template for another site, with or without its contents such as library documents, list items, and text. This is also a way to copy a site.

- **Reset Site Definition:** To remove all customizations from one or all pages in a site and reset the site to its original template definition. All changes made to the page or site will be lost.

- **Delete This Site:** To completely delete the site *and all its content*. All documents, libraries, lists, list items, discussions, surveys, calendars, settings, and unique permissions will be lost.

- **Site Web Analytics:** Collect and control the statistics relating to the use of the website. As you can see in Figure 3-11 showing the Summary report, the information is quite extensive and there are nine additional pages that are accessed from the column on the left.

CUSTOMIZING THE QUICK LAUNCH

(Continued)

CHANGE THE ORDER OF LINKS ON THE QUICK LAUNCH

1. From Site Settings Quick Launch, click **Change Order** at the top of the page.

2. In the page that was shown in Figure 3-8, select the numeric order of the headings and the links within the headings.

3. When you have the order the way you want, click **OK**.

4. If you want to move a link to a different heading, click the icon on the left of the link you want to move, click the **Heading** down arrow, select the heading you want, and click **OK**.

The result of these steps on the Planning Group Quick Launch is shown in Figure 3-12.

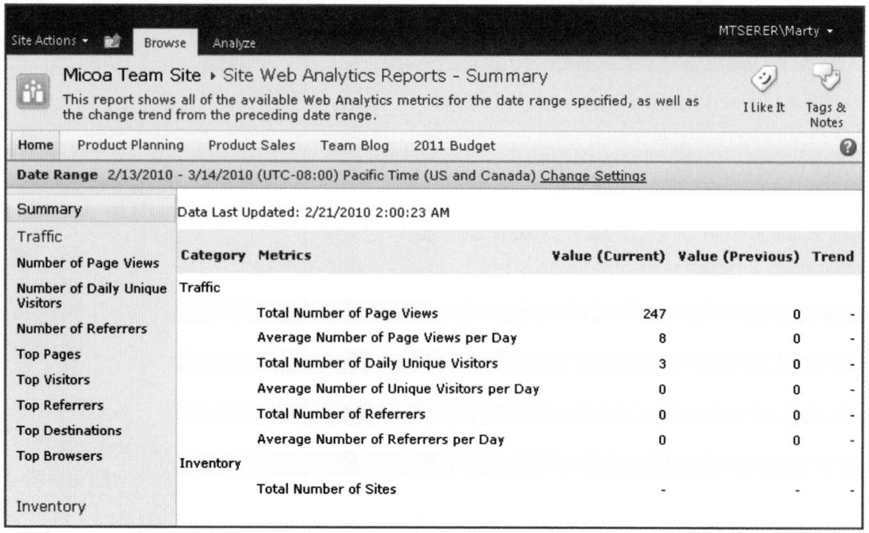

CHANGING THE HORIZONTAL NAVIGATION BAR

Second in importance to only the Quick Launch, the horizontal navigation bar needs to be a fully functioning navigation tool in your Web site. By default, the horizontal navigation bar only contains links to the subsites to this site. That's fine if you have subsites, but if you choose to build your site without them and just use pages, you might want the major pages on the horizontal navigation bar. Here's how.

Continued . . .

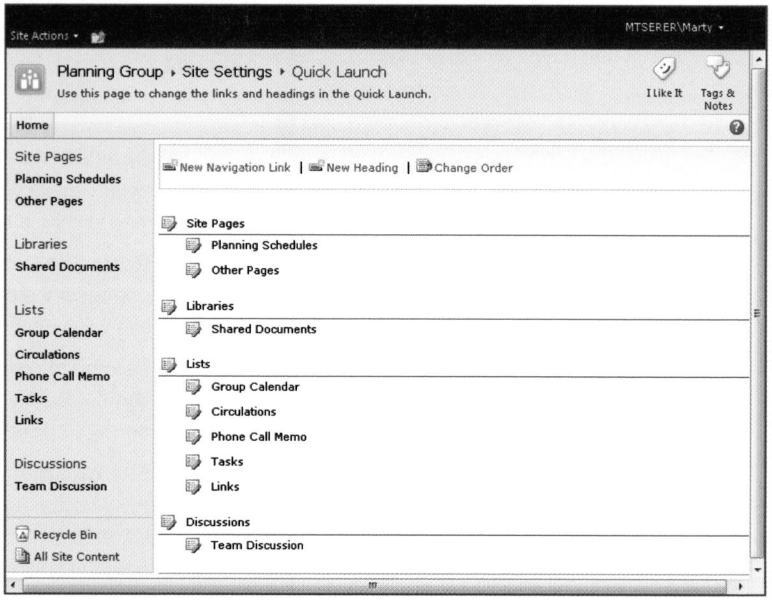

Figure 3-11: SharePoint automatically collects a significant amount of information about site usage.

Figure 3-12: Compare the Quick Launch here to earlier figures that show the Planning Group Quick Launch.

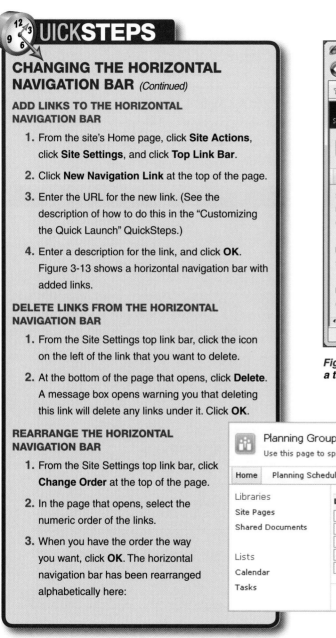

QUICKSTEPS

CHANGING THE HORIZONTAL NAVIGATION BAR *(Continued)*

ADD LINKS TO THE HORIZONTAL NAVIGATION BAR

1. From the site's Home page, click **Site Actions**, click **Site Settings**, and click **Top Link Bar**.

2. Click **New Navigation Link** at the top of the page.

3. Enter the URL for the new link. (See the description of how to do this in the "Customizing the Quick Launch" QuickSteps.)

4. Enter a description for the link, and click **OK**. Figure 3-13 shows a horizontal navigation bar with added links.

DELETE LINKS FROM THE HORIZONTAL NAVIGATION BAR

1. From the Site Settings top link bar, click the icon on the left of the link that you want to delete.

2. At the bottom of the page that opens, click **Delete**. A message box opens warning you that deleting this link will delete any links under it. Click **OK**.

REARRANGE THE HORIZONTAL NAVIGATION BAR

1. From the Site Settings top link bar, click **Change Order** at the top of the page.

2. In the page that opens, select the numeric order of the links.

3. When you have the order the way you want, click **OK**. The horizontal navigation bar has been rearranged alphabetically here:

Figure 3-13: This horizontal navigation bar has added links to a page, a calendar, a task list, and a document library.

NOTE

The horizontal navigation bar settings option to use links from the site's parent replaces all the current links with ones from the parent site. In effect, it deletes any links previously on the horizontal navigation bar.

Add and Manage Pages

All sites start with at least one page, the Home page, and some site templates have more. If you want more room for content, you can add a subsite, or you can add pages. Adding and managing pages is a bit simpler than adding sites. You need only determine the site in which you want to place the page and choose a template, but there are only two page templates.

Create ☐ ✕

Browse From:

| **Installed Items** > |
| Office.com |

Filter By:

▲

All Types
Library
List
Page >
Site

All Categories >

▼

Title ▲ Type

Page   Web Part Page

Search Installed Items

Page

Type: Page
Categories: Content, Blank & Custom

A page which can be easily edited in the web browser using Web Edit. Pages can contain text, images, and wiki links, as well as lists and other web parts. Pages are useful for collaborating on small projects.

Name

Create | More Options

- **Page** provides a blank page with only a blank text area at the top. The page can contain text, images, links, lists, libraries, and discussions.

- **Web Part Page** provides a number of different layouts of empty Web Part zones (areas into which you can insert Web Parts) on a page. The page contains the specified default Web Part zones, which in turn can hold lists, libraries, discussions, and surveys.

Add a Page

To add a page to a particular site:

1. From the Home page of the site in which you want the new page, click **Site Actions** and then click **More Options**.

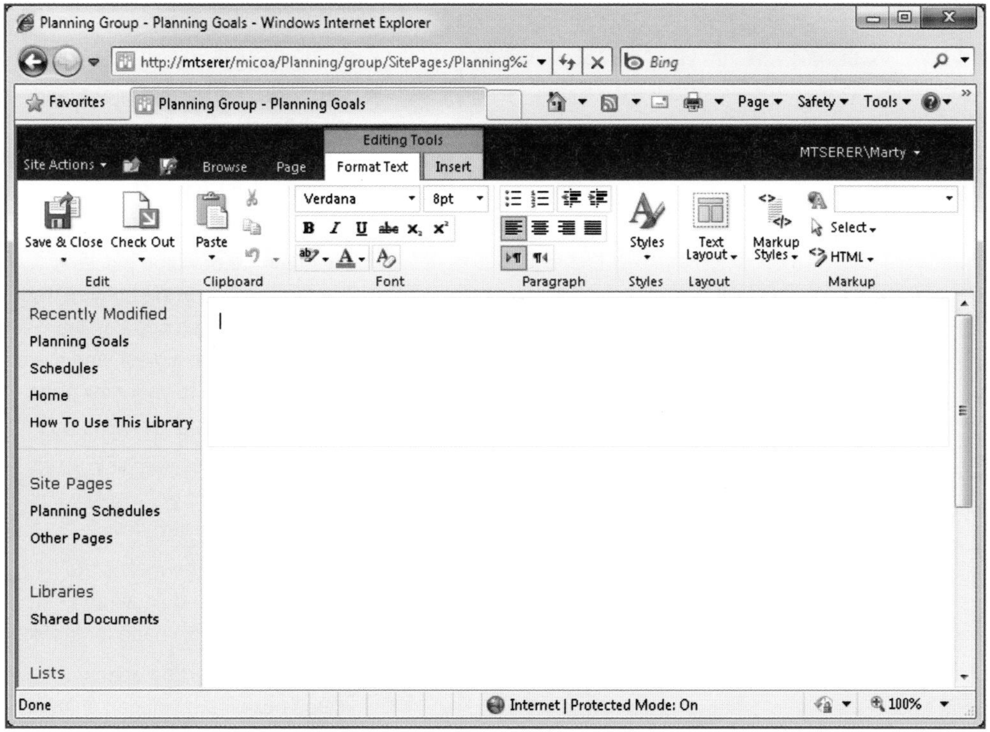

Figure 3-14: *The Page template gives you a blank page on which you can add any SharePoint element.*

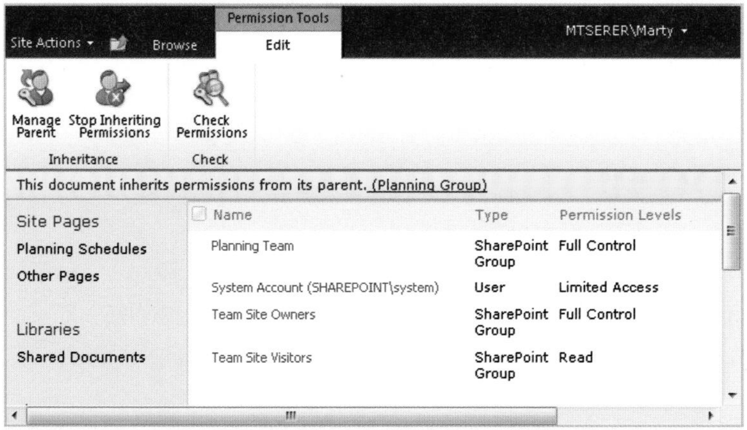

2. Click **Page** in the left column to see the two page templates shown earlier.

- Click the default **Page** template, type a name, and click **Create**. The new page will open with Editing Tools open in the ribbon, as shown in Figure 3-14.

  –Or–

- Click **Web Part Page**, and click **Create**. The New Web Part Page opens (see Figure 3-15). Enter a name for the page, and then review the layout options by clicking each and looking at the result in the middle column. Click the layout you want to use, select the library in which the page will reside, and click **Create**. The page will open with Page Editing open in the ribbon. An example of a resulting Web Part page is shown in Figure 3-16.

3. Click **Browse** and click **Home** to return there.

Configure a Page

Configuring a page is considerably simpler than configuring a site. The Page tab on the ribbon gives you the options that are available to tailor the page to meet your needs.

1. With a new page open, click the **Page** tab if it isn't already displayed.

2. Click **Edit Properties** to open a page where you can change the name of the page. If you do that, click **Save** to complete it.

3. Click **Permission** to open Permission Tools in the ribbon and display the permission groups active on this page. Initially, the permissions are inherited from the parent site. You can turn off inheriting permissions, add and remove members of a group, and delete a local group, all as explained in "Set Site Permissions" earlier in this chapter.

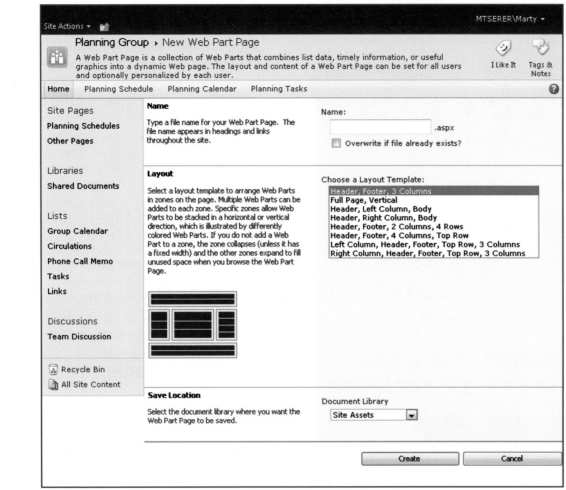

Figure 3-15: *When creating a Web Part page, you have a choice of eight different page layouts.*

4. The other options available on the Page tab include:

- **Versions**, **Approve**, **Reject**, and **Workflows** are used with pages that have workflows attached, as discussed in Chapter 6.

- **E-Mail A Link** opens an Outlook message window and places a link to the page in the body of the message. You can address the message, add a subject, and invite people to come to your new page.

- **Edit Mobile Page** opens a page where you can select the Web Parts that should be displayed on a mobile (and smaller) device.

- **Make Home Page** makes the current page the default (and, therefore, "Home") page for the site.

- **Title Bar Properties** opens a dialog box where you can change the page title, add a caption and a description, and add a link to an image you want in the title bar.

5. When you have finished configuring your new page, click **Stop Editing** to save your work and end the editing session.

Add and Work with Web Parts

As explained in Chapter 1, a Web Part is a container that can hold a list, a library, a discussion, a survey, a form, text, or an image. You can have none, or

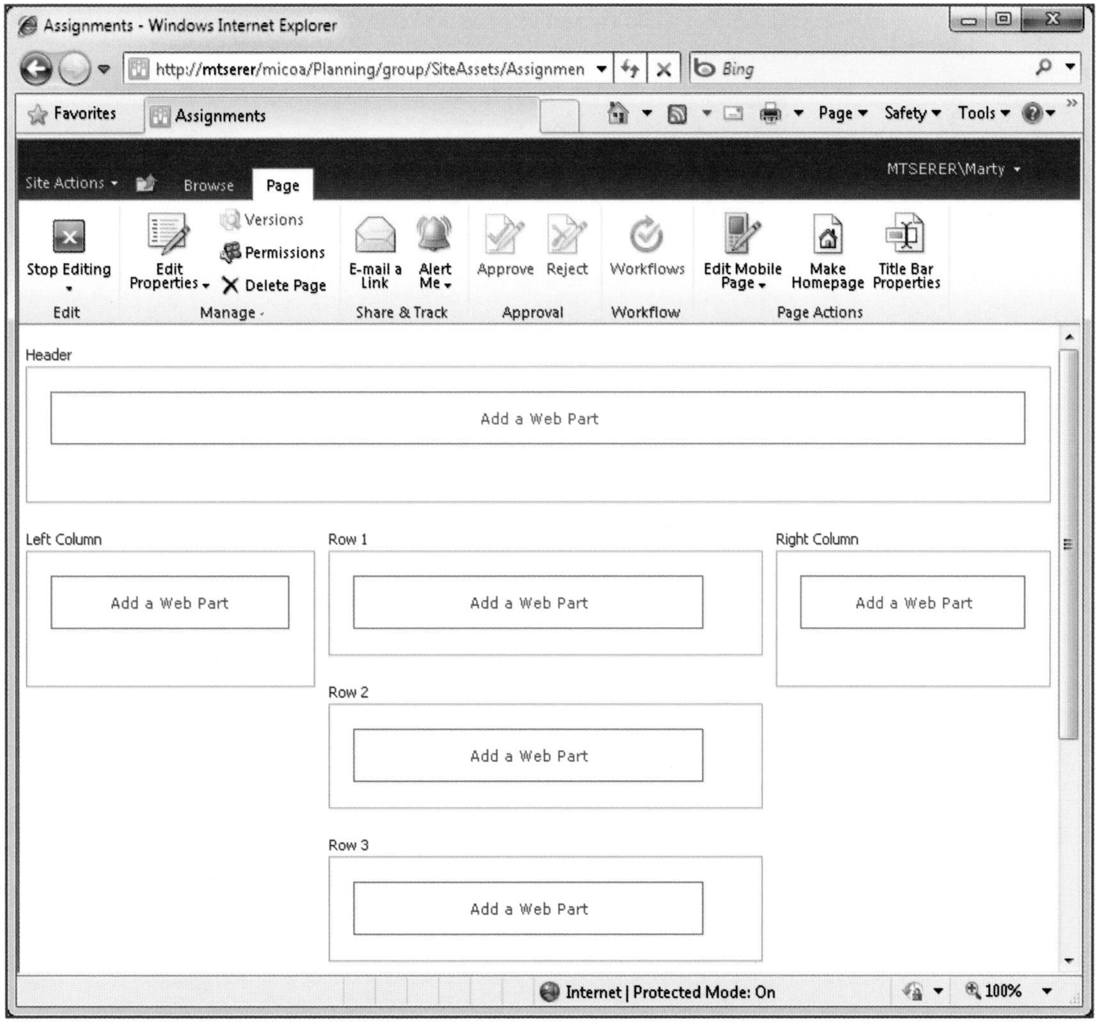

Figure 3-16: *A Web Part page allows you to place Web Parts in different areas of the page, depending on the layout you choose.*

many, Web Parts on a page. Web Parts help organize a page and encapsulate the various pieces of content to make them easier to work with. Chapters 4, 5, and 6 will talk a lot about working with the content of web parts; here, we'll talk about adding Web Parts to a page and to their configuration.

Add Web Parts

You can add Web Parts in two ways:

- By being incorporated in a template you have used, either with specific content, as you have seen in the Group Work Site template early in this chapter, or as an empty Web Part page, as you see in the Web Part Page template in Figure 3-16

- By manually adding a Web Part to a page

You've seen how to create sites and pages with templates that contain Web Parts, so here we'll talk about the manual addition of a Web Part to a page.

To add a Web Part to any page:

1. From your Home page, navigate to the page on which you want to add a Web Part.

2. Click the **Edit Page** icon 🖉 in the ribbon's tab bar. The Editing Tools tabs will open.

NOTE

This discussion pertains to adding Web Parts to a page that was created using the methods discussed in this chapter. You can use these techniques to add Web Parts to predefined areas of pages called *Web Part zones*. If there are no Web Part zones defined in a page, you will not be able to add Web Parts to them via the browser; instead, you have to use SharePoint Designer to add them.

3. Click the **Editing Tools | Insert** tab, and then click **Web Part**. The expanded Web Part selection will appear as follows:

4. Scan down and where needed, click the options under Web Parts to get an understanding of the Web Parts in the Lists And Libraries category. Note the explanation in the right pane. These are the lists and libraries that are available from other pages in your site.

5. Click each of the other categories, and look at the Web Parts that are available with them. These will be discussed further in the following chapters.

6. When you are ready, click the Web Part you want to add, and click **Add**. The Web Part appears on the page, like this:

Configure Web Parts

With a new Web Part on your page, review the options available to configure it to meet your requirements. There are two aspects of configuring a Web Part: configuring the Web Part itself, which we'll discuss here, and configuring the contents of the Web Part, which we'll discuss over the next several chapters.

1. If you currently do not have the Web Part on your screen, navigate to it so it is displayed.

2. Click the **Edit Page** icon in the ribbon's tab bar. The Editing Tools tabs will open.

3. Move the mouse over the right end of the Web Part until a check box appears on the far right. Click that check box. This selects the Web Part and its contents.

4. Two additional contextual tool tabs appear: one for the contents of the Web Part, discussed in later chapters, and one for the Web Part itself. Click the **Web Part Tools | Options** tab to open it in the ribbon.

5. Click **Web Part Properties** in the Web Part Tools | Options menu. This opens a task pane on the right of the browser window with a number of properties you can select or set, as shown in Figure 3-17. This is where you can change the text in the title bar above the Web Part by changing the text in the Title box in the Appearance section.

6. Scroll down through the Web Part properties task pane, opening each of the sections and looking at them. Make any necessary changes so that the Web Part looks and behaves the way you want. ("Edit Current View" in the first section edits the content, not the Web Part, and is discussed in Chapter 4.)

7. When you have completed the changes you wish to make in the Web Part properties task pane, click **OK** at the bottom of the pane. It will close.

8. With the Web Part Tool | Options tab still open in the ribbon (if it isn't, repeat steps 2 and 3) review the other options. Insert Related List is for the circumstance where you have two lists that reference one another and you want to include the second list on the page.

9. The Minimize, Restore, and Delete options are self-explanatory.

10. When you are done configuring the Web Part, click **Save And Close** to save your changes and close the editor.

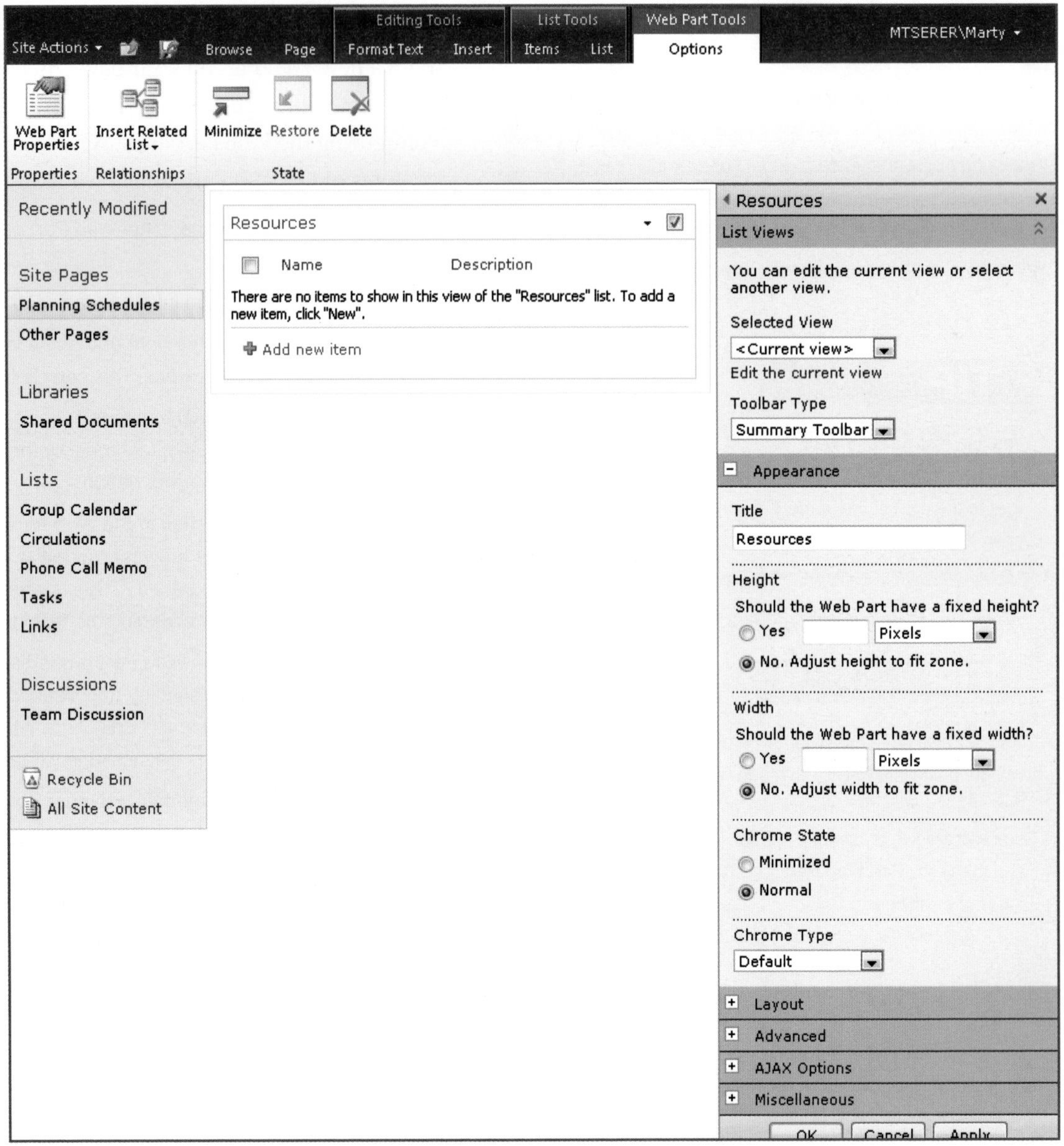

Figure 3-17: *The Web Part properties task pane provides a number of ways to tailor the Web Part to meet your needs.*

Chapter 4

Creating and Managing Lists

SharePoint lists form the backbone of the program. Lists are used for storing user data, SharePoint settings, and even storing the other elements such as web analytics and workflows. A list is a table, similar to a spreadsheet, and like a spreadsheet, it can contain anything that you would want to spread across a series of columns and over a number of rows. Think of a list as a series of columns of information, with each item in the list being a row. All items have the same categories of information, which are the columns, such as a last name, an address, or a part number. SharePoint actually has a Datasheet View for lists to confirm its similarity to spreadsheets.

In Chapter 3 you saw how to add information to lists. In this chapter we'll look at creating lists, then how to modify and customize them, and finally how to manage them, including establishing permissions for both lists and items, selecting and filtering a list, and creating and using views.

Create a List

Like most everything in SharePoint, lists are created with the use of a template. You start by defining what it is you need in a list, then selecting a template that is closest to what you want, and finally modifying it to get exactly what you want. SharePoint gives you many tools and options to do this.

Define a List

Defining a list is not difficult, but it needs to be done to assure that the list does what you want. Start by asking these questions:

- What is the purpose of the list; what is to be accomplished with it?
- What fields does the list require? Examples are name, title, description, start date, cost, item number, contact, and so on.
- What are the most important fields? You may want some views that show only some of the fields.
- What is the formatting of each field; do you show cents as well as dollars?
- Who is going to use the list, and what permission scheme is required?
- How is the list populated, from what source, and by whom?
- How is the list maintained, from what source, and by whom?
- What is the life of the list?

This is not meant to be an exhaustive list of questions to ask yourself, but the point is to fully think through the list before creating it. You may want to involve others if they will be using the list a lot.

Prepare to Add a List

There are at least three ways to add a list to a page, but, depending on the type of page you have, you may not always have all three choices.

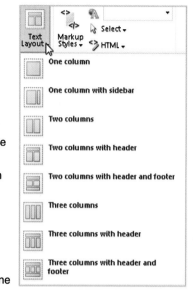

1. Navigate to the page on which you want the list.

2. **If it is a blank page** (the default when you create a new page without specifying a template) or content from a team template, click the **Edit** icon on the tab bar. Otherwise skip to step 5.

3. Consider if you want to keep the current layout, the default of a single column in a new blank page, or want some other layout. If so, in the Editing Tools I Formatting Text tab, click **Text Layout** to open a drop-down menu and select one of the layouts. You will see a faint outline around each Web Part zone.

4. Click in the Web Part zone in which you want the new list, click the **Editing Tools I Insert** tab, and click **New List**. The Create List dialog box will appear displaying libraries and lists. We'll talk about the libraries in the next chapter, and the lists in the next section of this chapter.

5. **If the page has content from a meeting template** or otherwise does not have the Edit page icon, click the **Page** tab on the tab bar, and click **Edit Page** on the left of the ribbon.

Create List

List Title:

Libraries	Communications	Tracking	Custom Lists
Record Library	Announcements	Links	Custom List
Document Library	Contacts	Calendar	Custom List in Datasheet View
Form Library	Discussion Board	Tasks	Status List
Wiki Page Library		Project Tasks	
Picture Library		Issue Tracking	
Data Connection Library			
Asset Library			
Slide Library			
Report Library			

OK   Cancel

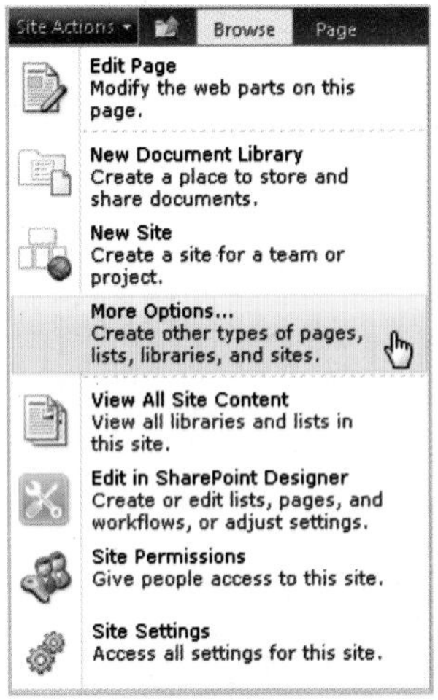

6. Click one of the **Add A Web Part** links that appear on the page to add a list there. The Web Parts menu will open below the ribbon and display the current lists and libraries that can be added.

7. **On any page**, click **Site Actions** and click **More Options**. In the Create dialog box that appears, click **Lists**. If you started in a site created with the Basic Meeting Workspace site template, the list templates will be as shown in Figure 4-1. If you started from a different type of site, you will not see the meeting list types such as Agenda and Decisions. (Figure 4-1 will look different if Silverlight is not installed.)

Select a List Template

Look at the available list templates, what they contain, and how close they are to your definition in Table 4-1 (it is expected that you may need to modify the list after selecting it).

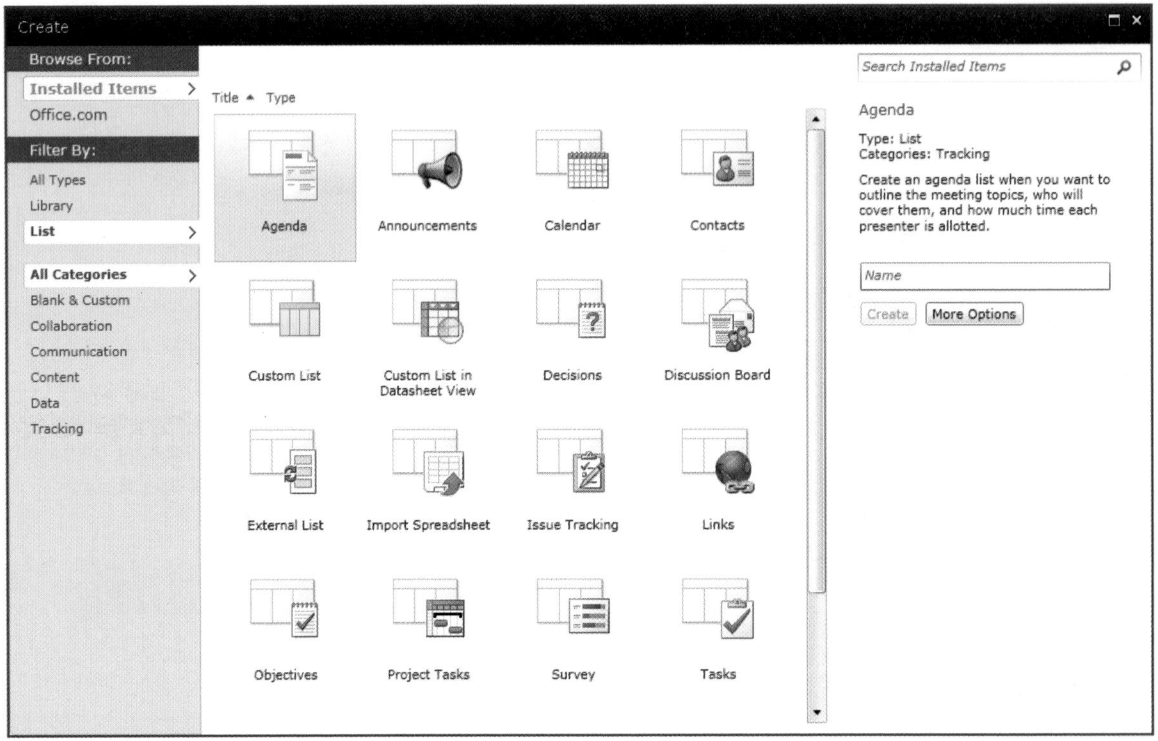

Figure 4-1: A meeting site adds five additional list types.

LIST	SITE TYPE	DESCRIPTION	DEFAULT COLUMNS
Agenda	Meeting	Outline meeting topics, who's responsible, allotted time	Subject, Owner, Time, Notes
Announcements	All	News items, statuses, short bits of information	Title, Body, Expires
Calendar	All	Upcoming meetings, events, and deadlines	Title, Location, Start Time, End Time, Attendees, Resources, Free/Busy, Description
Circulations	Group	Send information to team	Type, Body, Due Date, Time, Confidential, Editing, Recipients
Contacts	All	People the team works with	Last Name, First Name, Full Name, E-mail, Company, Job Title, Business Phone, Home Phone, Mobile Number, Fax Number, Address, City, State, ZIP, Country, Web Page URL, Notes
Custom List	All	A blank list to which columns can be added	Title
Custom List in Datasheet View	All	A blank spreadsheet (see Figure 4-2)	Title
Decisions	Meeting	Track decisions made at meeting	Decision, Contact, Status
Discussion Board	All	To hold a threaded discussion such as a news group	Subject, Body, Created By, Replies, Date Added
External List	All	View data in an external content type	Varies
Import Spreadsheet	All	Duplicates the columns and data of an existing spreadsheet	Varies
Issue Tracking	All	Issues for a project or team	Title, Assigned To, Status, Priority, Description, Category, Related Issues, Comments, Due Date, and Time
Links	All	Web pages and other resources	URL, Description, Notes
Microsoft IME Dictionary List	Group	A dictionary of "reading" fields to be converted to "display" fields using Microsoft's Input Method Editor (IME)	Reading, Display, Comment 1, Comment 2, Comment 3, URL, POS
Objectives	Meeting	Objective of meeting	Objective
Project Tasks	All	A Gantt chart view of tasks for Microsoft Project	Title, Predecessors, Priority, Status, % Complete, Assigned To, Description, Start Date, Due Date
Resources		Available resources	Name, Description
Survey	All	Create and hold responses to a list of questions (see Figure 4-3)	Varies
Tasks	All	Team or personal tasks	Title, Predecessors, Priority, Status, % Complete, Assigned To, Description, Start Date, Due Date
Text Box	Meeting	Add a block of text	Text
Things To Bring	Meeting	What an attendee should bring to be prepared	Item, Comment, Owner

Table 4-1: Available SharePoint Lists

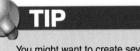

NOTE

You can only place a new Web Part, which is required for adding a list or library, in an existing Web Part zone. If you keep the default single-column layout, you can add several Web Parts in that column, but it is more difficult to get a proper and/or attractive separation of the various elements on the page without going into SharePoint Designer (see Chapter 8).

TIP

You might want to create several of the lists to fully explore their fields.

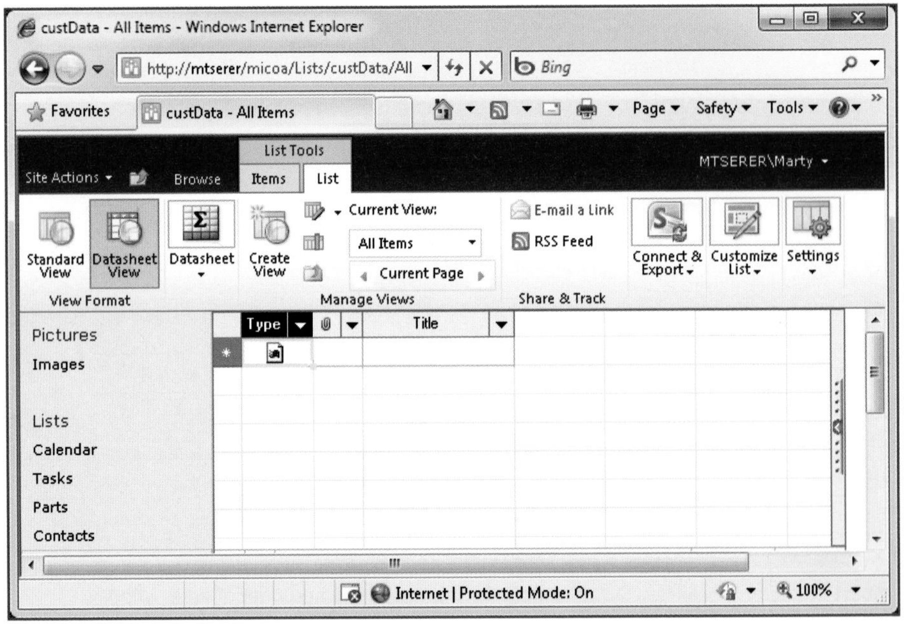

Figure 4-2: The Custom List In Datasheet View provides a spreadsheet-like view in which you can enter data.

Create a List

With a good definition of the list you want, a template in mind that supports that definition, and a location selected on the page that will hold it, create the list.

1. From the site Home page (if you are already looking at list templates, skip to step 5), navigate to the page on which you want the list, and click the **Page** tab.

2. Click **Edit** to display the Editing Tools tab and the Web Part zones on the page. If you don't see an Edit icon on the page to which you want to add a list, see the "Adding Lists" QuickSteps in this chapter and use the steps there in place of the remaining steps in this section.

3. If you haven't already selected the page layout you want, click **Text Layout** (if it is available), select the desired layout, and click in the region in which you want the list.

4. Click the **Insert** tab in the tab row, and click **New List** to display the list templates that are available for the page you have displayed.

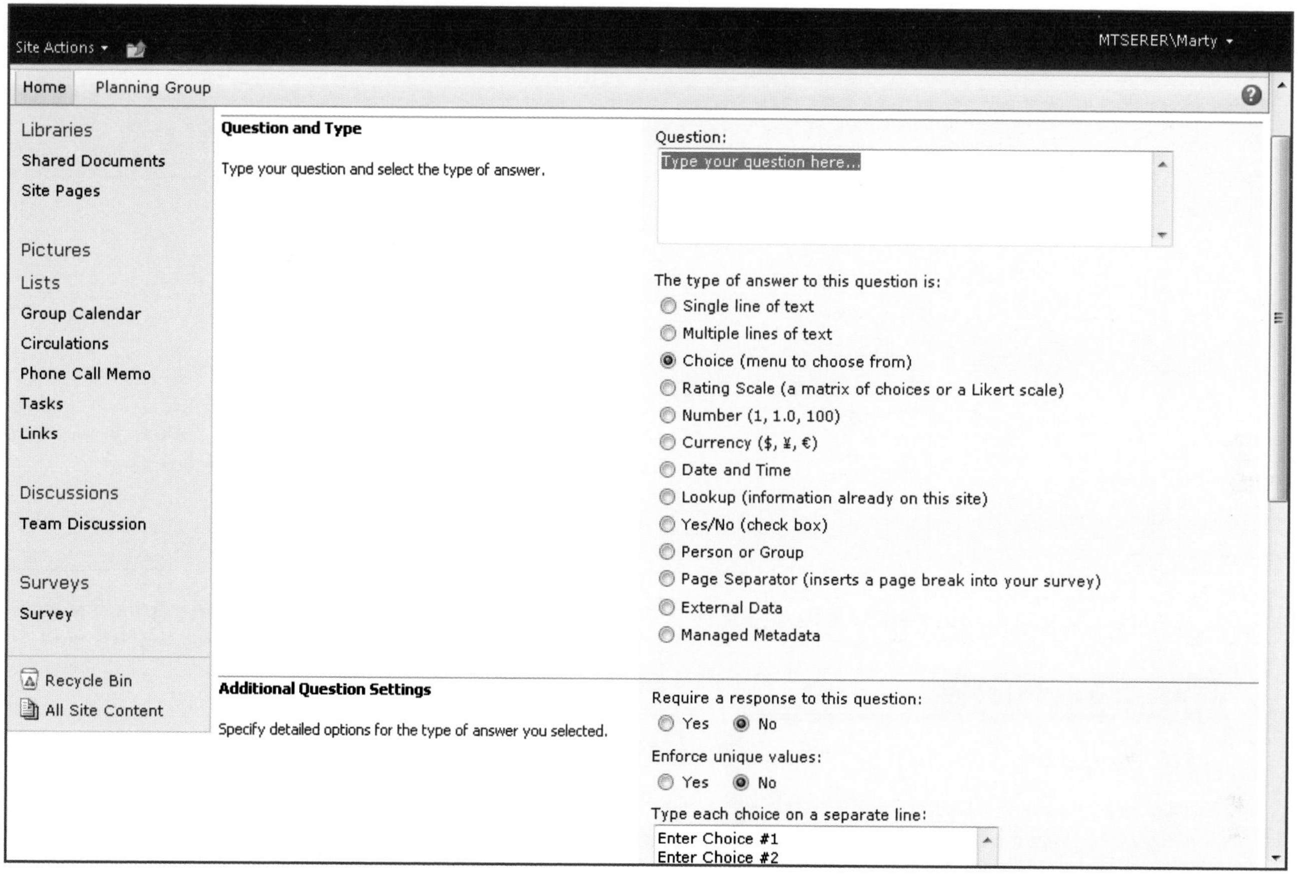

Figure 4-3: SharePoint provides for the creation and handling of reasonably complex surveys.

5. Enter the **List Title** that you want to use for this list. This name will become the title of the list on your page; it does not have to be the same as the template name.

6. Click the list template you want to use, and click **OK** to display the list on your page. Figure 4-4 shows an Issue Tracking list placed in the lower-left region of the page.

7. At this point, you can immediately begin to add items to your list, as described in Chapter 3, or you can modify or customize the list, as discussed in the next section.

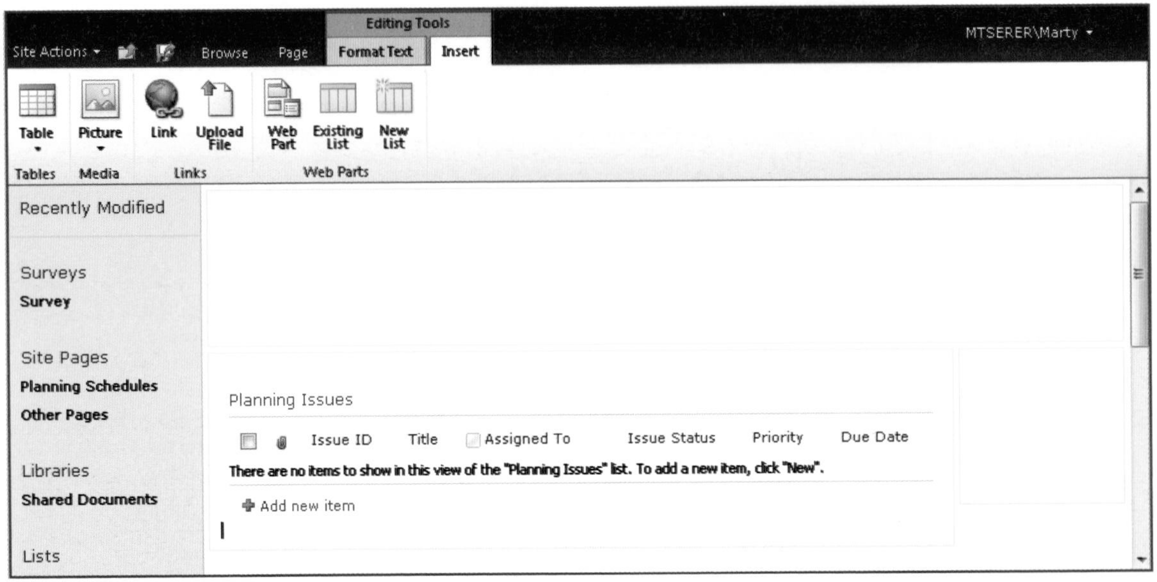

Figure 4-4: To place a list or other element in a particular location on a page, you must establish the layout first.

ADDING LISTS

As was mentioned elsewhere in this chapter, there are three methods to add lists to a site page:

- **Page Edit | Insert New | List**, as demonstrated in the "Create a List" section

- **Site Actions | More Options | Lists**

- **Add A Web Part**

Not all of these methods are available on all pages, and you may have to look at several to find one that works on your page. Here we'll review some of the considerations of each method and give examples of the other two.

Continued . . .

Create Specific Lists

SharePoint provides a variety of lists. Some are very simple, even blank; others are reasonably complex. Look at how several commonly used and unique lists are created. Many of the other lists look like the Announcements list, just with a different number of and names for the columns.

Begin the creation of each type of list by using the steps in either "Create a List" or "Adding a List" QuickSteps elsewhere in this chapter. The following sections will begin after you have clicked **Create**, **Add**, or **OK** in the previous steps.

QUICKSTEPS

ADDING LISTS (Continued)

USE THE EDIT PAGE

If you have a page with an Edit page icon on the tab bar, you may use it or the Page tab, Edit page steps used in the "Create a List" section to directly choose and add a list to the currently selected page. Unfortunately, not all pages have the Edit page button and when you use the Page tab, Edit page, the Editing Tools I Insert tab is not available. You must use one of the other choices in this situation.

The benefit of the Edit page icon, if you have it available, is that it allows you to put a new list in exactly the position on the page that you want with the steps in "Create a List."

One downside to the Edit page icon compared with the Site Actions option is that not all list templates available in Site Actions are available with the Edit Page option; three lists are missing: External List, Import Spreadsheet, and Survey. In addition, the meeting lists (Agenda, Decisions, Objectives, Text Box, and Things To Bring) are not available through the Edit page icon.

USE SITE ACTIONS

Site Actions is available in any site with any page and provides access to the most list templates. The negative is that it adds a list to the site, and you must separately add the list to the page where you want it. Here are the steps:

1. Navigate to the site in which you want a new list, click **Site Actions**, and then click **More Options**. The Create dialog box will appear.

2. Click **List** to limit the display of templates to lists, click the template you want, enter a name to be the title for the list (if appropriate), and click **Create**. If requested, enter any needed information for the particular template.

Continued . . .

CREATE AN ANNOUNCEMENTS LIST

The Announcements list will appear on the page with the List Tools I List tab displayed so you can customize the list. See "Modify a List" later in this chapter.

Click **Add New Announcement** to do that. Fill in the fields, and click **Save**.

QUICKSTEPS

ADDING LISTS (Continued)

3. The list will be added to the site, but not to a specific page. To do that, navigate to the page, click the **Page** tab, and click **Edit Page**. Add A Web Part boxes will appear on the page, as you see in Figure 4-5.

ADD A WEB PART

There are several instances when creating sites and pages that Add A Web Part boxes appear on a page, such as in a meeting site like the one in Figure 4-5. The Add A Web Part box can be used to add a list to the page, *but only lists that already exist in the site*. If the list you want to add to the page already exists in the site, use the following steps to add it to the page; otherwise, go back to "Use Site Actions" earlier in this Quick Steps to add the list to the site.

1. Click in the **Add A Web Part** box  where you want the new list. The Page Tools | Insert tab will appear and display the *existing* elements that are available to be added to the page, as shown in Figure 4-6.

2. In the Categories column on the left, click **Lists And Libraries** if it isn't already selected.

3. In the Web Parts column, click the list you want. If you don't see the list and you know it has been added to the current site, click the dark black arrow at the bottom of the list to display the balance of the list.

4. Click **Add** to place the list in the Add A Web Part box on the page.

TIP

There is also a fourth and more flexible way to add a list to a site page using SharePoint Designer, as will be discussed in Chapter 8.

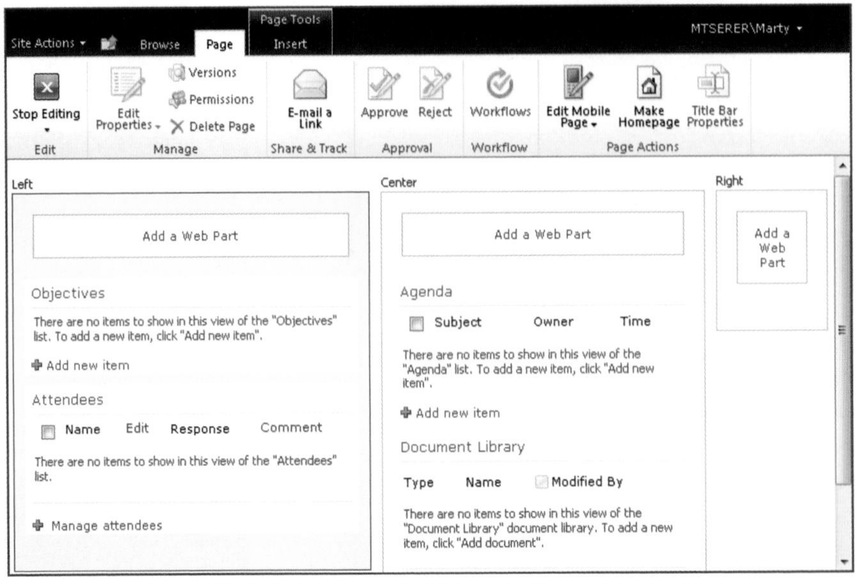

Figure 4-5: Some pages require you to add elements through a specific Web Part location.

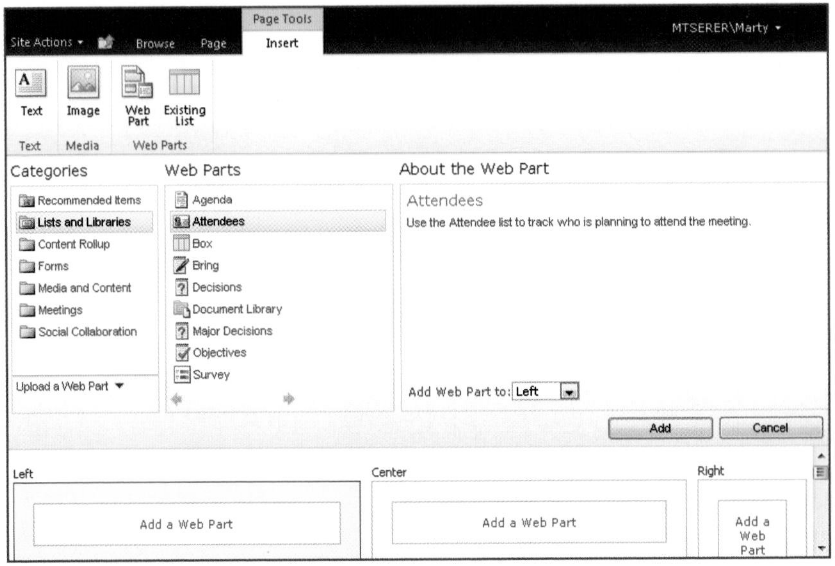

Figure 4-6: Only existing lists and other elements can be added within an existing Web Part zones.

CREATE A CALENDAR LIST

The Calendar list will appear on the page with the Calendar Tools | Calendar tab displayed (see Figure 4-7) so you can customize it. See "Modify a List" later in this chapter.

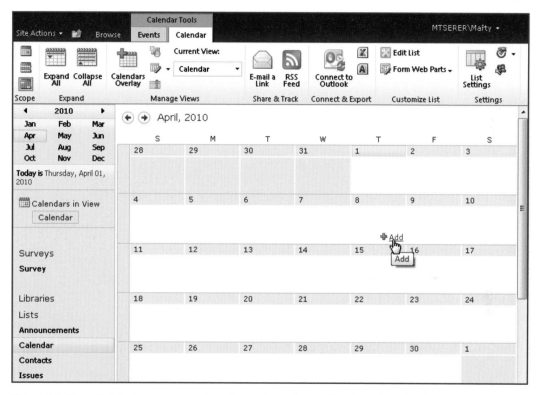

Figure 4-7: SharePoint gives you a number of ways to customize the view of a calendar.

Point in a day in which you want to add a calendar event, and click **Add**. Fill in the fields, and click **Save**.

CREATE A SURVEY LIST

The Survey list will open with a form, similar to what was shown in Figure 4-3 earlier in this chapter. The form lets you enter questions you want on the survey, choose how you want them answered, and specify the type of information you are expecting. You can also require that the question be answered, specify the choices for an answer, and choose how the question is displayed. After all the questions have been created and the list is inserted on your page, you can use Survey Settings to define branching logic that says if the answer to a question is one thing, then do A, but if it is another thing, then do B. List settings are discussed further in "Modify a List" later in this chapter.

Additional Question Settings

Specify detailed options for the type of answer you selected.

Require a response to this question:
○ Yes ● No

Enforce unique values:
○ Yes ● No

Type each choice on a separate line:

```
Enter Choice #1
Enter Choice #2
Enter Choice #3
```

Display choices using:
○ Drop-Down Menu
● Radio Buttons
○ Checkboxes (allow multiple selections)

Allow 'Fill-in' choices:
○ Yes ● No

Default value:
● Choice ○ Calculated Value

Branching Logic

Specify if branching is enabled for this question. Branching can be used to skip to a specific question based on the user response. A page break is automatically inserted after a branching enabled question. Learn about branching.

To define branching logic, add your questions and then, in the Survey Settings page, edit the questions to define the branching logic.

⊞ **Column Validation**

🖼 Respond to this Survey | Actions ▾ | Settings ▾

Survey Name:	Team Skillls
Survey Description:	Skill survey for use in assignments and support.
Time Created:	3/8/2010 10:44 PM
Number of Responses:	7

⊞ Show a graphical summary of responses
⊞ Show all responses

When the survey is open on your page, it is in the form of a summary, shown on the left. If you click **Respond To This Survey**, the survey questions will appear as shown in Figure 2-19 in Chapter 2. If you click **Show A Graphical Summary Of Responses**, you will see a chart of the results, as shown in Figure 2-20, also in Chapter 2.

As you are creating most lists, underneath the text box where you name the list, there is a More Options button. Clicking this opens a dialog box where, at a minimum, you can not only name the list, but also enter a description and determine whether the list will be on the Quick Launch. For some lists, there are also other options.

Modify a List

It is frequently the case that the list created with a template is not exactly what you want and you will need to modify it. When you finish creating a new list, it appears on the page with the List Tools | List tab open in the ribbon. From this tab you can:

- Add a column
- Create and change the view of the list
- Change other settings

By default, a new column will go at the end of the list's columns. To change that position or to make other changes to an existing column, see "Create and Change Views" in this chapter.

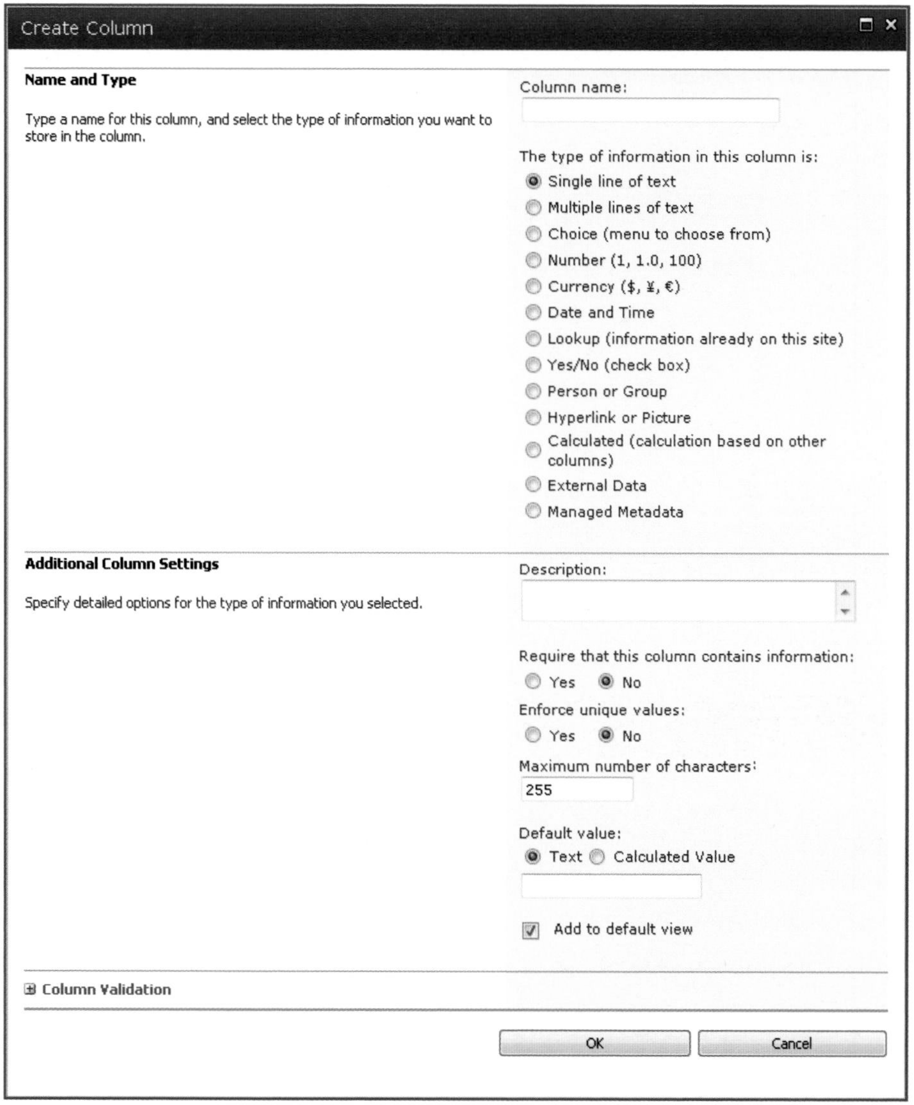

Figure 4-8: Adding a new column to a list is little more than naming and describing it.

Add a Column

The most common and easiest change to a list is to add a column to it. A column is a field in one item in the list, so if you have a name list, the first name might be a field for a person in the list and a column in the total list. You can add a column through the List Tools | List tab.

1. If you are not currently looking at the list to which you want to add a column, navigate to it.

2. If the List Tools | List tab is not displayed, click the check box on the right of the title bar of the list, and click the **List** tab.

3. Click **Create Column** [⊞ Create Column]. The Create Column page is displayed, as you can see in Figure 4-8.

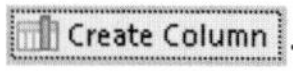

4. Enter the name of the new column. This will be used as the column heading in the list.

5. Choose the type of information the column will contain, enter a description, and complete the information requested. See "Adding a Calculated Column" QuickSteps and "Validating Column Data" QuickSteps in this chapter.

6. When you have completed entering all the needed information for a new column, click **OK**.

QUICKSTEPS

ADDING A CALCULATED COLUMN

Occasionally, you will want one column to contain a calculated result using the information in other columns. For example, the Value here is the product of the Cost times the Quantity:

Cost	Quantity	Value
$22.85	6	$137.10
$8.14	6	$48.84
$11.65	8	$93.20

To create a calculated column:

1. After naming the column, select **Calculated** as the type of column (see Figure 4-9).

2. After entering a description, enter a formula that is based on other columns in the same list. The values used in the formula will be taken from the same row. The formula can contain:

   - **Column names** from the current list. Add by clicking the name in the Insert Column list. They must be in square brackets if they contain a space, but can be either upper- or lowercase.

   - **Constants** such as 5 or 247

   - **Operators** such as + (addition) - (subtraction) * (multiplication) / (division) ^ (power of) < (less than) or > (greater than)

   - **Functions** such as Pi() in place of the constant 3.14159265, or If([quantity]<2, "Order", "OK") displays "Order" if the Quantity column is less than 2; otherwise, it displays "OK." See SharePoint Help "Formulas and Functions" for more information.

3. Select the data type returned by the formula and, if appropriate, the number of decimal places.

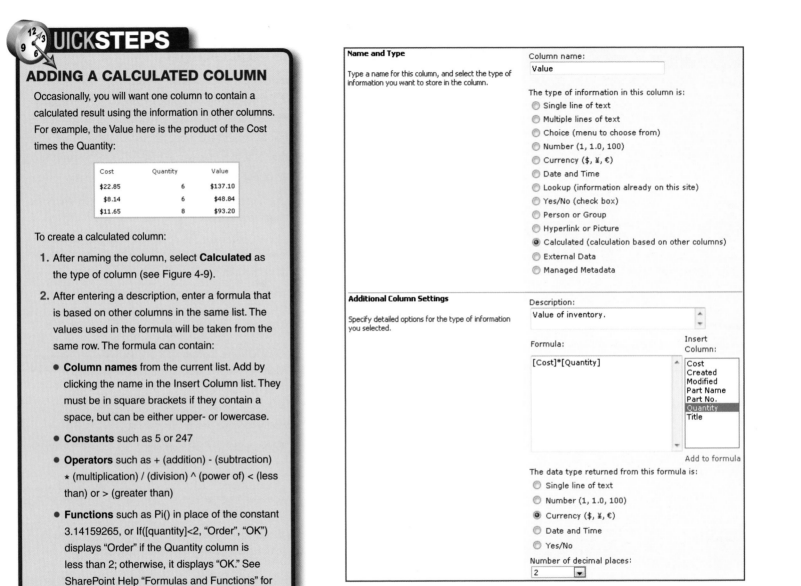

Figure 4-9: SharePoint has a powerful ability to calculate a value in a column based on values in other columns.

Create and Change Views

What you see on a site page often is not the full list that was created, but rather a subset of the available columns. Even many of the lists that are displayed as a result of using site and page templates are only summaries of the full list. The idea is that page real estate is valuable and you can always click the title of a list and see the full list in its own page. The key is to display just what is needed. For example, you could display a list of available products on your site's Home page with only the product name and a brief description, but display a detailed list of products, with detailed product descriptions, specification, and pricing on the inventory page. SharePoint gives you three potential ways to change the view: modifying the current view, creating a new view, and using Datasheet View.

MODIFY THE CURRENT VIEW

To modify the current list view:

1. If you are not currently looking at the view you want to modify, navigate to it.

2. If the List Tools | List tab is not displayed, click the check box on the right of the title bar of the list, and click the **List** tab.

3. Click **Modify View** . The Edit View page is displayed, as you can see in the two parts of Figure 4-10.

4. Select the columns to be displayed by clicking the **Display** check box next to each.

5. Determine the order, from left to right, by adjusting the number in the Position From Left column.

6. Enter the first two columns you want the list sorted on and the direction of the sort.

7. If you have a lot of items on your list, you may choose to view only the most important of them by filtering out the others. If so, select one or more columns for the filter and how you want it applied.

8. Review the eight other ways that your list can be customized, and determine if you want to use them.

9. When you have customized the list the way you want, click **OK**.

Site Actions ▾

MTSERER\Marty ▾

Micoa Team Site ▸ Announcements ▸ List Settings ▸ Edit View

To customize this view further, use a Web page editor compatible with Microsoft SharePoint Foundation.

I Like It   Tags & Notes

| Home | Product Planning | Product Sales | Team Blog | 2011 Budget | Product Development | |

Pictures

Images

Lists

Calendar

Tasks

Parts

Contacts

custData

Libraries

Site Pages

Shared Documents

Discussions

Team Discussion

Recycle Bin

All Site Content

[OK]   [Cancel]

Name

Type a name for this view of the list. Make the name descriptive, such as "Sorted by Author", so that site visitors will know what to expect when they click this link.

View Name:

All items

Web address of this view:

http://mtserer/micoa/Lists/Announcements/ AllItems

.aspx 🔊

This view appears by default when visitors follow a link to this list. If you want to delete this view, first make another view the default.

⊟ **Columns**

Select or clear the check box next to each column you want to show or hide in this view of this page. To specify the order of the columns, select a number in the **Position from left** box.

Display	Column Name	Position from Left
☑	Attachments	1
☑	Title (linked to item with edit menu)	2
☑	Modified	3
☐	Body	4
☐	Content Type	5
☐	Created	6
☐	Created By	7
☐	Edit (link to edit item)	8
☐	Expires	9
☐	Folder Child Count	10
☐	ID	11
☐	Item Child Count	12
☐	Modified By	13
☐	Title	14
☐	Title (linked to item)	15
☐	Type (icon linked to document)	16
☐	Version	17

Figure 4-10: The Edit View page of a list allows you to change just about everything about a list.

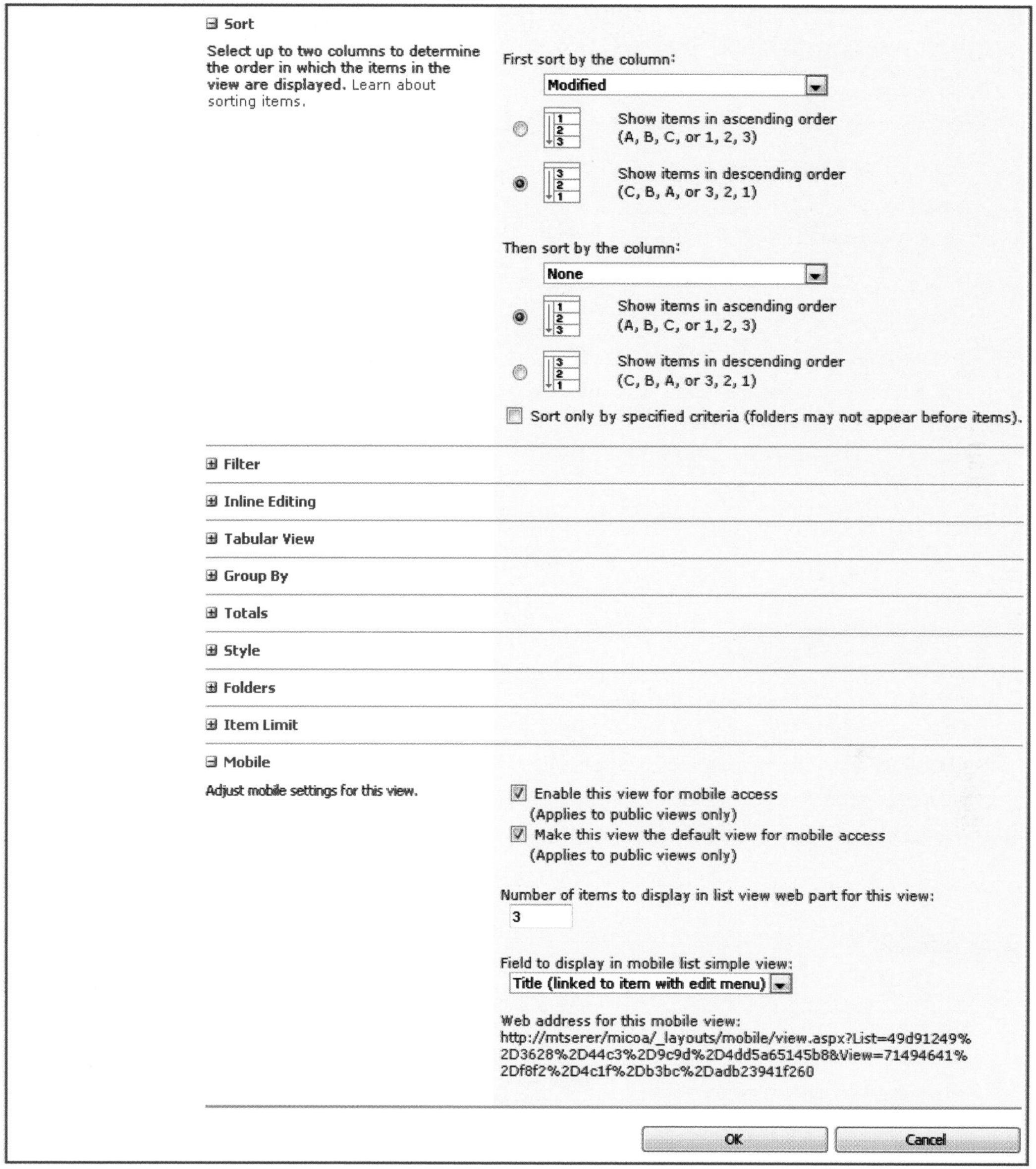

⊟ Sort

Select up to two columns to determine the order in which the items in the view are displayed. Learn about sorting items.

First sort by the column:

Modified

○ Show items in ascending order (A, B, C, or 1, 2, 3)

◉ Show items in descending order (C, B, A, or 3, 2, 1)

Then sort by the column:

None

◉ Show items in ascending order (A, B, C, or 1, 2, 3)

○ Show items in descending order (C, B, A, or 3, 2, 1)

☐ Sort only by specified criteria (folders may not appear before items).

⊞ Filter

⊞ Inline Editing

⊞ Tabular View

⊞ Group By

⊞ Totals

⊞ Style

⊞ Folders

⊞ Item Limit

⊟ Mobile

Adjust mobile settings for this view.

☑ Enable this view for mobile access (Applies to public views only)

☑ Make this view the default view for mobile access (Applies to public views only)

Number of items to display in list view web part for this view:

3

Field to display in mobile list simple view:

Title (linked to item with edit menu)

Web address for this mobile view:
http://mtserer/micoa/_layouts/mobile/view.aspx?List=49d91249%2D3628%2D44c3%2D9c9d%2D4dd5a65145b8&View=71494641%2Df8f2%2D4c1f%2Db3bc%2Dadb23941f260

OK   Cancel

Figure 4-10: The Edit View page of a list allows you to change just about everything about a list. (continued)

QUICK**FACTS**

VALIDATING COLUMN DATA

SharePoint gives you several ways to validate information entered into a list, as you can see in Figure 4-11.

- Require that a field be filled in
- Require that a field contain unique text or a value not in that field in any other item in the list
- Require a value between minimum and maximum values
- Enter a formula that is either true or false (see the "Adding a Calculated Column" QuickSteps for information entering formulas)

NOTE

To add validation to a column after it is created, click **List Settings** from the List Tools | List tab and click **Validation Settings**. The Formula and User Message boxes appear similar to what you saw in Figure 4-11.

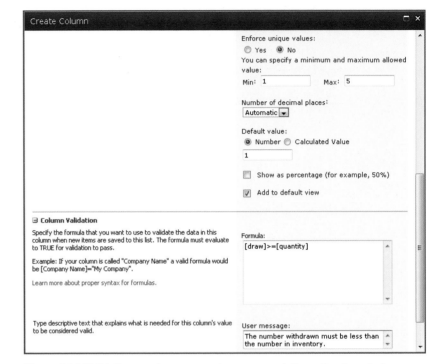

Figure 4-11: Validating a column prevents erroneous information from being entered in a list.

CREATE A NEW VIEW

Although modifying a view gives you a lot of options, there's nothing like a clean slate to give the maximum in flexibility to get what you want in a list view.

1. With the list on your screen and the List Tools | List tab open in the ribbon (if this is not the case, see the first two steps in "Modify the Current View" earlier in this chapter), click **Create View** in the ribbon.

2. Review the choices of views that are presented, and click the one that is correct for you (these steps will assume the Standard View was selected). The Create View window will open, the top part of which is shown in Figure 4-12.

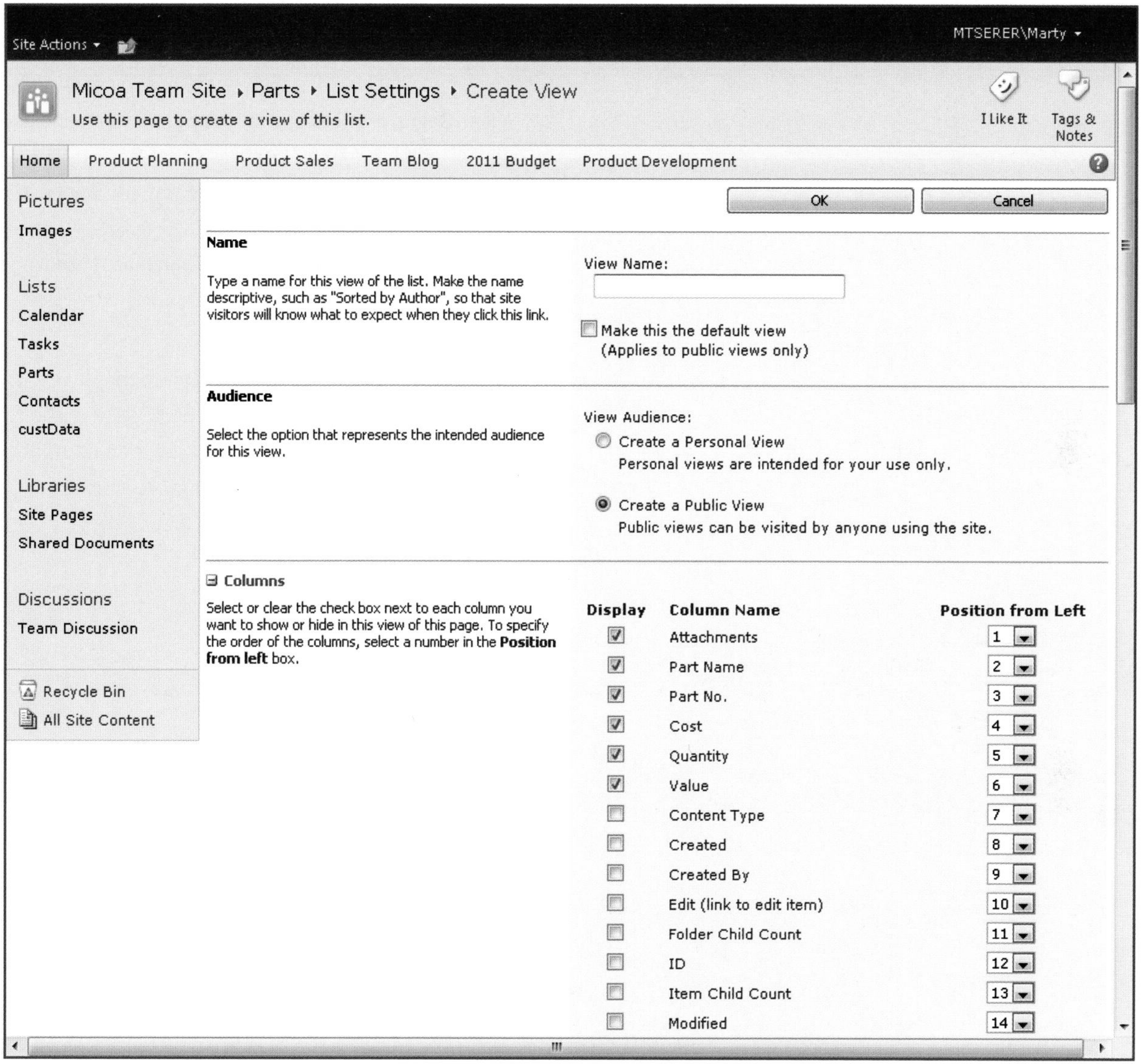

Figure 4-12: *Using Create View, you can easily create several specialized views for different purposes.*

3. Enter a view name, choose whether it will be the default view for the list, and whether this is a personal or public view.

4. Select the columns you want to display and the position in which you want to display them. Set up the sorting and filtering you want, and use any of the other settings you need to get the view you want.

5. When you have the view set up the way you want it, click **OK**.

6. To add validation to a column in a new view, click **List Settings** from the List Tools | List tab, and click **Validation Settings** (see "Validating Column Data" QuickFacts in this chapter).

USE DATASHEET VIEW

Some lists make more sense if they are displayed in a spreadsheet-like view called Datasheet View. The Datasheet View in the List Tools | List tab does that for you *if* you have Excel, Access, or a compatible program or Web App available to the computer. For example, this list:

		Part Name	Part No.	Cost	Quantity	Value
☐	📎	**Housing**	A-47-819	$22.85	6	$137.10
		Shaft	A-47-432	$8.14	6	$48.84
		Sprocket	A-47-621	$11.65	8	$93.20
		Controller	A-47-157	$64.21	5	$321.05
		Condenser	A-47-184	$42.50	6	$255.00

looks like this (shown left) in Datasheet View:

		Part Name	Part No.	Cost	Quantity	Value
Ⓐ	✎					
		Housing	A-47-819	$22.85	6	$137.10
		Shaft	A-47-432	$8.14	6	$48.84
		Sprocket	A-47-621	$11.65	8	$93.20
		Controller	A-47-157	$64.21	5	$321.05
		Condenser	A-47-184	$42.50	6	$255.00
✳						

To display a list in Datasheet View, display the list, open the **List Tools | List** tab, and click **Datasheet View**.

The Datasheet View provides several datasheet-centric tools, shown in Figure 4-13, including:

● A quick and easy way to edit multiple items without having to open each item separately. For example, you can paste a column of numbers directly from an Excel spreadsheet or other data source.

● A task pane with options for cutting, copying, pasting, undoing, sorting, filtering, and Help at the top and tracking, exporting, and reporting in an Office application (Access is shown in Figure 4-13).

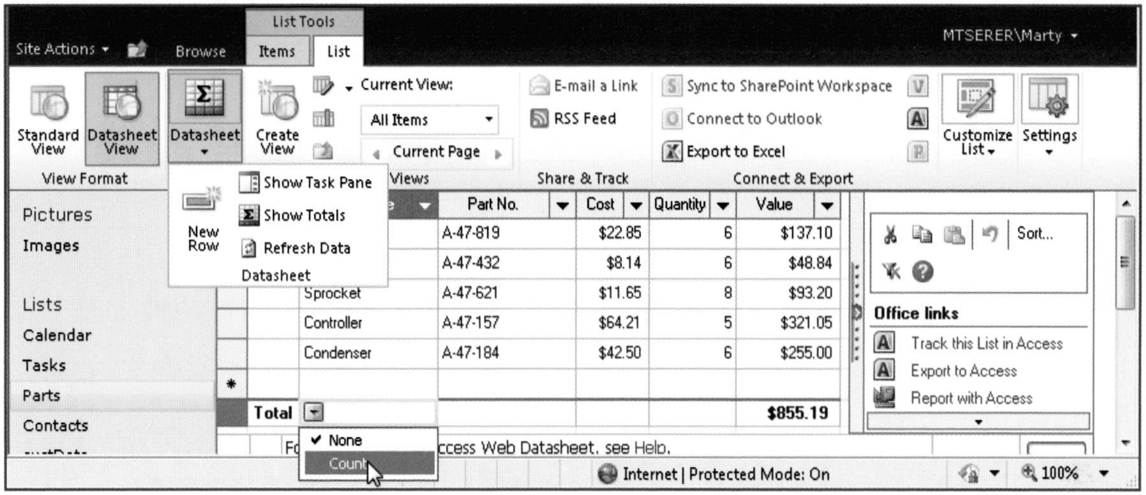

Figure 4-13: The benefits of Datasheet View include the Total row and the ability to export a list to other Microsoft Office programs.

- A Total row separate from the list that lets you count non-numeric columns and calculate the average, count, maximum, minimum, sum, standard deviation, and variance of a numeric column

- Add a row to the datasheet and refresh the view

- Sort and filter the list based on data in a column

TIP

If you have the Total row turned on, it is a good idea to turn it off before switching back to Standard List view. If you don't, you will get some spurious information in your list that is left over from the totals.

Manage Lists

With the importance of lists in SharePoint, the need to manage them becomes significant, and SharePoint provides the tools to handle that in the List Settings area. To work with these settings:

1. With the list on your screen and the List Tools | List tab open in the ribbon (if this is not the case, see the first two steps in "Modify the Current View" earlier in this chapter), click **List Settings** on the right of the ribbon.

2. Review the List Settings page that opens. It is quite comprehensive, as you can see in Figure 4-14. Here we'll look at using List Settings and setting permissions.

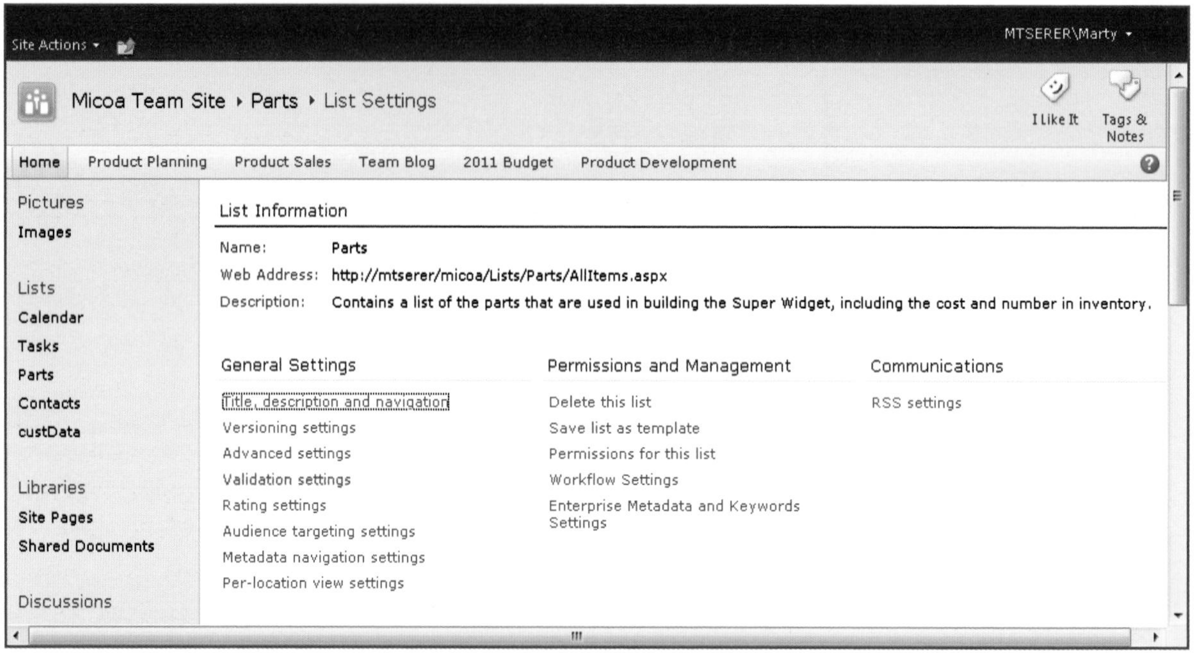

Figure 4-14: List Settings provides a comprehensive means of managing lists.

Use List Settings

As you can see in Figure 4-14, List Settings lets you change general items like name and description, control versioning and ratings, work with Advanced Settings, and delete the list.

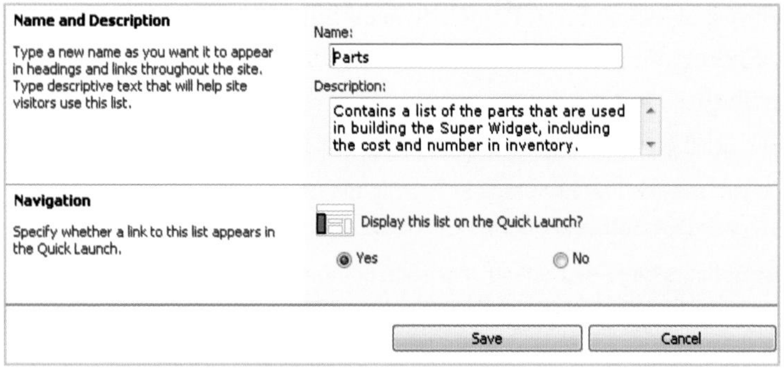

MANAGE GENERAL LIST SETTINGS

In this section we'll talk about the settings for the list title, description, navigation, metadata navigation, and per-location views. It is assumed that you are looking at the List Settings page shown in Figure 4-14.

1. Click **Title, Description, And Navigation**.

2. On the page that opens, you can change or enter the list name and description by clicking in the respective text boxes and entering your text.

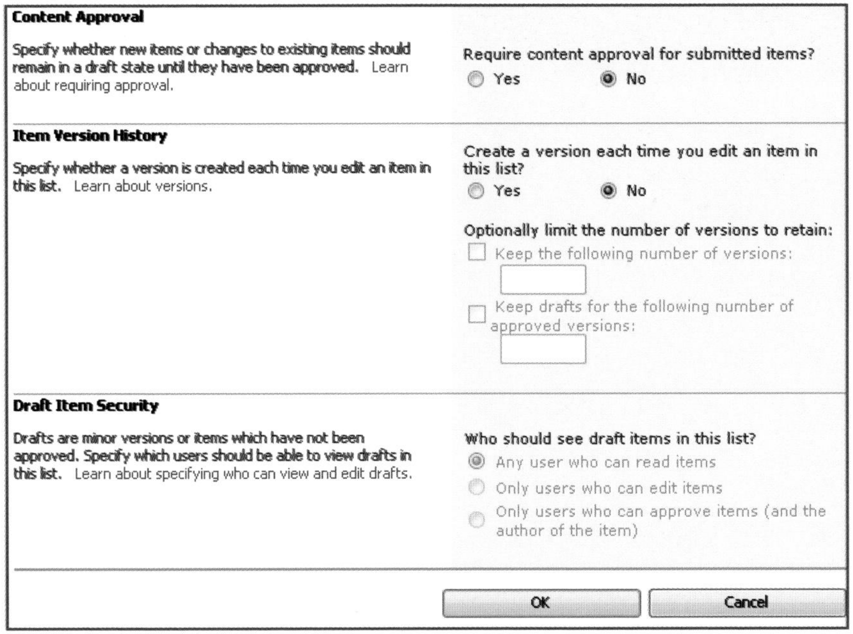

Content Approval

Specify whether new items or changes to existing items should remain in a draft state until they have been approved.   Learn about requiring approval.

Require content approval for submitted items?

◯ Yes   ◉ No

Item Version History

Specify whether a version is created each time you edit an item in this list.   Learn about versions.

Create a version each time you edit an item in this list?

◯ Yes   ◉ No

Optionally limit the number of versions to retain:

☐ Keep the following number of versions:

☐ Keep drafts for the following number of approved versions:

Draft Item Security

Drafts are minor versions or items which have not been approved. Specify which users should be able to view drafts in this list.   Learn about specifying who can view and edit drafts.

Who should see draft items in this list?

◉ Any user who can read items
◯ Only users who can edit items
◯ Only users who can approve items (and the author of the item)

[OK]   [Cancel]

Figure 4-15: SharePoint provides the means to track list changes and require approval if desired.

3. Choose whether you want this list on the Quick Launch. If not, how will you get to the list other than All Site Content?

4. When you are ready, click **Save**.

CONTROL LIST FEATURES

The list features discussed here will include versioning, rating, and audience targeting.

1. From the List Settings page, click **Versioning Settings**. As shown in Figure 4-15, choose:

   a. Whether changes to the list require approval

   b. Whether a version of the list is created each time a change is made to it and if and what the limit should be in keeping versions

   c. Who can see drafts of changes before they are approved

2. Make the necessary selections on the page, and click **OK** when ready.

3. Click **Audience Targeting Settings**. Choose whether to add a column to the list by the Content Query Web Part to filter the list based on the content the user has entered. Click **OK**.

WORK WITH ADVANCED SETTINGS

This section might be better titled "Miscellaneous Settings" because it is a potpourri of settings.

1. Click **Advanced Settings** and choose whether (see Figure 4-16):

   a. You want each type of content to have a unique set of columns and properties

   b. Readers with Read access can read all items or only those items they created, and readers with Create And Edit access can edit all items or only those they created

   c. Attachments can be added to items in this list

   d. The New Folder command is available

   e. Items in this list appear in a search

   f. Items in the list can be downloaded for offline use

   g. Items in this list can be edited in Datasheet View

   h. Forms can be launched in a dialog box or in a full page

2. Make the necessary selections on the page, and click **OK** when ready.

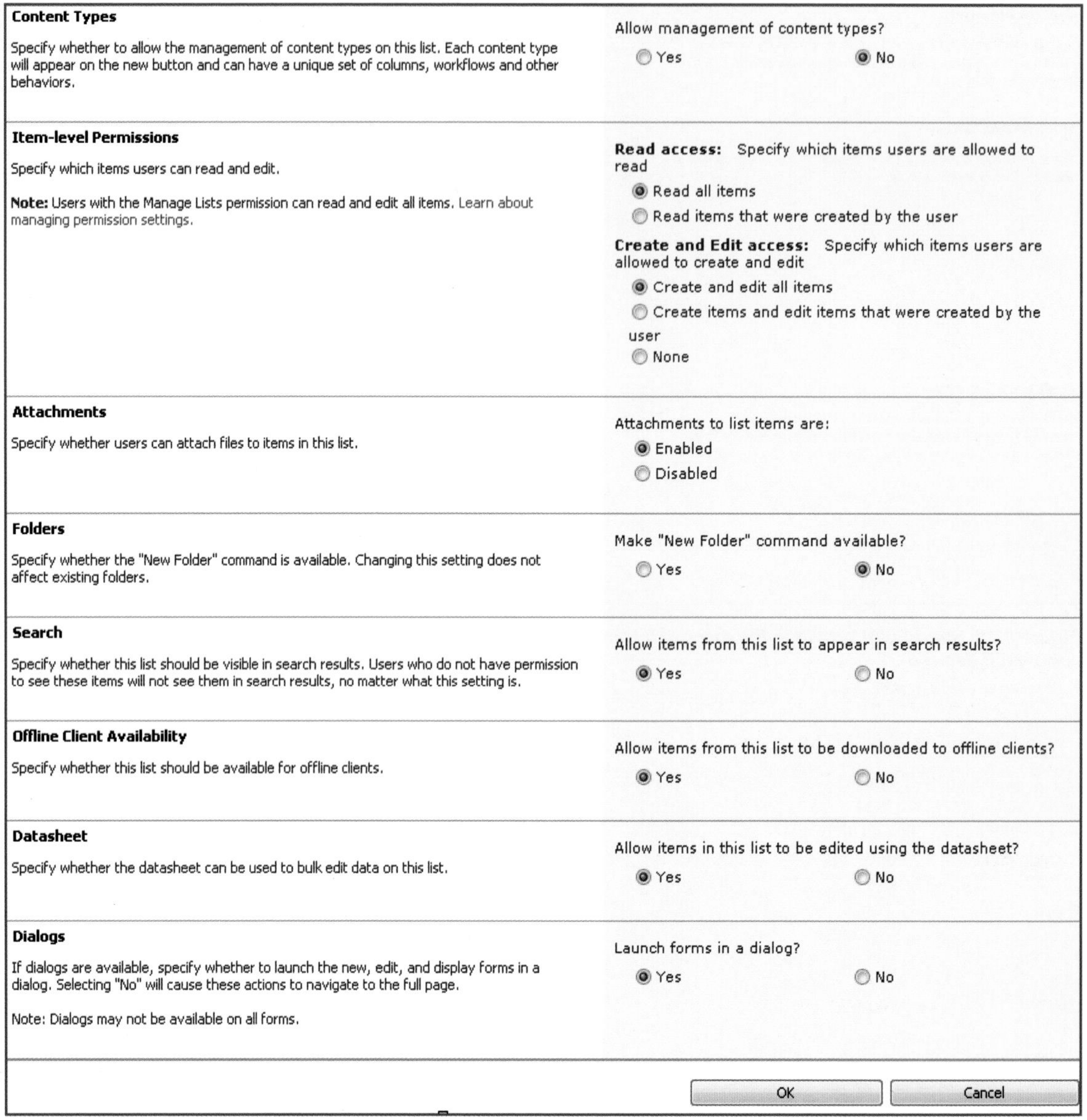

Content Types

Specify whether to allow the management of content types on this list. Each content type will appear on the new button and can have a unique set of columns, workflows and other behaviors.

Allow management of content types?

○ Yes   ● No

Item-level Permissions

Specify which items users can read and edit.

Note: Users with the Manage Lists permission can read and edit all items. Learn about managing permission settings.

Read access: Specify which items users are allowed to read

● Read all items
○ Read items that were created by the user

Create and Edit access: Specify which items users are allowed to create and edit

● Create and edit all items
○ Create items and edit items that were created by the user
○ None

Attachments

Specify whether users can attach files to items in this list.

Attachments to list items are:

● Enabled
○ Disabled

Folders

Specify whether the "New Folder" command is available. Changing this setting does not affect existing folders.

Make "New Folder" command available?

○ Yes   ● No

Search

Specify whether this list should be visible in search results. Users who do not have permission to see these items will not see them in search results, no matter what this setting is.

Allow items from this list to appear in search results?

● Yes   ○ No

Offline Client Availability

Specify whether this list should be available for offline clients.

Allow items from this list to be downloaded to offline clients?

● Yes   ○ No

Datasheet

Specify whether the datasheet can be used to bulk edit data on this list.

Allow items in this list to be edited using the datasheet?

● Yes   ○ No

Dialogs

If dialogs are available, specify whether to launch the new, edit, and display forms in a dialog. Selecting "No" will cause these actions to navigate to the full page.

Note: Dialogs may not be available on all forms.

Launch forms in a dialog?

● Yes   ○ No

[OK]   [Cancel]

Figure 4-16: Advanced Settings covers a myriad of settings about a list.

DELETE A LIST

Deleting a list is little more than clicking that option.

With the list to be deleted selected and its List Settings in view, click **Delete This List**. In response to the message asking if you are sure you want to delete this list, if you in fact do, click **OK**. The list goes into the Recycle Bin from which it can be retrieved, if desired.

Set Permissions

List permissions are in three segments:

- The definitions of what Read and Create And Edit permissions mean, as you saw in item b. of Advanced Settings
- Permissions for the list itself
- Permissions for each item in the list

By default, permissions for the list and for each item are inherited from the site parent unless you specifically turn off inheritance and set permissions for the list or for an item.

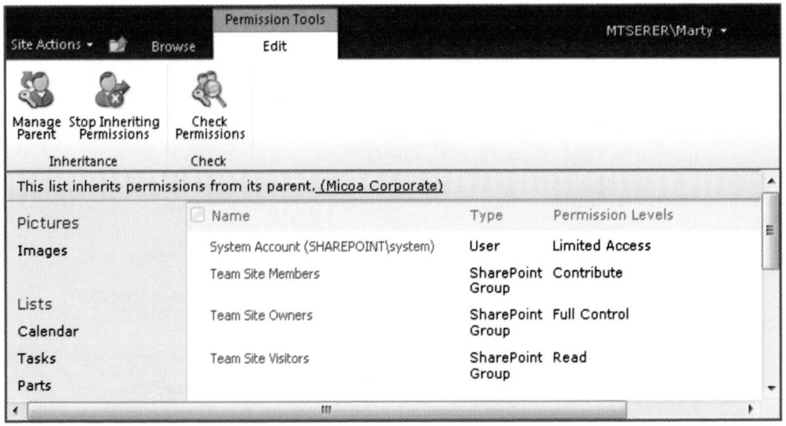

The process is exactly the same for both lists and list items, as it is for all other SharePoint elements, including sites, as was described in Chapter 3. Here, to change permissions, we'll present a summary version of the detail in Chapter 3.

Figure 4-17: Both list and item permissions start with inherited groups and permissions from the parent site.

1. **For lists**, begin with the list selected and the List Tools I List tab displayed, and then click **List Permissions** (or its 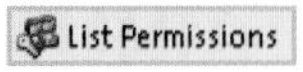 icon if you don't see the words).

   –Or–

   For items begin with the list in view, select the item for which you want to change the permissions, click the **List Tools I Items** tab, and then click **Item Permissions** or its icon.

   In both cases, the same page will appear with the same list of permissions, as shown in Figure 4-17 (except the one for items says "list item" instead of "list"), given that no one has made any changes from the default settings.

2. If you do not want to **use inherited permissions** and the limits they impose, click **Stop Inheriting Permissions**. A message box appears reminding you what this means. If you want to go ahead, click **OK**.

3. If you want to **change a group's permissions**, select the group (click its check box) and click **Edit User Permissions**. The Edit Permissions dialog box will appear with the four permission levels that have been inherited from the parent site.

Grant Permissions

Select Users

You can enter user names, group names, or e-mail addresses. Separate them with semicolons.

Users/Groups:

Grant Permissions

Select the permissions you want these users to have. You can add users to a SharePoint group that has already been granted the appropriate permission levels, or you can grant the users specific permission levels.

Adding users to a SharePoint group is recommended, as this makes managing permissions easier across multiple sites.

Grant Permissions

○ Add users to a SharePoint group (recommended)

Team Site Members [Design]

View permissions this group has on sites, lists, and items...

● Grant users permission directly

☐ Full Control - Has full control.

☐ Design - Can view, add, update, delete, approve, and customize.

☐ Contribute - Can view, add, update, and delete list items and documents.

☐ Read - Can view pages and list items and download documents.

OK   Cancel

Edit Permissions

Users or Groups

The permissions of these users or groups will be modified.

Users:
  Team Site Members

Choose Permissions

Choose the permissions you want these users or groups to have.

Permissions:

☐ Full Control - Has full control.

☐ Design - Can view, add, update, delete, approve, and customize.

☑ Contribute - Can view, add, update, and delete list items and documents.

☐ Read - Can view pages and list items and download documents.

4. Select the desired permission level for the group, and click **OK**.

5. To **add another user** to the group, click **Grant Permissions** to open that dialog box. Enter the name or names that you want in the group, and click the **Check Names** icon. Click the permissions you want to grant; adding them to a group is the recommended approach. When you have the correct set of users, click **OK**.

6. If you want to **remove *all* user permissions** from a particular group, select the group, click **Remove User Permissions**, and then click **OK** to confirm that.

7. If you want to **remove one or more members** of a particular group, click the group to display all the members, select the member(s), click **Actions**, and click **Remove Users From Group**. Click **OK** to confirm the removal.

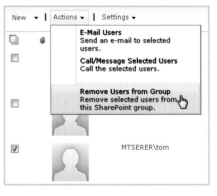

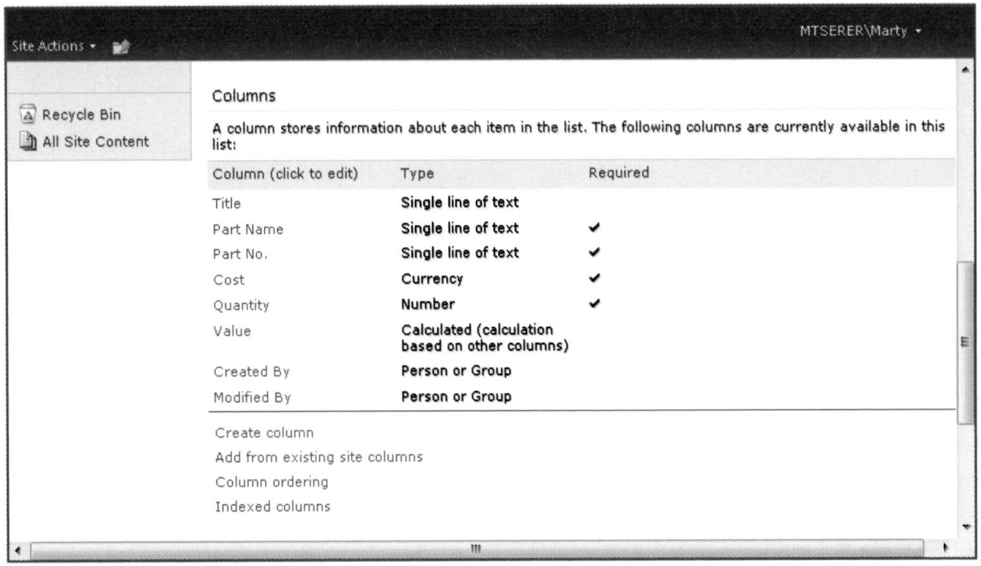

*Figure 4-18: **List Settings provides resources to change individual columns.***

Change Column Settings

On the lower part of the List Settings page, there are several resources for making changes to the columns in a list, as you see in Figure 4-18. These include changes to individual columns and adding and ordering columns.

CHANGE INDIVIDUAL COLUMNS

In the List Settings page there is a list of columns, with the column name being a link you can use to access the detailed column information.

1. To make changes to or delete a column, click the column name. The Change Column page will be displayed, as shown in Figure 4-19.

2. From the Change Column page, you can:

- Change the column name, information type, and description

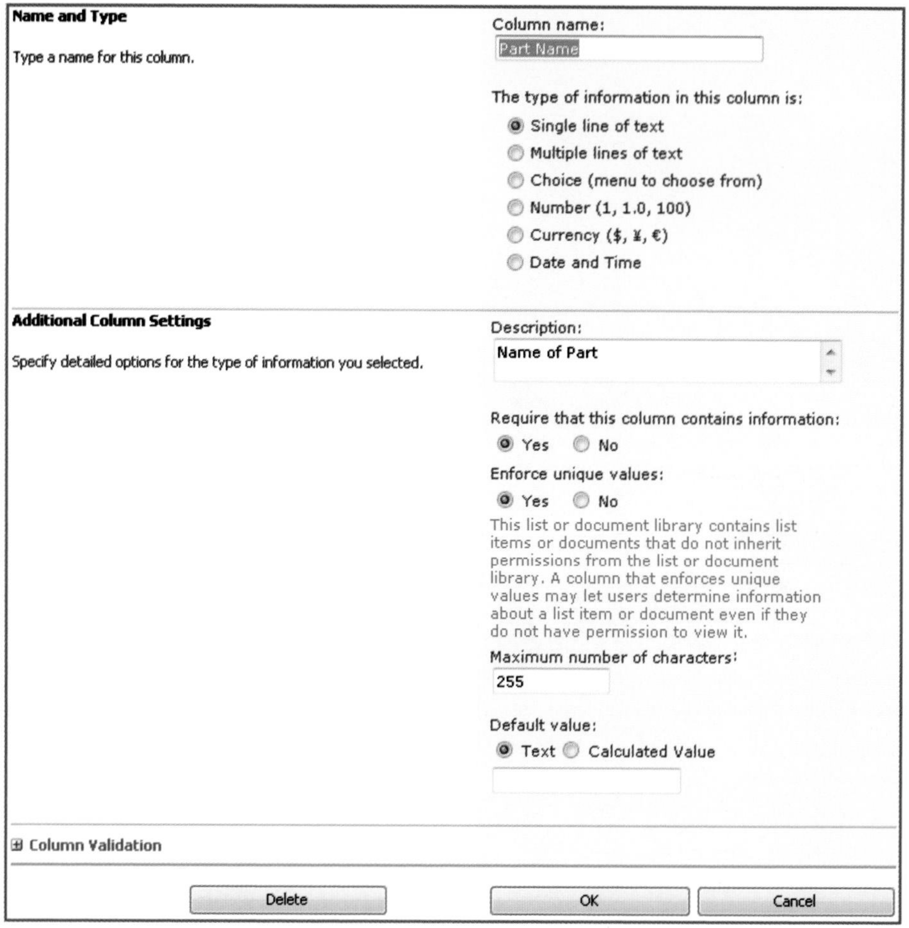

Figure 4-19: *You can change every aspect of a column, including deleting it, if you wish.*

NOTE

You can only delete columns that are not mandatory. Some original default columns that come from the template cannot be deleted. For example, the URL field in a Links list cannot be deleted, but the Notes field can be deleted.

- Change the requirement to fill in the column and to make the content unique among all items

- Change the maximum number of characters, the default value, and the validation formula and text (see the "Validating Column Data" QuickFacts earlier in this chapter).

3. To delete a column, click **Delete** at the bottom of the page, and click **OK** to confirm it.

4. After making the column changes that you want, click **OK** to return to the List Settings page.

ADD AND ORDER COLUMNS

Below the list of columns are the following options for working with columns:

- **Create Column** opens the same page that was discussed in "Add a Column" earlier in this chapter.

- **Add From Existing Site Columns** opens a page that lets you select columns from other lists in the site so that you can add the same column to the current table. This doesn't add any content from the originating list, just the column and its settings, the latter of which you can change.

- **Column Ordering** allows you to select the order in which the columns will appear in the list.

- **Indexed Columns** displays the columns in the current list that are an index. Clicking the column name opens Edit Index, where, under certain circumstances, you can create a secondary column for this index or delete the original index. Clicking Create

Index also opens the Edit Index page, but now you can change both the primary and secondary columns to choose a new column to index.

> Use this page to view and change the indexing settings for this list. You can create a new index or remove an existing one.
> Learn more about column indices.
>
> **You have created 2 of maximum 20 indices on this list.** These indices are:
>
> 1. Part Name
> 2. Part No.
>
> Create a new index

> Use this page to create a new index, or delete an existing one. Certain indices are created by the system and cannot be deleted.
>
> **Primary Column**
>
> Select the primary column for this index.
>
> Primary column for this index:
>
> Content Type ▾
>
> **Secondary Column**
>
> Select the secondary column for this index. If this is left blank, then this index will be a single column index on the selected Primary column. If a secondary index is specified, then this index becomes a compound index. Only certain field types can participate in compound indices.
>
> Secondary column for this index:
>
> (none) ▾
>
> [Create]   [Cancel]

NOTE

Indexed columns are pre-analyzed on the server to make them faster for visitors to view. However, indexed columns also take up more resources in the database. Therefore, it is common to index columns only on very large lists (say, with 2,000 or more items) and only to index the columns that you expect visitors to sort or filter by. Filtering by an indexed column enhances performance more than filtering by a column that has not been indexed.

At the bottom of the List Settings page there is a section that lists existing views and gives you the Create View option. Clicking a view name opens the Edit View page, while clicking Create View opens the Choose A View Format page and then the Create View page, all of which were discussed earlier in this chapter.

In the next chapter we'll discuss the second most important element in SharePoint, libraries, which allow you to share and archive documents, pictures, surveys, and forms.

Chapter 5

Adding and Handling Libraries

Libraries in SharePoint, like real-life libraries, are repositories for documents; or in terms of computers, SharePoint libraries are like folders that contain files, the files being documents of all types (you can have actual folders in both libraries and lists). Libraries hold written documents, such as those that might be produced by Microsoft Word; spreadsheets, such as those from Excel; forms created in several different programs including SharePoint; presentations like those created with PowerPoint; pictures and graphic files of many different types, including photographs, flow charts, architectural drawings, organizational charts, and Gantt charts; and audio and video files of a number of types.

5

The primary purpose of SharePoint libraries is to have a single place to put all the information needed and used by a team or project so everybody on the team or project can have immediate access to the same material. This lets everyone know what information is available and eliminates the hunting and searching to find who has what document or trying to determine where it has been stored.

In this chapter we'll discuss the various types of libraries; how to create, search, and manage them; and how to connect or relate different documents.

Create a Library

SharePoint libraries are closely related to SharePoint lists, and in some ways a library can be thought of as a list of documents. Each document in a library has identifying information connected to it that is the same as an item in a list with fields and columns that can be modified, arranged, and sorted. Many of the list functions that you saw in Chapter 4 are also used with libraries. Like lists, libraries are created with the use of a template, and you should start a library in the same way as a list: by defining what it is you want in the library, then selecting a template that is closest to what you want, and finally modifying it to get exactly what you want.

Define a Library

Defining a library is important to assure that it provides what you want. Start by asking these questions:

- What is the purpose of the library; what is it to contain?
- How does the new library relate to existing libraries? Does it duplicate what exists?

- What fields are required by the library? Examples are title, description, created by, created date, modified by, modified date, and so on.

- What are the most important fields? You may want some views that show only some of the fields.

- Who is going to use the library, and what permission scheme is required?

- Who can add to the library, and do additions require approval?

- Who can modify library documents, and do modifications require approval?

- What is the archiving plan? When should documents be moved to archival storage, and who will do that?

The objective is to think through the proposed library to make sure it is well defined and needed. You will probably want to involve others who will be using the library in this definition process.

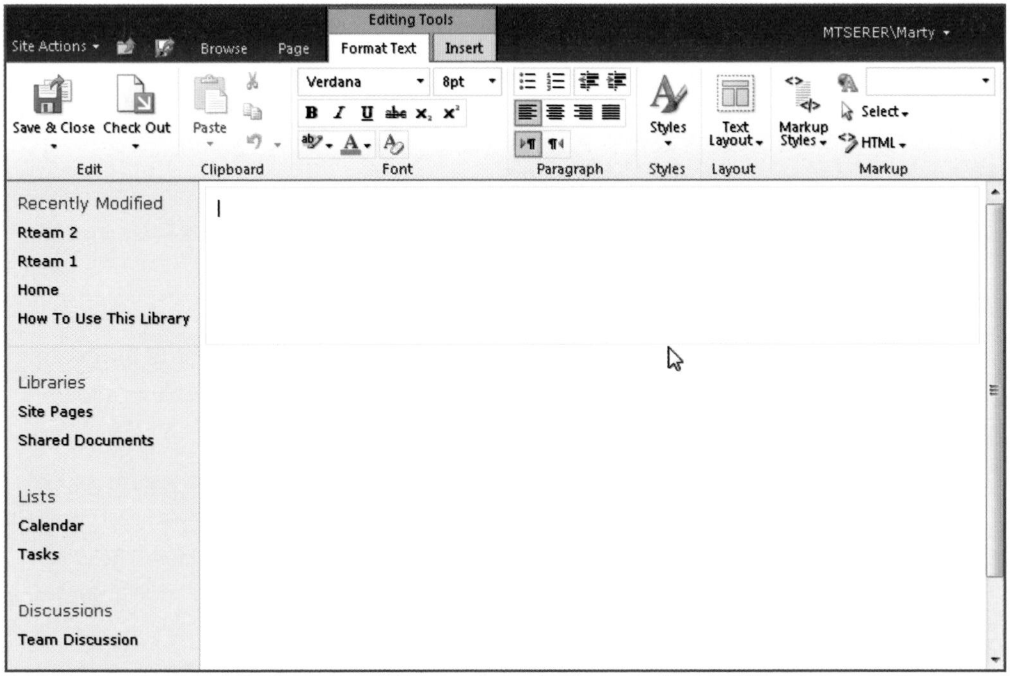

Figure 5-1: *A standard page has an Edit icon in the tab bar and the ability to change the layout.*

Prepare to Add a Library

Depending on the page on which you want to add a library and the templates that were used to create the site and page, there are different opportunities to prepare for a new library. The key distinction is whether the page is a:

- **Standard page**, which when it is blank has a single Web Part zone on it, but in all cases has an Edit Page icon. When you click the **Edit** icon, the Web Part zone becomes apparent, as you can see in Figure 5-1.

- **Web Part page**, which when it is blank has multiple Web Part zones with an "Add A Web Part" box in them and it does *not* have an Edit Page icon. To edit the page, you must click the **Page** tab and then click **Edit Page** to see the Web Parts and Web Part zones shown in Figure 5-2.

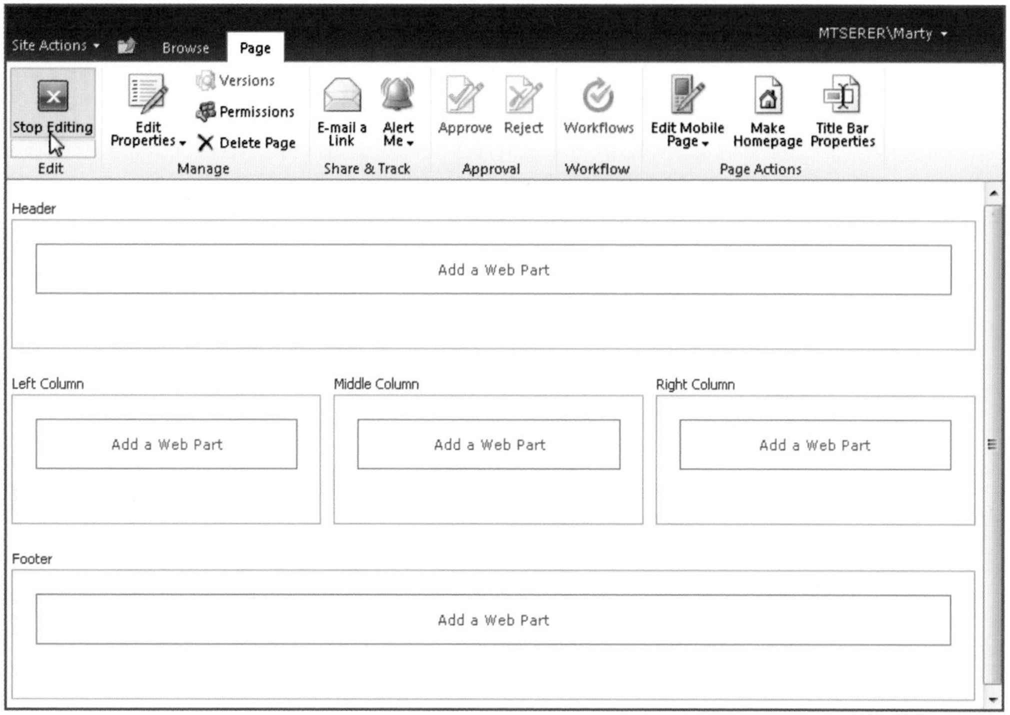

Figure 5-2: *A Web Part page does not have an Edit icon, and the layout has predefined Web Part zones.*

In either case, navigate to or create the page on which you want the library.

PREPARE A STANDARD PAGE

If the page to which you will add a library has an Edit Page icon in the tab bar, it is a standard page, independent of whether it has existing content; and you can directly change the layout of the page to give you a location for adding a library.

1. Click the **Edit** icon on the tab bar. A page similar to Figure 5-1 will appear.

   Consider if you want to keep the current layout or want a different one. If so, in the Editing Tools I Formatting Text tab, click **Text Layout** to open a drop-down menu, and select one of the layouts. You will see a faint outline around each cell in the table that is created to help align content.

2. Click in the table cell where you want the library.

PREPARE A WEB PART PAGE

A Web Part page has less flexibility, and you will need to use one of the existing Web Part zones in which to add your library. Also, you will be able to add only existing libraries or other elements.

1. Click the **Page** tab on the tab bar, and click **Edit page**. If it is a blank page, it will open as you saw in Figure 5-2.

2. Click one of the **Add A Web Part** links on the page to add a library there. The Web Parts menu will open below the ribbon and display the current lists and libraries that can be added.

NOTE

Team sites tend to use a standard page with the Edit icon, while meeting sites tend to use Web Part pages.

TIP

If you want to add a library that does not currently exist to a Web Part page, add it first to the site and then to the Web Part page.

Add Libraries

Adding a library to a page can be done in several different ways, depending on the page and the type of library you want. There are four methods to add libraries to a site page in addition to using SharePoint Designer (see Chapter 8):

- **Site Actions | New Document Library**
- **Site Actions | More Options | Libraries**
- **Edit | Insert | New List**
- **Add A Web Part**

The first two and fourth methods are available on all pages. The third method is available only on standard pages.

USE SITE ACTIONS | NEW DOCUMENT LIBRARY

This is the simplest method to add a basic document library. You can use it on any page, although the resulting library will be created on the site and not on an existing page; to get the library on a page, you will have to separately use the steps in "Add a Web Part" later in this chapter. To create a new document library:

1. On any page in the site, click **Site Actions** and then click **New Document Library**. The Create dialog box will appear, as shown in Figure 5-3.

2. Enter a name and description, choose whether you want the library shown on the Quick Launch and whether a new document version is created each time the document is edited, and choose a document template to use for new documents in the library.

3. When you are ready, click **Create**.

USE SITE ACTIONS | MORE OPTIONS

Site Actions | More Options gives you a choice of up to nine library templates. These are added to the site, and you must separately add the library to the page where you want it. Here are the steps:

1. From the site in which you want a new library, click **Site Actions**, and then click **More Options**. The Create dialog box will appear.

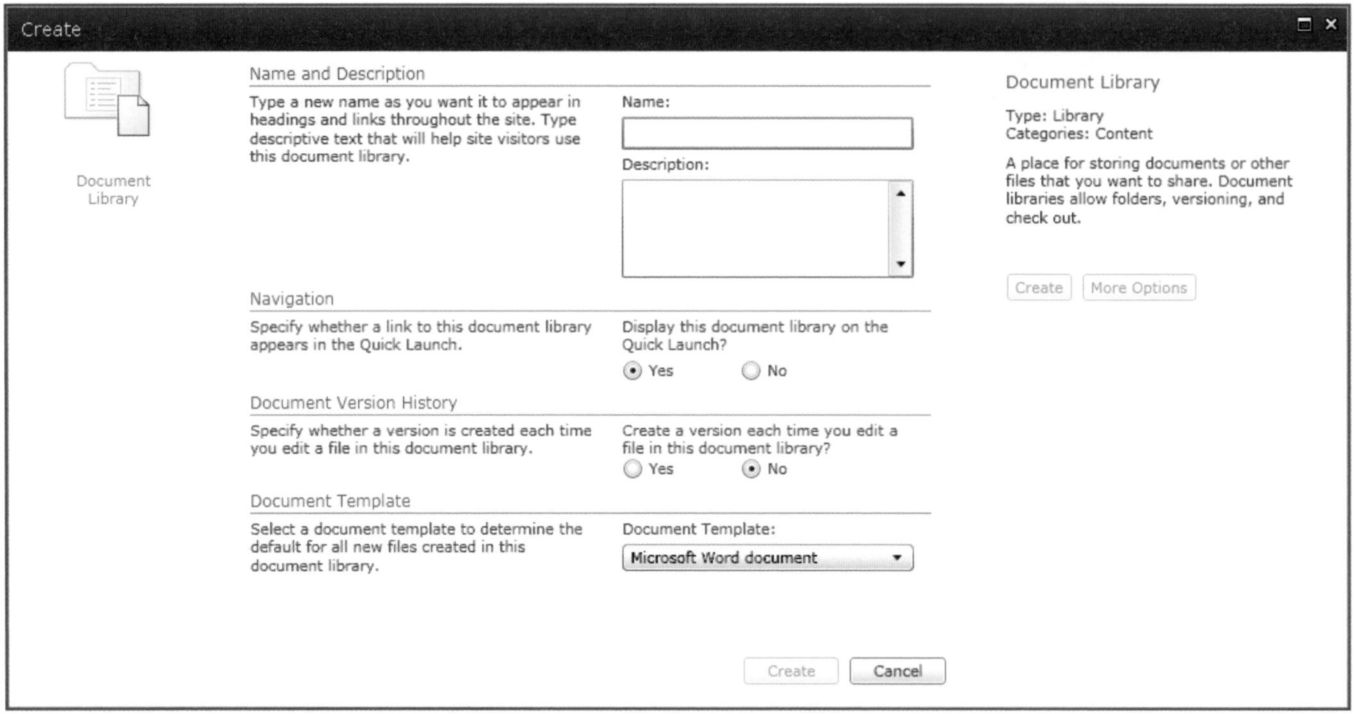

Figure 5-3: *Creating a basic document library is probably what you will most often do because it provides what is needed most of the time.*

2. Click **Library** to limit the display of templates to libraries (see Figure 5-4), click the template you want, for all but the slide library enter a name for the library, and click **Create**. If requested, enter any needed information for the particular template.

3. The library will be added to the site, but not to a specific page. To do that, see "Add a Web Part" later in this chapter.

USE EDIT | INSERT | NEW LIST

If you have a page with an Edit Page icon on the tab bar, such as a page created with the standard page template, you may use it with the Editing Tools | Insert tab's New List option, where you can select any of the nine library templates, as

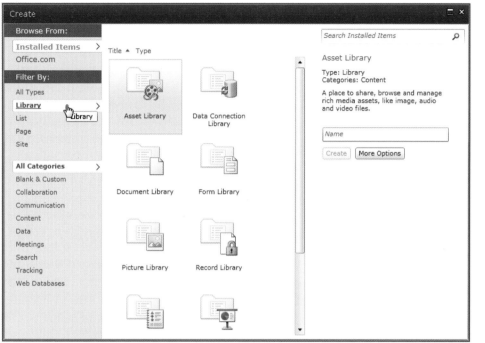

Figure 5-4: *SharePoint provides templates for up to nine different libraries.*

Create List

List Title:

Libraries	Communications	Tracking	Custom Lists
Record Library	Announcements	Links	Custom List
Document Library	Contacts	Calendar	Custom List in Datasheet View
Form Library	Discussion Board	Tasks	Status List
Wiki Page Library		Project Tasks	
Picture Library		Issue Tracking	
Data Connection Library			
Asset Library			
Slide Library			
Report Library			

OK   Cancel

Figure 5-5: *Although the dialog box is titled "New List," it includes new library templates.*

you can see in Figure 5-5. On a page with the Edit Page icon, you can alternatively click the Page tab **Edit** option to display the Insert tab's New List option from which you can get the same selection of library templates.

The "Create a Library" section later in this chapter will demonstrate how to directly choose and add a library to the currently selected page using the Edit Page icon with the Editing Tools | Insert tab | New List.

The benefit of the Edit Page option, if you have it available, is that it allows you to put a new library in exactly the position on the page that you want with the steps in "Create a Library."

ADD A WEB PART

There are several instances when creating sites and pages that Add A Web Part boxes appear on a page when it is being edited, like the ones in Figure 5-6. The Add A Web Part box can be used to add a library to the page, *but only libraries that already exist in the site.* If the library you want to add to the page already exists in the site, use the following steps to add it to the page; otherwise, go back to either "Use Site Actions | New Document Library" or "Use Site

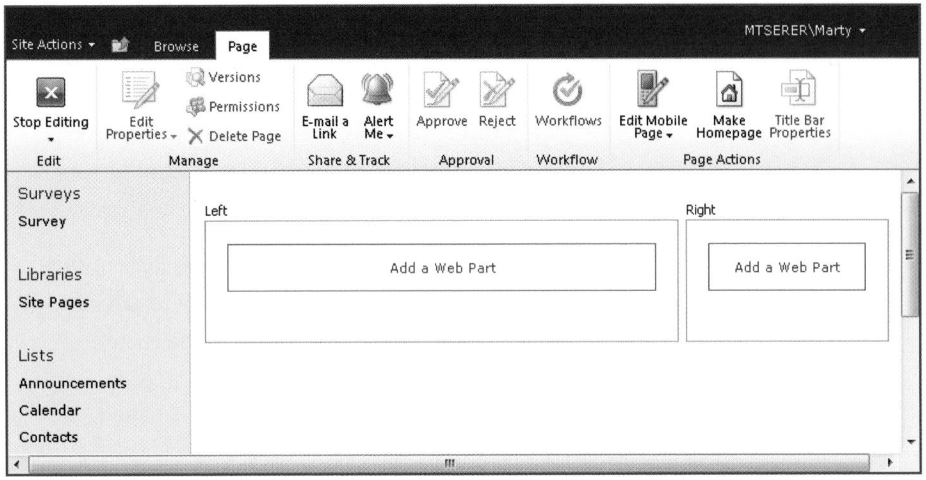

Figure 5-6: *Some pages require you to add elements through a specific Web Part location.*

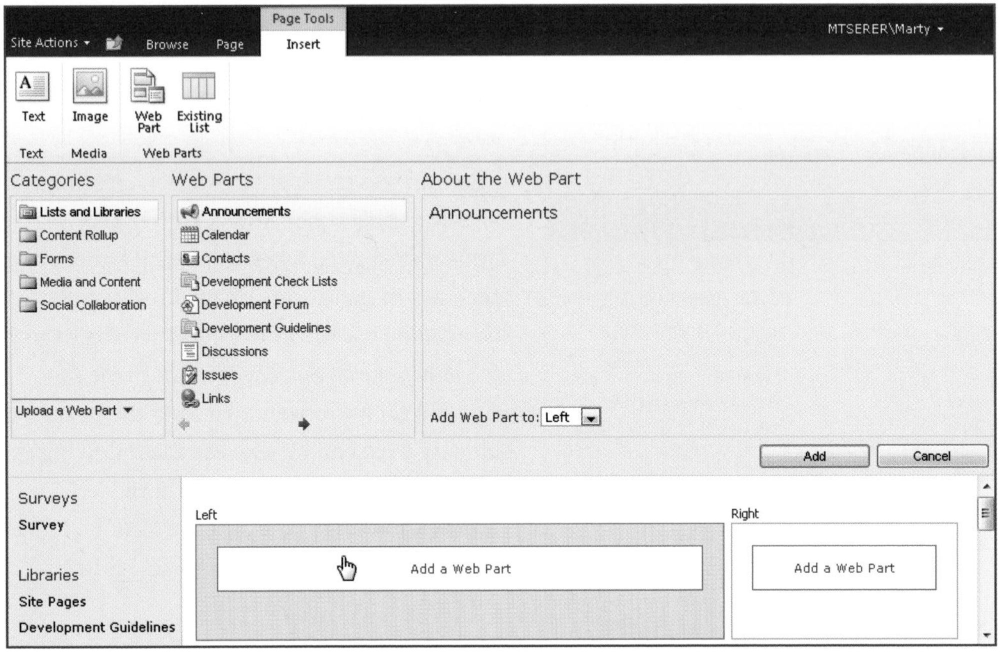

Figure 5-7: *Only existing libraries and other elements can be added within an existing Web Part zone.*

Actions | Other Options" earlier in this chapter to add the library to the site, and then come back here to add it to the page.

1. Click in the **Add A Web Part** box where you want the new library. The Page Tools | Insert tab will appear and display the *existing* elements that are available to be added to the page, as shown in Figure 5-7.

2. In the Categories column on the left, click **Lists And Libraries** if it isn't already selected.

3. In the Web Parts column, click the library you want (in Figure 5-7, there are three libraries in the middle of the Web Parts list, all beginning with the word "Development"). If you don't see the library and you know it has been added to the current site, click the dark black arrow at the bottom of the list to display the balance of the list.

4. When you have selected a library, click **Add** to place the library in the Add A Web Part box on the page.

Select a Library Template

The more popular library templates and what they contain are shown in Table 5-1. All of the library templates are similar to the Document Library template in that they store files and link each file with a list entry containing a name, who created it, who modified it, and who checked it out. Most also allow folders to partition the library, to

LIBRARY	DESCRIPTION	DEFAULT COLUMNS
Document Library	Store documents and other files to be shared	Type, Name, Modified, Title, Created By, Modified By, Checked Out To
Form Library	Manage business forms of all types compatible with InfoPath	Type, Name, Modified, Title, Created By, Modified By, Checked Out To
Picture Library	Store, locate, and share pictures, images, and other graphics	Type, Name, Size, Title, Date Taken, Description, Keywords, Created By, Modified By, Checked Out To
Slide Library	Manage, store, locate, and reuse PowerPoint slides	Thumbnail, Name, Presentation, Description, Modified, Title, Created By, Modified By, Checked Out To
Wiki Page Library	Contain an interconnected set of editable pages with text, graphics, and Web Parts.	Wiki Content, Created By, Modified By, Checked Out To

Table 5-1: *More popular SharePoint Libraries*

use versioning to track who and when a document was modified, and to have their contents be checked out.

TIP

You might want to create several of the libraries to fully explore how they function.

Create a Library

With a definition of the library you want, a supporting template in mind, and a location selected on the page that will hold it, create the library.

1. From the site Home page (if you are already looking at library templates, skip to step 5), navigate to the page on which you want the library and click the **Page** tab.

2. Click **Edit** to display the Editing Tools tab and the Web Part zones on the page. If you don't see an Edit icon on the page to which you want to add a library, see "Add Libraries" in this chapter and use the steps there in place of the remaining steps in this section.

3. If you haven't already selected the page layout you want, click **Text Layout** (if it is available), select the desired layout, and click in the region in which you want the library.

4. Click the **Insert** tab in the tab row, and click **New List** to display the library templates that are available for the page you have displayed.

5. Enter the **List Title** that you want to use for this library. This name will become the title of the library on your page; it does not have to be the same as the template name.

6. Click the library template you want to use, and click **OK** to display the library on your page.

7. Click **Save & Close** to complete the process.

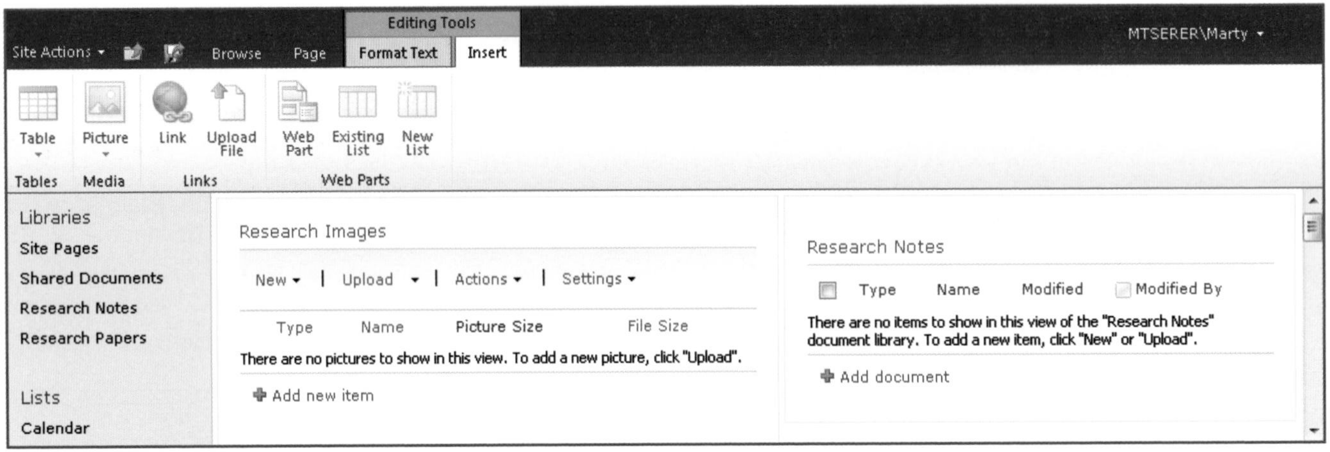

Figure 5-8: *To have your pages reflect a particular design, you must establish the layout first and then place a library or other element in a particular Web Part zone.*

You can immediately add documents to your library, as described in Chapter 3, or you can modify or customize the library, as discussed later in this chapter.

Work with Specific Libraries

SharePoint libraries have more commonalities than differences. The document library is the common denominator and has been covered here and in Chapter 3. The form, picture, and slide libraries are similar to the document library, although they do differ in the type of files they contain, some of the fields in the library entries, and, most importantly, how the files are handled once they are in the library. Handling library content for forms and slides is discussed in Chapter 7 as it relates to Microsoft InfoPath and PowerPoint. Here we'll focus on picture and wiki page libraries.

Begin working with each type of library by using the steps in "Add Libraries" and "Create a Library" earlier in this chapter. The following sections will begin after you have completed the previous steps.

Edit

Save | Cancel | Paste | Cut / Copy | Delete Item

Commit | Clipboard | Actions

ⓘ The document was uploaded successfully. Use this form to update the properties of the document.

Name * SV400896[1]   .JPG

Preview

Title

Date Picture Taken   6/11/2009   1 AM ▼ 39 ▼

Description

Figure 5-9: As you add pictures to your site, keep in mind that you may want to search for this picture in the future, so enter the name, description, and keywords accordingly.

WORK WITH A PICTURE LIBRARY

A new Picture library will come on the page, as shown on the left in Figure 5-8. You can immediately add a picture, or you can perform a number of other actions.

1. **To add pictures to the library**, click **Add New Item**
   ⊕ Add new item to open the Select Picture dialog box. Enter or browse to a file path and name, and click **OK**. The image will open in a preview window, as you see in Figure 5-9.

   Select Picture

   Upload Document

   Browse to the picture you intend to upload.

   Name:
   [   ] Browse...

   Upload Multiple Files...
   ☑ Overwrite existing files

   OK   Cancel

2. Enter a title, make any desired changes in the date and time, enter a description and keywords, and click **Save**.

3. **To work with the library**, click the library title to open its preview and display the picture library menu, as you can see in Figure 5-10.

4. **To add a new folder** to the library, click **New**, enter a name, and click **Save**. Click the new folder to open it, and observe the same menu bar uploading and so on.

   New ▼ | Upload ▼ | Actions ▼ | Set

   New Folder
   Add a new folder to this picture library.

5. **To add multiple pictures** at the same time, click **Upload** and click **Upload Multiple Pictures**. The Microsoft Office Picture Manager will open (see Figure 5-11).

   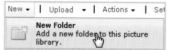

   Upload ▼ | Actions ▼ | Settings ▼

   Upload Picture
   Upload a picture from your computer to this library.

   Upload Multiple Pictures
   Upload multiple pictures from your computer to this library.

Site Actions ▾

MTSERER\Marty ▾

🏢 Research Team ▸ Research March ▸ All Pictures ▾

I Like It   Tags & Notes

Home

Search this site... 🔍 ❓

New ▾ | Upload ▾ | Actions ▾ | Settings ▾

View: All Pictures ▾

Libraries
Site Pages
Shared Documents
Research Notes
Research Papers

☐ SV400896   ☐ SV400897   ☐ SV400898

Lists
Calendar
Tasks

Discussions
Team Discussion

☐ SV400899   ☐ SV400900   ☐ SV400905

🗑 Recycle Bin
📄 All Site Content

Figure 5-10: Opening a picture library on its own page previews the pictures and provides options for working with them.

6. Select the location of the pictures, and then select the pictures by clicking the first picture, holding **SHIFT** and clicking the last picture, or holding **CTRL** and clicking individual pictures.

7. When all pictures have been selected, click **Upload And Close**. When you are returned to SharePoint, click **Go Back To Picture Library**.

8. **To edit, delete, download, e-mail, view, and drag and drop pictures**, click the check box of the picture you want to work with, and then click the option you want. Various message, dialog boxes, or applications open; simply follow the instructions to carry out the desired action. For example, to delete a picture, click **OK** to confirm you want to do that.

Actions ▾ | Settings ▾

Edit
Open pictures in a picture editor.

Delete
Delete selected pictures. 🖱

Download
Copy pictures from this library to your computer.

Send To
Insert pictures into an e-mail or document.

View Slide Show
View pictures in a slide show format.

Open with Windows Explorer
Drag and drop files into this library.

Connect to Outlook
Synchronize items and make them available offline.

Sync To Computer
Make a synchronized copy of this library available on your computer.

View RSS Feed
Syndicate items with an RSS reader.

Alert Me
Receive notifications when items change.

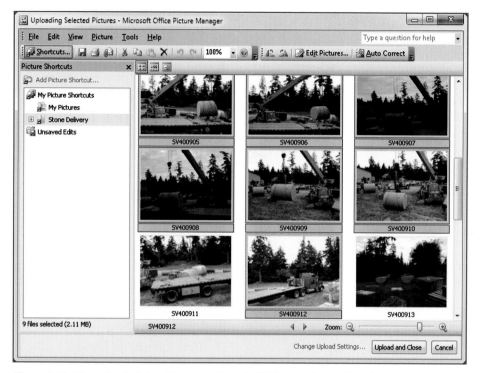

Figure 5-11: *SharePoint picture library options facilitate opening both a picture manager and a picture editor.*

9. To create a view of a picture library, click **Settings** and then click **Create View**. Click the view format you want to use (normally Standard), enter a view name, select or clear the check boxes to identify the columns that are to be used (see Figure 5-12), choose how you want to sort and filter the view, determine and set any other options you want, and click **OK**.

Display	Column Name	Position from
☐	Selection Checkbox (select a picture)	6
☐	Type (icon linked to document)	7
☑	Name (linked to display items)	2
☑	Picture Size	4
☑	File Size	5
☑	Required Field (must be selected for picture library details view)	8
☐	Check In Comment	9
☐	Checked Out To	10
☐	Content Type	11
☐	Copy Source	12
☐	Created	13
☑	Created By	3
☐	Date Picture Taken	14
☐	Description	15
☐	Edit (link to edit item)	16
☐	File Type (File extension)	17
☐	Folder Child Count	18
☐	ID	19
☐	Item Child Count	20
☐	Keywords	21
☐	Modified	22
☐	Modified By	23
☐	Name (for use in forms)	24
☐	Name (linked to document with edit menu)	25
☐	Name (linked to document)	26
☐	Picture Height	27
☐	Picture Width	28
☐	Preview	29
☑	Thumbnail	1
☐	Title	30
☐	Version	31
☐	Web Preview	32

Figure 5-12: *There is a wide selection of columns that you can add to the list attached to a picture library.*

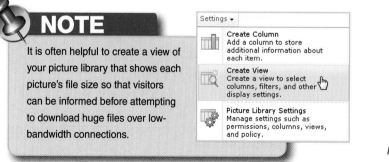

NOTE

It is often helpful to create a view of your picture library that shows each picture's file size so that visitors can be informed before attempting to download huge files over low-bandwidth connections.

Settings ▾

Create Column
Add a column to store additional information about each item.

Create View
Create a view to select columns, filters, and other display settings.

Picture Library Settings
Manage settings such as permissions, columns, views, and policy.

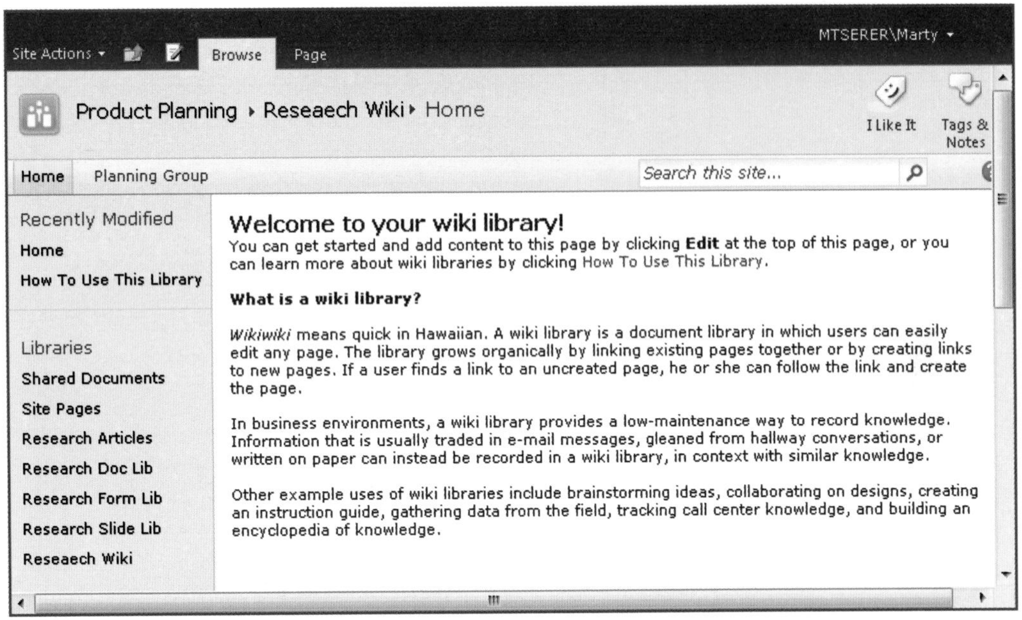

Figure 5-13: *SharePoint provides a lot of help in using a wiki page library.*

WORK WITH A WIKI PAGE LIBRARY

A *wiki page library* is a library of pages, with each page containing an essay (writing on a particular topic). Depending on permissions, anybody on the team can create a wiki page essay, and anybody can modify it. A wiki library grows organically by someone starting a topic and others adding to it, either directly or by adding links to another wiki page or to other elements in SharePoint, or to other web sites, or to shares (shared drives) available to the team. The purpose of a wiki page library is to share knowledge within a team. To be successful, everybody on the team must willing, and take the time, to add their information to the library.

When you create a new wiki library and open it, you see a Welcome To Your Wiki Library message (see Figure 5-13) with a link to "How To Use This Wiki Library." Here we'll look at adding and editing pages, and creating and viewing links.

1. **To add a wiki page**, click **Site Actions** and then click **New Page** (if you don't see New Page, click **More Options**, click **Page**, and then click the **Page** template).

2. Enter the name of the page, click **Create**, enter the essay you want to write using the options in the Editing Tools tabs, and then click **Save & Close**.

3. **To edit a wiki page**, to either correct something or add content, navigate to the page so it is displayed, click the **Edit Page** icon in the tab bar (if you don't see the Edit icon, click the **Page** tab and click **Edit Page**), enter any corrections or additions using editing tools as needed, and click **Save & Close**.

5

TIP

The linking notation discussed with wiki page libraries can be used on any page that can be edited (that has an edit icon in the tab bar).

QUICKSTEPS

ADDING MULTIPLE DOCUMENTS AT ONCE

In Chapter 2 you saw how to add single documents to a library. SharePoint also provides a way to add multiple documents at one time.

1. Open the site and navigate so that the library is displayed.

2. Click **Add New Document**. The Upload Document dialog box appears.

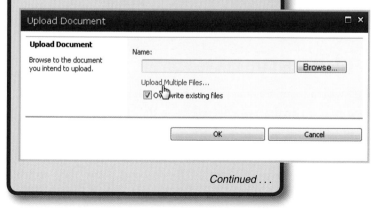

Continued . . .

4. **To create a link**, open the page in Edit mode, and enter the page or element to which you want to link enclosed in two pairs of square brackets, for example:

- To link to another page in the current folder and site: type [[Research]] for a page named "Research."

- To create a new page and link to it: type [[Testing Data]] to create a new page named "Testing Data" in the current site and enter a link to it.

- To link to another page in a subfolder in the current site: type [[Development/Research]] for a page named "Research" in a folder named "Development."

- To link to an item in a list in the current site: type [[List:Tasks/Testing]] for an item named "Testing" in the "Tasks" list.

- To have a link display a name other than the page being linked to: type [[Testing|Load Testing]] to display "Load Testing" for a link to a page named "Testing."

5. After typing the opening pair of square brackets, SharePoint will suggest a list of site pages and elements, as you can see in Figure 5-14. After clicking an entry, that lone entry will be displayed in what used to be the list, or use the arrow keys to select the entry. Press **ENTER** to confirm the selection and automatically add the closing square brackets.

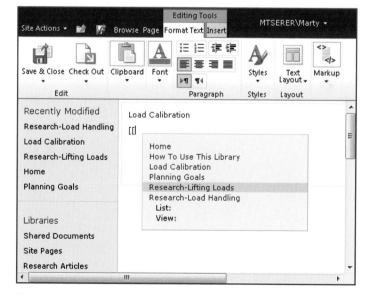

Figure 5-14: SharePoint makes creating links to other pages easy.

ADDING MULTIPLE DOCUMENTS AT ONCE *(Continued)*

3. Click **Upload Multiple Files**. The Upload Multiple Documents dialog box appears, as you see in Figure 5-15.

4. Open Windows Explorer and navigate to where you can see the files you want in the right pane of the Explorer.

5. Adjust the position of Windows Explorer and the SharePoint Upload Multiple Documents dialog box so that both are visible on your screen.

6. In Windows Explorer select the files you want to transfer by selecting the first file and pressing and holding **SHIFT** while clicking the last file in a contiguous group, or pressing and holding **CTRL** while clicking individual files that can be in any order.

7. When all the files you want to transfer are selected, drag them from Windows Explorer to the Upload Multiple Documents dialog box.

8. When all the files you want to transfer are in the dialog box, click **OK**. The files will be transferred.

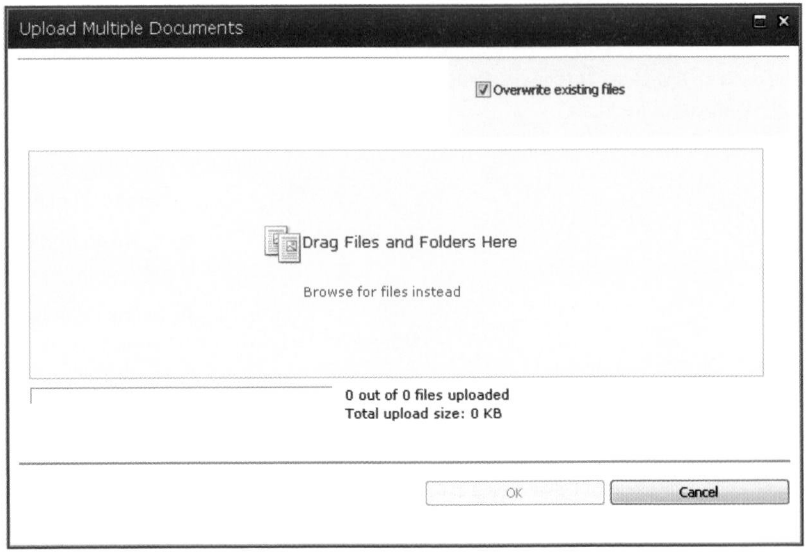

Upload Multiple Documents ☐ ×

☑ Overwrite existing files

Drag Files and Folders Here

Browse for files instead

0 out of 0 files uploaded
Total upload size: 0 KB

OK   Cancel

Figure 5-15: Multiple documents can be easily dragged and dropped to a SharePoint library.

6. When the links are the way you want them, click **Save & Close**. The pair of square brackets will disappear.

7. **To view the links coming into a page**, click the **Page** tab, and then on the Page ribbon, click **Incoming Links**. A list of the pages that have links to the current page is displayed, like this:

The following pages link to this page:
Research-Load Handling
Research-Lifting Loads
Load Calibration

Modify a Library

A library created with a template may not be exactly what you want, and you will need to modify it. To do that, you need to open the library for editing.

1. Click the title of the library so it opens in its own page and the Library Tools tabs appear.

2. Click the **Library Tools | Library** tab to open it in the ribbon, as shown in Figure 5-16.

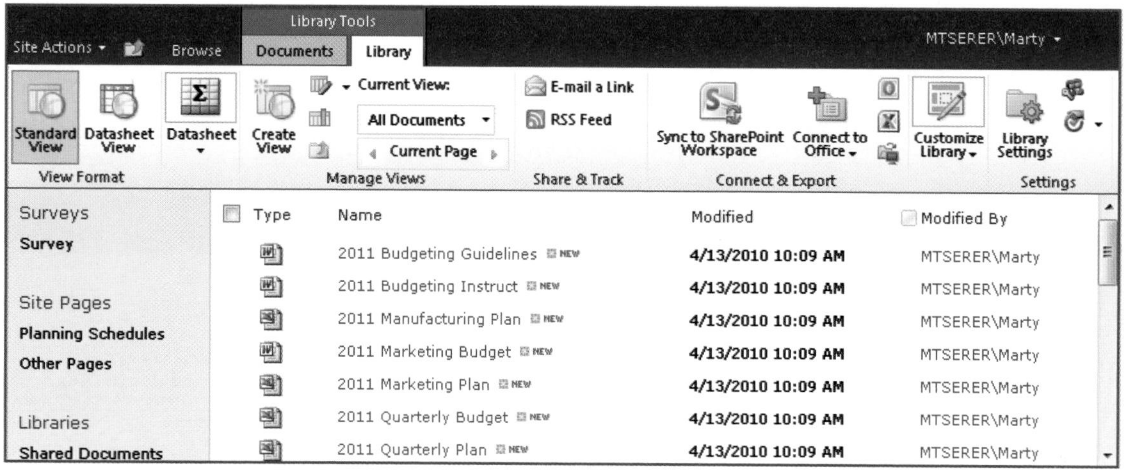

Figure 5-16: *The Library tab has many of the same options as the List tab.*

Among the actions that you can undertake from the Library tab are:

- Create and change the view of the library
- Add a column
- Change other settings

Create and Change Views

The normal document library view displays the type icon, title, modified date, and modified by name. This is generally true both for a library on a summary page and for a library in its own page. SharePoint gives you several ways to change the library view, but most important of these are by modifying the current view and by creating a new view.

MODIFY THE CURRENT VIEW

To modify the current library view:

1. If you are not currently looking at the view you want to modify, navigate to it.

2. If the Library Tools | Library tab is not displayed, click the check box on the right of the title bar of the library, and click the **Library** tab.

3. Click **Modify View** [⟦ Modify View ▾]. The Edit View page is displayed, the top part of which is shown in Figure 5-17. The bottom part is exactly the same as the bottom part of the list Edit View page shown in Chapter 4.

4. Select the columns to be displayed by clicking the **Display** check box next to each.

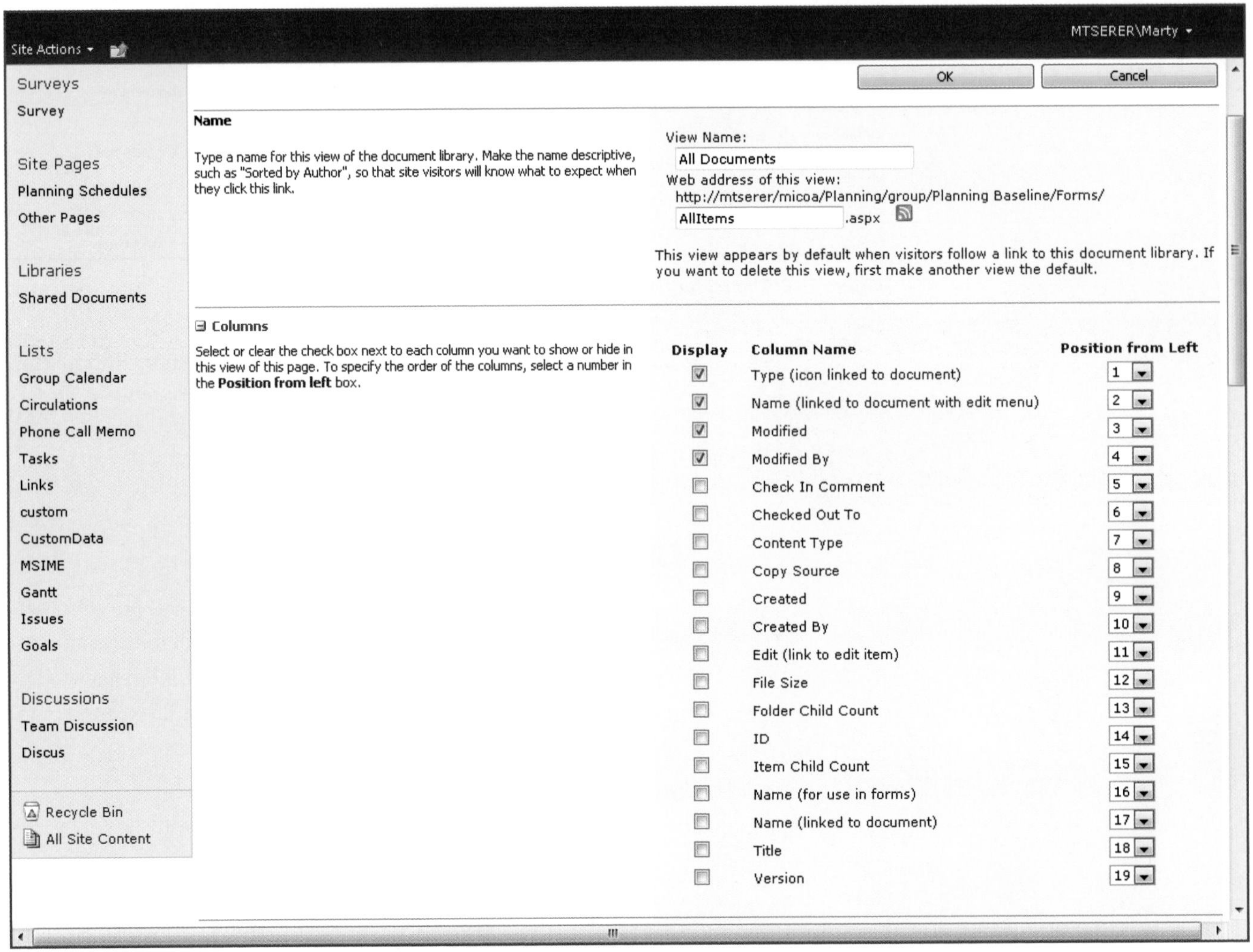

Figure 5-17: The top part of the library Edit View page allows you to change the columns displayed in a library document listing.

5. Determine the order, from left to right, by adjusting the number in the Position From Left column.

6. Enter the first two columns you want the library sorted on and the direction of the sort. After the first two columns are filled in, an option appears to add another.

7. If you have a lot of items on your library, you may choose to view only the most important of them by filtering out the others. If so, select one or more columns for the filter and how you want them applied.

8. Review the eight other ways that your library can be customized, and determine if you want to use them.

9. When you have customized the library the way you want, click **OK**.

CREATE A NEW VIEW

Besides modifying a view, you can also start from scratch and create exactly the library view you want.

1. With the library on your screen and the Library Tools I Library tab open in the ribbon (if this is not the case, see the first two steps in "Modify the Current View" earlier in this chapter), click **Create View** in the ribbon.

2. Review the choices of views that are presented, and click the one that is correct for you (these steps will assume the Standard View was selected). The Create View window will open, the top part of which is shown in Figure 5-18.

3. Enter a view name, choose whether it will be the default view for the library, and whether this is a personal or public view.

4. Select the columns you want to display and the position in which you want to display them. Set up the sorting and filtering you want, and use any of the other settings you need to get the view you want.

5. When you have the view set up the way you want it, click **OK**.

Add a Column

You can add a column to the list produced for a library. Common ones are a description column and a keywords column to provide more information on a document and a more granular filter, respectively.

1. If you are not currently looking at the library to which you want to add a column, navigate to it.

TIP

As with lists, you can add validation to a column in a new view by clicking **Library Settings** from the Library Tools I Library tab and clicking **Validation Settings** (validating column data is discussed in Chapter 4).

NOTE

While you can display a library in Datasheet View, it generally is not helpful. The meat of a library is in the document being stored, and Datasheet View does not help you see that. But if you want to quickly edit a custom field in a document library, such as Owner Name or Category, the Datasheet View can make it easy to edit those fields.

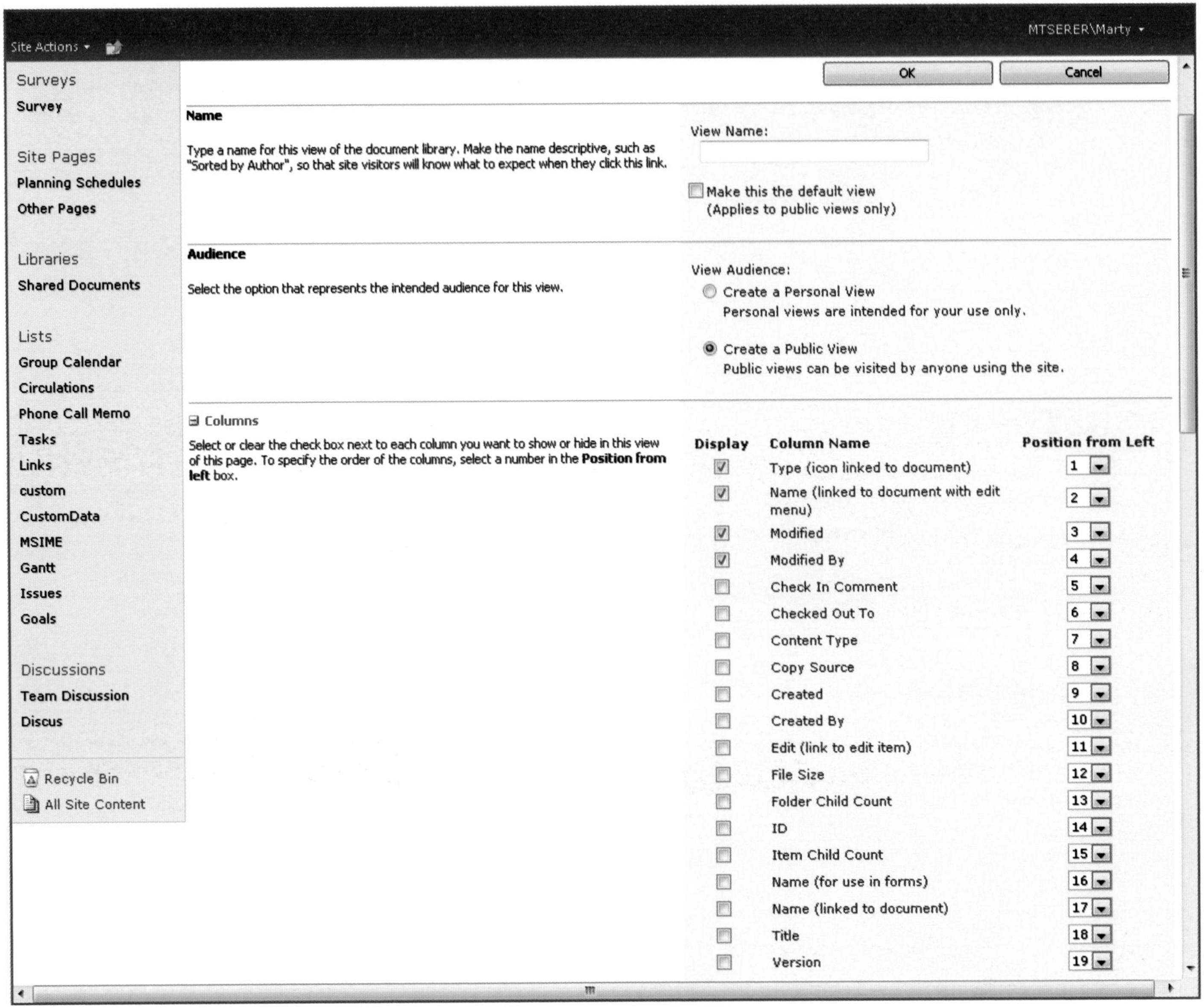

Figure 5-18: The Create View page allows you to create specialized view of a library.

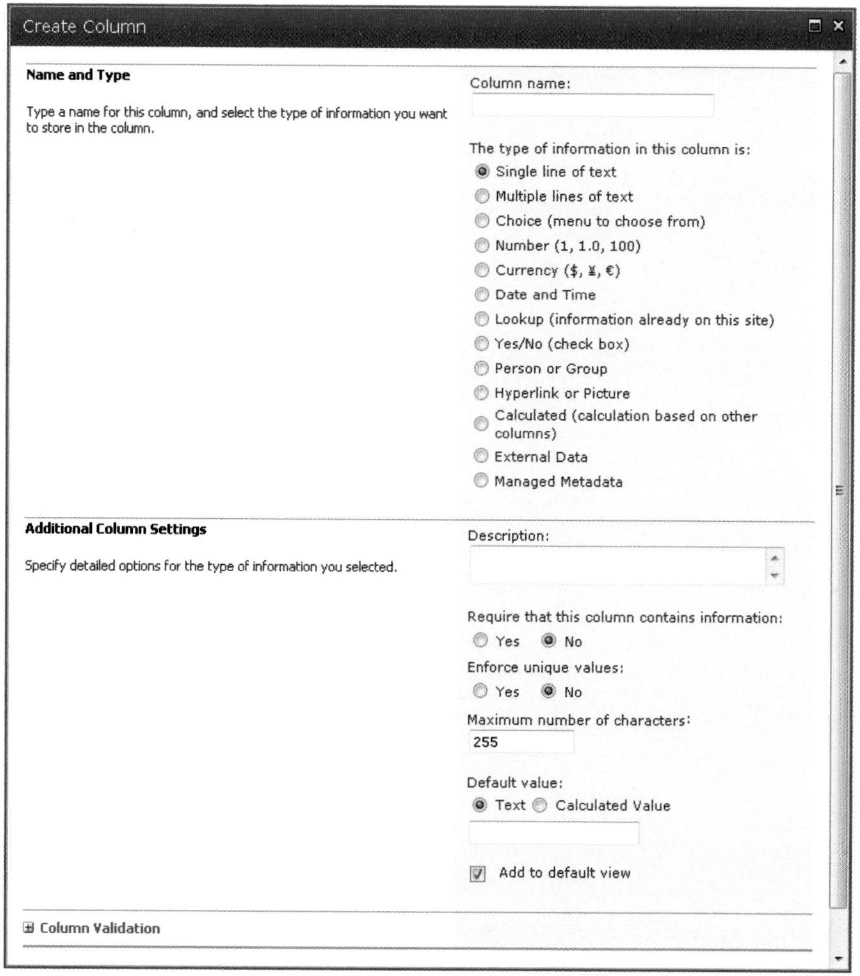

Figure 5-19: Adding a new column to a library can provide a description of a document.

TIP

By default, a new column will go at the end of the library's columns. To change that position or to make other changes to an existing column, see "Create and Change Views" in this chapter.

2. If the Library Tools | Library tab is not displayed, click the check box on the right of the title bar of the library, and click the **Library** tab.

3. Click **Create Column** [🔳 Create Column]. The Create Column page is displayed, as you can see in Figure 5-19.

4. Enter the name of the new column. This will be used as the column heading in the library.

5. Choose the type of information the column will contain, enter a description, and complete the information requested (see Chapter 4).

6. When you have completed entering all the needed information for a new column, click **OK**.

Manage Libraries

SharePoint libraries are an important element and need to be managed accordingly. The tools to do this are in library settings. For the most part, library settings are similar to list settings, so the review here will go at a quicker pace than that in Chapter 4 on lists. Refer back to that chapter for the added detail.

1. With the library on your screen and the Library Tools | Library tab open in the ribbon (if this is not the case, see the first two steps in "Modify the Current View" earlier in this chapter), click **Library Settings** on the right of the ribbon.

2. Review the Library Settings page that opens. It is quite comprehensive, as you can see in Figure 5-20. Here we'll look at using library settings and setting permissions.

Use Library Settings

As you can see in Figure 5-20, library settings let you change general items like name and description, control versioning and ratings, work with advanced settings, and delete the library.

QUICKSTEPS

HANDLING LIBRARY APPROVAL AND VERSIONING

While library approval and versioning is also similar to that for lists, there are some slight differences that warrant their own review.

1. From the Library Settings page, click **Versioning Settings**. The page shown in Figure 5-21 will open.

2. Choose whether or not additions or changes to library require approval.

3. Determine if a version of a document should be created each time a change is made to it and, if so, should SharePoint keep track of just major (approved) versions by numbering them 1, 2, 3,…, or should SharePoint keep track of both major and minor (drafts prior to approval) versions by numbering them 1.0, 1.1, 1.2, 2.0, 2.1…. If versioning is turned on, what should the limit be in the number of versions that are kept for both major versions, and, if enabled, for drafts?

4. Choose who can see drafts of changes before they are approved.

5. Determine if documents have to be checked out before they can be edited.

6. After making the necessary selections on the page, and click **OK**.

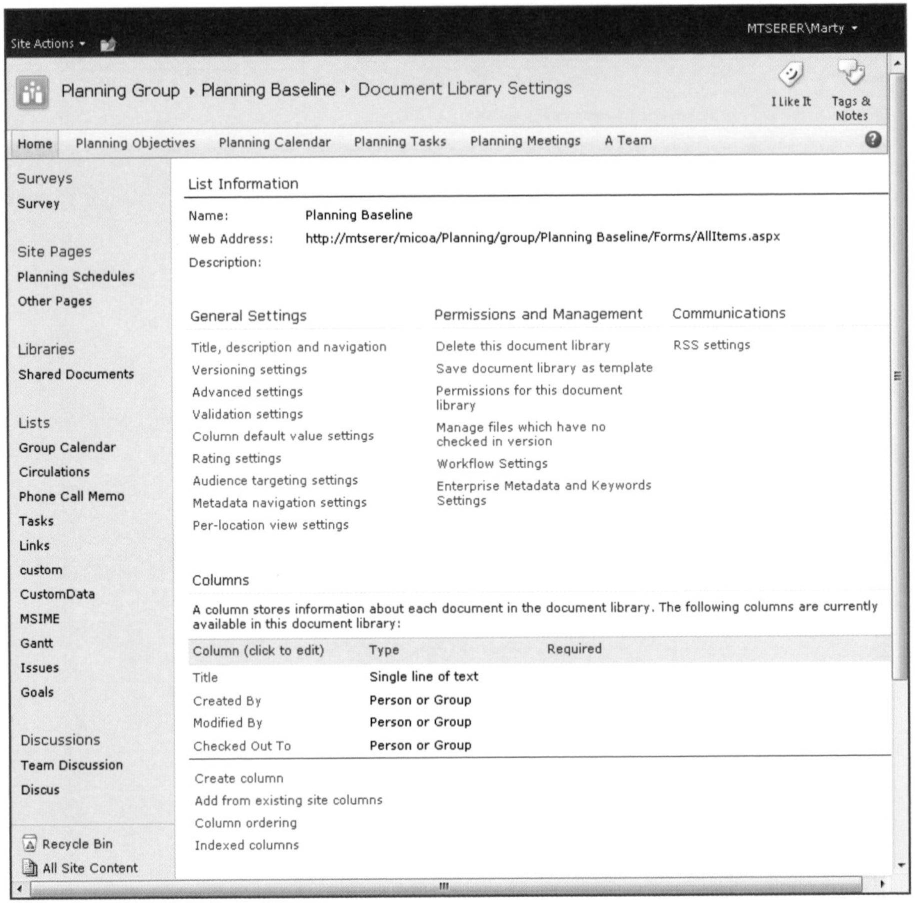

Figure 5-20: *Library settings are almost a duplicate of list settings.*

MANAGE GENERAL LIBRARY SETTINGS

The settings for the library title, description, navigation, validating, rating, audience targeting, metadata navigation, and per-location views are similar to what was described in Chapter 4. Please see that chapter for the discussion of those options.

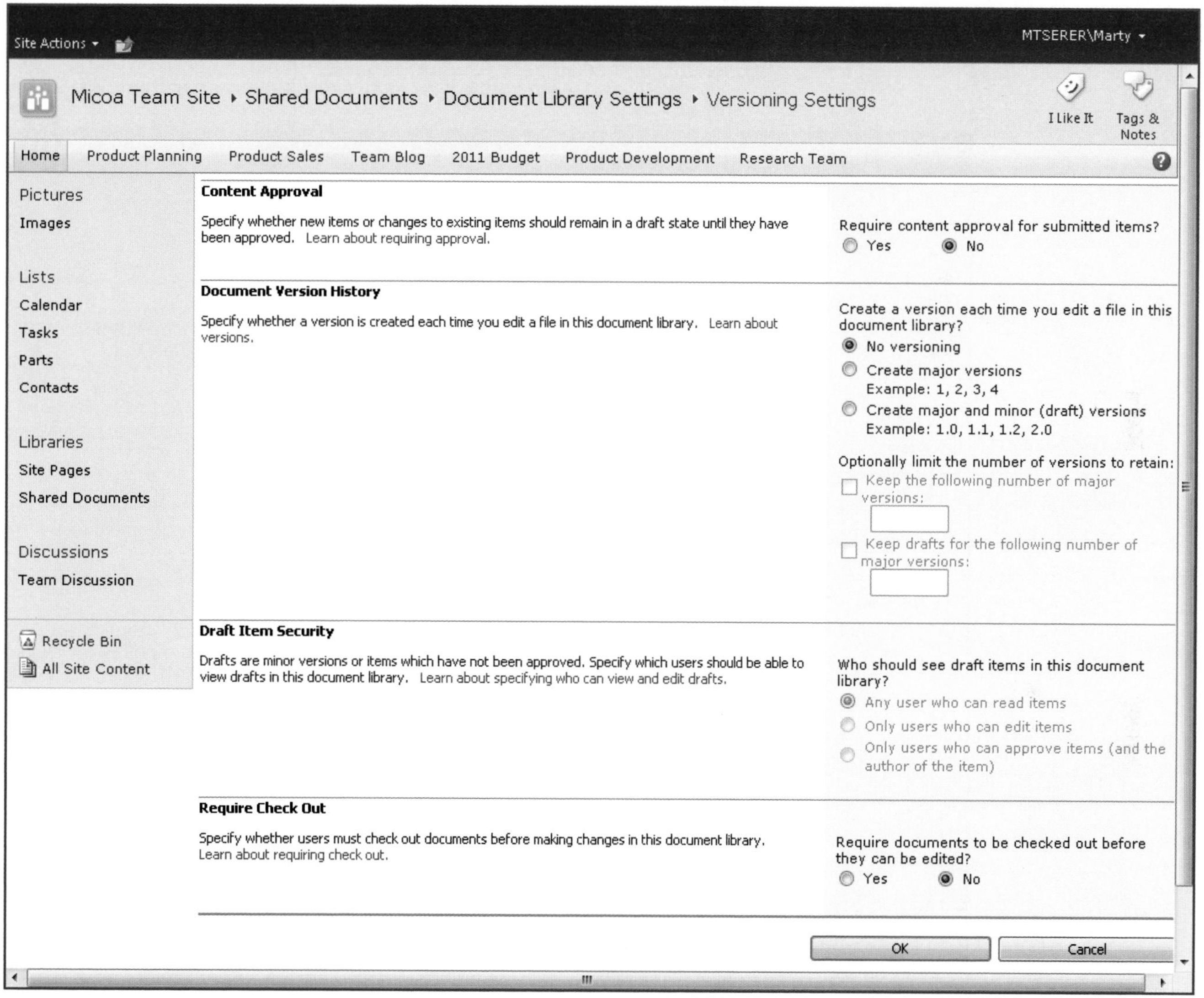

Site Actions ▾ 📝

MTSERER\Marty ▾

🏛 Micoa Team Site ▸ Shared Documents ▸ Document Library Settings ▸ Versioning Settings

🏷 I Like It   🏷 Tags & Notes

| Home | Product Planning | Product Sales | Team Blog | 2011 Budget | Product Development | Research Team |

❓

Pictures
Images

Lists
Calendar
Tasks
Parts
Contacts

Libraries
Site Pages
Shared Documents

Discussions
Team Discussion

🗑 Recycle Bin
📄 All Site Content

Content Approval

Specify whether new items or changes to existing items should remain in a draft state until they have been approved. Learn about requiring approval.

Require content approval for submitted items?
○ Yes   ● No

Document Version History

Specify whether a version is created each time you edit a file in this document library. Learn about versions.

Create a version each time you edit a file in this document library?
● No versioning
○ Create major versions
   Example: 1, 2, 3, 4
○ Create major and minor (draft) versions
   Example: 1.0, 1.1, 1.2, 2.0

Optionally limit the number of versions to retain:
☐ Keep the following number of major versions:
   [   ]

☐ Keep drafts for the following number of major versions:
   [   ]

Draft Item Security

Drafts are minor versions or items which have not been approved. Specify which users should be able to view drafts in this document library. Learn about specifying who can view and edit drafts.

Who should see draft items in this document library?
● Any user who can read items
○ Only users who can edit items
○ Only users who can approve items (and the author of the item)

Require Check Out

Specify whether users must check out documents before making changes in this document library. Learn about requiring check out.

Require documents to be checked out before they can be edited?
○ Yes   ● No

[OK]   [Cancel]

Figure 5-21: SharePoint can track document versions and require approval of changes.

WORK WITH ADVANCED SETTINGS

Library advanced settings have several options that are unique to libraries, as you can see in Figure 5-22. Here we will discuss just those. See Chapter 4 for the balance.

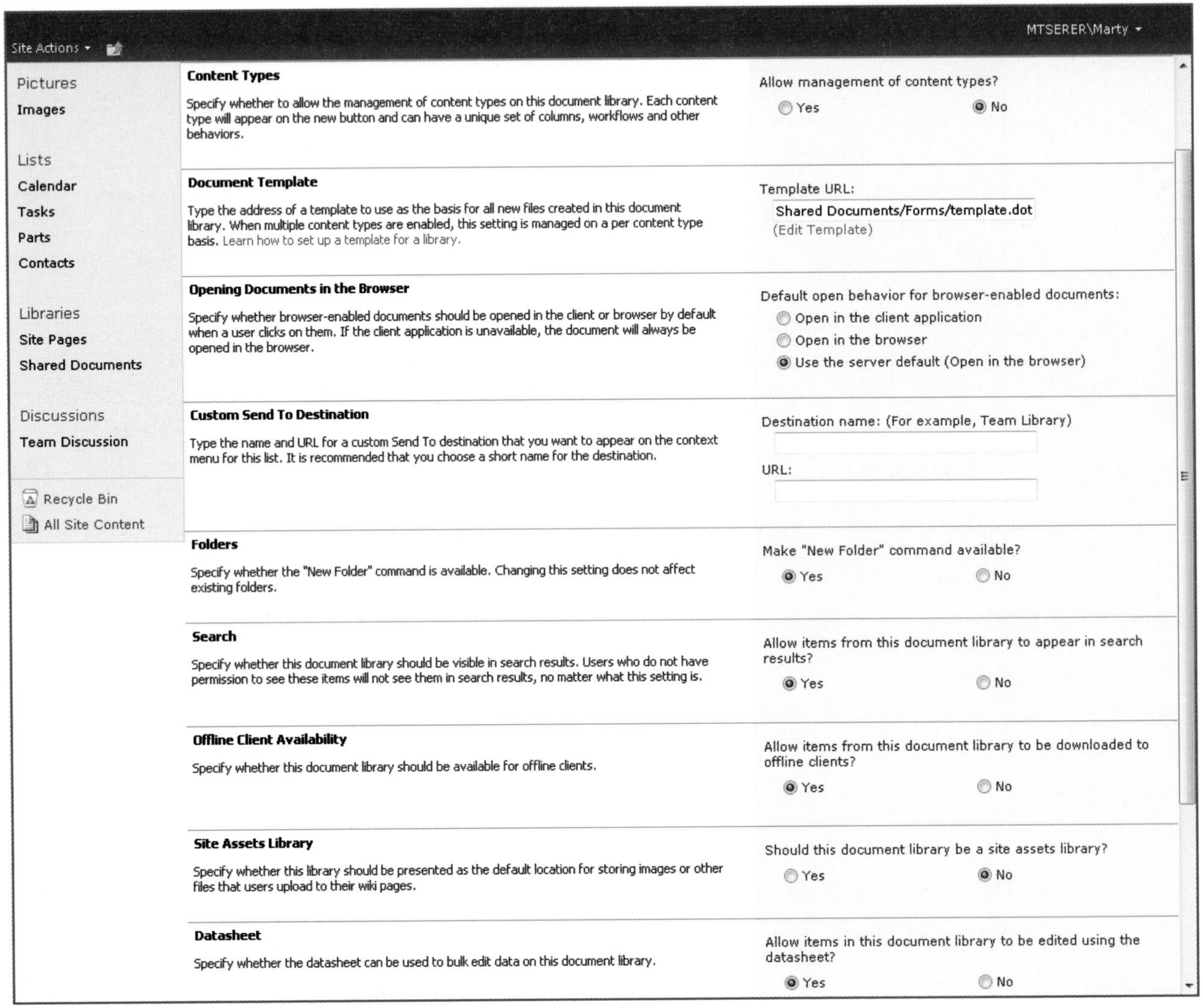

Figure 5-22: *Advanced settings contains several settings that are unique to libraries.*

1. Click **Advanced Settings** and choose the setting you want for the following library-specific options:

   a. **Document Template**: Enter the URL for the default template that will be used for new files created in the library.

   For example, if you have created an Expense Reports document library, you could point to your organization's expense report template in Excel. When users choose to create a new document in your document library, it would open that Excel template for them to start with; when they are finished, it will save the completed spreadsheet in your document library.

   b. **Open Documents In The Browser**: Choose if you want library documents to open in applications residing on the client's computer—for example, using the client's own copy of Excel—or if they should open in the browser using browser-based applications such as Excel Web Apps.

   c. **Custom Send To Destination**: Enter a short name, such as "Research," that will appear in a context menu, and a URL for the location to which library documents are often sent. This allows you to right-click a document and click the **Send To** *<name you entered>* to send the file to that destination.

   d. **Site Assets Library**: Choose whether the current library should be the site assets library.

2. Make the necessary selections on the Advanced Settings page, and click **OK** when ready.

DELETE A LIBRARY

To delete a library *and all of its documents* and place them in the Recycle Bin:

With the library to be deleted selected and its library settings in view, click **Delete This Library**. In response to the message asking if you are sure you want to delete the library and its contents, if you in fact do, click **OK**.

Set Permissions

Library permissions are similar to list permissions, which are introduced in Chapter 3 and further described in Chapter 4. You can set permissions for both libraries and the documents they contain.

For libraries, begin with the library selected and the Library Tools | Library tab displayed, and then click **Library Permissions** (or its icon if you don't see the words).

–Or–

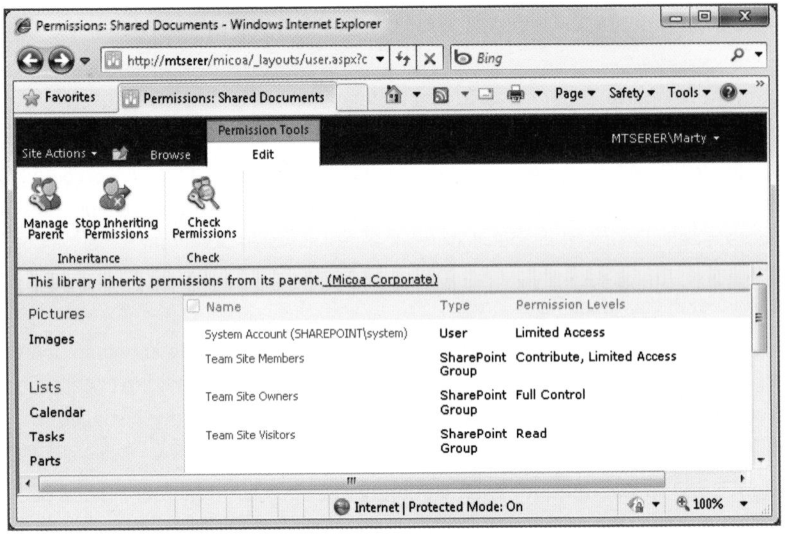

Figure 5-23: *Both library and document permissions start with inherited groups and permissions from the parent site.*

For documents, begin with the library in view, select the document for which you want to change the permissions, click the **Library Tools | Document** tab, and then click **Document Permissions** or its icon.

In both cases, the same page will appear with the same list of permissions, as shown in Figure 5-23, given that no one has made any changes from the default settings.

To change the handling of permissions, see Chapter 4.

Change Column Settings

On the lower part of the Library Settings page, there are several resources for making changes to the columns in a library, as you see in Figure 5-24. These include changes to individual columns and adding and ordering columns. The handling of these changes is the same as for list columns, described in Chapter 4.

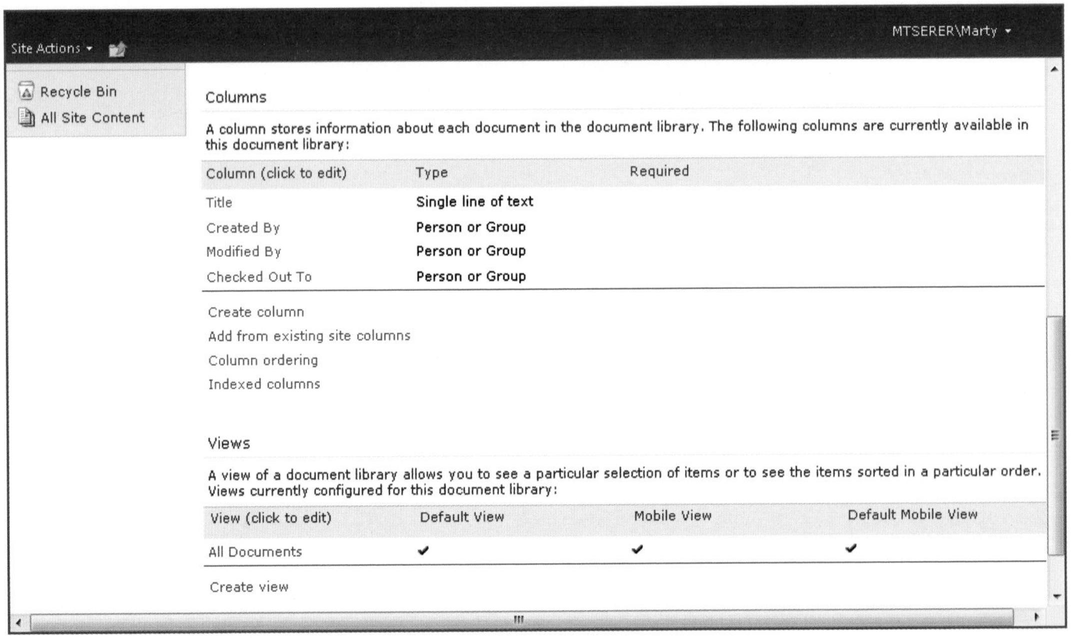

Figure 5-24: *Library settings provide resources to change individual columns.*

Chapter 6

Working with Other SharePoint Elements

While lists and libraries demand a large amount of attention due to their widespread use, SharePoint offers six other elements that can be useful for their function. These are alerts, blogs, discussions, surveys, meetings, and workflows. While these are not all in the same category or at the same level of importance, they are brought together here as useful elements of SharePoint. They will all be discussed in this chapter in terms of how they are created and how they are used.

Set Up and Manage Alerts

SharePoint alerts tell you if something has changed. You are told via e-mail, and the "something" can be:

- A change to a list or to a library
- A change to a list item or to a library document
- A change in the results of a search

Set Up Alerts

Alerts are set from the individual element for which you want to be alerted. So we'll separately review alerts for lists and libraries, items and documents, and searches.

Shared Documents - New Alert

	OK	Cancel

Alert Title

Enter the title for this alert. This is included in the subject of the notification sent for this alert.

Shared Documents

Send Alerts To

You can enter user names or e-mail addresses. Separate them with semicolons.

Users:

MTSERER\Marty ;

Delivery Method

Specify how you want the alerts delivered.

Send me alerts by:
- ● E-mail
- ○ Text Message (SMS)
  - ☐ Send URL in text message (SMS)

Change Type

Specify the type of changes that you want to be alerted to.

Only send me alerts when:
- ● All changes
- ○ New items are added
- ○ Existing items are modified
- ○ Items are deleted

Send Alerts for These Changes

Specify whether to filter alerts based on specific criteria. You may also restrict your alerts to only include items that show in a particular view.

Send me an alert when:
- ● Anything changes
- ○ Someone else changes a document
- ○ Someone else changes a document created by me
- ○ Someone else changes a document last modified by me

When to Send Alerts

Specify how frequently you want to be alerted. (mobile alert is only available for immediately send)

- ● Send notification immediately
- ○ Send a daily summary
- ○ Send a weekly summary

Time:
Sunday | 7:00 PM

SET UP ALERTS FOR LISTS AND LIBRARIES

Lists and libraries can alert you when:

- New items or documents have been added
- Existing items or documents have changed
- Existing items or documents have been deleted

To set an alert for a list or library:

1. Navigate to the list or library, and click its title to open it in its own page.

2. Click the **List** or **Library** tab in the ribbon, click **Alert Me** in the Share & Track group, and then click **Set Alert On This List** or **Set Alert On This Library**. The New Alert page will open, as you can see in Figure 6-1.

3. Enter an alert title. This is in the subject of the alert e-mail.

4. In the Send Alerts To box, enter the user names and/or e-mail addresses of the people to get the alert, and in the Delivery Method section choose whether to send the alert via e-mail or text message.

5. In the Change Type and Send Alerts For These Changes sections, choose the type and circumstances of the changes for which you want an alert.

6. When you have finished configuring the alert, click **OK**.

SET UP ALERTS FOR ITEMS AND DOCUMENTS

List items and library documents can alert you when:

- Someone else has changed an item or document
- Someone else has changed an item or document you wrote
- Someone else has changed an item or document you modified

Figure 6-1: *Alerts can save you from having to go through all new postings to a list or a library.*

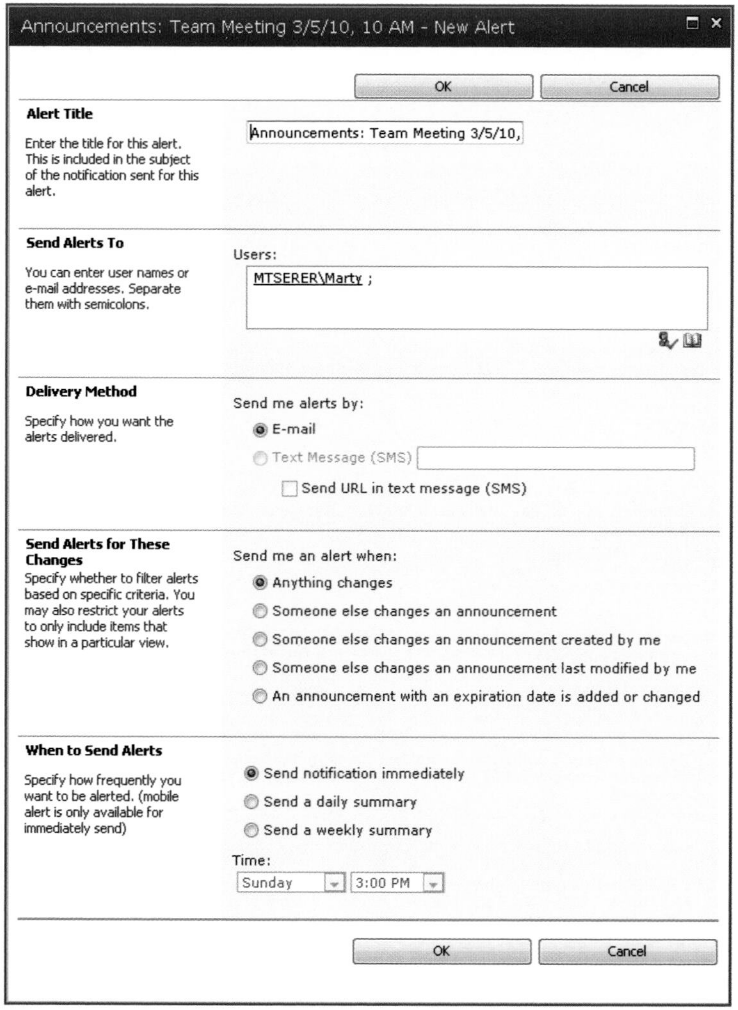

Announcements: Team Meeting 3/5/10, 10 AM - New Alert □ ×

[OK] [Cancel]

Alert Title

Enter the title for this alert. This is included in the subject of the notification sent for this alert.

Announcements: Team Meeting 3/5/10,

Send Alerts To

You can enter user names or e-mail addresses. Separate them with semicolons.

Users:

MTSERER\Marty ;

Delivery Method

Specify how you want the alerts delivered.

Send me alerts by:

◉ E-mail

○ Text Message (SMS) [ ]

☐ Send URL in text message (SMS)

Send Alerts for These Changes

Specify whether to filter alerts based on specific criteria. You may also restrict your alerts to only include items that show in a particular view.

Send me an alert when:

◉ Anything changes

○ Someone else changes an announcement

○ Someone else changes an announcement created by me

○ Someone else changes an announcement last modified by me

○ An announcement with an expiration date is added or changed

When to Send Alerts

Specify how frequently you want to be alerted. (mobile alert is only available for immediately send)

◉ Send notification immediately

○ Send a daily summary

○ Send a weekly summary

Time:
Sunday ▾ 3:00 PM ▾

[OK] [Cancel]

*Figure 6-2: **Alerts for changes to items and documents are more specific and, therefore, more valuable.***

To set an alert for an item or document:

1. Navigate to the list or library with the desired item or document, and select the item or document so its check box is checked.

2. Click the **Items** or **Documents** tab in the ribbon, click **Alert Me** 🔔 Alert Me ▾ in the Share & Track group, and then click **Set Alert On This Item** or **Set Alert On This Document**. The New Alert page will open, as you can see in Figure 6-2.

3. Enter an alert title, the user names and/or e-mail addresses of the people to get the alert, and choose whether to send the alert via e-mail or text message.

4. Choose the circumstances of the changes for which you want an alert, and then select when you want the alert sent.

5. When you have finished configuring the alert, click **OK**.

SET UP ALERTS FOR SEARCHES

You can be alerted when the results of searching on a given criteria change as a result of:

● New items appearing in the search result

● Existing items changing

● Any change in the search result

To set an alert for a search:

1. From the site in which you want the search, click in the **Search This Site** text box on the right of the tab bar. Type your search criteria, and click **Search** (the magnifying glass icon).

2. In the Search Results page that opens (see Figure 6-3), refine the search by clicking the options that are available on the left.

3. When the search is the way you want it, click **Alert Me** in the upper-right corner of the Search Results page. The New Alert page will open, as you can see in Figure 6-4.

4. Enter an alert title, the user names and/or e-mail addresses of the people to get the alert, and choose whether to send the alert via e-mail or text message.

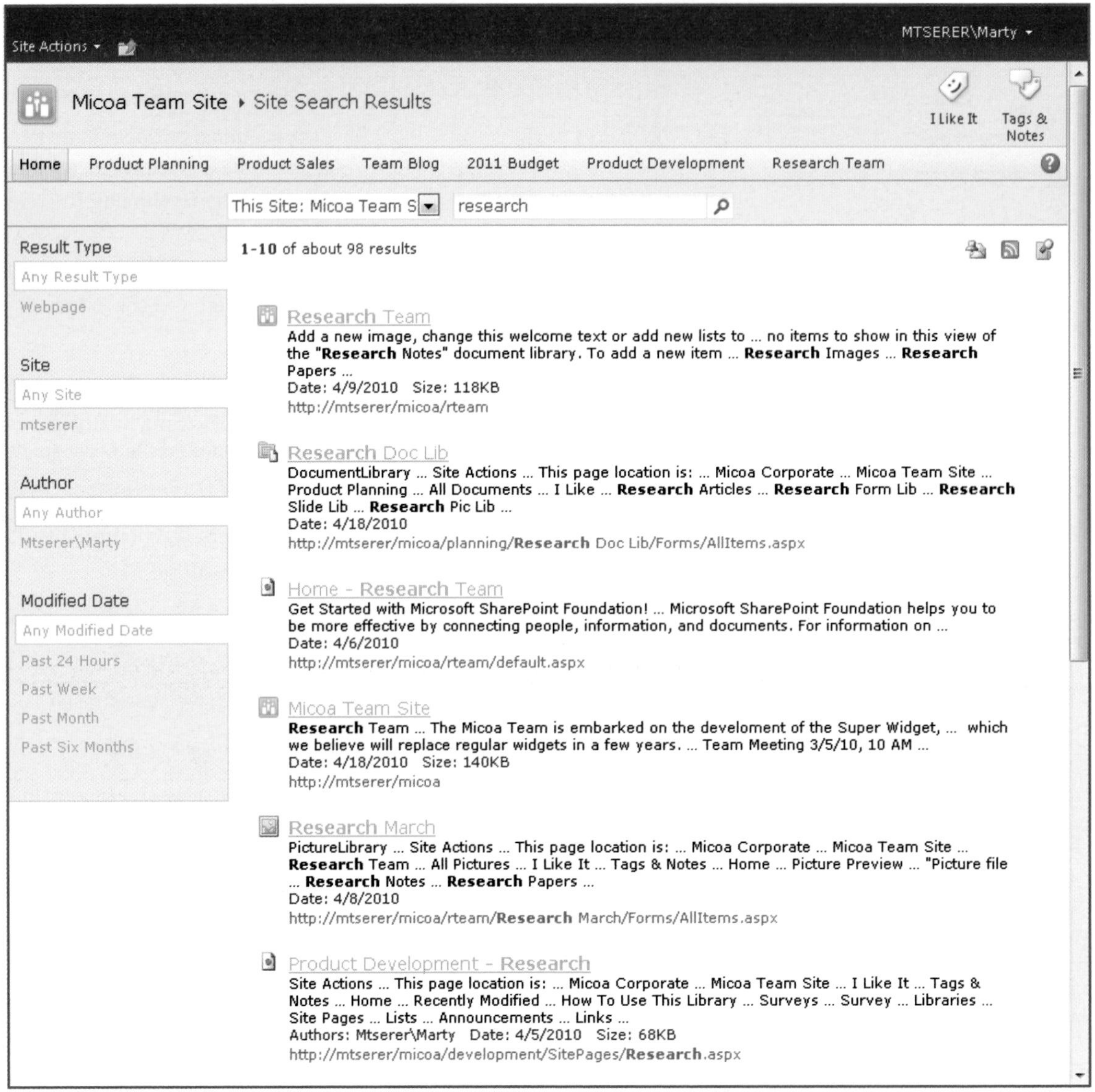

Site Actions ▾

MTSERER\Marty ▾

Micoa Team Site ▸ Site Search Results

I Like It   Tags & Notes

| Home | Product Planning | Product Sales | Team Blog | 2011 Budget | Product Development | Research Team |

This Site: Micoa Team S ▾   research

1-10 of about 98 results

Result Type

Any Result Type

Webpage

Site

Any Site

mtserer

Author

Any Author

Mtserer\Marty

Modified Date

Any Modified Date

Past 24 Hours

Past Week

Past Month

Past Six Months

Research Team
Add a new image, change this welcome text or add new lists to ... no items to show in this view of the "**Research** Notes" document library. To add a new item ... **Research** Images ... **Research** Papers ...
Date: 4/9/2010   Size: 118KB
http://mtserer/micoa/rteam

Research Doc Lib
DocumentLibrary ... Site Actions ... This page location is: ... Micoa Corporate ... Micoa Team Site ... Product Planning ... All Documents ... I Like ... **Research** Articles ... **Research** Form Lib ... **Research** Slide Lib ... **Research** Pic Lib ...
Date: 4/18/2010
http://mtserer/micoa/planning/**Research** Doc Lib/Forms/AllItems.aspx

Home - Research Team
Get Started with Microsoft SharePoint Foundation! ... Microsoft SharePoint Foundation helps you to be more effective by connecting people, information, and documents. For information on ...
Date: 4/6/2010
http://mtserer/micoa/rteam/default.aspx

Micoa Team Site
Research Team ... The Micoa Team is embarked on the develoment of the Super Widget, ... which we believe will replace regular widgets in a few years. ... Team Meeting 3/5/10, 10 AM ...
Date: 4/18/2010   Size: 140KB
http://mtserer/micoa

Research March
PictureLibrary ... Site Actions ... This page location is: ... Micoa Corporate ... Micoa Team Site ... **Research** Team ... All Pictures ... I Like It ... Tags & Notes ... Home ... Picture Preview ... "Picture file ... **Research** Notes ... **Research** Papers ...
Date: 4/8/2010
http://mtserer/micoa/rteam/**Research** March/Forms/AllItems.aspx

Product Development - Research
Site Actions ... This page location is: ... Micoa Corporate ... Micoa Team Site ... I Like It ... Tags & Notes ... Home ... Recently Modified ... How To Use This Library ... Surveys ... Survey ... Libraries ... Site Pages ... Lists ... Announcements ... Links ...
Authors: Mtserer\Marty   Date: 4/5/2010   Size: 68KB
http://mtserer/micoa/development/SitePages/**Research**.aspx

*Figure 6-3: **Alerts can be used to see what has changed instead of repeating a search.***

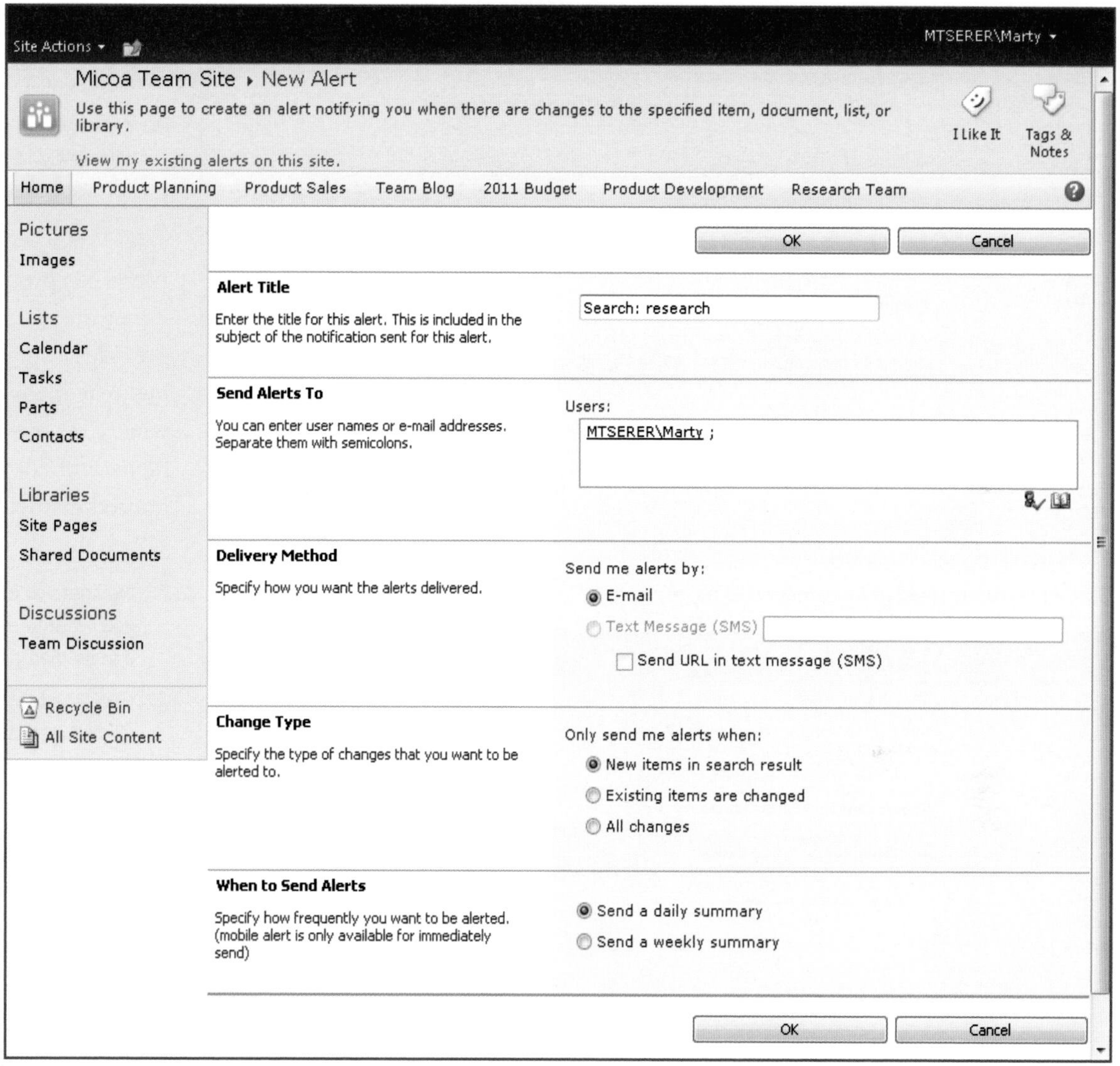

Site Actions ▾

MTSERER\Marty ▾

Micoa Team Site ▸ New Alert

Use this page to create an alert notifying you when there are changes to the specified item, document, list, or library.

I Like It

Tags & Notes

View my existing alerts on this site.

| Home | Product Planning | Product Sales | Team Blog | 2011 Budget | Product Development | Research Team |

Pictures

Images

Lists

Calendar

Tasks

Parts

Contacts

Libraries

Site Pages

Shared Documents

Discussions

Team Discussion

Recycle Bin

All Site Content

[OK]   [Cancel]

Alert Title

Enter the title for this alert. This is included in the subject of the notification sent for this alert.

Search: research

Send Alerts To

You can enter user names or e-mail addresses. Separate them with semicolons.

Users:

MTSERER\Marty ;

Delivery Method

Specify how you want the alerts delivered.

Send me alerts by:

◉ E-mail

◯ Text Message (SMS)

☐ Send URL in text message (SMS)

Change Type

Specify the type of changes that you want to be alerted to.

Only send me alerts when:

◉ New items in search result

◯ Existing items are changed

◯ All changes

When to Send Alerts

Specify how frequently you want to be alerted. (mobile alert is only available for immediately send)

◉ Send a daily summary

◯ Send a weekly summary

[OK]   [Cancel]

Figure 6-4: *Search alerts can be useful when you are not sure where an item will appear.*

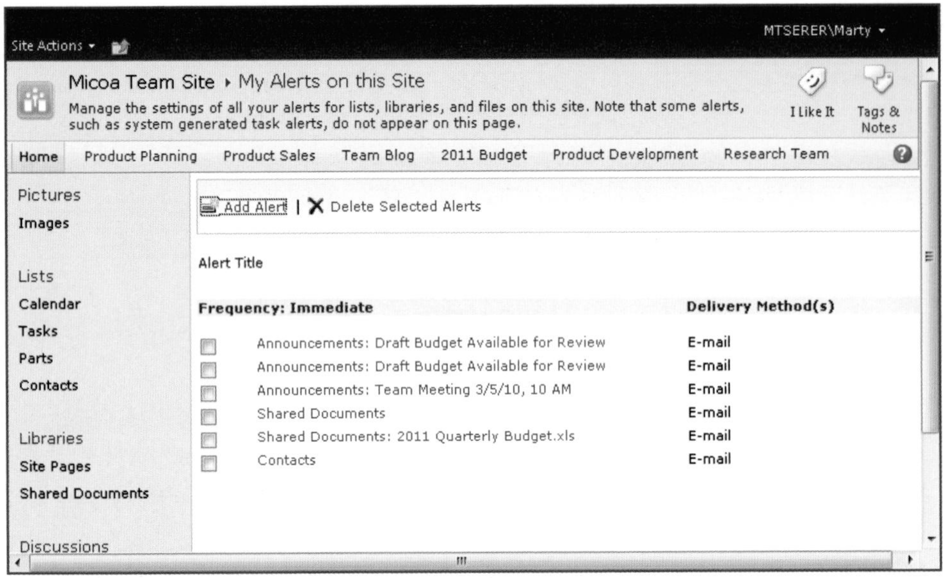

Figure 6-5: *Alerts need to be managed to be effective.*

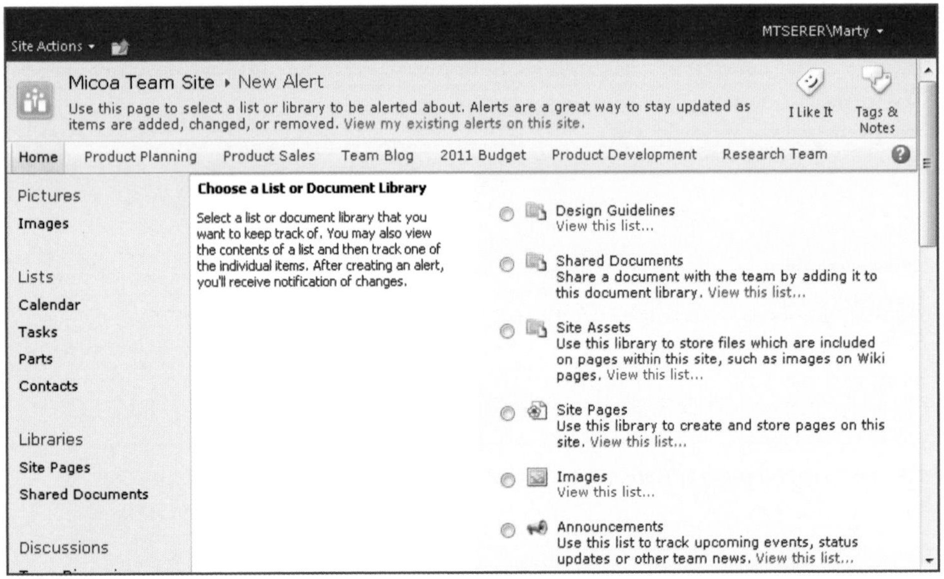

Figure 6-6: *Alerts can be added for several lists, libraries, items, and documents from Manage My Alerts.*

5. Choose the type of the changes for which you want an alert, and then select when you want the alert sent.

6. When you have finished configuring the alert, click **OK**.

Manage Alerts

Alerts can produce a lot of unwanted e-mail if they are not managed properly. SharePoint provides a summary of your alerts in a site (see Figure 6-5), giving you a single place to manage what you have placed in various lists, libraries, items, and documents. You have probably noticed that when you click **Alert Me** in the ribbon that there is a Manage My Alerts option.

1. Navigate to a list or library in the site whose alerts you want to manage. Click the list or library to open it in its own page.

2. Click the **List** or **Library** tab to open its ribbon. Click **Alert Me** and then click **Manage My Alerts**. A page similar to Figure 6-5 will open.

3. To delete an existing alert, click its check box to select the alert, and then click **Delete Selected Alerts**. Click **OK** to confirm the deletion.

4. To add a new alert, click **Add Alert**. A list of the lists and libraries in the site will open, as shown in Figure 6-6.

   a. To add an alert for changes to a list or library, click its option button, and click **Next**. In the New Alert page that opens, follow the steps in "Set Up Alerts for Lists and Libraries" earlier in this chapter.

DELETING ALERTS FOR OTHERS

Since you can add alerts for others by adding their e-mail address in the New Alert page, you can also delete alerts for others if you have the appropriate administrative privileges.

1. Navigate to the site for which you want to manage alerts.

2. Click **Site Actions**, click **Site Settings**, and under Site Administration, click **User Alerts**.

3. Click the **Display Alerts For** down arrow, select the user for whom you want to manage alerts, and click **Update**.

4. Click the check box for the alert or alerts you want to delete, and click **Delete Selected Alerts**.

5. Click **OK** to confirm the deletion.

NOTE

An alternative to using alerts is to use an RSS (Really Simple Syndication) feed, which is a subscription to receive text and graphic information over the Internet or an intranet. RSS feeds are discussed further in Chapter 7. The difference between alerts and RSS feeds is that RSS feeds, which are automatically created for each SharePoint list or library in the site, produce a lot of information and are displayed in other programs like Internet Explorer, Outlook, or an RSS viewing program, whereas alerts are tailored to your needs and come to you via e-mail or text messages. Alerts are often preferable to RSS feeds because if you have time to browse RSS feeds, you would probably have time to go to the site to view what's new.

b. **To add an alert for a change to a particular item or document**, click **View This List** under the list or library the item or document is in. Click the check box for the item or document, click **Alert Me**, and click **Set Alert On This Document**. In the New Alert page that opens, follow the steps in "Set Up Alerts for Items and Documents" earlier in this chapter.

5. **To edit an existing alert**, click the alert title on the Manage My Alerts page. In the Edit Alert page that opens, follow the steps for the particular type of alert as described earlier in this chapter.

Create and Manage Blogs

A *blog* (short for web log) is a series of articles, a journal, or chronicle, generally by a single person, but sometimes by a team, on a particular subject. In a business environment, it is meant to educate and inform an audience. The use of a blog within a team or organization can be a valuable tool to spread knowledge from a person (or persons) more knowledgeable on a subject to those who are less so.

Each major entry or article in the blog is called a *post*, and is generally shown with the most recent first. In addition to posts, which are added by the blog creator(s) (called a *blogger*), readers of the blog can add comments, which creates a written conversation.

Create and Customize a Blog Site

Blogs are created and used through a blog site template, as described in Chapter 3. The resulting site, shown in Figure 6-7, is tailored to blogging with several unique features.

- A primary column for the blog posts and comments
- A secondary column for general information and links
- A special Quick Launch providing categorization and monthly archiving of blog posts
- A set of blog tools to create and manage both posts and comments

NOTE

There can be some confusion between blogs and wikis. Blogs are an ongoing series of articles, most often by a single person on a single subject. Wikis are articles on a number of subjects by a number of people, often with a number of people contributing to a single article. Blogs are often created and managed by a single person and are thought of as "her or his blog." Wikis are the result of many people collaborating to produce a comprehensive work. For example, if you wanted to get feedback about a job description, a wiki would be suitable if you wanted to gather edits and feedback from a variety of people. Your thoughts about what it is like to perform a specific job, however, would be best suited to a blog.

*Figure 6-7: **SharePoint provides a complete blog template with all the necessary tools.***

The blog site template produces a complete blogging environment that can be used as-is, or it can be significantly modified to fit the blogger's wishes, as you can see in Figure 6-8.

CREATE A BLOG SITE

A blog site can be created like other sites—using its template.

1. Navigate to the site that will be the parent site for the blog site.

2. Click **Site Actions**, click **New Site**, click the **Blog** template, enter a title and a URL, and click **Create**.

The blog site will open, as shown in Figure 6-7.

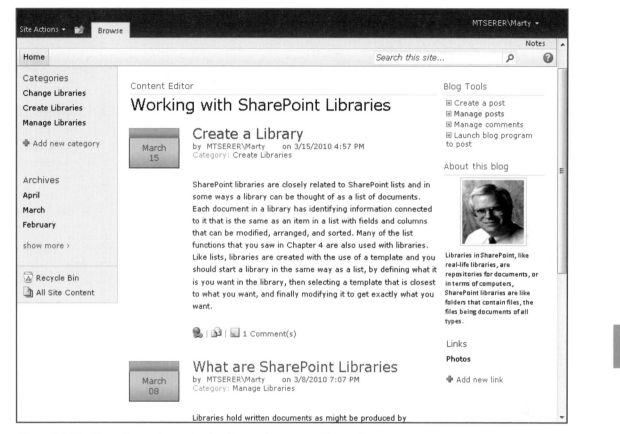

Figure 6-8: **The blog site can be customized to meet your specific needs.**

CUSTOMIZE A BLOG SITE

Although the blog site has many special features, it is highly customizable. You can:

- Add your own blog title

- Add your own picture

- Add your own welcome message

- Add your own category titles

- Add a theme to change the colors used

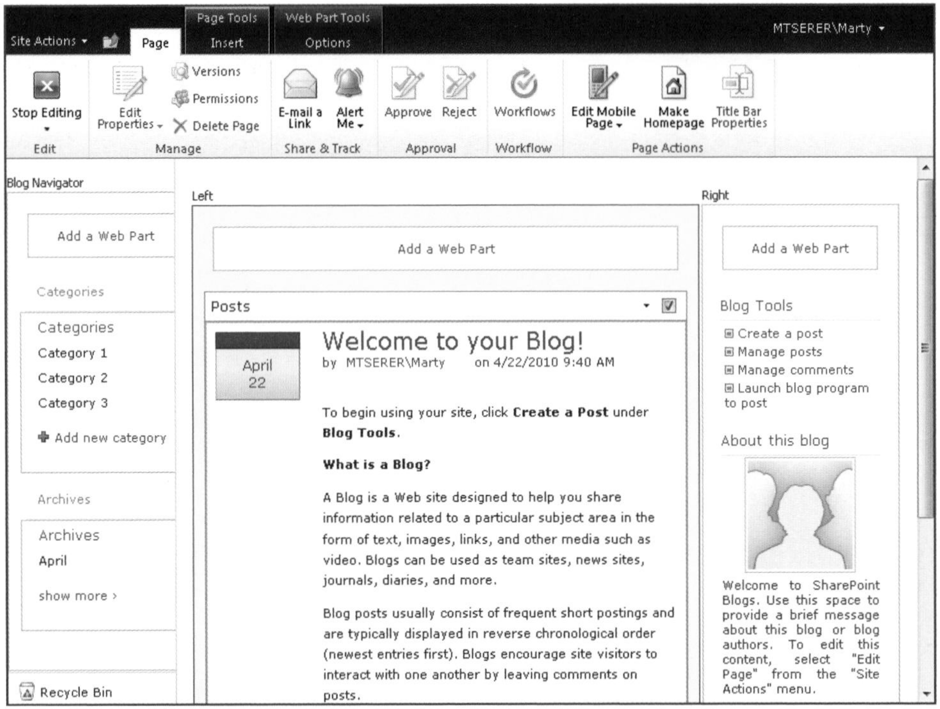

Figure 6-9: *The blog site page can be edited like any other SharePoint page.*

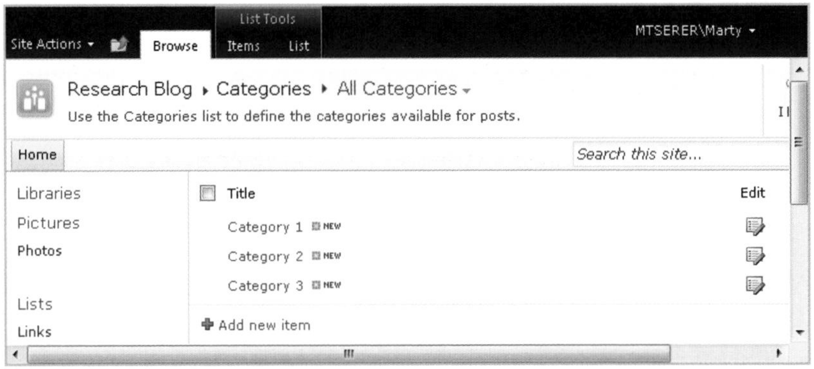

And all of that is in addition to adding your own articles. To customize the blog site:

1. With the blog site open on your screen, click **Site Actions**, and click **Edit Page**. The blog page will open in edit mode, as you can see in Figure 6-9.

2. **To add a title**, click **Add A Web Part** in the primary (left) column. Click the **Page Tools | Insert** tab, and click **Text**. Click **Click Here To Add New Text** and type the title. While the insertion point is still at the end of the title, press SHIFT+HOME to select the title, and use the formatting options in the Format Text tab to format the title.

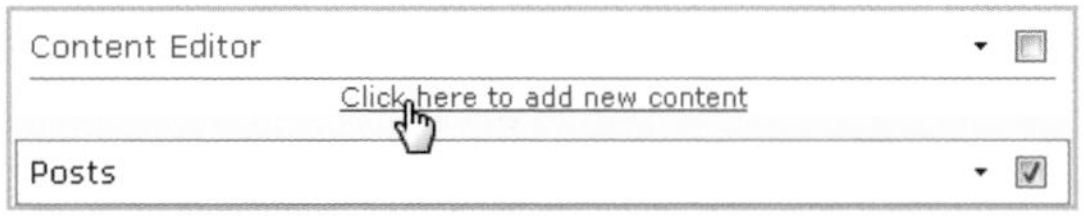

3. **To add your own picture**, while still in edit mode, click the picture placeholder in the right column, click **Picture Tools | Design** tab, click the **Change Picture** down arrow, and click **From Computer**. Browse to and double-click the picture you want to use, and click **OK**. In the Photos dialog box that appears, click **Save**.

4. **To change the welcome message** below the picture, drag across the existing text and type the new message you want to use. If you want to change the formatting of the new text, select it and use the Format Text tab tools as needed.

5. When you have completed customizing the two right columns, click the **Page** tab, and click **Stop Editing** to save your changes.

6. **To change the category titles**, click the **Categories** heading to open the categories in their own page. Opposite the category whose title you want to change, click the **Edit** icon, select the current title, type the replacement, and click **Save**.

CAUTION

When you have finished editing a blog page (or any page), it is important that you return to the Page tab and click **Stop Editing** *before* going to a different area on the same page (like the Quick Launch) or to a different page or site. This saves your changes; otherwise, they will be lost.

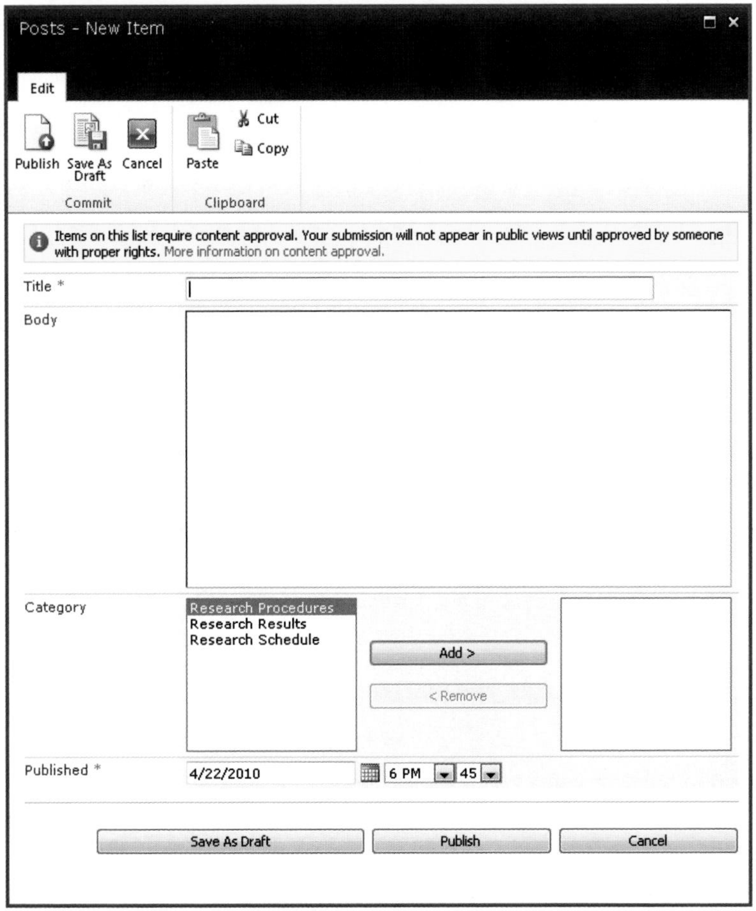

Posts - New Item

Edit

Publish Save As Cancel Paste
          Draft

Cut
Copy

Commit   Clipboard

ⓘ Items on this list require content approval. Your submission will not appear in public views until approved by someone with proper rights. More information on content approval.

Title *

Body

Category

Research Procedures
Research Results
Research Schedule

Add >

< Remove

Published * 4/22/2010   6 PM 45

Save As Draft   Publish   Cancel

Figure 6-10: **You can directly enter a blog post (but you don't have any formatting tools), or you can use Word to create a post.**

Use and Manage a Blog

To be truly useful, a blog must be kept up to date, well managed, and archived. SharePoint automatically handles the archiving, but it is up to you to handle the updating and managing, although SharePoint gives you good tools to do that.

POST ARTICLES TO A BLOG

To post articles to a blog:

1. With the blog site's Home page open on your screen, click **Create A Post** in the Blog Tools area on the right. The Posts – New Item dialog box appears, as shown in Figure 6-10.

2. Enter the title of the article, enter the body (you can also cut and paste it and use Word; see the "Using Word to Post an Article" QuickSteps).

3. Click the category in which you want the article, and click **ADD**.

4. Change the date and time as needed, and click **Publish**.

ADD COMMENTS TO A POST

Often, the readers of a blog have comments they would like to add to a post, and even the blog creator may want to comment either on his or her own post, or on another's comment. To add a comment to a post:

1. On the blog page with the post to be commented on, click **Comment(s)** beneath the post. Existing comments will be displayed, and beneath them an area for adding comments will appear, as you see in Figure 6-11.

2. Click in the **Title** text box, and type a title for the comment. Then click in the body, and type the comment.

3. After completing the comment, click **Submit Comment**.

MANAGE POSTS AND COMMENTS

Blog posts and comments are special lists that have unique views and their own set of controls within Blog Tools. The managing of

USING WORD TO POST AN ARTICLE

You can use Microsoft Word 2010 to directly compose and publish articles to a SharePoint site. This gives you the benefit of the full Word editor with all its capabilities, as well as the ability to load and edit existing content and then publish it to your blog.

To use Word to post an article:

1. From the blog site's Home page, click **Launch Blog Program To Post** in the Blog Tools area on the right. Your default word-processing program will open. Most likely, this is Microsoft Word, either the stand-alone version on your computer (see Figure 6-12) or the Web Apps browser version.

2. Click **Enter Post Title Here**, and type the title of your current blog post.

3. Click at the left side of the bottom line, and type the post using the formatting tools in Word.

4. In the Blog Post tab, click **Insert Category** in the Blog group, click the down arrow opposite category, and choose the one you want.

5. When the post is the way you want it, click **Publish**. If you are done with Word, click **Close**. Back in your blog, click **Refresh** (the pair of arrows) at the right end of the address bar to see your latest post.

NOTE

The "Account → Research Blog" appears in Figure 6-12 because the site collection of which the Research Blog is a member has multiple blogs, which can be selected by clicking **Research Blog** and getting a drop-down list of the blogs.

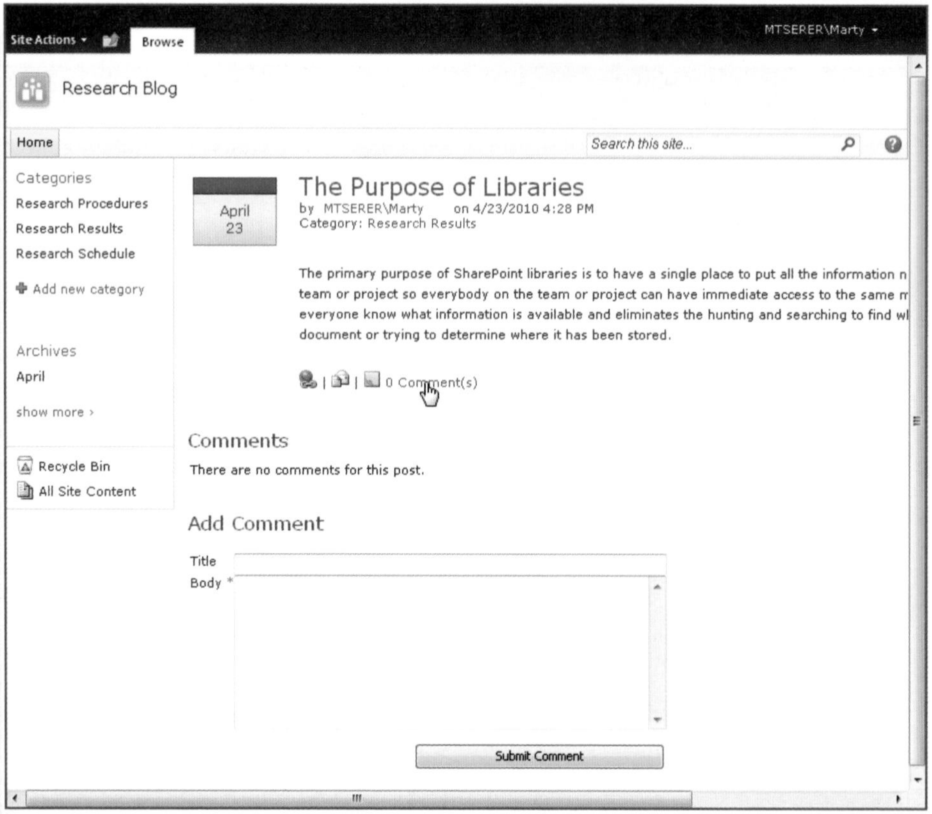

Figure 6-11: *Comments can be added easily to posts within a blog.*

posts and comments are the same, and we'll combine our discussion by looking at the managing of posts.

1. From the blog site's Home page, click **Manage Posts** in the Blog Tools on the right. The list of posts will appear with the List Tools tabs in the ribbon.

2. Click the check box on the left of a post you want to work with. The List Tools | Items tab will open, as you see in Figure 6-13. From here you can view, edit, delete, and set permissions and alerts for the post, as well as approve or reject a post with the appropriate permission, all of which are similar to what was discussed in Chapter 4 for other types of list items.

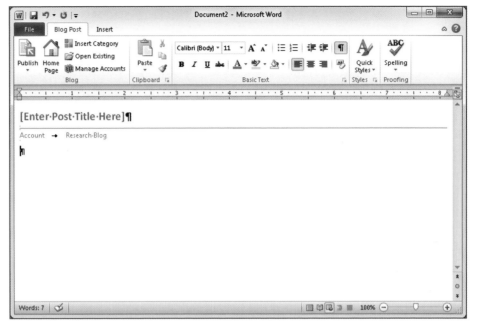

*Figure 6-12: **Using Word for a blog post gives you a full set of formatting tools and spelling checker.***

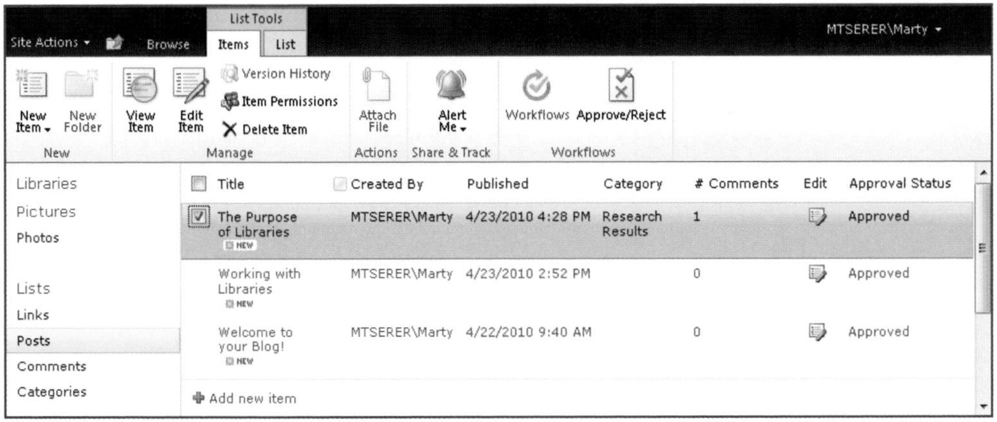

*Figure 6-13: **Managing blog posts is similar to managing a SharePoint list.***

3. Click either **Edit Item** in the ribbon or the **Edit** icon in the item to open the Posts dialog box, which was shown earlier in Figure 6-10. This allows you to edit the title and body of the post, change or add categories, and change the date and time.

4. When you have made the desired changes to the post, click **Publish**.

5. When you have completed the blog management tasks you wanted to do, click **Browse** and then click **Home** to return to the blog Home page.

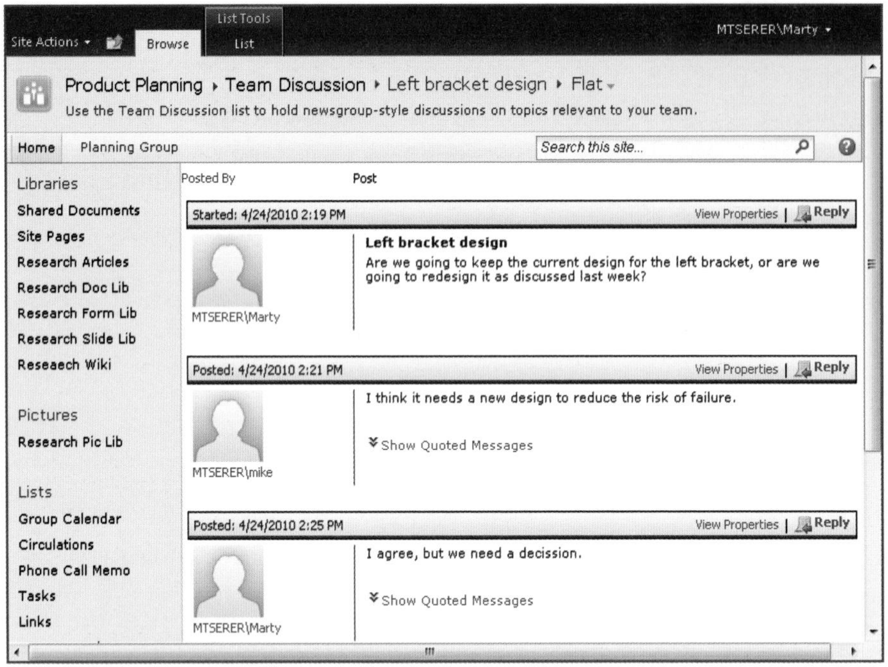

Figure 6-14: *Discussions are similar to online forums and are a useful form of online communication.*

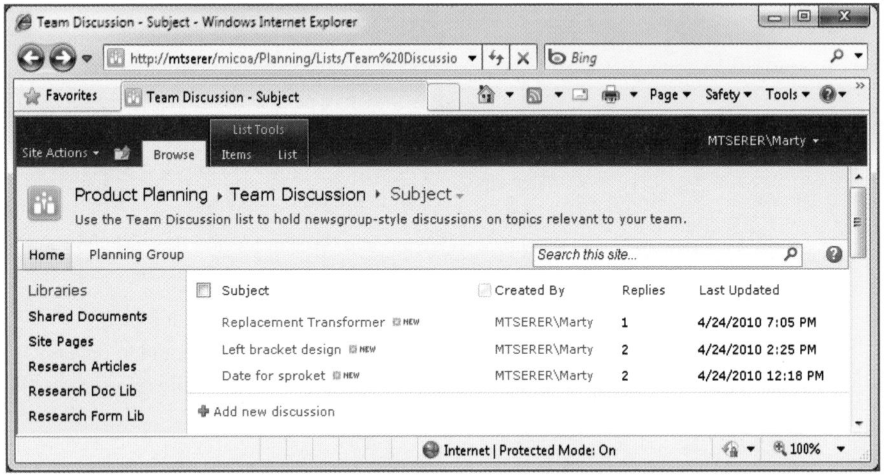

Add and Handle Discussions

Discussions, also called "discussion boards," are lists of threaded messages on specific topics. Someone starts a discussion on a particular topic by adding a message on that topic and thereby beginning a thread. Someone else adds to that discussion and thread by entering a message in reply on the same topic. Other people can reply to either the first message or the first reply to it, or to any subsequent reply, and extend the discussion and thread in so doing, as shown in Figure 6-14.

Discussion boards are in essence a list (see Figure 6-15), although they are treated as a separate element, with the individual discussions being the items in the list. Several site templates, most importantly the team site, include a discussion board, and you can add a new discussion board to a site, as you would add a list (see Chapter 4).

Add Discussions

In a discussion, you either start a new discussion or reply to an existing one, and the reply can be either to the original message or to one of the replies.

Figure 6-15: *In the default view of a discussion board, it is easy to see it is a list.*

NOTE

SharePoint blogs are created as separate subsites, whereas discussions are SharePoint lists within an existing site or subsite. Therefore, discussions are often used to insert threaded conversations into existing pages to augment existing content, whereas blogs are usually linked to as separate entities.

NOTE

Discussions can be configured to use e-mail if this feature has been set up (a SharePoint administrator's task). A site's discussion board will have its own e-mail address and each new e-mail message will become a new discussion, while replies to that e-mail message will be replies to the discussion.

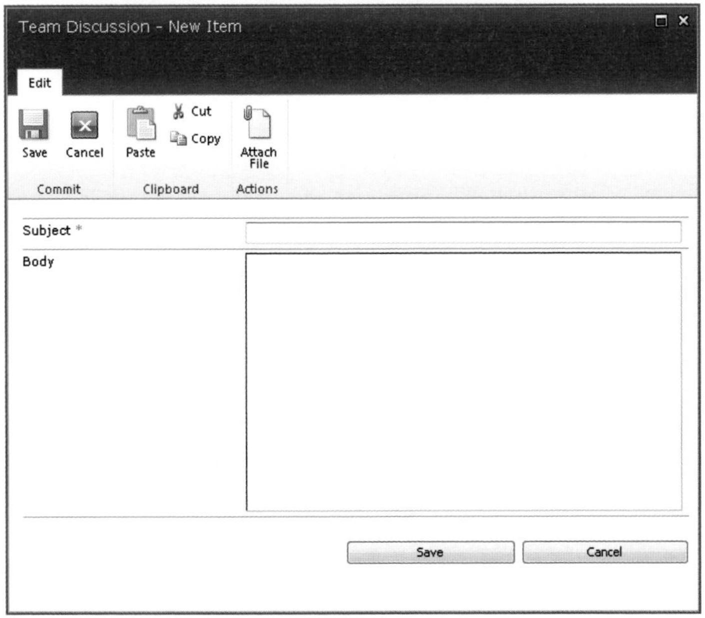

Figure 6-16: ***A SharePoint discussion is a series of messages related to a single subject.***

START A NEW DISCUSSION

To start a new discussion in an existing discussion board:

1. Navigate to the discussion board to which you want to add a new discussion.
2. Click **Add New Discussion** at the bottom of the discussion list. The Team Discussion dialog box will appear, as shown in Figure 6-16.
3. Enter the discussion subject, the topic you'll be discussing, and then enter the body of your message.
4. When you are satisfied with your message, click **Save**. You are returned to the discussion list where you can see your new discussion.

VIEW AND REPLY TO A DISCUSSION

To view and reply to a discussion:

1. Navigate to the discussion board with the discussion you want to view and potentially reply to.
2. Click the subject of the discussion you want to view to open the Flat view of it, as you saw earlier in Figure 6-14.
3. **To reply** to either the original message or another reply message, click **Reply** on the right of the message heading. The discussion reply dialog box will appear.
4. Type your reply and, when done, click **Save**.

Handle Discussions

The handling of discussions is not a significant task. There are several different views that you will usually want to use, and there are the standard property setting and editing tasks that are similar to working with all SharePoint lists.

WORK WITH DISCUSSION VIEWS

There are three built-in views of discussions:

- **Subject view** of a discussion board, which is shown in Figure 6-15, is the default view that you get when you click a discussion board in the Quick Launch or elsewhere.

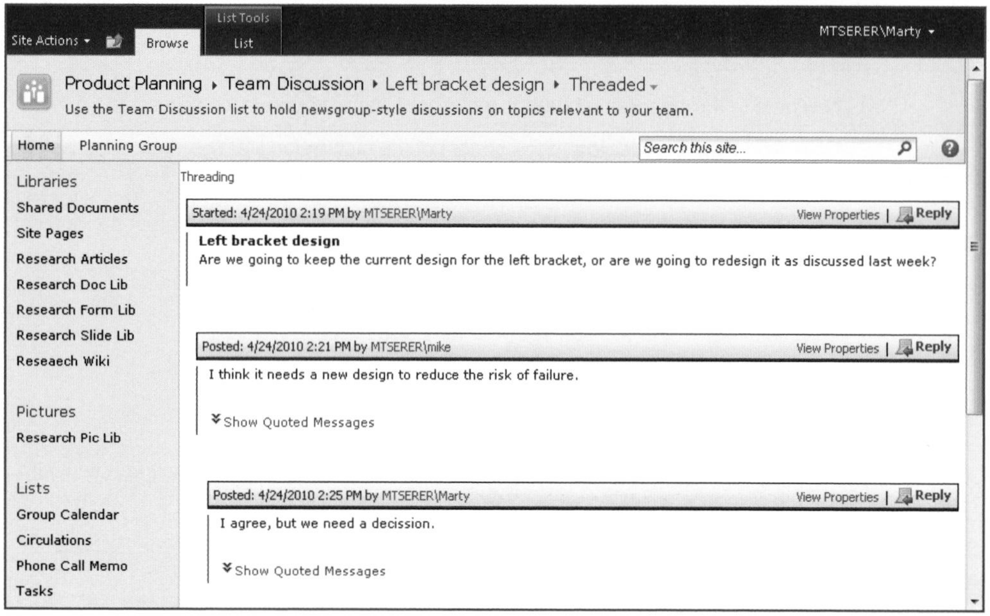

Figure 6-17: *The Threaded view is closer to what most forums look like.*

- **Flat view** of a discussion thread, which is shown in Figure 6-14, is the default view that you get when you click the subject of a discussion in Subject view.

- **Threaded view** of a discussion thread, shown in Figure 6-17, is an alternative view that you can select by opening the List tab's **Change View** drop-down list and clicking **Threaded**.

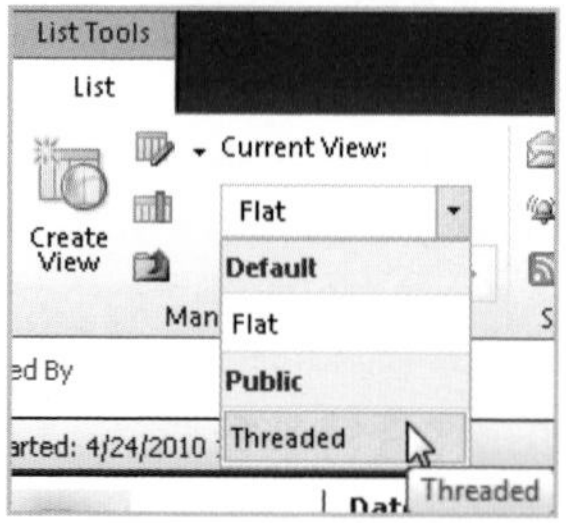

You can, of course, create your own view, as you can for any list, using the steps described in Chapter 4.

SET DISCUSSION PROPERTIES

Discussion properties are not much different from those you can set for lists and their items.

1. **To set properties for a discussion board**, navigate to it. What you see should be in Subject view.

2. Click the **List Tools | List** tab, and click **List Settings**. The Discussion Board Settings page will open, as you see in Figure 6-18. The options that you see here are the same as you saw for list properties in Chapter 4, although there are fewer options here. Use the discussion in Chapter 4 to guide you in the settings here.

3. When you have completed making any changes to the discussion properties, click your discussion in the breadcrumb navigation to return to it.

Site Actions ▾

MTSERER\Marty ▾

Product Planning ▸ Team Discussion ▸ Discussion Board Settings

Home   Planning Group

Libraries
Shared Documents
Site Pages
Research Articles
Research Doc Lib
Research Form Lib
Research Slide Lib
Reseaech Wiki

Pictures
Research Pic Lib

Lists
Group Calendar
Circulations
Phone Call Memo
Tasks
Links
Support Tasks

Discussions
Team Discussion

Surveys
Survey

🔄 Recycle Bin
📄 All Site Content

List Information

Name:	Team Discussion
Web Address:	http://mtserer/micoa/Planning/Lists/Team Discussion/AllItems.aspx
Description:	Use the Team Discussion list to hold newsgroup-style discussions on topics relevant to your team.

General Settings	Permissions and Management	Communications
Title, description and navigation	Delete this discussion board	RSS settings
Versioning settings	Save discussion board as template	
Advanced settings	Permissions for this discussion board	
Validation settings	Workflow Settings	

Content Types

This list is configured to allow multiple content types. Use content types to specify the information you want to display about an item, in addition to its policies, workflows, or other behavior. The following content types are currently available in this list:

Content Type	Visible on New Button	Default Content Type
Discussion	✔	✔
Message	✔	

Add from existing site content types
Change new button order and default content type

Columns

A column stores information about each item in the list. Because this list allows multiple content types, some column settings, such as whether information is required or optional for a column, are now specified by the content type of the item. The following columns are currently available in this list:

Column (click to edit)	Type	Used in
Body	Multiple lines of text	Discussion, Message
Subject	Single line of text	Discussion, Message
Created By	Person or Group	
Modified By	Person or Group	

Figure 6-18: **The discussion board settings are the same as those for a list.**

Team Discussion - Replacement Transformer

View

Edit Item

Version History

Manage Permissions

Delete Item

Manage

Open

Open

Alert Me

Actions

Subject	Replacement Transformer
Body	When is the replacement transformer supposed to arrive?

Content Type: Discussion
Created at 4/24/2010 4:48 PM by MTSERER\Marty
Last modified at 4/24/2010 4:48 PM by MTSERER\Marty

Close

4. **To set the properties of a particular discussion**, from the discussion board's Subject view, click the check box on the left of the discussion. The List Tools | Items tab will open. Here you can set permissions, alerts, workflows, and approvals. All of these are discussed elsewhere in either Chapter 4 or in this chapter.

5. **To set the properties for a particular message** within a discussion, click the discussion subject to open it in Flat view.

6. For the message whose properties you want to set, click **View Properties** on the right of the message heading bar. The discussion message will open in its own dialog box. Here you can set permissions and alerts.

7. When you are done setting the needed message permissions, click **Close**.

Create and Work with Surveys

SharePoint surveys allow you to create a questionnaire, have others to fill it out, and then summarize and analyze the information collected. SharePoint gives you a lot of flexibility in doing this. Surveys also allow you to have branching questions, which allows you to design the list so that the next question presented depends on the answer given to a previous question. For example, if you want to find out what menu choices should change in the company cafeteria, if the first question asks whether the respondent is a vegetarian, then all of the subsequent questions about meat choices could be skipped if they responded that they are vegetarian. A SharePoint survey would make it easy to design such a questionnaire.

A SharePoint survey is another form of a list, defined by a list template, in which the questions on the questionnaire are the columns for the list and each response that is received is an item in the list.

Create a Survey

In creating a survey questionnaire, you are defining a list by laying it out and specifying what each column will contain. The columns are questions, and the responses are the answers to the questions. Creating a questionnaire, then, is stating the questions and defining the types of answers that are allowed. To create a survey:

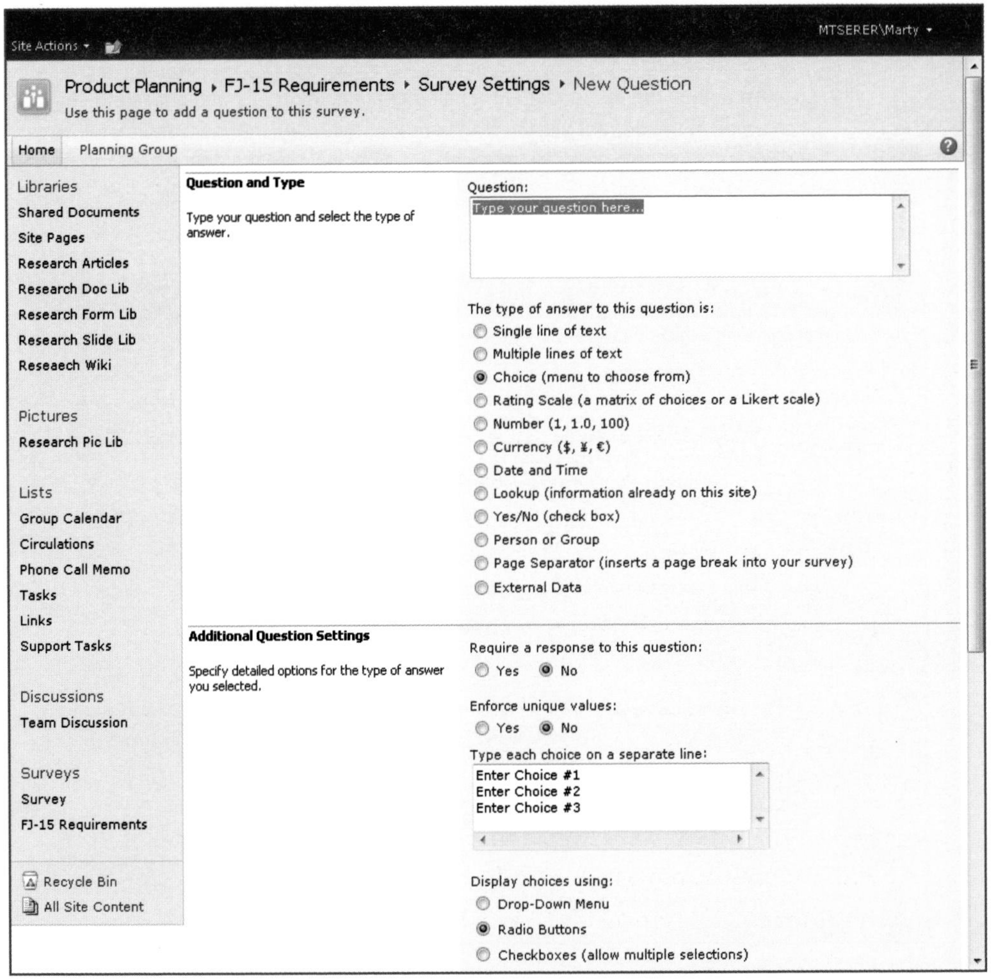

1. Navigate to the site in which you want the survey. Click **Site Actions**, click **More Options**, click **List** in the left column, scroll through the center column, and click **Survey**.

2. Click in the **Name** text box, and enter a survey name. If you wish to enter a description and specify the navigation, click **More Options**, make the desired entries, and, in any case, click **Create**. The New Questions page will open where you can create the first questions, as you can see in Figure 6-19.

3. Begin by typing the question you want to ask. Then review the types of answers to pick the one you want to use. There is a wide range of answer types. The best way to understand them is to select each of the types at least once and look at the Additional Question Settings area, which provides an explanation and related settings for the answer type chosen. Here are some considerations on the various answer types:

   - **Single line of text** allows for any typed answer so long as it fits within a stated number of characters.

   - **Multiple lines of text** provides for a larger typed answer that can optionally be formatted, but must fit within a stated number of lines.

   - **Choice** allows the respondent to choose from among several choices that can be presented in several forms.

*Figure 6-19: **SharePoint surveys can contain many different types of questions and possible answers.***

USING BRANCHING LOGIC

Branching logic is the ability to conditionally ask questions based upon the answers to other questions. For example, consider the following simple questionnaire:

- Can you come to a meeting on May 14th at 2 P.M.?
- If so, can you report on your team's progress?
- If not, what date and time is best for you?

The second and third questions depend on the answer to the first. SharePoint's survey branching logic gives you this ability. To do this, you need to create all the questions first, and then come back and specify the branching. Here is how that is done with the simple questionnaire:

1. Create a survey based on the steps in "Create a Survey" section in this chapter.

2. Enter the following three questions:

   a. Enter <u>Can you come to a meeting on May 14th at 2 pm?</u> Click **Yes/No**, leave the default value of **Yes**, and click **Next Question**.

   b. Enter <u>Can you report on your team's progress?</u> Click **Yes/No**, leave the default value of **Yes**, and click **Next Question**.

   c. Enter <u>What date and time is best for you?</u> Click **Date And Time**, click Yes to require a response, leave the default No to not enforce a unique value, click **Date & Time** to request both, enter as the default values <u>4/14/2011</u> and <u>2 pm</u>, and click **Finish**.

3. When you have completed all the questions and clicked **Finish**, you are taken to the Survey Settings page, shown in Figure 6-20, because you asked a Yes/No or multiple choice question that could lead to branching.

Continued . . .

- **Rating Scale** asks the respondent to rate a series of additional questions or statements on a numeric scale with a stated scale meaning.

- **Number** provides for a numeric answer to the question that can be limited to a particular range.

- **Currency** provides for a numeric answer to the question in a particular currency that can be limited to a stated range.

- **Date And Time** allows a date, a time, or a date and time answer to a question with an optional default value.

- **Lookup** directs the respondent to an element (list, library, or calendar) and set of columns in the current site where the respondent can choose a value as their answer.

- **Yes/No** provides for a binary answer with a default value. It appears as a check box on the questionnaire.

Figure 6-20: **To set up branching, you need to first add all questions and complete the questionnaire; then from Survey Settings, select the questions that need to have branching added.**

UICKSTEPS

USING BRANCHING LOGIC (Continued)

4. Under Questions, click the question for which you want to add branching logic. The Edit Question page will open for that question and give you two branching logic choices for Yes and for No.

5. Click the **Yes** down arrow, and click **Can You Report On Your Team's Progress?** to jump to that question on a Yes answer.

Possible Choices	Jump To
Yes	No Branching
No	No Branching
	Can you report on your team's progress?
	What date and time is best for you?
	Content Type

6. Click the **No** down arrow, and click **What Date And Time Is Best For You?** to jump to that question on a No answer.

7. Click **OK** to return to the Survey Settings page. Make any other change on this page, considering any needed changes to permissions so the people you want can respond to this survey.

8. When you are ready, click **Home** to leave the survey.

TIP

If one or more of your possible branching logic choices are to not go to another question, select **Content Type** as your choice.

TIP

When you add branching to a question, a page break is added after that question because the next question is unknown.

● **Person Or Group** allows the entry of a person or group that is a registered user of the SharePoint site or is a member of a SharePoint group.

● **External Data** directs the respondent to specific type of content, for example a SQL database, and a specific field in that type of content, where the respondent can choose a value as their answer.

● **Page Separator** places a page separation in the questionnaire.

4. Click the answer type that you want to use and determine if answering the questions is required. For many of the answer types, select whether each respondent's answer must be different from every other respondents'.

5. Fill in the remaining Additional Question Settings topics as needed for the particular answer type you have chosen. See the "Using Branching Logic" QuickSteps for a discussion of how branching logic is used in a survey.

6. When you have finished the settings for the current question, click **Next Question**, if there is one, and repeat steps 3 through 6; or click **Finish** if you have completed the last question. In the latter case you are returned to the survey overview.

Respond to a Survey

Responding to a survey is simply filling out the questionnaire online.

1. Navigate to the Home page of the site with the survey. If it is in the Quick Launch, click it. If not, click **All Site Content**, scroll down to **Surveys**, and click the one you want.

2. Click **Respond To This Survey** just above the overview. The questionnaire will open. Here is the simple branching questionnaire:

NOTE

If you want to get to the Survey Settings page when you are not automatically taken there, from the Home page, click the survey in the Quick Launch, click **Settings** just above the survey overview, and click **Survey Settings**.

TIP

By default, a person is allowed to respond to a survey only once. You can change this in Survey Settings | General Settings, as explained in "Manage a Survey" in this chapter.

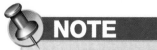

3. Answer the questions that are posed. If branching is involved, click **Next** and continue to answer the questions that are there.
4. When you have answered all the questions, click **Finish**. You are returned to the survey overview.

Analyze a Survey

SharePoint provides tools to summarize and analyze the information collected with a survey. There are two built-in reports that can be easily opened.

1. Navigate to the Home page of the site with the survey. If it is in the Quick Launch, click it. If not, click **All Site Content**, scroll down to **Surveys**, and click the one you want.
2. Click **Show A Graphical Summary Of Responses** below the survey overview. Such a summary will open, as shown in Figure 6-21.

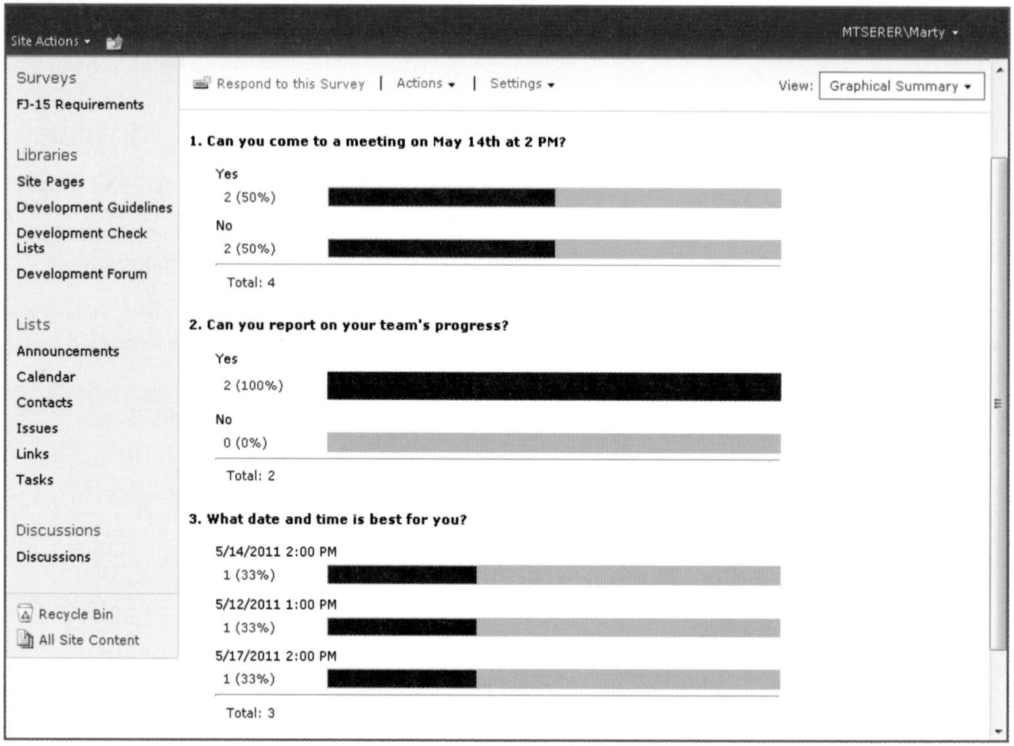

Figure 6-21: ***The graphical summary actually gives you both a visual representation as well as the numeric result.***

3. Click the **View** drop-down arrow in the upper-right corner of the page, and click **All Responses**. A list of responses will be displayed.

4. Click **View Response #** and some number to look at the detailed answers for that response, one example of which is shown next:

	Close
Edit Response	X Delete Response	Manage Permissions	Alert Me	
Can you come to a meeting on May 14th at 2 PM? No	
Can you report on your team's progress?	
What date and time is best for you? 5/17/2011 2:00 PM	
Created at 4/27/2010 4:39 PM by MTSERER\tom	Close
Last modified at 4/27/2010 4:40 PM by MTSERER\tom	

5. When you are ready, click **Close**.

Manage a Survey

Like all lists, surveys have a number of settings that you can change to tailor them to your needs. Unlike the setting for some of the other list elements, which are not different from the standard list settings, those for surveys have some uniqueness. Review these next.

1. From the overview view of the survey whose settings you want to review and possibly change, click **Settings** and then click **Survey Settings**. The Survey Settings page will open as was shown earlier in Figure 6-20.

2. Click **Title, Description And Navigation** to open the General Settings page, shown in Figure 6-22. The Name, Description, and Navigation sections are all standard to other lists. The Survey Options section is unique and should be reviewed to determine if the user names are to be shown in the results and if you want to allow one person to respond multiple times. Click **Save** when you are done.

Name and Description

Type a new name as you want it to appear in headings and links throughout the site. Type descriptive text that will help site visitors use this survey.

Name:
FJ-15 Requirements

Description:

Navigation

Specify whether a link to this survey appears in the Quick Launch.

Display this survey on the Quick Launch?
◉ Yes   ○ No

Survey Options

Specify whether users' names will appear in survey results and whether users can respond to the same survey multiple times.

Show user names in survey results?
◉ Yes   ○ No

Allow multiple responses?
○ Yes   ◉ No

Save   Cancel

Figure 6-22: **Under most circumstances, you do not want someone to respond more than once to a survey.**

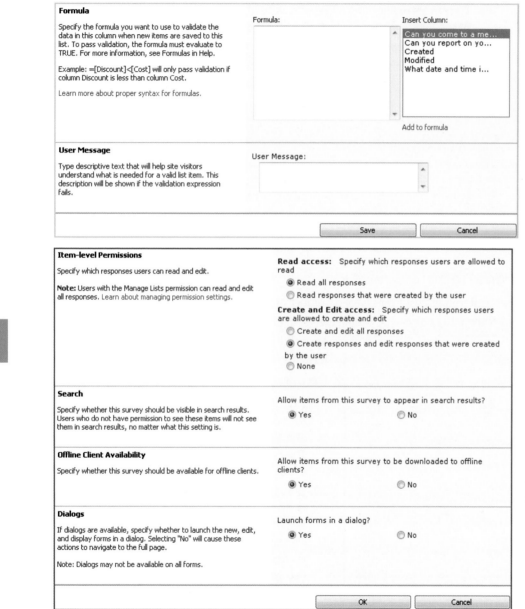

Formula

Specify the formula you want to use to validate the data in this column when new items are saved to this list. To pass validation, the formula must evaluate to TRUE. For more information, see Formulas in Help.

Example: =[Discount]<[Cost] will only pass validation if column Discount is less than column Cost.

Learn more about proper syntax for formulas.

Formula:

Insert Column:

Can you come to a me...
Can you report on yo...
Created
Modified
What date and time i...

Add to formula

User Message

Type descriptive text that will help site visitors understand what is needed for a valid list item. This description will be shown if the validation expression fails.

User Message:

Save   Cancel

Item-level Permissions

Specify which responses users can read and edit.

Note: Users with the Manage Lists permission can read and edit all responses. Learn about managing permission settings.

Read access: Specify which responses users are allowed to read

◉ Read all responses
◯ Read responses that were created by the user

Create and Edit access: Specify which responses users are allowed to create and edit

◯ Create and edit all responses
◉ Create responses and edit responses that were created by the user
◯ None

Search

Specify whether this survey should be visible in search results. Users who do not have permission to see these items will not see them in search results, no matter what this setting is.

Allow items from this survey to appear in search results?

◉ Yes   ◯ No

Offline Client Availability

Specify whether this survey should be available for offline clients.

Allow items from this survey to be downloaded to offline clients?

◉ Yes   ◯ No

Dialogs

If dialogs are available, specify whether to launch the new, edit, and display forms in a dialog. Selecting "No" will cause these actions to navigate to the full page.

Note: Dialogs may not be available on all forms.

Launch forms in a dialog?

◉ Yes   ◯ No

OK   Cancel

Figure 6-23: **Surveys require special attention to how permissions are set so they are most useful.**

3. Click **Advanced Settings** to open that page (see Figure 6-23). Here, determine the types of permissions the normal user will have with the particular survey, whether or not survey data should be included in searches and available for download, and whether the survey should be displayed in a dialog box or in a full browser page. Click **OK** when you are ready.

4. Click **Validation Settings** to open the Validation Settings page. Select a column (or question) whose answer you want to validate, and enter a formula to calculate the validation. See the discussions in Chapter 4 on validating column data and adding a calculated column for how to create a validation formula. Enter a message to the user explaining the purpose of the validation. When you are ready, click **Save**.

5. The remainder of the settings on the Survey Settings page are common to other lists and have been discussed in Chapter 4. Click **Home** to leave the Survey Settings page.

Set Up and Hold Meetings

SharePoint provides five meeting workspace sites that provide for the planning, organizing, announcing, running, and decision making in a meeting. These meeting workspaces are:

- **Basic Meeting Workspace** To plan, organize, and capture the results of a meeting with Agenda, Attendees, and Objectives lists

- **Blank Meeting Workspace** To create a custom meeting site with an Attendees list

- **Decision Meeting Workspace** For decision-making and status-checking meetings with Agenda, Attendees, Decisions, Objectives, and Tasks lists

- **Multipage Meeting Workspace** To plan, organize, and capture the results of a meeting with Agenda, Attendees, and Objectives lists and two additional pages

- **Social Meeting Workspace** To organize a social gathering with Attendees, Directions, and Things to Bring lists

There is a lot of similarity among the five types of meeting sites. As a result, the discussions here apply to all five.

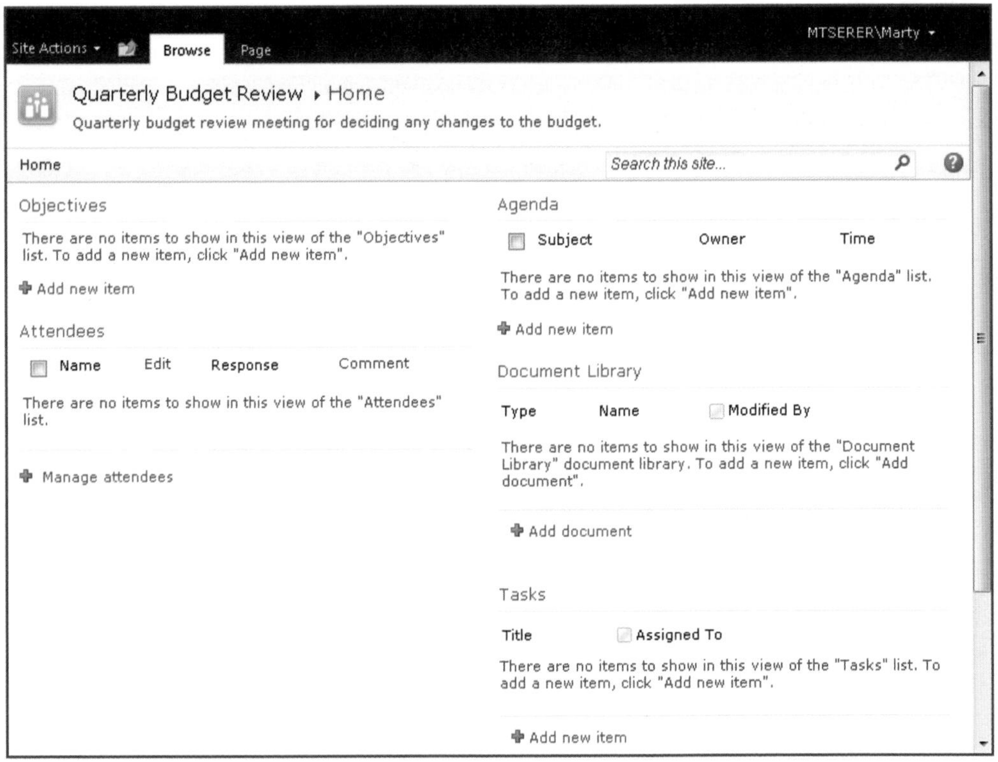

Set Up a Meeting

Setting up a meeting involves the creation of a meeting workspace site, customizing that site, and adjusting the properties settings as needed for the site itself and for each of the elements in the site.

1. Navigate to the Home page of the site that will be the parent of the meeting workspace site.

2. Click **Site Actions** and click **New Site** if it is on the Site Actions menu. If it isn't on the menu, click **More Options**, and click **Site**.

3. Click **Decision Meeting Workspace**, click in the **Title** text box, enter a title, press **TAB**, enter a URL, and click **More Options**.

4. Click in the **Description** text box, and enter a description for the meeting. Consider if you want unique permissions for this site and, if so, click **Use Unique Permissions**, and click **Create**. The site will open, as you see in Figure 6-24.

Figure 6-24: *The Decision Meeting Workspace site provides a number of elements to set up and manage a meeting.*

5. A meeting site can be customized like any other by clicking the **Page** tab and clicking **Edit Page**. From here you can use the Edit Web Part links to add text and other elements to the page, as described in Chapter 3. When you have made the changes you want, click **Stop Editing** in the Page tab.

6. The settings for the individual elements and their Web Parts can be changed by clicking the check box on the right of a Web Part, clicking the **List Tools | List** tab, clicking **Settings**, and clicking **List Settings**. This opens the List Settings page, which has been discussed in both this chapter and Chapter 4. After completing the settings you want to make, click **Home** to return to the site Home page.

7. To change the settings for the site itself, click **Site Actions** in the tab bar, and click **Site Settings**. On the Site Settings page that opens, you can change permissions, manage alerts, determine what is on the top navigation bar, apply a new theme, and manage site features, all of which have been described earlier in this chapter and in previous chapters.

8. When the site and its settings are the way you want them, click **Home**.

Hold a Meeting

When the meeting site is set up, the next step is to populate the various lists that are on the site. Do that as you would any other list.

1. **For the Objectives, Agenda, Tasks, and Decisions list elements**, click **Add New Item** to open the form to enter an item in a list. Type the information or choose the setting in the fields that are either required or pertinent to you, and click **Save**.

2. **For Attendees**, click **Manage Attendees**, click the **List Tools | Items** tab, and click **New Item** to open the Attendee – New Item dialog box. Enter one name, any comments you wish to make, any response you have had, whether their attendance is required, and then click **Save**.

3. As the meeting approaches, is held, and the assigned tasks are completed, the status fields of the various lists need to be updated to show attendance, task, and decision status, as well as task assignments, percentage completion, and start and end dates.

Use and Manage Workflows

As you read in Chapter 1, a *workflow* divides a process into steps that are measured and reported upon to better manage the process. In SharePoint a workflow is a feature that you can associate with a list, library, list item, or document to track progress, approval, or disposition of the item. The standard workflows available in SharePoint are shown in Table 6-1.

For example, if a document needs to be approved by the marketing department first, then after their comments are consolidated into another draft, the legal department needs to approve it before it is published, the Approval workflow can help manage the process.

To use a workflow, it must be:

- **Activated** by an administrator for a site collection containing your site
- **Added** to a list or library
- **Assigned** to a particular document or list item

Workflow activation at the site collection level is generally a task for an administrator. If you don't see any workflows, or only the Three-State workflow, check with your administrator. With the proper permissions, you should be able to add a workflow and assign it to a document or list item.

WORKFLOW	DESCRIPTION	SOURCE
Approval	Routes a document for approval, which can be approved, rejected, reassigned, or changes requested	SharePoint Server
Collect Feedback	Routes a document for reviewer comments, which are sent to the originator	SharePoint Server
Collect Signatures	Accumulates signatures for final completion of a document	SharePoint Server
Disposition Approval	Tracks the retention and expiration of a document to determine when to delete it	SharePoint Server
Publishing Approval	Routes a document for approval, which can be approved, rejected, reassigned, or changes requested	SharePoint Server
Three-State	Tracks the status of an item as being in one of three states, such as assigned, completed, and accepted	SharePoint Foundation

Table 6-1: Standard Workflows Available in SharePoint

Add and Assign Workflows

By adding a workflow to a list or library, you are making it available to the items and documents in the list or library. You can add multiple workflows to a library or list. In the process, you are creating two new lists: a task list to keep track of the tasks that the workflow will help manage, and a history list to keep a record of what was accomplished or approved with the workflow.

ADD A WORKFLOW TO A LIST OR LIBRARY

In the following steps, we'll use a library as our example, but we could just as well have used a list; the steps apply equally to both, simply replace "library" with "list" and "document" with "item." To add a workflow to a library or list:

1. Navigate to the site with the library. Click in the title bar of the library so a check mark appears on the right and the Library Tools tabs appears in the ribbon.

2. Click **Library Tools I Library** tab, and click **Workflow Settings** on the right of the ribbon to open the Workflow page.

3. In most cases, you want the workflows to apply to all content types, but you can select one for the particular workflow you are adding if you want the workflow to apply to one content type and not another.

4. Click **Add A Workflow** to open that page, shown in Figure 6-25.

5. The first task is to choose the type of workflow you want to use. Review Table 6-1 and compare each workflow's description with what you want your workflow to accomplish.

6. Type a unique name for the workflow, and then either select an existing task list and history list or have a new one created for you.

7. Finally, choose whether to start the workflow manually or automatically, with several options for each.

8. When you are ready, click **Next** (or click **OK** if you choose Disposition Approval). The page that opens next depends on the workflow you have chosen. Figure 6-26 shows

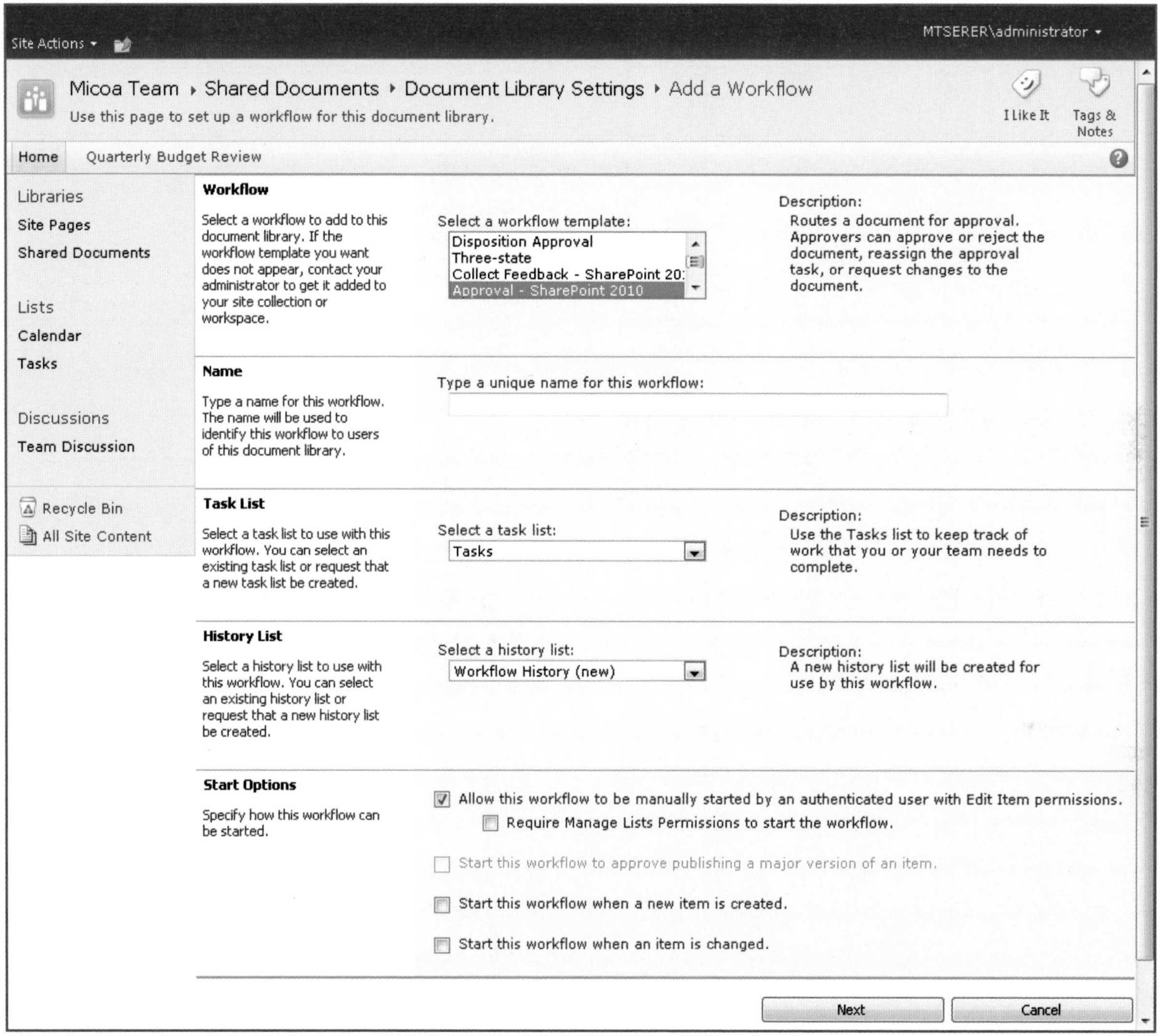

Site Actions ▾

MTSERER\administrator ▾

Micoa Team ▸ Shared Documents ▸ Document Library Settings ▸ Add a Workflow

Use this page to set up a workflow for this document library.

I Like It   Tags & Notes

| Home | Quarterly Budget Review | | ? |

Libraries
Site Pages
Shared Documents

Lists
Calendar
Tasks

Discussions
Team Discussion

▲ Recycle Bin
▣ All Site Content

Workflow

Select a workflow to add to this document library. If the workflow template you want does not appear, contact your administrator to get it added to your site collection or workspace.

Select a workflow template:

| Disposition Approval |
| Three-state |
| Collect Feedback - SharePoint 20: |
| Approval - SharePoint 2010 |

Description:
Routes a document for approval. Approvers can approve or reject the document, reassign the approval task, or request changes to the document.

Name

Type a name for this workflow. The name will be used to identify this workflow to users of this document library.

Type a unique name for this workflow:

Task List

Select a task list to use with this workflow. You can select an existing task list or request that a new task list be created.

Select a task list:

Tasks

Description:
Use the Tasks list to keep track of work that you or your team needs to complete.

History List

Select a history list to use with this workflow. You can select an existing history list or request that a new history list be created.

Select a history list:

Workflow History (new)

Description:
A new history list will be created for use by this workflow.

Start Options

Specify how this workflow can be started.

☑ Allow this workflow to be manually started by an authenticated user with Edit Item permissions.

☐ Require Manage Lists Permissions to start the workflow.

☐ Start this workflow to approve publishing a major version of an item.

☐ Start this workflow when a new item is created.

☐ Start this workflow when an item is changed.

Next   Cancel

Figure 6-25: **The first step you can take to use a workflow is to add a workflow template to a library or list.**

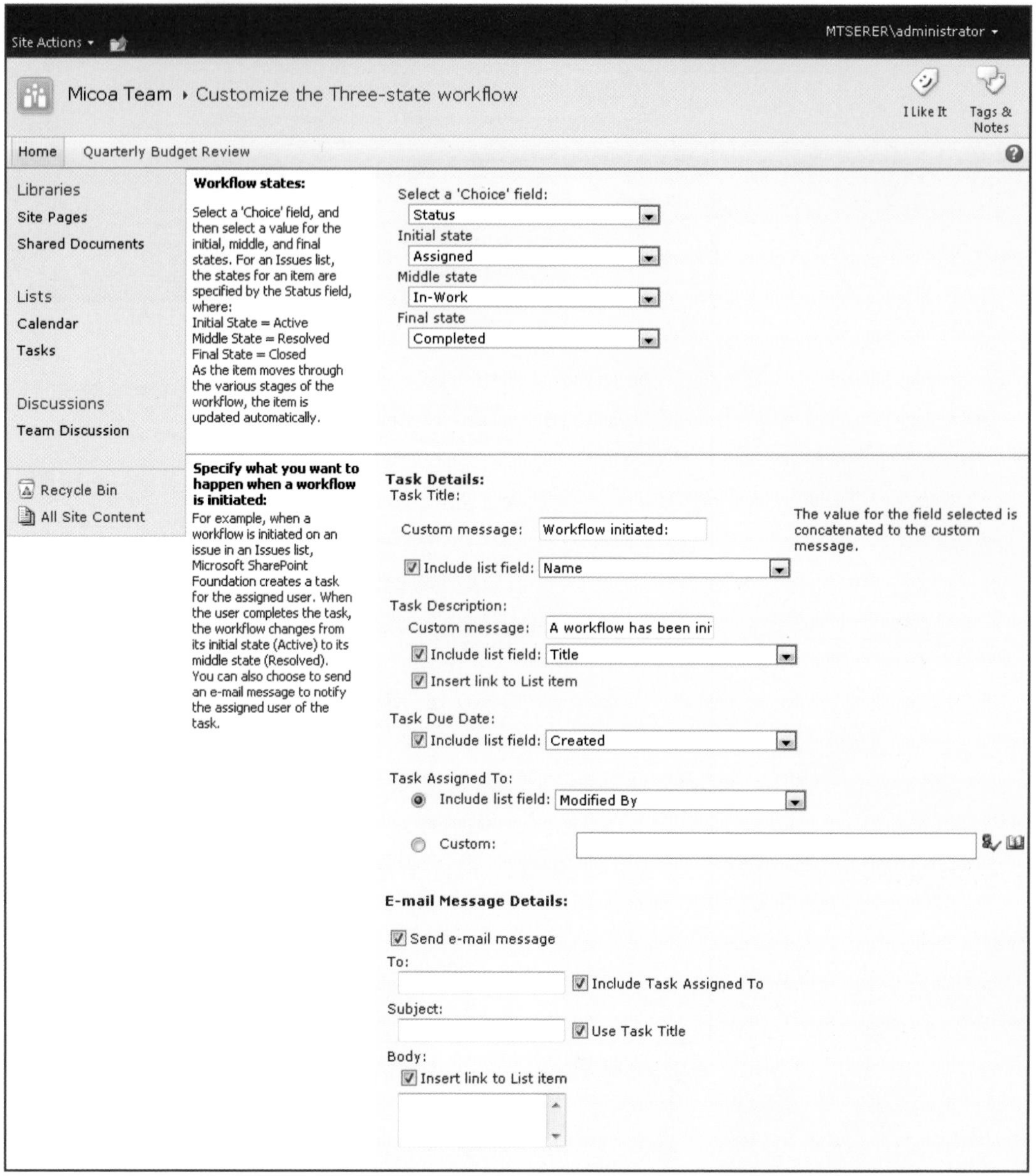

Figure 6-26: **The Three-State workflow requires a choice field in the library or list it is added to.**

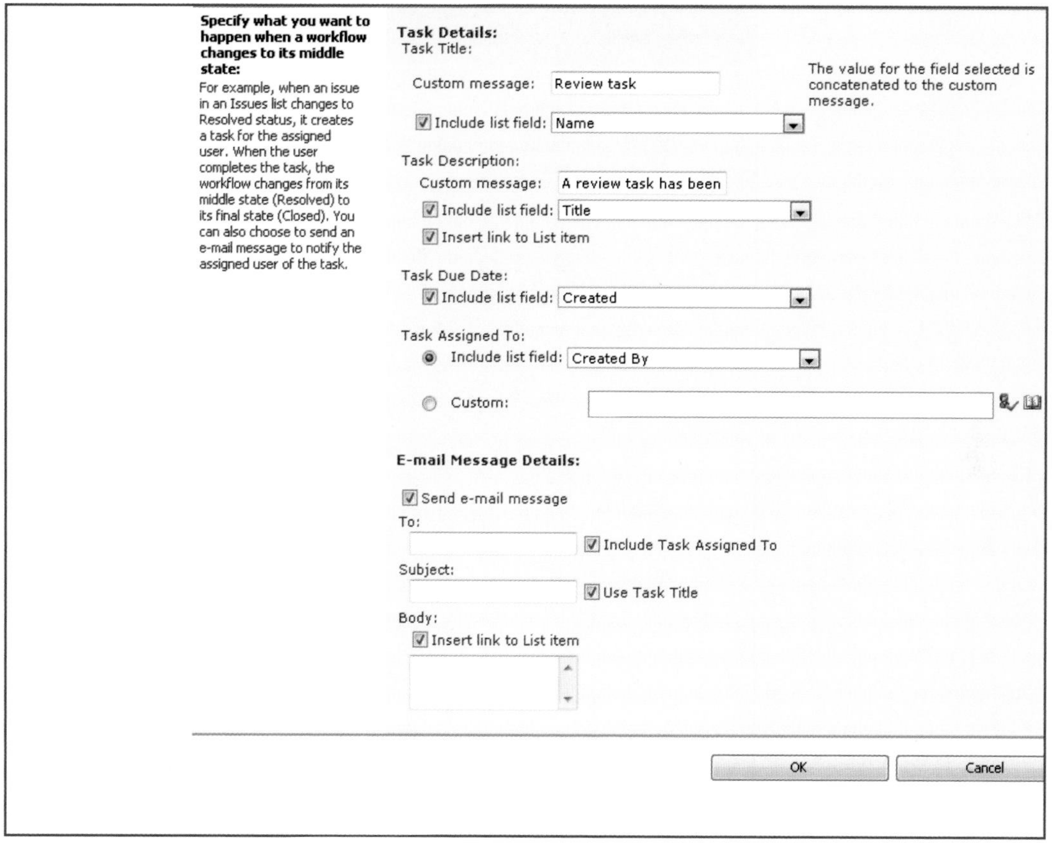

Specify what you want to happen when a workflow changes to its middle state:

For example, when an issue in an Issues list changes to Resolved status, it creates a task for the assigned user. When the user completes the task, the workflow changes from its middle state (Resolved) to its final state (Closed). You can also choose to send an e-mail message to notify the assigned user of the task.

Task Details:
Task Title:

Custom message: `Review task`

The value for the field selected is concatenated to the custom message.

☑ Include list field: `Name` ⌄

Task Description:
Custom message: `A review task has been`
☑ Include list field: `Title` ⌄
☑ Insert link to List item

Task Due Date:
☑ Include list field: `Created` ⌄

Task Assigned To:
◉ Include list field: `Created By` ⌄

○ Custom: `_____` 🖋 📖

E-mail Message Details:

☑ Send e-mail message
To:
`_____` ☑ Include Task Assigned To
Subject:
`_____` ☑ Use Task Title
Body:
☑ Insert link to List item
`_____`

[OK] [Cancel]

*Figure 6-26: **The Three-State workflow requires a choice field in the library or list it is added to.** (continued)*

the Three-State customization page, while Figure 6-27 shows the settings for the Approval workflow.

9. Work your way through the settings, configuring them as appropriate. When all the fields that you want have been set, click **Save** or **OK** depending on your workflow.

ASSIGN A WORKFLOW TO A DOCUMENT OR ITEM

After adding one or more workflows to a library or list, you can then assign them to a document or item and, in that process, start the workflow. We'll continue

NOTE

Some workflows, such as the Three-State workflow, require a "choice" field that has several states, like "Assigned," "In-Work," and "Completed." You may have to add such a field and can choose your own names for the states.

Site Actions ▾ 📝

Micoa Team ▸ Shared Documents ▸ Document Library Settings ▸ Change a Workflow ▸
Document Approval
To finish associating the workflow, use the submit button in the form below.

I Like It   Tags & Notes

Home   Quarterly Budget Review

Search this site...   🔍   ❓

Approvers	**Assign To**		**Order**
		👤 📖	One at a time (serial) ▾

☐ Add a new stage
Enter the names of the people to whom the workflow will assign tasks, and choose the order in which those tasks are assigned. Separate them with semicolons. You can also add stages to assign tasks to more people in different orders.

Expand Groups	☑ For each group entered, assign a task to every member of that group.
Request	
	This message will be sent to the people assigned tasks.
Due Date for All Tasks	📅
	The date by which all tasks are due.
Duration Per Task	
	The amount of time until a task is due. Choose the units by using the Duration Units.
Duration Units	Day(s) ▾
	Define the units of time used by the Duration Per Task.
CC	👤 📖
	Notify these people when the workflow starts and ends without assigning tasks to them.
End on First Rejection	☐ Automatically reject the document if it is rejected by any participant.
End on Document Change	☐ Automatically reject the document if it is changed before the workflow is completed.
Enable Content Approval	☐ Update the approval status after the workflow is completed (use this workflow to control content approval).

Save   Cancel

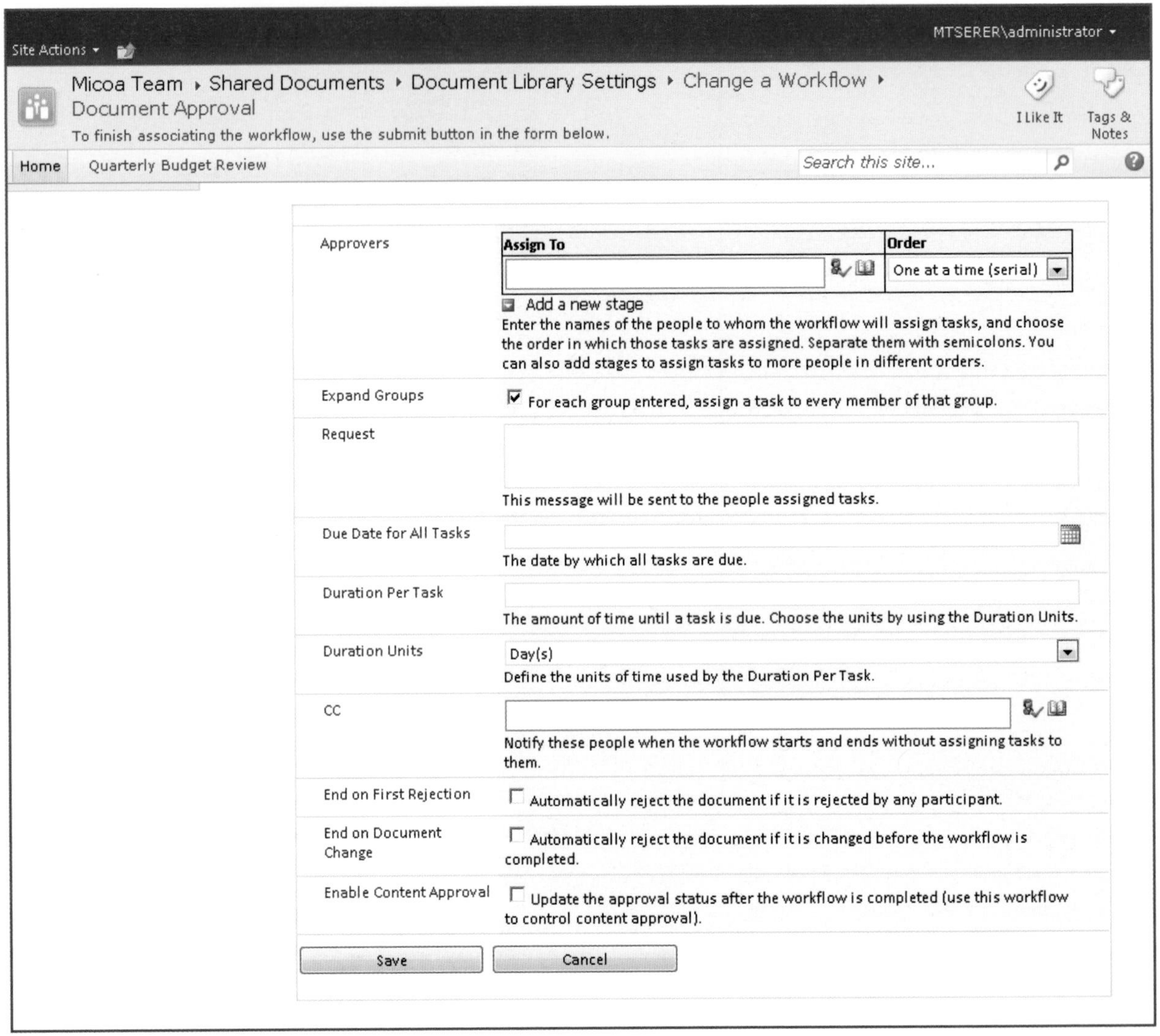

Figure 6-27: **The Approval workflow can require one or multiple people to give their approval.**

with the library and document example, but remember that these steps apply equally to lists and items.

1. Click the check box on the left of the document that the workflow will be assigned to.

2. In the Library Tools | Document tab, click **Workflows**. The Start A New Workflow page will open, like this:

3. Click a workflow that you want to use with this document. The detail settings for the workflow will open, allowing you to make any changes needed for this particular document.

4. When you are ready, click **Start** to initiate the workflow. You will see a message that the workflow is being started.

Manage Workflows

Once you have assigned a workflow to a document or list, you can check on and change its status, as well as change the settings, report on it, and remove the original workflow in the library or list, given that you have the appropriate permissions.

Start a New Workflow

	Work Status
	Use this workflow to track items in a list.

Workflows

Select a workflow for more details on the current status or history.

Name	Started

Running Workflows

Document Approval	5/1/2010 4:15 PM

Completed Workflows

There are no completed workflows on this item.

Workflows

		Workflows in Progress
	Workflow Name (click to change settings)	
	Document Approval	1
	Work Status	0

These workflows are configured to run on items of this type:

All ▼

(Selecting a different type will navigate you to the Workflow Settings page for that content type.)

- Add a workflow
- Remove a workflow
- View workflow reports

CHECK A WORKFLOW STATUS

To look at the status of a workflow attached to a document or list item (once more, we'll talk in terms of a document, but this applies to items as well):

1. Click the check box on the right of the document whose workflow you want to check.

2. In the Library Tools | Library Documents tab, click Workflows and click Workflows a second time.

3. Under Running Workflows, click the workflow whose status you want to check.

4. The Workflow Status page opens, as you can see in Figure 6-28. This page gives you a comprehensive picture of the workflow and lets you:
   - Open the document the workflow applies to
   - Add or update approvers
   - Cancel all approval tasks
   - Update approval tasks
   - Terminate the workflow

5. When you have completed your work on the workflow status page, click **Home** to return there.

CHANGE AND REMOVE A WORKFLOW

To change and/or remove a workflow at the library or list level:

1. Click in the title bar of the library, click **Library Tools | Library** tab, and click **Library Settings**. The Library Settings page will open.

2. Under Permissions And Management, click **Workflow Settings**. A list of workflows and their progress will appear. Don't do it now, but note that you can click **Remove A Workflow** to do that if desired.

3. Click the workflow you want to work with. The Add A Workflow page you saw in Figure 6-25, now renamed "Change A Workflow," will open and allow you to change many aspects of the workflow, including the name, the two lists, and how it is started.

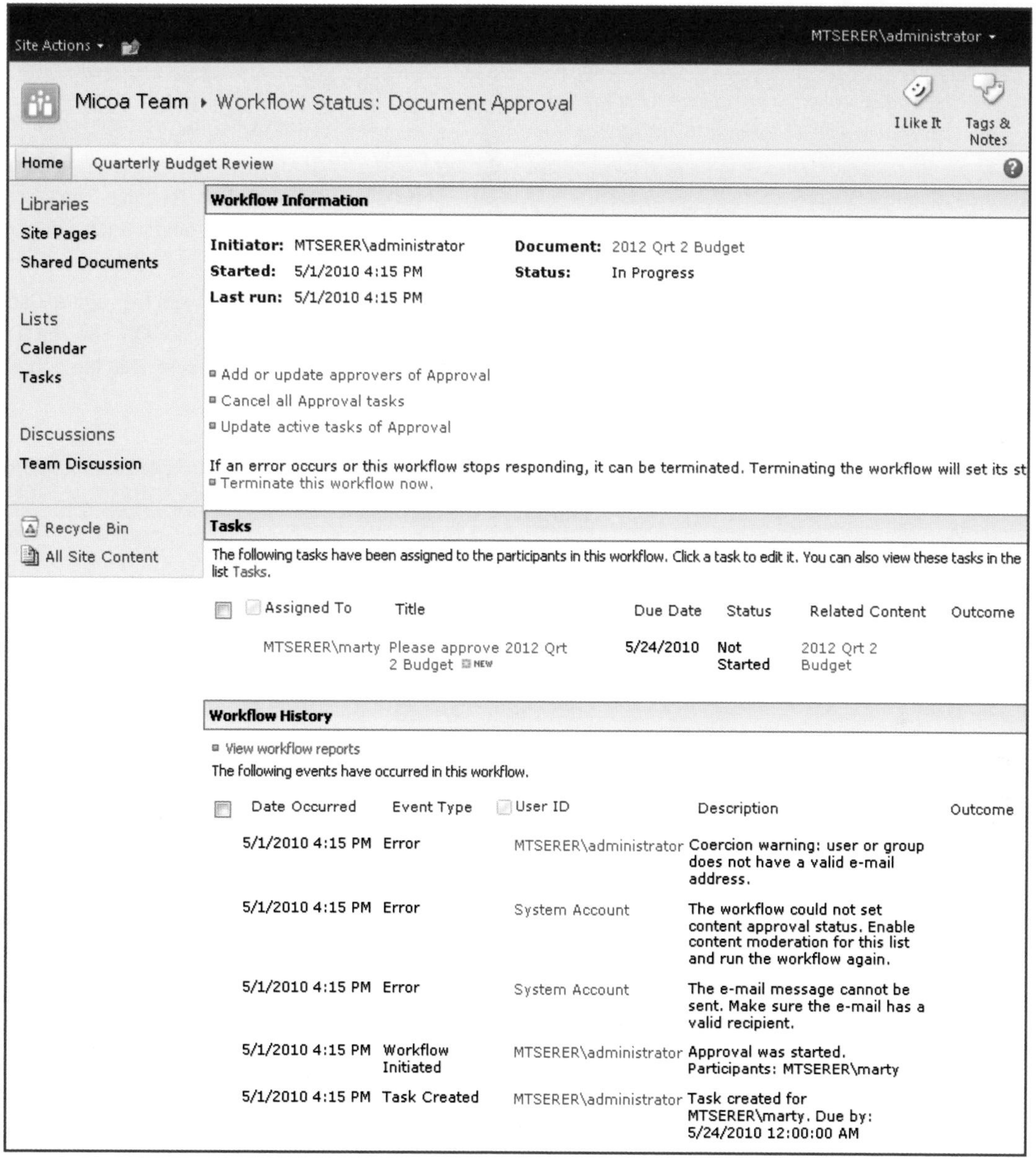

Site Actions ▾ 📝

MTSERER\administrator ▾

👥 **Micoa Team** ▸ Workflow Status: Document Approval

I Like It   Tags & Notes

| Home | Quarterly Budget Review | ❓ |

Libraries

Site Pages

Shared Documents

Lists

Calendar

Tasks

Discussions

Team Discussion

🗑 Recycle Bin

📄 All Site Content

Workflow Information

Initiator: MTSERER\administrator   **Document:** 2012 Qrt 2 Budget
Started: 5/1/2010 4:15 PM   **Status:** In Progress
Last run: 5/1/2010 4:15 PM

▫ Add or update approvers of Approval
▫ Cancel all Approval tasks
▫ Update active tasks of Approval

If an error occurs or this workflow stops responding, it can be terminated. Terminating the workflow will set its st
▫ Terminate this workflow now.

Tasks

The following tasks have been assigned to the participants in this workflow. Click a task to edit it. You can also view these tasks in the list Tasks.

	Assigned To	Title	Due Date	Status	Related Content	Outcome
☐	MTSERER\marty	Please approve 2012 Qrt 2 Budget ☐ NEW	5/24/2010	Not Started	2012 Qrt 2 Budget	

Workflow History

▫ View workflow reports
The following events have occurred in this workflow.

	Date Occurred	Event Type	User ID	Description	Outcome
☐	5/1/2010 4:15 PM	Error	MTSERER\administrator	Coercion warning: user or group does not have a valid e-mail address.	
	5/1/2010 4:15 PM	Error	System Account	The workflow could not set content approval status. Enable content moderation for this list and run the workflow again.	
	5/1/2010 4:15 PM	Error	System Account	The e-mail message cannot be sent. Make sure the e-mail has a valid recipient.	
	5/1/2010 4:15 PM	Workflow Initiated	MTSERER\administrator	Approval was started. Participants: MTSERER\marty	
	5/1/2010 4:15 PM	Task Created	MTSERER\administrator	Task created for MTSERER\marty. Due by: 5/24/2010 12:00:00 AM	

Figure 6-28: **The Workflow Status page provides a comprehensive view of the workflow.**

NOTE

The workflow reports are presented as Excel spreadsheets that use PivotTables to give you further flexibility in viewing them. If you are unfamiliar with PivotTables or how to use Excel 2010, get *Microsoft Excel 2010 QuickSteps* by John Cronan and published by McGraw-Hill Professional.

NOTE

Custom workflows can be created and managed using Microsoft Visual Studio or SharePoint Designer.

4. Make the desired changes, and click **Next**. The workflow customization page will open, similar to what you saw in Figures 6-26 and 6-27, and allow you to make any desired changes.

5. Click **Save** or **OK** when you are ready. You are returned to the Workflows list you saw in step 2.

6. Click **View Workflow Reports**. The Workflow Reports page will open, displaying the reports that you can get for each workflow you have added to the library, as you can see in Figure 6-29.

7. Click the report you want to prepare. Click **Browse** to select where you want to store the report, and then click **OK**. You see a message that the report is in process and then a second one saying that the operation completed successfully. Click **OK** again.

Site Actions ▾

MTSERER\administrator ▾

Micoa Team ▸ **Shared Documents** ▸ **Document Library Settings** ▸ View Workflow Reports

Use these reports to monitor how your business processes are running based on the history information of those workflows.

I Like It   Tags & Notes

Home   Quarterly Budget Review   Search this site...

Libraries
Site Pages
Shared Documents

⊟ **Document Approval**

Activity Duration Report
Use this report to see how long it is taking for each activity within this workflow to complete, as well as how long it takes each instance to complete.

Cancellation & Error Report
Use this report to see which workflows are being canceled or encounter errors before completion.

Lists
Calendar
Tasks

Discussions
Team Discussion

⊟ **Work Status**

Activity Duration Report
Use this report to see how long it is taking for each activity within this workflow to complete, as well as how long it takes each instance to complete.

Recycle Bin
All Site Content

Cancellation & Error Report
Use this report to see which workflows are being canceled or encounter errors before completion.

Figure 6-29: **SharePoint provides two reports to help you keep track of what is happening with a workflow.**

Chapter 7
Using SharePoint with Microsoft Office

As you might imagine, with SharePoint and Office both coming from Microsoft, there is a significant amount of synergy between the two. SharePoint facilitates the collaborative use of Word, Excel, and PowerPoint, which can all be opened from within SharePoint. SharePoint has several e-mail and calendar functions that coordinate with Outlook, lists can be transferred to both Excel and Access, and SharePoint facilitates working with InfoPath forms. We'll look at all of these areas in this chapter.

Collaborate with Word, Excel, and PowerPoint

The first thing that comes to mind when SharePoint is mentioned is collaboration. While collaboration takes place in many ways in SharePoint, one of the most common and important collaborative processes is in the production, editing, and review of Microsoft Word, Excel, and PowerPoint documents.

Save Documents to SharePoint

You've seen in earlier chapters how you bring an existing file into a SharePoint library. However, the simplest way to get a new Word, Excel, or PowerPoint document into a SharePoint library is to save it there directly from the Office application. You can start either from the Office application or from SharePoint.

START NEW DOCUMENTS IN OFFICE

1. From your desktop, open the Office application (we'll use Word in this instance) and create the document as you normally would, with all the formatting and other features.

NOTE

In this and elsewhere in this book, when we are talking about Microsoft Office, we are talking about Office 2010. Both Office 2003 and Office 2007 have many of the features for integration with SharePoint, just not as finely developed. If you are using one of the earlier versions of Office, look for the equivalent steps to those presented here for Office 2010.

2. When you have completed the document, open your browser and your SharePoint site, navigate to the library to which you want to add the new document, and open the library in its own page. Note the address, or URL, in the browser's address bar, and perhaps drag across it and press **CTRL+C** to copy the address to the Clipboard. The URL should look something like:
http://*server name/site name/library name/*Forms/Allitems.aspx.
You want to use this address through the library name and its slash, and then add the file name and extension.

3. Back in Word, click the **File** tab, click **Save & Send**, and click **Save To SharePoint**. The first time you save a file to SharePoint, you won't have the Current Location and Recent Locations (see Figure 7-1), so click **Browse For A Location** and then click **Save As**.

Figure 7-1: After you have saved one or more files to SharePoint, it becomes easy to do so again because the path to recently accessed SharePoint libraries is displayed and can be simply clicked to save again to the same library.

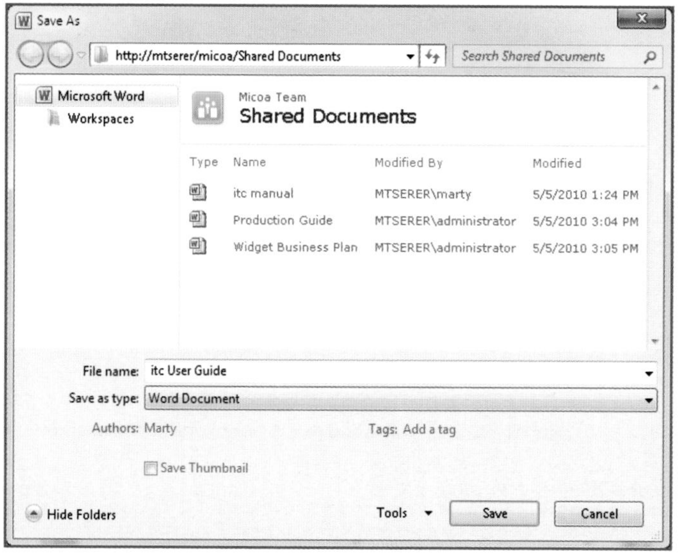

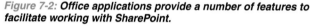

Figure 7-2: ***Office applications provide a number of features to facilitate working with SharePoint.***

4. In the Save As dialog box that appears, click the down arrow at the right end of the address bar at the top of the dialog box, and then click the same arrow again to select the existing contents. In that address bar, either type your URL or paste what you copied and delete the "Forms/Allitems.aspx," as shown in Figure 7-2.
5. In the File Name text box type the file name and click **Save**. Return to your SharePoint site in your browser, and refresh your library page (click the two curved arrows on the right end of the address bar). Your newly saved file should appear as you see in Figure 7-3.

START NEW DOCUMENTS IN SHAREPOINT

You can start the creation of a new Office document from within SharePoint.

1. Open SharePoint, navigate to the library where the document will reside, click the library's title bar to open it in its own page and make the Library Tools tab available.

QUICKFACTS

USING WEB APPS VERSUS STAND-ALONE OFFICE

Microsoft offers Office on two platforms beginning with Office 2010:

- The original stand-alone version that is resident on the computer where it is being used, called the "desktop" version, also runs on laptop computers. This is the same platform that Office has used since its inception.
- The new Web Apps version that is resident on a server somewhere and available to you through your browser. Generally with SharePoint, Web Apps is being hosted on your organization's servers. It is also available with Microsoft's cloud computing (live.com) and possibly elsewhere.

Continued . . .

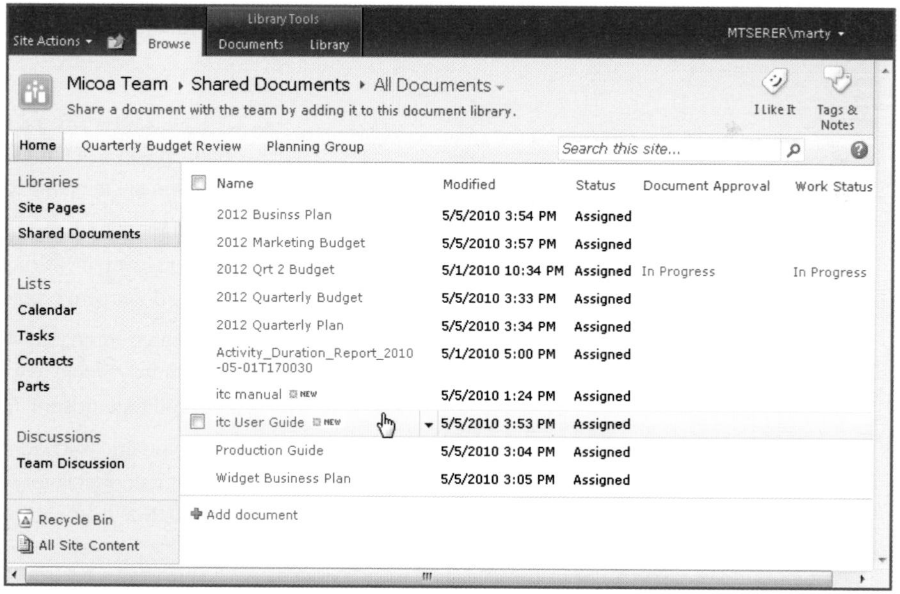

Figure 7-3: ***Files saved from Office to a SharePoint library look and behave exactly the same as those that are uploaded from SharePoint.***

USING WEB APPS VERSUS STAND-ALONE OFFICE *(Continued)*

Web Apps provides a reduced set of features that are fine for reviewing and lightly editing most documents or for creating fairly simple documents. For all major document creation and for heavy editing, however, you want to use the Office stand-alone version.

In this chapter we'll assume that when reviewing and editing a document you initially will open it in Web Apps, if it is available to you, because that is the normal and default setup. From Web Apps you can easily open the document in stand-alone Word by clicking that option, as shown in Figure 7-4. If you don't have Web Apps available, the stand-alone version will automatically open. From the standpoint of this book, it really doesn't matter which version of Office you use.

Micoa Team ▸ Shared Documents ▸ itc manual.docx   MTSERER\marty ▾

Microsoft Word Web App

File | Home | Insert | View

Arial | 18 | B *I* U abc x₂ x² | A ▾ | caption AaBbCc | AaBbC H 1 | AaBbCc H 4 | ABC Spelling | Open in Word

Clipboard | Font | Paragraph | Styles | Spelling | Office

- What are the most important fields? You may want some views that show only some of the fields.
- What is the formatting of each fields, do you show cents as well as dollars?
- Who is going to use the list and what permission scheme is required?
- How does the list get populated, from what source, by whom?
- How does the list get maintained, from what source, by whom?
- What is the life of the list?

This is not meant to be an exhaustive list of questions to ask yourself, but the point is to fully think through the list before creating it. You may want to involve others if they will be using the list a lot.

(2)Prepare to Add a List

There are at least three ways to add a list to a page, but, depending on the type of page you have, you may not always have all three choices.

1. Navigate to the page on which you want the list.
2. **If it is a blank page**, click the **Edit** icon on the tab bar.
3. Consider if you want to keep the default of a single column or want some other layout. If so, in the Editing Tools Formatting Text tab, click **Text Layout** to open a drop-down menu and select one of the layouts. You will see a

*Figure 7-4: **Although the Office Web Apps may initially load when you open a library document, you can easily switch to the stand-alone application.***

2. Click the **Library Tools I Documents** tab. Click **New Document** on the left of the ribbon. If you see a message that some files may harm your computer and asking about the file template .dotx, that is the standard template, so click **OK**.

3. If the stand-alone application is available on the computer you are using, that is what will open, even if Web Apps is available. At the top of the document window, you may see the document properties in addition to the document.

4. If you see a Protected View warning, click **Enable Editing**. Create your document as you normally would, using all of the needed tools available in the application, and then, if desired and present, fill in the document properties, as shown in Figure 7-5.

5. When you are ready to save the document, click the **File** tab, click **Save & Send**, and if the correct library is shown under Save To SharePoint, click it. Otherwise, click **Browse For A Location**. In either case, click **Save As**.

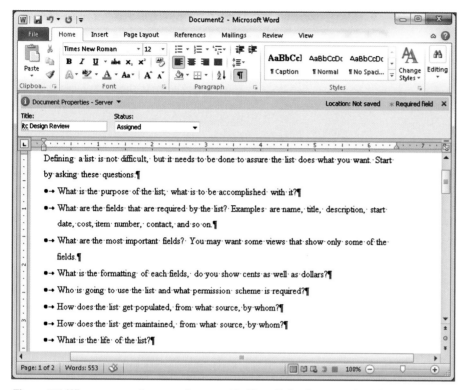

Figure 7-5: *When you create a new document in SharePoint, it opens the Office stand-alone version.*

TIP

If you would like more information about Microsoft Office products such as Word, Excel, PowerPoint, and Outlook, check out *Microsoft Office 2010 QuickSteps* for a good overview of all these products, or for more in-depth coverage, look at one or all of the four separate books: *Microsoft Office Word 2010 QuickSteps*, *Microsoft Office Excel 2010 QuickSteps*, *Microsoft Office PowerPoint 2010 QuickSteps*, and *Microsoft Office Outlook 2010 QuickSteps*, all published by McGraw-Hill/Professional.

6. In the Save As dialog box that appears, if the correct folder is not shown in the address bar at the top of the dialog box, click the down arrow at the right end and then click it again to select the existing contents. Then type your URL or paste what you copied and delete the "Forms/Allitems.aspx" (see the earlier discussion under "Start New Documents in Office").

7. In the File Name text box, type the file name and click **Save**. Return to your SharePoint site in your browser, and refresh your library page. Your newly saved file should appear.

Review and Edit Office Documents

Although collaboration may occur while creating a document with several people involved in the process, that situation is even more likely with the review and editing. To facilitate collaboration, SharePoint must be appropriately set up.

SET UP SHAREPOINT COLLABORATION

Setting up SharePoint for collaboration means that permissions and controls have been established that are appropriate for your organization. In some organizations, collaboration can effectively take place without special permissions and controls. In other organizations, editing and approval permissions need to be set, versioning needs to be turned on and parameters set, and possibly workflows assigned. Both sides can successfully argue their philosophy, so there is no "right" way. You need to determine what is correct for you. All three—permissions, versioning, and workflows—have been discussed in depth in other chapters, so here we'll just go through a quick summary. Start by turning on versioning and adding workflows for the library and then setting permissions and assigning workflows for the document.

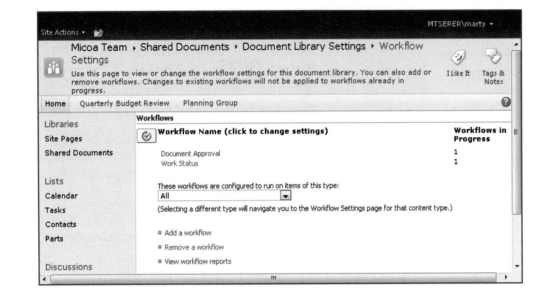

Figure 7-6: *Workflows enable you to track and control a collaborative process.*

1. Navigate to the site and page with the library you will work with. Click the library header to open it in its own page and have the Library Tools tabs appear.

2. **To add workflows to the library**, click **Library Tools | Library** tab and click **Workflow Settings** 🔄 ▾ in the Settings group on the right of the ribbon to open the Workflow Settings page (see Chapter 6 for a detailed discussion of workflows). At the top of the detail area you'll see the workflows that are currently available to the documents in this library, as shown in Figure 7-6.

3. Click **Add A Workflow**, select the workflow you want to use, type a unique name for it, identify the task and history lists to use, choose the start option to use, and, if applicable, click **Next**; otherwise, click **OK**. If you clicked **Next**, fill in the parameters unique to the workflow you are using, and click **Save**.

4. **To set up versioning in a library**, click **Document Library Settings** in the breadcrumb navigation to open the Library settings page. Click **Versioning Settings**, choose if the library documents require approval and, if so, click **Yes**. Choose and click appropriately if you want major versions only, major and minor versions, or no versioning. Determine who should see draft versions of the documents and if they require checkout. Click **OK**.

5. **To add unique permissions to a document**, click your library name in the breadcrumb navigation to return to the library's page. Click the check box of the document you want to set permissions for, in the Library Tools | Documents tab click **Document Permissions** 🔏, click **Stop Inheriting Permissions**, click **OK**, and click **Grant Permissions** to open the Grant Permissions dialog box (see Figure 7-7).

6. Enter the users you want to give permission to, leave **Add Users To A SharePoint Group** unselected, click the permissions you want the users to have, choose whether to send an e-mail to the user and type the message it should contain, and then click **OK**.

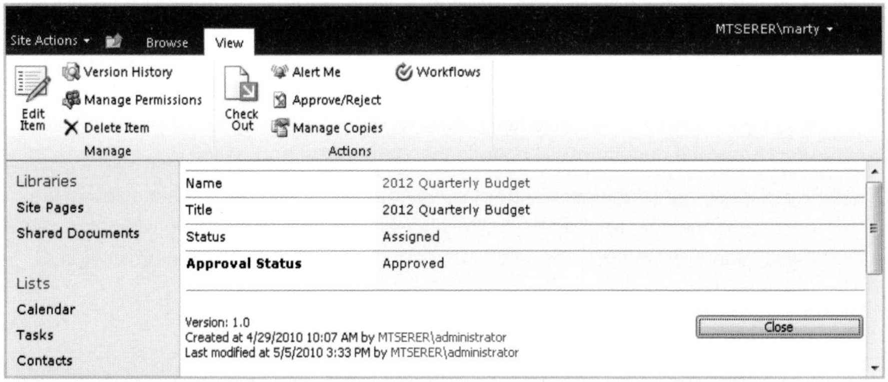

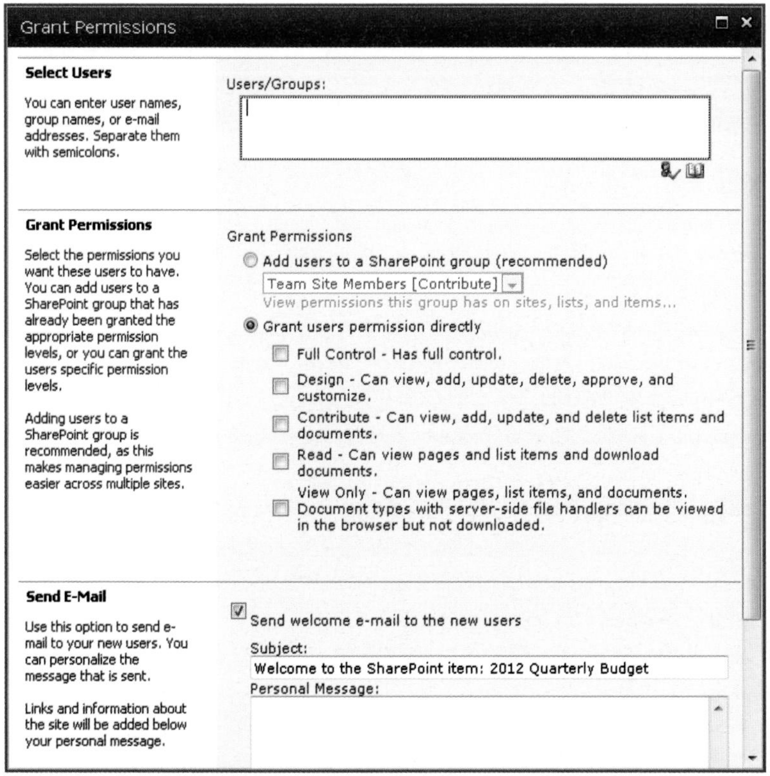

Figure 7-7: *Setting unique permissions for a document means first turning off inherited permissions. Only then can you grant permissions.*

7. **To assign a workflow to a document**, click **Navigate Up** in the tab row and click the name of your document to open its properties page. Click **Workflows** and click the workflow you want to use. The detail page of the workflow that you saw when you clicked **Next** in step 3 will reopen so that you can change any of the settings. Do that and then click **Start** to enable the workflow for your document.

You are now ready to begin collaboratively working with the document using unique permissions and versioning within the workflows you have selected.

COLLABORATIVELY REVIEW AND EDIT DOCUMENTS

Collaboratively reviewing and editing a document can have a number of definitions, depending on the objective. One or more people can:

- Approve, reject, or reassign the document
- Review the document and separately prepare notes
- Review the document and leave comments within it
- Edit the document and make any needed changes, with or without tracking them
- Add content to the document, with or without tracking
- Maintain version control of the document
- Handle any assigned workflow requirements

The versioning and workflow handling need to be set up as described in the previous section. Once that has been done, here is how to review, edit, add content to, approve, and handle workflow; all with Track Changes turned on, or off if you don't want to use this feature (see the "Tracking Changes in Word, Excel, and PowerPoint" QuickSteps in this chapter). In this discussion we'll use Word as the application, but Excel and PowerPoint could also be used.

TIP

You can view a consolidated list of all of the workflows you have running or completed by clicking **Site Actions**, clicking **View All Site Content**, and then clicking **Site Workflows**.

1. Navigate to the site, page, and library with the document that you want to review/edit/approve. Click the title to open the document.

   - If your server has Office Web Apps running with SharePoint, then your document will open in the Web Apps Reading View, as shown in Figure 7-8. If you don't have Web Apps, the document will open in the stand-alone application.

   - If you only want **to review the document for approval** or for notes outside of the document and you are in Web Apps Reading View, then you can do what you want there. When you are done, click **Back** in the upper-left corner of the browser, and skip to step 3.

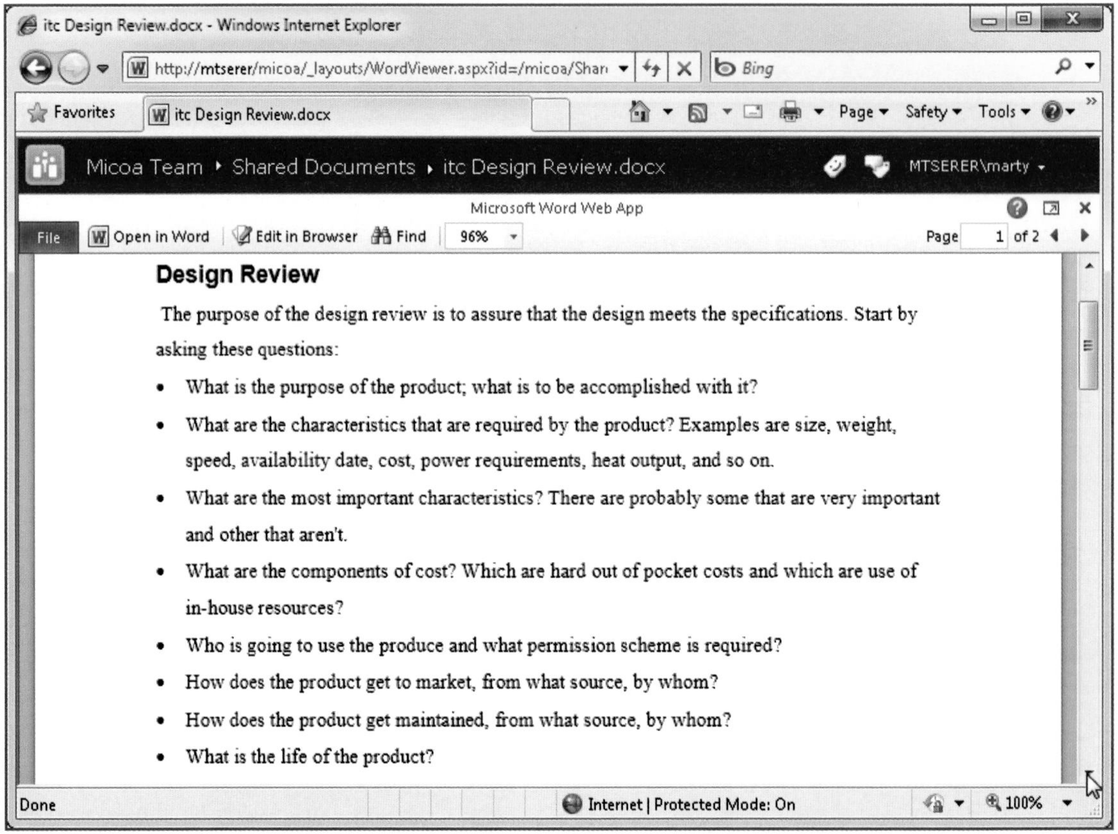

*Figure 7-8: **Office Web Apps Reading View allows you to review a document and take notes outside of the application.***

- If you only want **to do some light editing** and tracking the changes is not important, you can do that in Web Apps by clicking **Edit In Browser** and making the changes you want, as shown in Figure 7-9. When you are done with the changes, click **Save** in the upper-left corner, click **Back** in the upper-left corner of the browser, and skip to step 3.

- If you want **to make substantial changes to the document** and keep track of them, you need to open it in the stand-alone application. Do that from Web Apps by clicking **Open In Word**, clicking **OK** to open the file, and then turning on Track Changes (see the "Tracking Changes in Word, Excel, and PowerPoint" QuickSteps in this chapter).

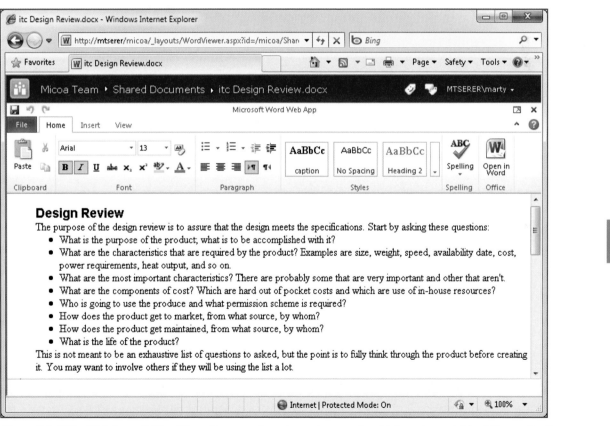

*Figure 7-9: **Office Web Apps Editing View allows you to review a document and take notes outside of the application.***

2. In the stand-alone application with Track Changes enabled, carry out the additions, editing, and commenting as needed. When you are finished, click **Save** in the Quick Access toolbar in the upper-left corner, close the application, and reopen your SharePoint site in your browser.

3. In your SharePoint site with your library open in its own page, click the check box on the left of the document you are working with.

4. To approve or reject the document, in Library Tools | Documents, click **Workflows** and then click **Approve/Reject** to open that dialog box. Click Approved, Rejected, or leave Pending selected; enter a comment; and click **OK**.

Approve/Reject ☐ ✕

Approval Status

Approve, reject, or leave the status as Pending for others with the Manage Lists permission to evaluate the item.

○ Approved. This item will become visible to all users.

○ Rejected. This item will be returned to its creator and only be visible to its creator and all users who can see draft items.

● Pending. This item will remain visible to its creator and all users who can see draft items.

Comment

Use this field to enter any comments about why the item was approved or rejected.

[OK]   [Cancel]

Version History ☐ ✕

Delete All Versions | Delete Draft Versions

No. ↓	Modified	Modified By	Size	Comments
4.0	5/10/2010 10:17 PM	MTSERER\marty	24.1 KB	
3.0	5/10/ ⟶ View	MTSERER\marty	25.9 KB	
2.0	5/10/2010 3:24 PM Restore	MTSERER\marty	25.9 KB	
	Approval Status Pending			

This is the current approved version

1.0	5/5/2010 7:35 PM	MTSERER\marty	25.7 KB	
	Title	itc Design Review		
	Status	Assigned		
	Approval Status	Approved		

5. To review the version history, with the document selected (its check box selected), in Library Tools | Documents, click **View Properties**, and in the document properties dialog box click **Version History**. In the Version History dialog box that appears you can see the versions of the document that have been kept, as well as the latest approved version. By clicking the date and time of a version, you can view and restore that version, and if it isn't the latest version, you can delete it. When you are ready, click **Close** in the upper-right corner.

6. To review the workflow status, with the document selected, in Library Tools | Documents click **Workflows** and then click **Workflows** again. The Workflows page will open showing the running workflows. Click the running workflows that you want to review.

QUICKSTEPS

TRACKING CHANGES IN WORD, EXCEL, AND POWERPOINT

When two or more people work on a document, it is helpful to see what the other people did without having to read every word and accurately remembering what it was before it was changed. All three Office products—Word, Excel, and PowerPoint—have the ability to show you what has been changed in a document. Both Word and Excel have Track Changes that directly show you the changes that several people have made by making each person's changes a different color. In PowerPoint you can compare two documents and display the differences. PowerPoint's comparison ability is only available in PowerPoint 2010, while both Word and Excel have Track Changes in both 2003 and 2007 versions.

USE TRACK CHANGES IN WORD

Track Changes identifies the changes (additions or deletions) made to a document by everyone who works on it. Each person is automatically assigned a color, and their changes are noted in that color. For example, Figure 7-11 shows a section of a Word document in the editing process. After all the changes are made, they can be accepted or rejected, either one at a time or all together.

To use Track Changes in Word, you must turn it on. Prior to doing that, anything anyone types looks like ordinary text, and there is no way of telling the difference between the new text and what was on the page before the change was made. Once Track Changes is turned on, however, anything anyone types or does to the document will be shown in the color automatically assigned to that person; furthermore, the changes are fully reversible, if desired. To turn on Track Changes:

1. Start Word and open the document in which you want to track changes.

Continued . . .

The detail Workflow Information page will open, as you see in Figure 7-10. Here you can see the tasks that have been assigned and the events that have taken place, as well as add or update reviewers and update or cancel tasks, plus terminate the workflow. Carry out the appropriate actions, and when you are ready, click **Close** in the upper-right corner.

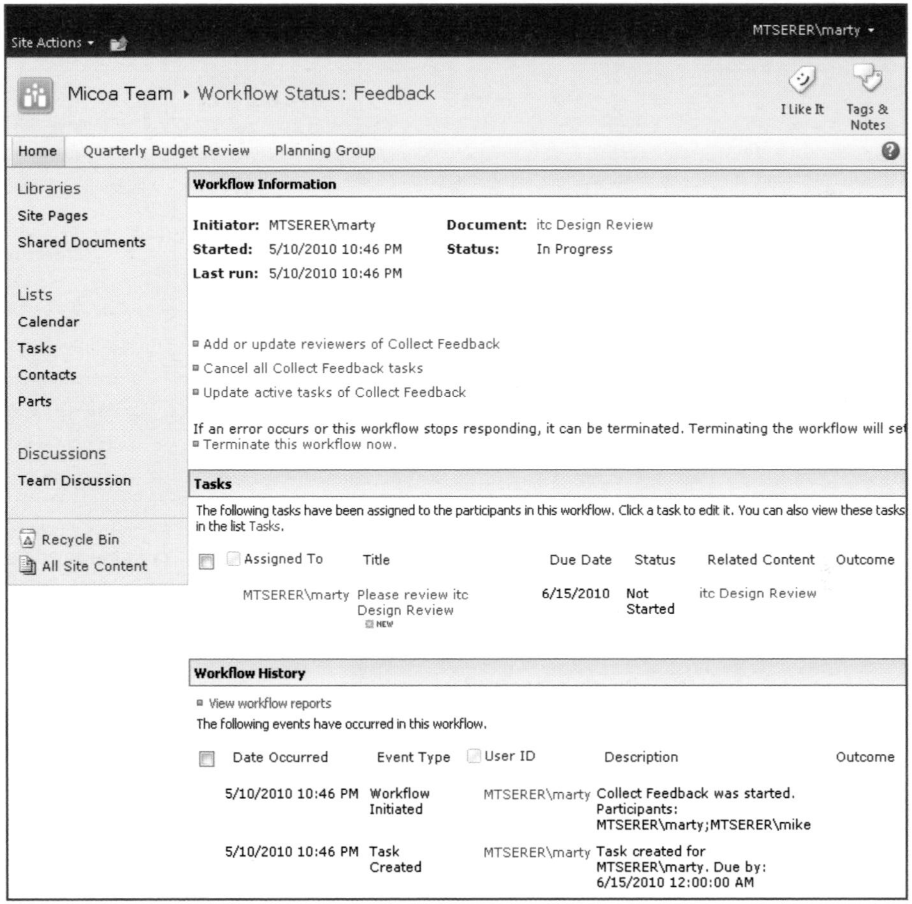

Figure 7-10: *Workflows can gather a significant amount of information.*

TRACKING CHANGES IN WORD, EXCEL, AND POWERPOINT (Continued)

2. In the Review tab Tracking group, click the upper part of the **Track Changes** button.

- –Or–
- Press **CTRL+SHIFT+E**.

The Review tab provides a number of features that you can use as you and others edit a document, as shown in Figure 7-12.

Word gives you a number of options for how changes are displayed and how one can review and accept or reject the changes. To learn more about Track Changes in Word, see *Microsoft Office Word 2010 QuickSteps*, published by McGraw-Hill/Professional.

USE TRACK CHANGES IN EXCEL

Track Changes in Excel also shares the workbook and uses the Review tab. To enable them both:

1. In the Review tab Changes group, click **Track Changes** and click **Highlight Changes** to open the Highlight Changes dialog box.

Continued . . .

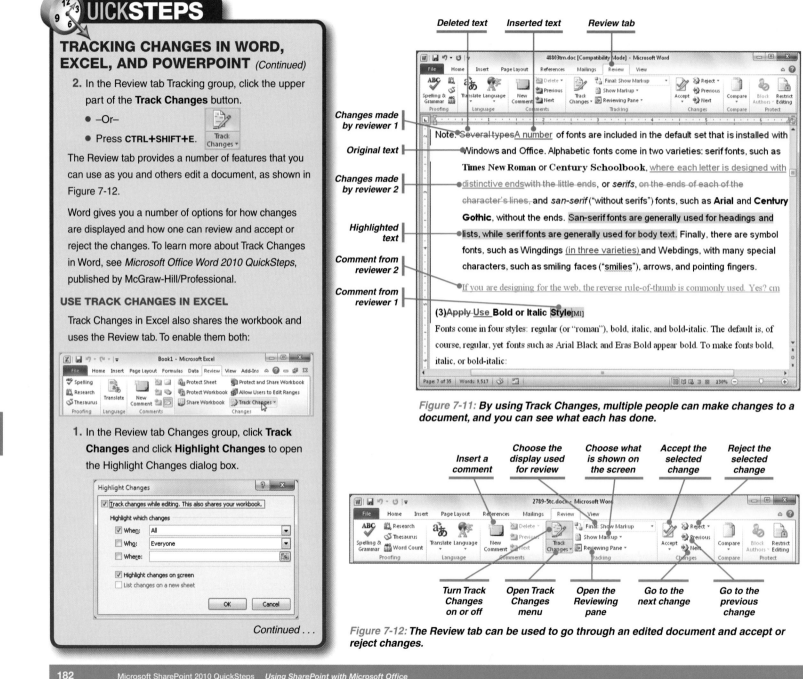

Deleted text **Inserted text** **Review tab**

Changes made by reviewer 1
Original text
Changes made by reviewer 2
Highlighted text
Comment from reviewer 2
Comment from reviewer 1

Figure 7-11: **By using Track Changes, multiple people can make changes to a document, and you can see what each has done.**

Insert a comment · Choose the display used for review · Choose what is shown on the screen · Accept the selected change · Reject the selected change

Turn Track Changes on or off · Open Track Changes menu · Open the Reviewing pane · Go to the next change · Go to the previous change

Figure 7-12: **The Review tab can be used to go through an edited document and accept or reject changes.**

TRACKING CHANGES IN WORD, EXCEL, AND POWERPOINT *(Continued)*

2. If it isn't already checked, click **Track Changes While Editing**.

- To highlight all changes, deselect the **When**, **Who**, and **Where** check boxes.

- To selectively highlight changes, select options from the When and/or Who drop-down list boxes, and/or click the **Where** text box, and select the range where you want changes highlighted.

- To view changes onscreen, select **Highlight Changes On Screen**.

- To view changes on a separate worksheet, select **List Changes On A New Sheet**. After saving your workbook, a History worksheet is added to the workbook, as shown in Figure 7-13.

3. Click **OK** to close the Highlight Changes dialog box. Click **OK** again to acknowledge that no changes were found meeting the default settings (assuming you didn't make any); or in the case of a new workbook, name and save the file in the Save As dialog box that appears.

USE COMPARE IN POWERPOINT

PowerPoint 2010 allows you to compare two presentations, one designated to contain the merged changes. This is useful, for instance, when you have a presentation that has been reviewed by others and you want to select and merge desired edits. You compare changes slide by slide, seeing what is different between the slides and accepting those from the secondary file to be merged onto the designated presentation.

Continued . . .

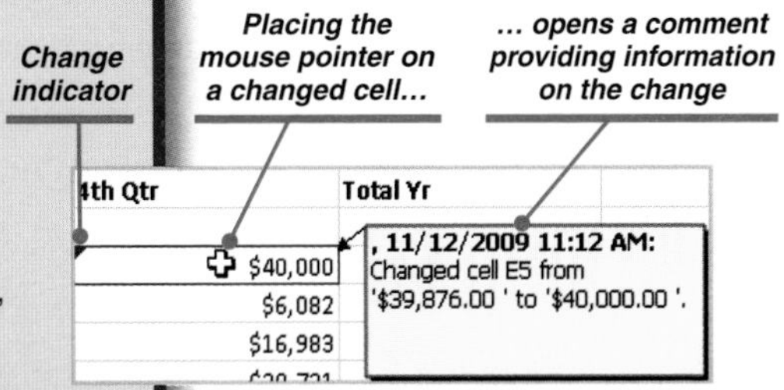

7. Click **Navigate Up** and choose the level you want to go to, to continue your work.

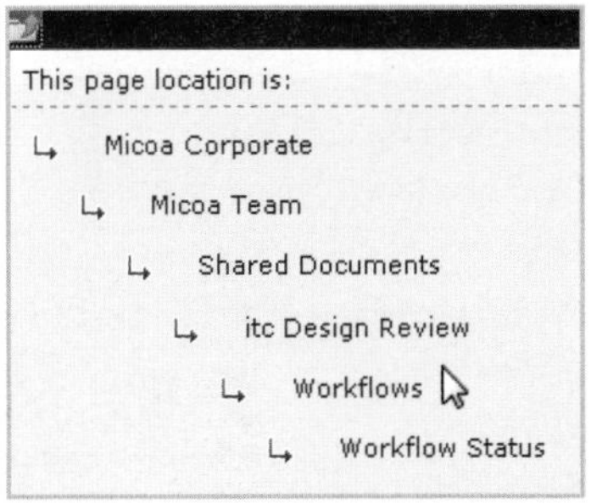

If your objective is to **keep** a complete record of what has happened and is scheduled to happen in the creation, review, and approval of a document, then SharePoint satisfies that objective very well.

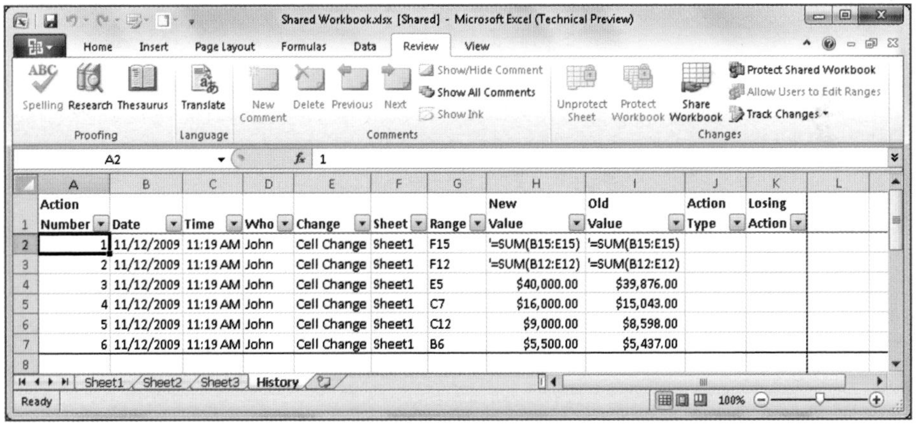

Placing the mouse pointer on a changed cell... **... opens a comment providing information on the change**

Change indicator

Figure 7-13: In shared workbooks, you can opt to have changes recorded on a separate History worksheet.

QUICKSTEPS

TRACKING CHANGES IN WORD, EXCEL, AND POWERPOINT *(Continued)*

1. In PowerPoint, open the slide show containing the slides to be updated. This file will contain the merge results.

2. On the Review tab, click **Compare** in the Compare group. The Choose File To Merge With Current Presentation dialog box appears.

3. Find the presentation containing the changed slides, and click **Merge**. The Compare view will be displayed (see Figure 7-14). Also, when you have done this, more of the commands in the Compare group become available.

4. You have these options:

   • Click **Slides** on the Revisions pane to see the slide being compared.

   • Click the **Revision** icons to see the list of changes to a slide. Place a check mark next to the changes you want to retain and merge into the primary file. If you change your mind, you can clear the check box and restore the original.

   • Once you have identified those changes you want to merge, click **Accept** in the Compare group. If you want to reject them, click **Reject**.

   • Click **Previous** and **Next** in the Compare group to see the previous and next slide with changes, respectively.

   • Click **Reviewing Pane** to toggle the pane on and off.

5. When you are finished with the merge, click **End Review** and save your file. Click **Yes** to verify that you do indeed want to end the compare process.

Work with Outlook

Outlook generally represents an individual's information—an individual's e-mail, calendar, contacts, and tasks—while SharePoint represents similar information for a group. Microsoft has provided a number of areas where the two programs can transfer and/or link information between them, as well as connect to and/or create elements in SharePoint from Outlook. Among these are:

• Connecting with a list or library

• Linking discussions

• Transferring contacts

• Linking calendars

• Linking meetings

• Transferring events

• Using e-mail and RSS

Link and Transfer Information

Many users make heavy use of Outlook and SharePoint, so it is important that you can easily connect, transfer, and/or link elements between the two applications.

CONNECT WITH LISTS AND LIBRARIES

From Outlook you can connect to a SharePoint list or library, synchronize items between the two, and view and edit offline (when you are not connected with the SharePoint server) the content of the list or library in Outlook.

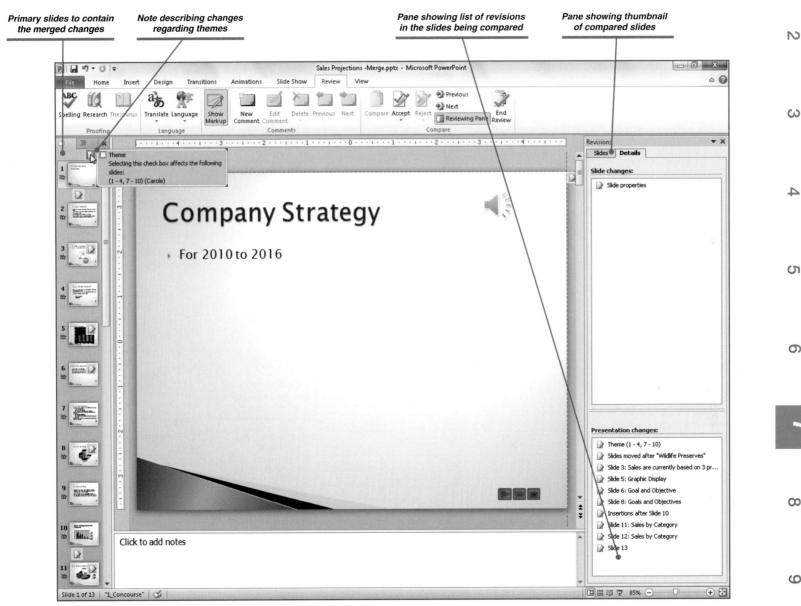

Primary slides to contain the merged changes

Note describing changes regarding themes

Pane showing list of revisions in the slides being compared

Pane showing thumbnail of compared slides

Figure 7-14: **The Compare feature in PowerPoint allows you to compare slides from two presentations and select which changes should be merged with the primary presentation.**

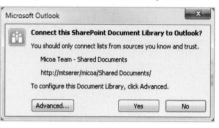

1. In SharePoint, navigate to the list or library to which you want to connect. Click the list or library title to open it in its own page and make the Library Tools tabs available.

2. Click **Library Tools | Library**, in the ribbon that opens click **Connect & Export**, and then click **Connect To Outlook**, or just click **Connect To Outlook** if your window is large enough.

3. Click **Allow** to allow the SharePoint server to open Outlook, and then click **Yes** to confirm you want to connect the list or library to Outlook.

4. Outlook will open and display the list or library from SharePoint, as shown in Figure 7-15. From here you can do most of the things you can do with the list items or library documents that you can do in SharePoint, including viewing and editing the items offline.

*Figure 7-15: **Outlook provides a way to view and work with SharePoint lists and libraries offline.***

5. **To work with a list item or library document**, double-click the item in Outlook. Depending on the item and your security settings, you may be asked if you want to enable access to the item. If you do, click **Enable**. If you are working offline, you will be told that to modify the item you'll have to edit it offline. Click **Edit Offline** and then click **OK** to temporarily store the document offline. The item or document is saved in a SharePoint Drafts folder and will open in its application, as you can see in Figure 7-16.

6. Edit or change the item and then save it, if offline, on your local computer at the location suggested. The next time you are online with your SharePoint server, you can upload the item or document you changed. You can tell the items or documents that need to be uploaded by the icon in the lower-right corner.

itc User Guide.docx	Wed 5/5	
MTSERER\marty		

NOTE

If you get an error trying to save or resave a document back to SharePoint, that means you have to go to the SharePoint site and upload the file as a new file; you can't replace the existing file.

Please review itc Design Review - Task

File | Task | Insert | Format Text | Review | Add-Ins

Save & Close | Delete | Forward | Open in Browser | OneNote | Task | Details | Reply | Reply All | Forward | Open this Task | Address Book | Check Names | Categorize | Follow Up | Zoom

Actions | Show | Respond | Manage Task | Names | Tags | Zoom

Assigned To... | MTSERER\marty

Subject: | Please review itc Design Review

Start date: | Tue 5/11/2010 | Status: | Not Started
Due date: | Tue 6/15/2010 | Priority: | Normal | % Complete: | 0%

Reminder: | None | None

Task assigned by MTSERER\marty on 5/10/2010.

Due by 6/15/2010.
Please proment.vide feedback on this docu
To complete this task:

1. Review itc Design Review.docx.
2. Perform the specific activities required for this task.
3. Open this task to mark the task as completed.

In Shared Folder: | Micoa Team - Tasks | Last modified by System Account on Mon 10:46 PM

*Figure 7-16: **Downloading your tasks from SharePoint to Outlook is a good way to keep track of what you have to do.***

TIP

You can check your connection between Outlook and SharePoint. In Outlook click the **File** tab, if it isn't open, click **Info** on the left, and then click **Account Settings** twice. In the Account Settings dialog box that appears click the **SharePoint Lists** tab.

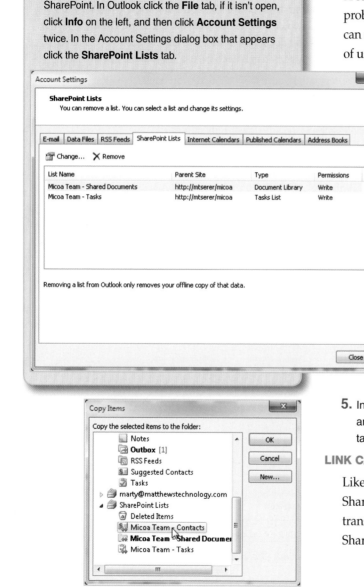

LINK AND TRANSFER CONTACTS

A contact list is, of course, central to Outlook's e-mail operation, and you probably have one with both professional and personal addresses in it. SharePoint can also maintain a contact list that is generally limited to professional contacts of use to many of the people using the site. Therefore, it makes sense to transfer some of your contacts to the SharePoint list if those contacts are useful to other site users and you may want access to SharePoint's contacts. Here's how:

1. In SharePoint, navigate to the contact list to which you want to add some of your contacts and open it in its own page with the List Tools tabs displayed.

2. Click **List Tools | List** to open it in the ribbon. Click **Connect & Export** and then click **Connect To Outlook**; or just click **Connect To Outlook** if it is visible.

3. Click **Allow** and click **Yes** to open Outlook and display the SharePoint Contacts list. You can now use this list in Outlook as you would other contact lists.

4. To transfer some of your contacts to the SharePoint Contacts list, open your contacts list in Outlook, select the contacts you want to transfer (hold down **SHIFT** to select a contiguous group of contacts or hold down **CTRL** to select separate contacts), right-click one of the selected contacts, click **Move**, and click **Copy To Folder**, as shown in Figure 7-17.

5. In the Copy Items dialog box, scroll down to and select the SharePoint Contacts list and then click **OK**. Click **Yes** to continue the transfer. If you are online, the transfer will take place immediately and your contacts will be available to other site users.

LINK CALENDARS AND EXCHANGE EVENTS

Like contacts, in Outlook you probably maintain your personal calendar, while SharePoint keeps your team's schedule, and it is reasonable that there is some transference between the two, even to the extent that you want to create a SharePoint meeting workspace site from Outlook.

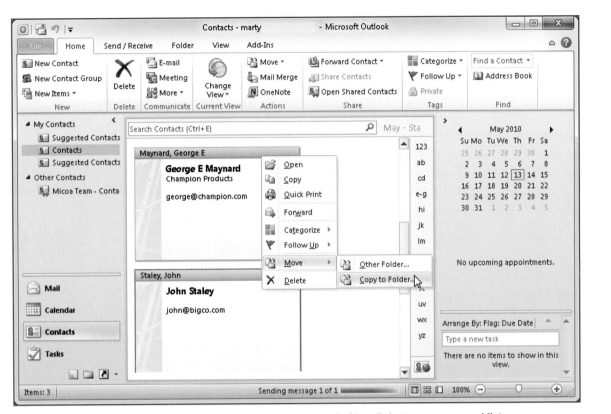

Figure 7-17: **You can move your contacts to SharePoint and those in SharePoint to your personal list.**

1. In SharePoint, navigate to the calendar you want to share with Outlook and open it in its own page. Click the **Calendar Tools I Calendar** tab, and click **Connect To Outlook**.

2. Click **Allow** and click **Yes** to open Outlook. In the default view, the two calendars will open side by side, where you can drag appointments between the two calendars, as shown in Figure 7-18.

3. When you drag a SharePoint event to Outlook, it is copied there. If it is a recurring event, you will be asked if you want its recurrence transferred. When you drag an Outlook event to SharePoint, you are asked if you want to continue. Click **Yes**.

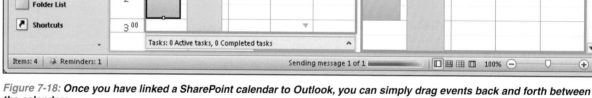

Figure 7-18: *Once you have linked a SharePoint calendar to Outlook, you can simply drag events back and forth between the calendars.*

NOTE

To fully use e-mail and RSS feeds with SharePoint, SharePoint must be set up for both incoming and outgoing mail at three levels. Two of the levels, at the server farm and at the Central Administration site, must be done by a SharePoint administrator. The third level, lists and libraries, you can control, as described in this chapter.

Use E-mail and RSS

SharePoint allows you to send e-mail to its various lists and libraries, and they can send you e-mail, as well as provide RSS (Real Simple Syndication) feeds to you. As you read in Chapter 6, SharePoint alerts can send you both e-mail and RSS feeds, and discussion boards can be posted to via e-mail. Here we'll look a bit more at alerts and discussions, as well as how to set up any list or library to receive e-mail, and in some instances send it.

![Screenshot of SharePoint RSS settings page]

Site Actions ▾

MTSERER\marty ▾

Micoa Team ▸ Site Settings ▸ RSS
Use this page to enable/disable RSS feeds for this site collection

I Like It   Tags & Notes

Home   Quarterly Budget Review   Planning Group

Libraries
Site Pages
Shared Documents

Lists
Calendar
Tasks
Contacts
Parts
Issues

Discussions
Team Discussion

Enable RSS

☑ Allow RSS feeds in this site

Allow RSS feeds in this site

Advanced Settings
Specify the site-wide channel elements for the RSS feeds.

Copyright:

Managing Editor:

Webmaster:

Time To Live (minutes):
60

OK   Cancel

*Figure 7-19: **While RSS should be running by default, check to make sure it hasn't been turned off.***

ENABLE AND USE RSS FEEDS

By default, RSS is enabled on new sites, lists, and libraries, so unless it has been turned off, it should be available to you. We'll check that and set up and use RSS in the next set of steps.

1. Confirm with your SharePoint administrator that sending e-mail and RSS feeds has been enabled at the server farm and site collection levels. The following steps assume that they have.

2. Navigate to the site Home page with the lists and/or libraries for which you want to send e-mail and RSS feeds.

3. Click **Site Actions** and then click **Site Settings**. Under Site Administration, click **RSS**. In the RSS settings page that opens, confirm that **Allow RSS Feeds In This Site** is checked, as shown in Figure 7-19. If not, click it; then, in any case, click **OK**.

4. Click **Home** and navigate to the list or library from which you want an RSS feed, and click the title bar to open it in its own page with the List or Library Tools available. (We'll continue with a library, but this procedure could apply to a list.)

5. Click **Library Tools | Library** and in the ribbon that opens, click **Settings** and then click **Library Settings**. Under Communications, click **RSS Settings**.

6. In the RSS Settings page that opens (see Figure 7-20), confirm that **Yes** is checked under Allow RSS For This List. Leave the default settings for RSS Channel Information and Document Options, click the columns that you want in the feed, make any desired changes to the Item Limits, and click **OK**.

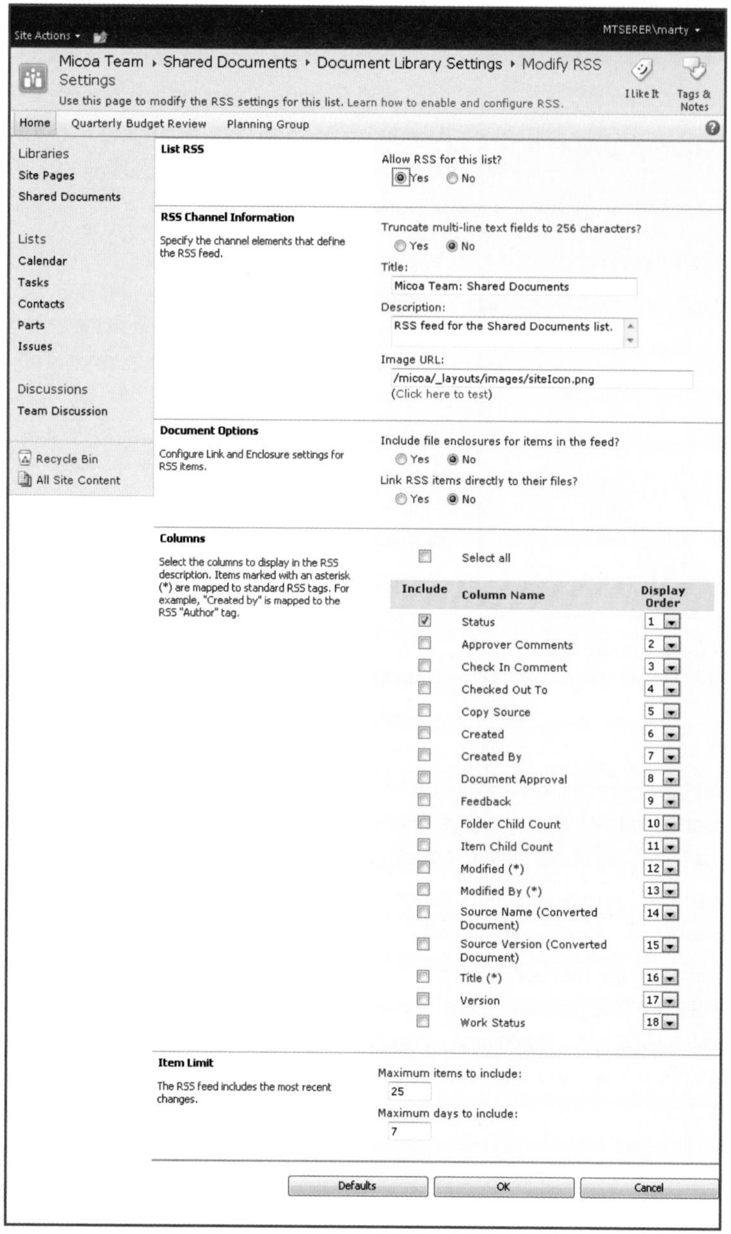

Figure 7-20: *You can select the information that an RSS feed sends out.*

7. To view the RSS feed for the library, click the library name in the breadcrumb navigation, click **Library Tools I Library**, and in the ribbon that opens, click **RSS Feed**. The library's RSS feed page opens, as shown in Figure 7-21.

8. Click **Subscribe To This Feed** to open a dialog box of that name. If desired, click **Add To Favorites Bar**, and then click **Subscribe**.

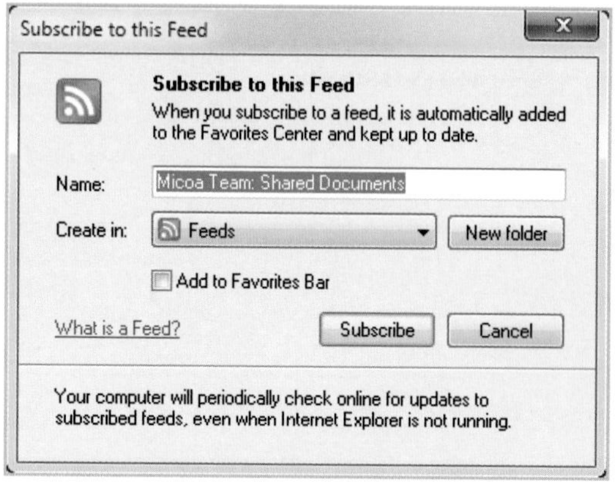

9. Without necessarily being in your SharePoint site, you can open Internet Explorer, click the RSS feed icon on the right of Internet Explorer's tab bar, and click your library's feed to see it.

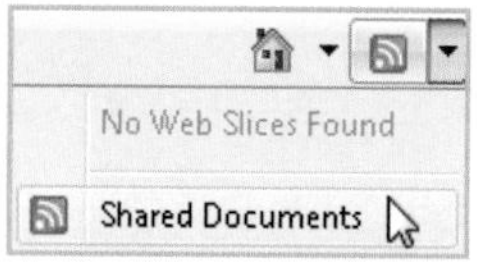

ENABLE E-MAIL

Some lists (such as tasks and issues) can send e-mail to you when list items change, which is enabled at the list level. Here's how to set that up.

1. Navigate to the list from which you want to send e-mail. Click its title to open the list in its own page.

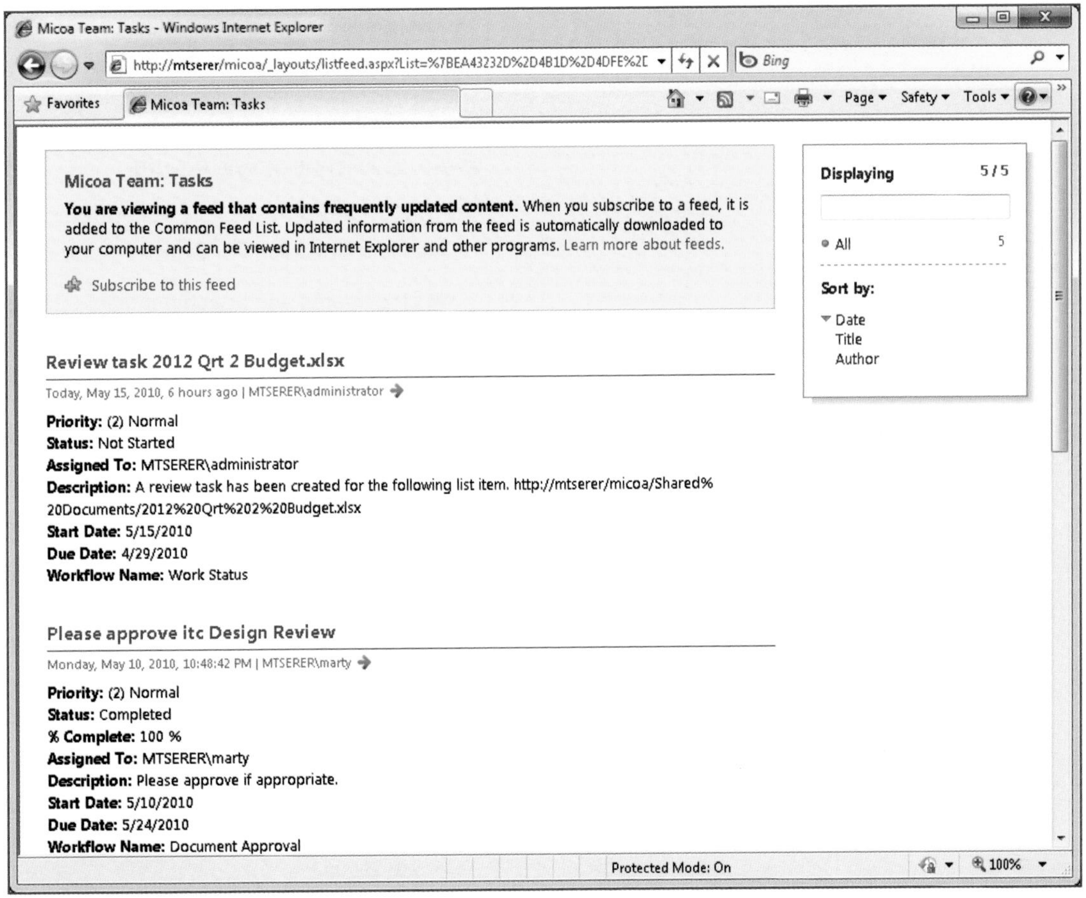

Figure 7-21: *RSS feeds can send you a large amount of information that might be easier to obtain on your SharePoint site.*

TIP

You can also view RSS feeds in Outlook. Just copy the URL for the feed (shown in Figure 7-21), right-click the RSS symbol in your Outlook Inbox, and then choose **Add A New RSS Feed**.

2. Click the **List Tools | List** tab, click **List Settings**, and click **Advanced Settings**. Under E-mail Notification, confirm that Yes is selected to send e-mail when ownership is assigned or an item has been changed.

E-Mail Notification	
Send e-mail when ownership is assigned or when an item has been changed.	Send e-mail when ownership is assigned? ● Yes ○ No

3. Make any other changes desired, scroll to the bottom of the page, and click **OK**. Click the list in the breadcrumb navigation to return to the list itself. Changes made to items assigned to you or new assignments should be sent automatically to your e-mail address.

ENABLE AND RECEIVE E-MAIL

Your SharePoint site can be configured to receive e-mail that adds content to lists and libraries. For example, you can e-mail:

- **Documents and attachments** to a library in lieu of uploading them
- **An entry** to a blog
- **An announcement** to an announcement list
- **A new discussion or a comment** to a discussion board
- **A meeting request** to a team calendar
- **A task** to a task list

To do this, you need to add an e-mail address to the list or library you want to send e-mail to. Before you can do that, however, the SharePoint server must be configured to facilitate e-mail service and SharePoint Central Administration needs to be set up to handle incoming e-mail. Both of these tasks require, at a minimum, a SharePoint administrator, and probably an IT professional is required to add e-mail service to the server.

1. Check with your SharePoint administrator to see if your server and SharePoint Central Administration are set up to handle incoming e-mail. What follows assumes that they are set up.

2. Navigate to the list or library (we'll use a list here) to which you want to send e-mail. Click the title bar to open the list in its own page.

Communications
Incoming e-mail settings
RSS settings

3. Click **List Tools I List** and click **List Settings**. Under Communications, click **Incoming E-mail Settings**.

4. In the E-mail Settings page that opens (see Figure 7-22), click **Yes** to allow incoming e-mail, enter a mail box name for the list, and then review and change as needed the remaining settings on the page. Not all elements will have the same settings, but they are all reasonably explained.

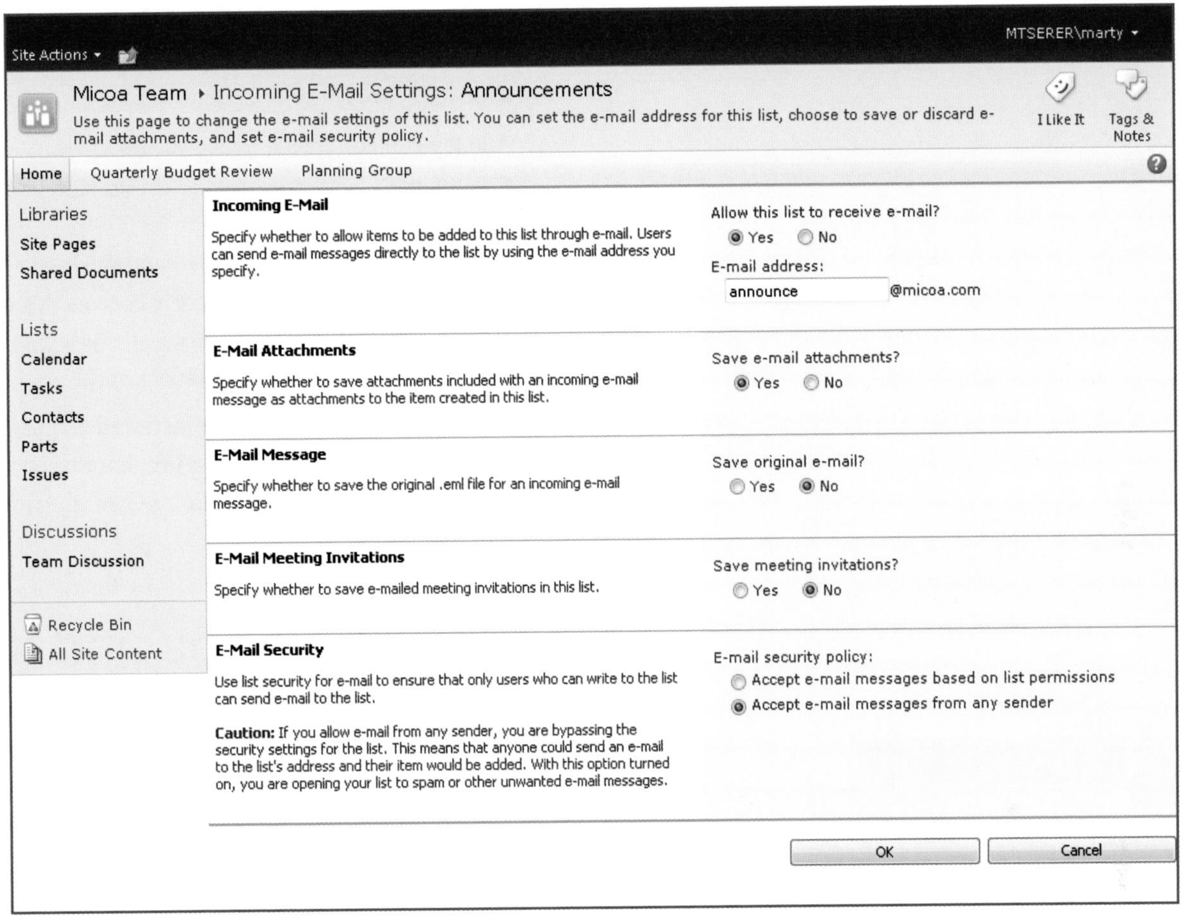

*Figure 7-22: **Setting up such lists as Announcements and Tasks to receive e-mail allows you to update them remotely.***

5. When you have completed the settings you want, click **OK**. Note that the full e-mail address you will need to use to send mail has been added at the top under List Settings.

List Information	
Name:	Announcements
Web Address:	http://mtserer/micoa/Lists/Announcements/AllItems.aspx
Description:	Use this list to track upcoming events, status updates or other team news.
E-Mail Address:	announce@micoa.com

6. To send an e-mail to a list or library, open Outlook (or any e-mail program), open a new message window, and fill out the message as follows:

- **In the To or Cc** text boxes, enter the full e-mail address noted in step 5.
- **In the subject**, enter anything you want, it is not used by SharePoint.
- **In the body**, enter content to go in lists, such as announcements and tasks, or the post to discussions and blogs.
- **In appointments or meeting requests** (Outlook only), enter events for calendars.
- **Add attachments** that you want to become files added to libraries.

7. When the message is ready, click **Send**. If all is working correctly, the content of your message should appear in your list or library.

If the information is not being transferred from e-mail to SharePoint, you will need to talk to your SharePoint administrator because there are a number of settings at the server and SharePoint Central Administration levels that need to be set correctly.

Work with Forms and InfoPath

SharePoint and InfoPath jointly provide a powerful way to create, distribute, fill out, and handle completed forms. SharePoint provides a form library that is specifically set up to work with InfoPath forms, and is used for distributing the forms and handling them and their data when they are returned. InfoPath provides tools for creating and filling out forms that work well with SharePoint and provide data that can be easily extracted and analyzed.

InfoPath is actually two programs: one to design and build forms, and one to fill them out. For the work in this section, you will need InfoPath Designer on the local client computer you are using (it comes with Office Professional Plus). With SharePoint Server available to you, you do not need InfoPath Filler (which comes with InfoPath Designer) because SharePoint Server converts InfoPath forms into ones that can be filled out in a browser. Also, InfoPath must be set up in SharePoint Central Administration, which is a job for a SharePoint administrator.

TIP

SharePoint Server 2010 comes with more than 20 form templates that are primarily used with workflows and include collecting signatures, routing tasks, approving, and publishing. These form templates must be installed by a SharePoint administrator in SharePoint Central Administration.

Once that is done, a SharePoint form library needs to be created and a form template needs to be created and published to the library. Then others can fill out forms based on the template and SharePoint can store and manage the returns. These are the tasks discussed here.

Prepare a Form Library for Use

To prepare a form library for use, it must be created and then a form template added, either by uploading one or creating a new one with InfoPath (the recommended approach). The process that works the best is to have a forms library for a single forms template that is repeatedly used to generate forms that are filled out and stored in the library. The library and template are linked, and the completed forms and the template are linked.

CREATE A FORM LIBRARY

Creating a form library is like creating any other element in SharePoint, a task you have now done numerous times. Here we will assume that you want the form library on its own page, but there is nothing requiring this.

1. In SharePoint, from the Home page of the site in which you want the form library, click **Site Actions** and click **New Page**.

2. In the New Page dialog box, enter a page name and click **Create**. The new page will open with the Editing Tools tabs enabled and a table with a single cell at the top of the page.

3. Assuming that you want to add a title and narrative on how you want the forms used, enter and format those now.

4. When you have entered the desired text, click the **Editing Tools I Insert** tab, click **New List**, enter a list title, under Libraries click **Form Library**, and click **OK**.

5. The new form library will appear. Click **Save & Close** in the tab bar.

NOTE

You could store forms in any library, but by using the Form Library template you get a connection to InfoPath, as well as a number of unique forms-related settings. In addition, when users submit InfoPath forms to a form library, the field data from the form can become the columns displayed on the form library views pages. You choose which fields to display when you publish your InfoPath form to the form library.

Site Actions ▾ | Browse | Page | MTSERER\administrator ▾

Planning Forms
Home
How To Use This Library

Planning Forms

Please use these forms for planning purposes.

Libraries
Site Pages
Shared Documents
Forms

Forms

	Type	Name	Modified	Modified By	Checked Out To

There are no items to show in this view of the "Forms" document library. To add a new item, click "New" or "Upload".

➕ Add document

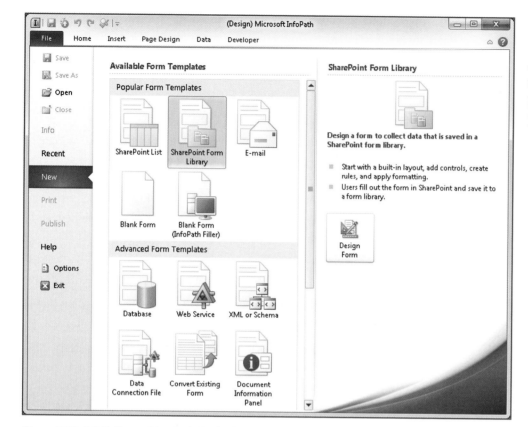

Figure 7-23: *InfoPath provides tools for both creating and filling out forms.*

CREATE A FORM IN INFOPATH

You can create forms in Word, Excel, or Adobe Acrobat and upload them to a SharePoint form library. But to get the full benefit of what is available to you with InfoPath, create a form there.

1. From your desktop or Start menu, double-click **Microsoft InfoPath Designer 2010**. In InfoPath, click the **File** tab and, if it isn't already displayed, click **New**. The available form templates will be displayed, as you can see in Figure 7-23.

2. Review the templates that are available, select several promising forms, and read their description in the right column. Click the form template you want to use, and then click **Design Form**.

3. Type or paste the URL for your SharePoint site, click **Next**, type the name of the SharePoint list you'll be creating, click **Next**, and then click **Finish**.

4. InfoPath will open in design mode. Use the tools and options available in the tabs to create your form. The majority of the tools and options are the same as those in other Microsoft Office products. If you find something you are unfamiliar with, try it out and see if it does what you want; if not, use Undo to get rid of it.

5. At any time you can click **Preview** to see how your finished form will look. Figure 7-24 shows what the form under construction on the left looks like in a preview on the right. Click **Close Preview** when you are ready.

6. While the form is under construction and not yet ready for use, save it as you would any other Office file on your hard disk or to a server share, but not to SharePoint yet.

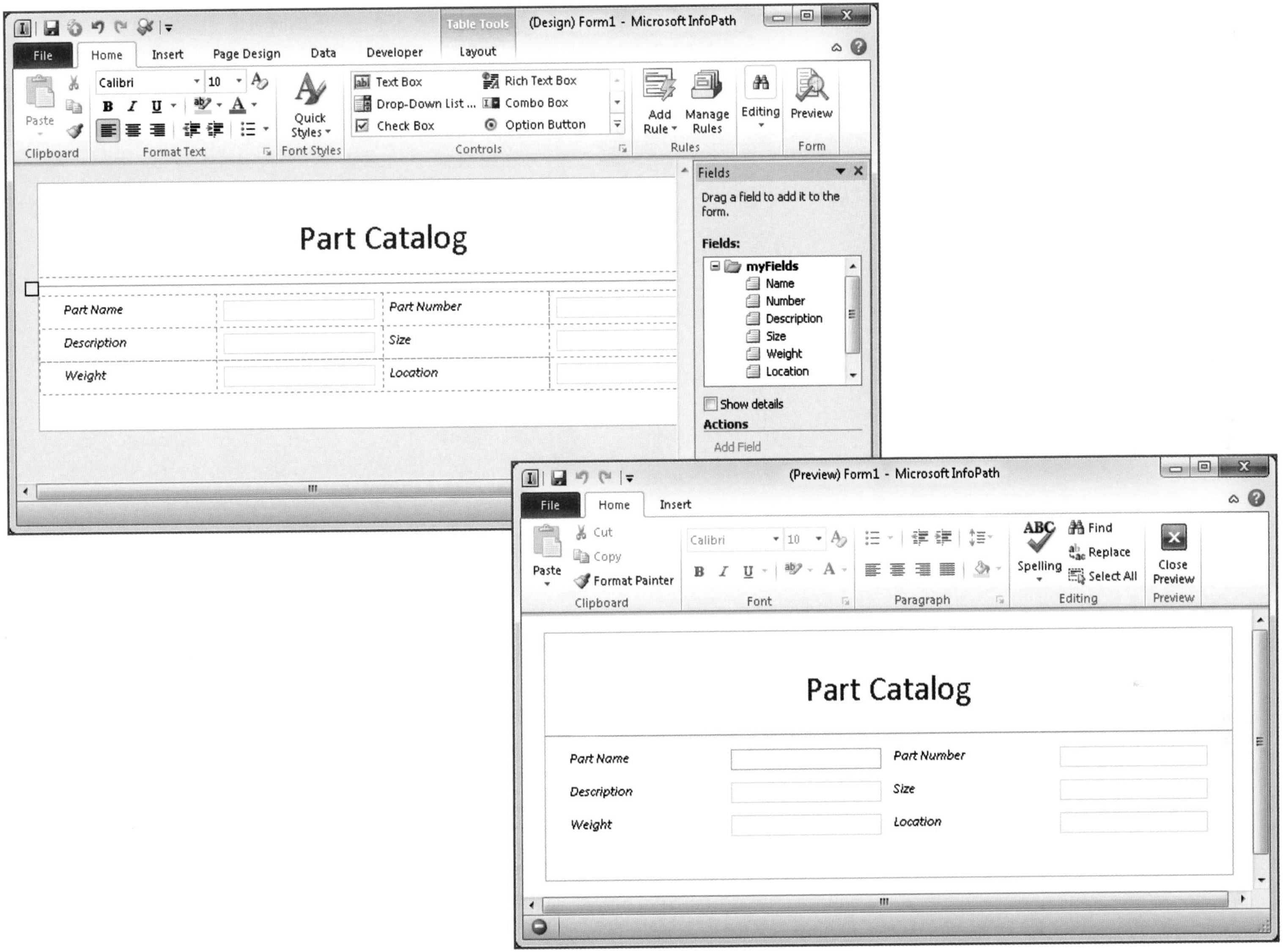

Figure 7-24: *It can be helpful to preview your form as you go along.*

7. When your form is finished and is ready to use, publish it to SharePoint by clicking the **File** tab, clicking **Publish**, and clicking **SharePoint Server** or **SharePoint List** if you chose that template.

8. The Publishing Wizard will open. Enter the URL for your forms library, which you can see in the address bar when you display the library in its own page in SharePoint, and click **Next**.

9. Choose if you want the form to be filled out in a browser (in most cases, you do), and if so, check that box.

10. Accept **Form Library** (the default) to store the form in the new form library, and click **Next**. This publishes the form as a template that will generate the forms that are filled out.

11. Choose whether you want to create a new form library or to store the form in an existing library. If the latter, select the library; otherwise, enter the name and description of the new library. In either case, click **Next**.

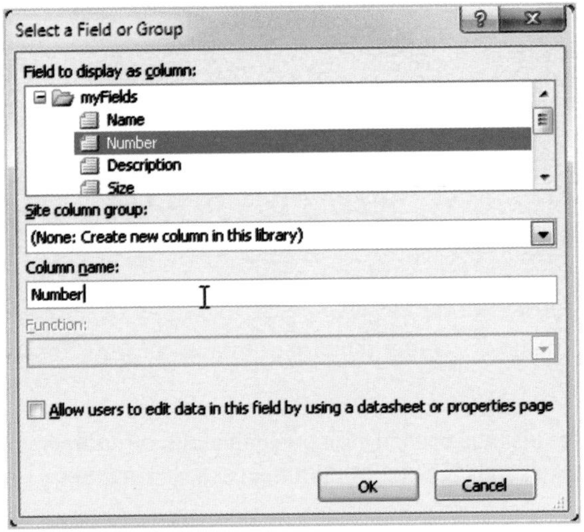

12. Click **Add** to add a form field as a working column in the SharePoint site. In the Select A Field Or Group dialog box that appears, select a field and select a column name if one exists; otherwise, in the Site Column Group, select **None; Create New Column In This Library**, enter a new column name, and click **OK**. Repeat this for each column you want.

13. When you have added all the columns you want, click **Next** and then click **Publish**. Choose if you want to e-mail the form to recipients and/or open the form library in which you stored the form. Finally, click **Close** and then close InfoPath.

Use and Manage a Form Library

When you create a form and save it in a SharePoint form library, you are saving a template that is then used to create the actual form someone can fill out. When a form is filled out, the completed form is also stored in the same SharePoint form library with the template.

Here we'll look at how forms can be filled out and how a forms library is managed.

FILL OUT A FORM

There are two ways in which a form can be filled out: in the InfoPath Filler program, or in a web browser. When the form comes from the InfoPath Designer, it is created for use with the InfoPath form filler program. SharePoint Server, however, has a built-in capability to convert the form for use with a web browser, so the person filling out the form does not need access to InfoPath Filler.

1. Navigate to the form library where you stored the InfoPath form(s) created in the previous section. It looks like there isn't anything there, but click **Add Document**. Your form will open in your browser, as you can see in Figure 7-25.

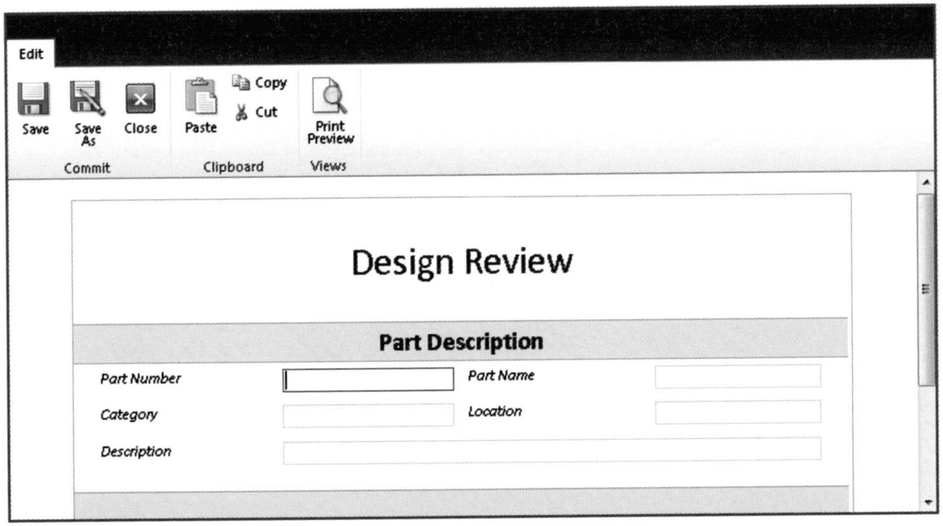

Figure 7-25: The browser-based version of your form looks and acts the same as it does in InfoPath Filler.

NOTE

The form library in SharePoint, when used with InfoPath forms, serves as a repository for filled in forms. Under most circumstances, you want to store a single form template and the filled-in copies in a single forms library.

2. Fill in the form, typing the text entries and using the other controls. When you have completed the form, click **Save**.

3. Enter a file name that both identifies the form and the person filling it out (for example, with their initials), and click **Save**.

4. Back in the form, click **Close**. Back in the SharePoint page with your form library, you'll see the form you filled out.

MANAGE A FORM LIBRARY

Like other lists and libraries, a form library has an extensive number of settings, some common to other libraries and a number that are unique to a forms library, as you can see in Figure 7-26.

1. With the form library you want to manage opened in its own page, click the **Library Tools I Library** tab, click **Settings**, and click **Library Settings**; or just click **Library Settings** if it is visible.

2. In the Forms Library Settings page that opens, the following settings groups have settings unique to forms. Click the groups and then review and change as needed the settings required for your situation.

- **Advanced Settings** has two important forms-related settings: **Document Template**, which allows you change and edit the template for that library, and **Open Documents In The Browser**, which gives you the choice of opening a form in the application that created it (InfoPath here), in a browser, or in the server default (the default selection).

- **Validation Settings**, while not unique to forms, are important because they allow you to establish validation formulas that assure the entered data is correct. See Chapter 4 for a discussion of validation settings. (InfoPath also has validation settings that you can assign on a per-field basis, so you may not need to touch this setting in SharePoint.)

Site Actions ▾   MTSERER\administrator ▾

Planning Group ▸ Forms ▸ Form Library Settings

I Like It   Tags & Notes

Planning Group

Libraries	List Information		
Site Pages			
Shared Documents	Name:	Forms	
Forms	Web Address:	http://mtserer/micoa/Planning/Planning Forms/Forms/AllItems.aspx	
	Description:		
Lists			
Calendar	General Settings	Permissions and Management	Communications
Tasks	Title, description and navigation	Delete this form library	Incoming e-mail settings
	Versioning settings	Save form library as template	RSS settings
Discussions	Advanced settings	Permissions for this form library	
Team Discussion	Validation settings	Manage files which have no checked in version	
	Column default value settings	Relink documents to this Library	
Recycle Bin	Rating settings	Workflow Settings	
All Site Content	Audience targeting settings	Enterprise Metadata and Keywords Settings	
	Metadata navigation settings	Generate file plan report	
	Per-location view settings	Information management policy settings	
	Form settings	Record declaration settings	

Figure 7-26: A form library has a number of unique settings.

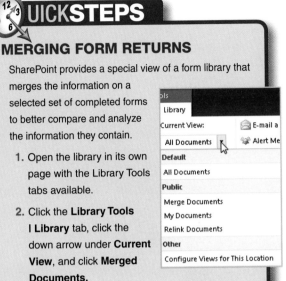

SharePoint provides a special view of a form library that merges the information on a selected set of completed forms to better compare and analyze the information they contain.

1. Open the library in its own page with the Library Tools tabs available.

2. Click the **Library Tools I Library** tab, click the down arrow under **Current View**, and click **Merged Documents.**

3. In the page that opens (see Figure 7-27), click the **Merge** check boxes for the forms you want to merge. (The original forms remain and are not changed. Rather, a new form with the merged data is created.)

4. Click the **Library Tools I Documents** tab, click **Merge** in the actions group, and click **OK** to confirm that you want to do that.

5. The InfoPath Filler will open and display the merged data on the form. If you want to save this information, click **File**, click **Save As**, enter the name you want, and click **Save.**

Menu items shown in inset:
ols
Library
Current View: E-mail a
All Documents   Alert Me
Default
All Documents
Public
Merge Documents
My Documents
Relink Documents
Other
Configure Views for This Location

You can create special views of a forms library to help analyze it.

- **Form Settings** looks like it would be an important grouping, but it has no function in InfoPath.

- **Relink Documents To This Library** attaches a completed form to its template. Normally, following the steps in this chapter, a completed form is automatically linked to its template, but if you upload a completed form by e-mail, they will not be linked. This settings group allows you to re-establish the link.

3. When you have completed each group of settings, click **OK** to return to the Form Library Settings page.

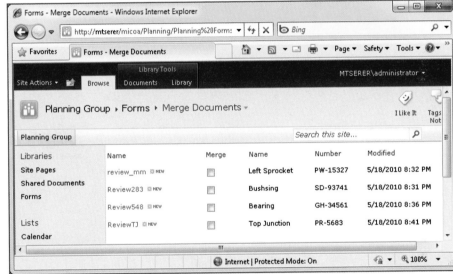

*Figure 7-27: **SharePoint allows you to merge the information on selected completed forms.***

Chapter 8
Customizing with SharePoint Designer

In this chapter you gain a better understanding of when and how to use SharePoint Designer 2010 to edit your SharePoint site. You will learn how to open your site, tackle a few common emergency tasks that sometimes come up, and get an overview of how to customize content and change site styles and master pages.

Determine When to Use SharePoint Designer

Microsoft SharePoint Designer 2010 has evolved over the years from a product called FrontPage that was an early what-you-see-is-what-you-get (WYSIWYG) Web page editing and site creation tool. SharePoint Designer 2010 can be used to make simple cosmetic changes to your SharePoint site or to enable professional developers to create or deeply modify Web Parts, pages, and more.

Plan Your Customizations

The fact is that sites created directly by SharePoint contain enough features and functionality to make them perfectly adequate for many team sites, as you've seen in the preceding chapters of this book. However, after using a SharePoint site for a time, many individuals and groups want to do more with the site. Here are some customizations to SharePoint sites that can be accomplished using SharePoint Designer.

- Move files from one document library to another or from one folder to another.
- Copy files from one SharePoint site to another.
- Remove a file's checked-out status so that others can open it once again.
- Create new pages in the site, including pages that combine simple text or graphics with Web Parts.
- Add text or graphics to pages, including images with clickable hot spots or hover effects.
- Customize the display of Web Parts in pages. For example, in a sales Web Part you can use conditional formatting to tell SharePoint to display a green light if sales goals were met and a red light if they weren't.
- Customize SharePoint workflow. SharePoint Designer 2010 includes a robust workflow editor to allow teams to modify the out-of-the-box SharePoint Approval, Feedback, and Signatures workflows.
- Change the look of your site to coordinate with your organization's branding. For example, you can use the colors in your organization's logo as the colors on your SharePoint site.
- Change the structure of pages on your site to suit your needs. For example, you can display a graphic or logo on the left navigation of every page in your site.

Identify Authorized SharePoint Designer Users

SharePoint Designer 2010 is a powerful tool that makes site customizations easy and immediate. There is no publishing required when you edit a SharePoint site with SharePoint Designer 2010; you make your change and then save it, and the update is then live and ready for site visitors to see. Therefore, you will want to make sure that only trustworthy individuals with some technical expertise are authorized to make site changes with SharePoint Designer 2010.

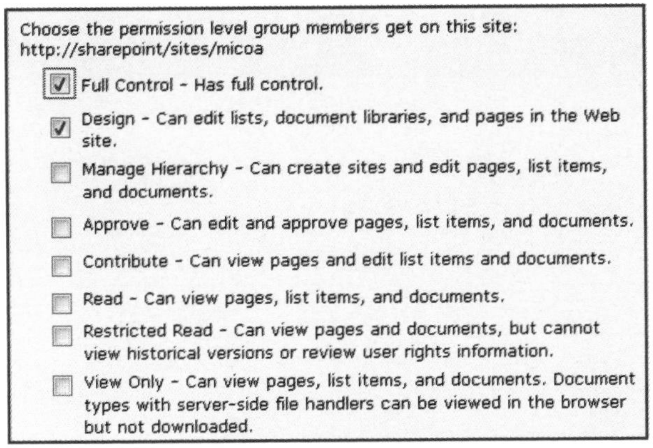

Choose the permission level group members get on this site:
http://sharepoint/sites/micoa

☑ Full Control - Has full control.

☑ Design - Can edit lists, document libraries, and pages in the Web
site.

☐ Manage Hierarchy - Can create sites and edit pages, list items,
and documents.

☐ Approve - Can edit and approve pages, list items, and documents.

☐ Contribute - Can view pages and edit list items and documents.

☐ Read - Can view pages, list items, and documents.

☐ Restricted Read - Can view pages and documents, but cannot
view historical versions or review user rights information.

☐ View Only - Can view pages, list items, and documents. Document
types with server-side file handlers can be viewed in the browser
but not downloaded.

*Figure 8-1: It is important to set the appropriate permissions
for those who will use SharePoint Designer.*

SET PERMISSIONS TO EDIT IN SHAREPOINT DESIGNER

Remember the discussion of site permissions in Chapter 3? Site groups allow us to give groups of users the same level of permissions. In order to be able to open a site with SharePoint Designer, you need to have Full Control or Design permissions. Figure 8-1 shows the permission levels that are available.

To determine your site's permissions:

1. With your site's Home page displayed on your screen, click **Site Actions** in the ribbon's tab bar.

2. Click **Site Permissions**. Figure 8-2 shows the list of groups and their permission levels.

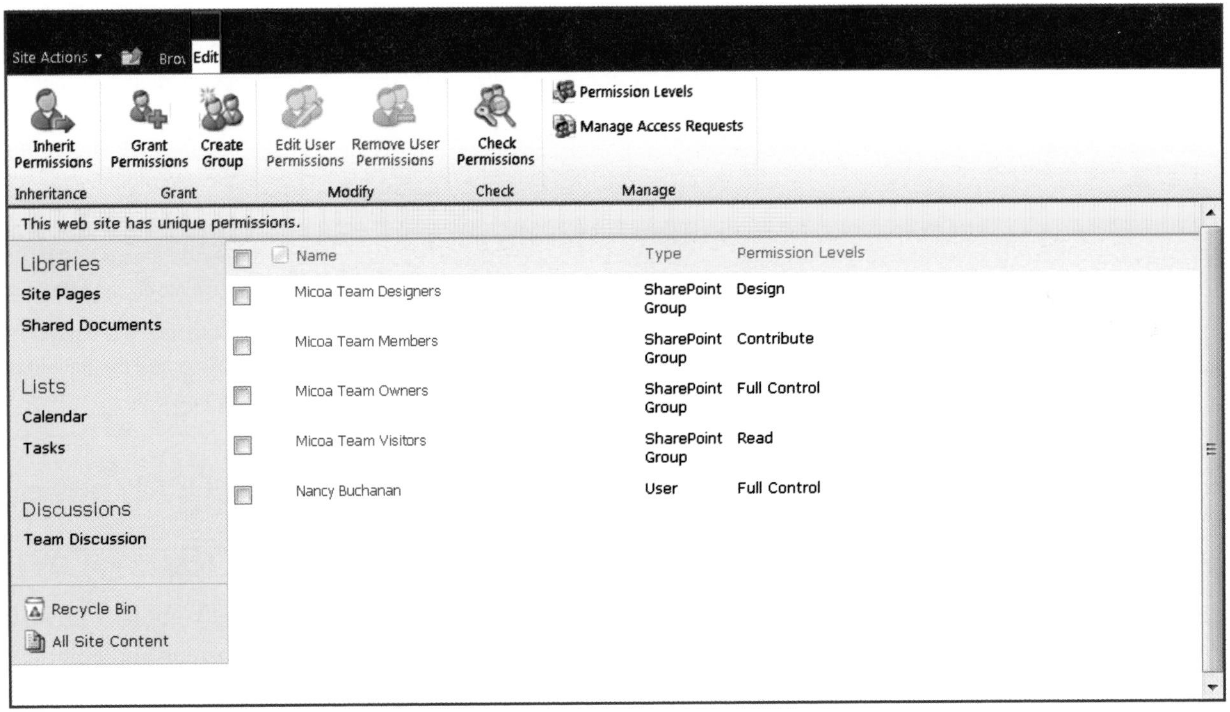

Figure 8-2: A default set of SharePoint groups is used to set permissions for sites.

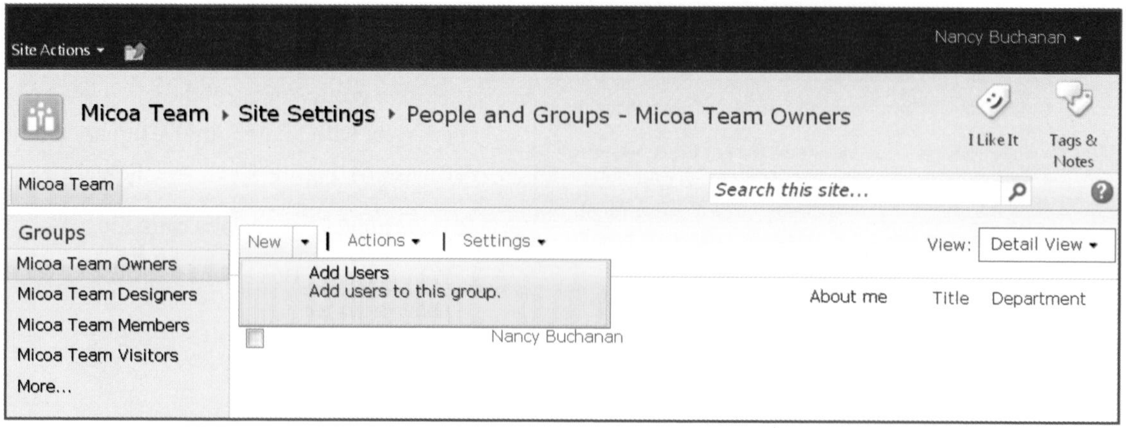

Figure 8-3: **Normally, new users are added to existing groups and are not directly assigned permissions.**

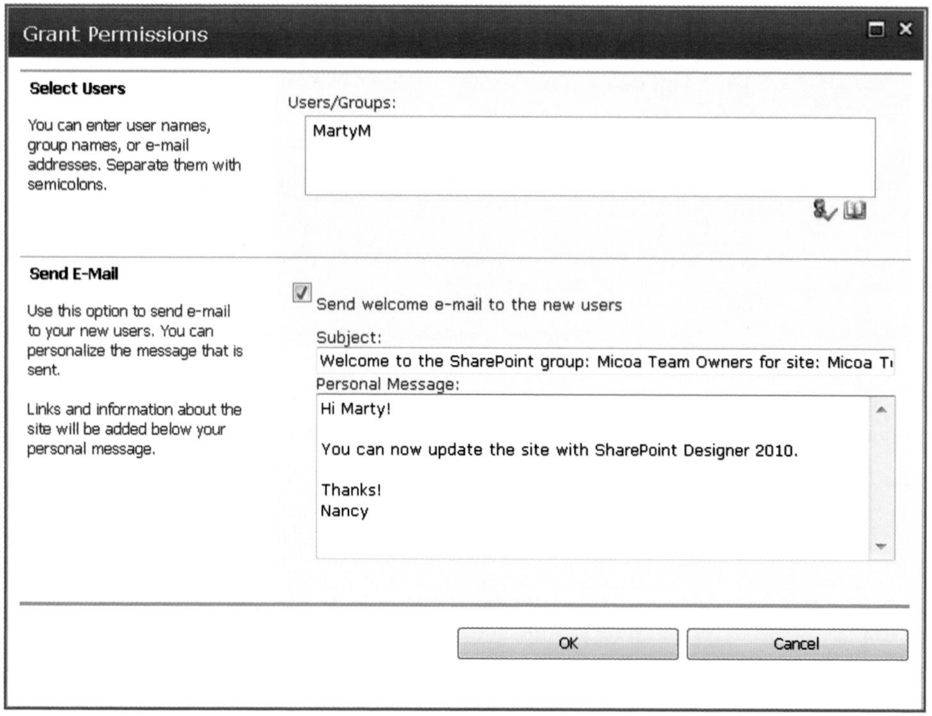

Grant Permissions

Select Users

You can enter user names, group names, or e-mail addresses. Separate them with semicolons.

Users/Groups:

MartyM

Send E-Mail

Use this option to send e-mail to your new users. You can personalize the message that is sent.

Links and information about the site will be added below your personal message.

☑ Send welcome e-mail to the new users

Subject:

Welcome to the SharePoint group: Micoa Team Owners for site: Micoa T

Personal Message:

Hi Marty!

You can now update the site with SharePoint Designer 2010.

Thanks!
Nancy

OK   Cancel

3. You need to have at least Design or Full Control permissions in order to open the site in SharePoint Designer, so you can click either the **Designers** group or the **Micoa Team Owners** group (the sample organization used in this book) in order to see who is in the group or to add a user.

4. To add a user to the group, click **Add Users** on the New menu, as shown in Figure 8-3.

5. Complete the Grant Permissions form, and then click **OK** to add the new user to the group, as shown in Figure 8-4.

Get Started with SharePoint Designer

Many Web site administrators are accustomed to opening and editing single pages and then following a publishing process to post them to

Figure 8-4: **Permission to use SharePoint Designer should be carefully thought out.**

TIP

A quick way to start SharePoint Designer and open your site at the same time is to click **Start** and then in the Search text box type <u>spdesign</u> plus the URL for your site, such as <u>spdesign http://sharepoint/sites/micoa</u>, and then press **ENTER**. This simple command opens SharePoint Designer and the site.

a production server. SharePoint 2010 sites are easier to manage than that because you can open the entire site at once, and after you edit and then save a page or other element on the site, it is updated immediately on the site. This section steps you through how to open a site in SharePoint Designer, how to open a page, and how to organize site content.

Open Your Site

Before you open your SharePoint site in SharePoint Designer, you will need to know its URL. Generally speaking, the URL to use is the complete site address without the page or folder part of the URL. For example, if you normally browse to http://*server name*/*site name*/SitePages/Home.aspx, the site URL to open in SharePoint Designer is http://*server name*/*site name*/SitePages. Once you have the URL, you can open your site in SharePoint Designer (see the Tip in this section).

1. If you don't use the Tip in this section, click **Start**, click **All Programs**, scroll down to and click **SharePoint**, and click **Microsoft SharePoint Designer 2010**.

2. On the File tab, click **Sites** and in the Open SharePoint Site section, click **Open Site**. The Open Site dialog box appears, as shown in Figure 8-5.

3. If you see your site in the list on the right, click it; otherwise, type or paste your site's URL in the Site Name box, and then click **Open**. The site opens in SharePoint Designer, as shown in Figure 8-6.

Open a Page in Your Site

The Site Objects pane on the left in SharePoint Designer 2010 makes it easy to switch back and forth between key site elements like Site Pages (the new default folder where new pages created via the browser are stored),

*Figure 8-5: **SharePoint Designer opens and works with an entire site, including all pages, graphics, and attachments.***

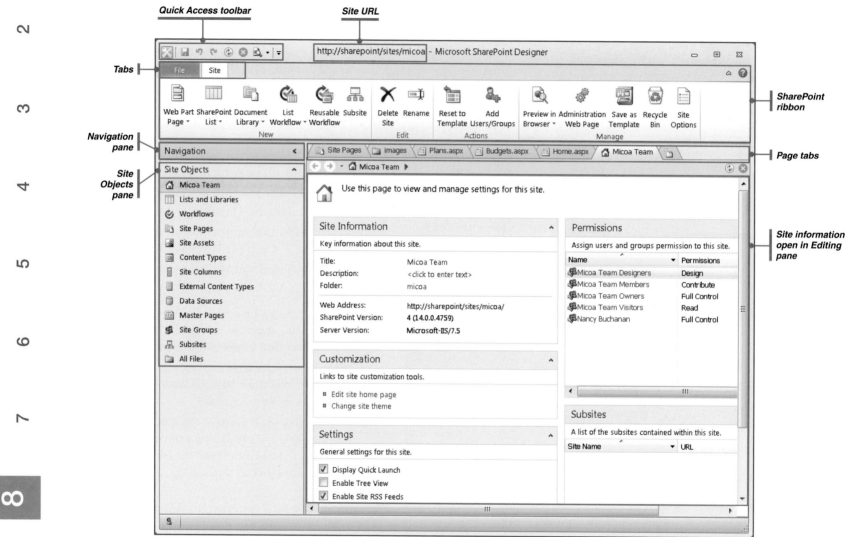

*Figure 8-6: **A site may open with this information page or displaying the Home page.***

1

2

3

4

5

6

7

8

9

Subsites, and All Files. When you click All Files, for example, a list of all folders in the site is displayed in the Editing pane, as shown in Figure 8-7.

If, in the Site Objects task pane, you move the mouse over a section and click the **Pin** icon 📌, such as All Files, an expanded view of files for that section appears below the Site Objects task pane, as shown in Figure 8-8. This is especially handy if you want to keep a folder open while you work with it.

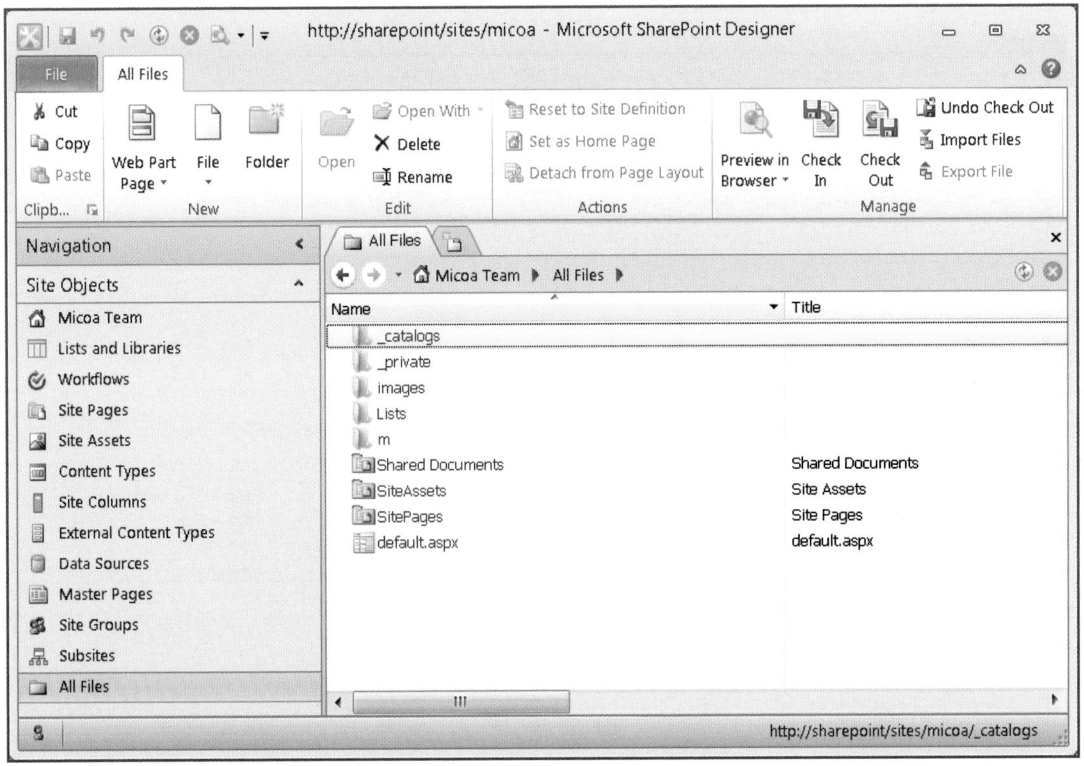

Figure 8-7: *SharePoint Designer provides easy navigation among elements such as Site Pages and All Files.*

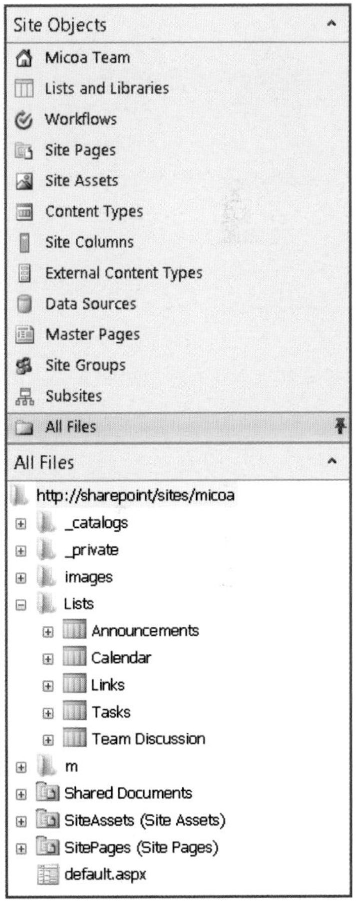

Figure 8-8: *The Pin feature is a handy way to keep a folder open.*

TIP

You can identify SharePoint document libraries in the All Files task pane by the icon to the left of the folder name 📁. Similarly, SharePoint lists are identified by this icon 📋 and the fact that they are located in the Lists folder, not at the root of the site like document libraries are.

TIP

The Home page might be located at the root of the site, but it might be in the Site Pages or other folder as well. You can identify the Home page by the icon to the left of the file name 🏠 in SharePoint Designer.

To open a page in your site:

1. Click **All Files** in the Site Objects task pane.

2. Click the page you want to open. (You may have to click to open folders to locate the file if it is located in a folder or folders. For example, the Home page in this example is in the Site Pages folder.)

3. Double-click the file; or click the file and click **Open** on the SharePoint ribbon, as shown in Figure 8-9.

4. If you try to immediately edit the page you will find that you aren't able to. That's because SharePoint Designer opens pages by default in Standard Mode, which doesn't allow edits. To change to Advanced Mode where you can edit the page, click **Advanced Mode** toward the right side of the SharePoint ribbon, as shown in Figure 8-10.

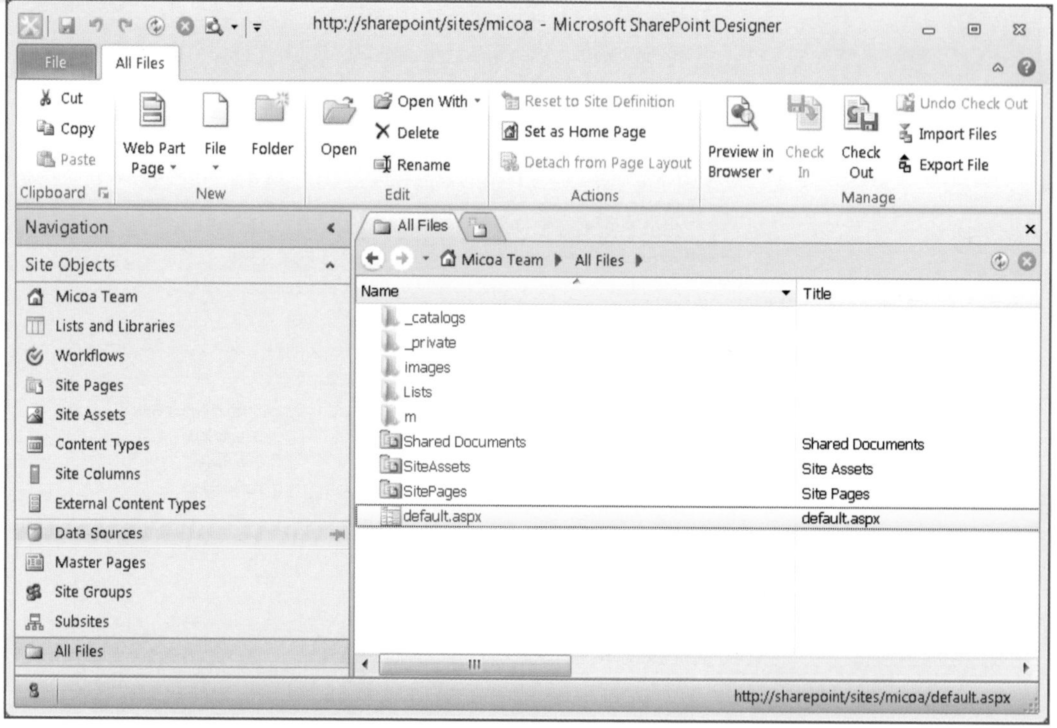

Figure 8-9: **To edit a page in SharePoint Designer means to open the page and work with both the elements on the pages as well as the code behind them.**

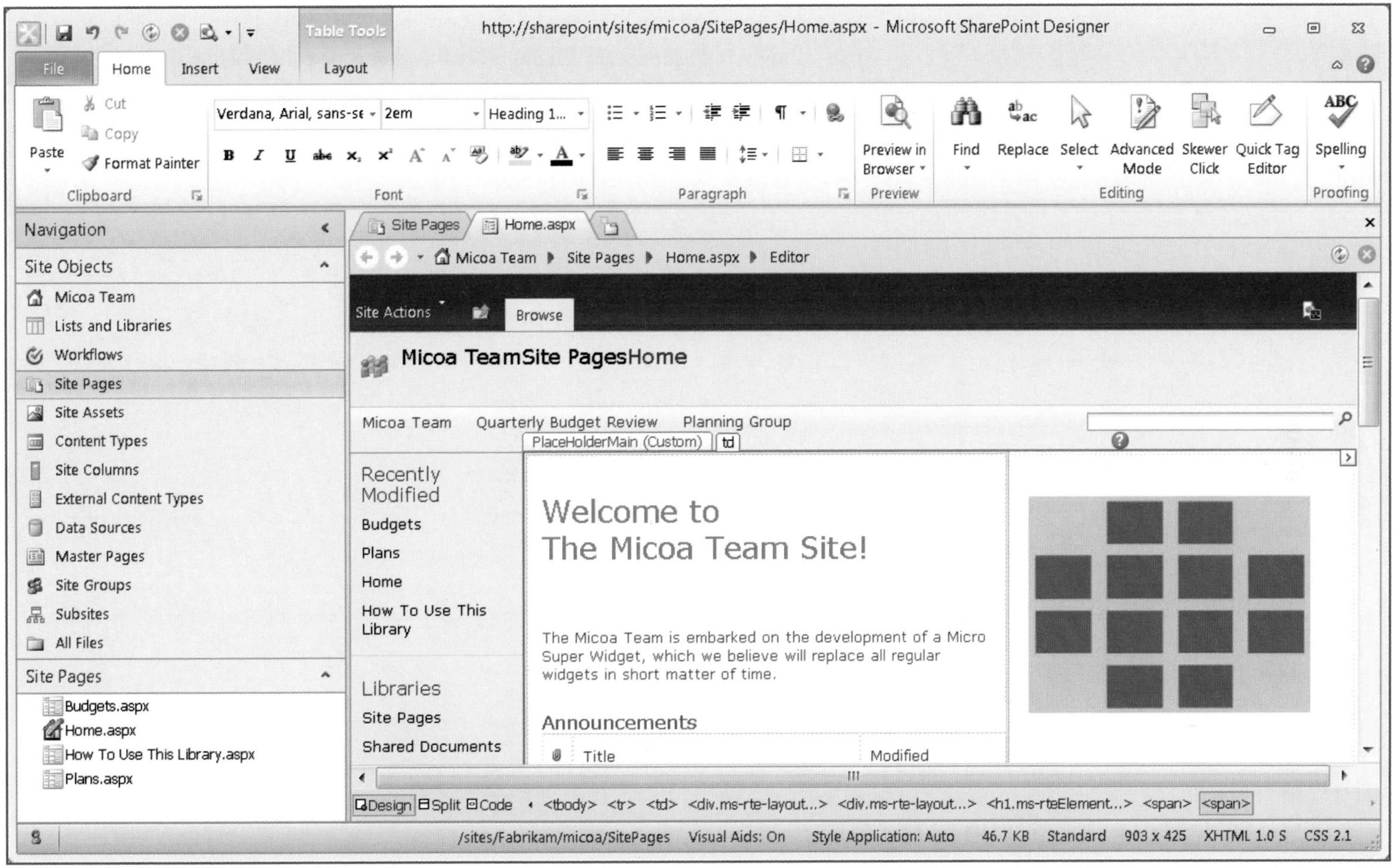

Figure 8-10: *Page opened in SharePoint Designer Editing pane, but at this point the content is not yet editable.*

TIP

Now that you know about Advanced Mode, you can save time when opening files by simply right-clicking them and then choosing **Edit File In Advanced Mode**.

CHANGE VIEWS

One of the great things about SharePoint Designer is how easily you can switch from what-you-see-is-what-you-get *Design View*, to a notepad-like *Code View*, to the combination *Split View*. The View options are located in the bottom-left area of the Editing pane when you have a page opened, and switching views is as easy as clicking **Design** or **Split** or **Code** ⎕Design ⊟Split ⊡Code . The Split View is shown in Figure 8-11. When you edit code in the code portion of the Split View, the update is instantly reflected in the design portion, making it fast even for coding experts to visualize their changes.

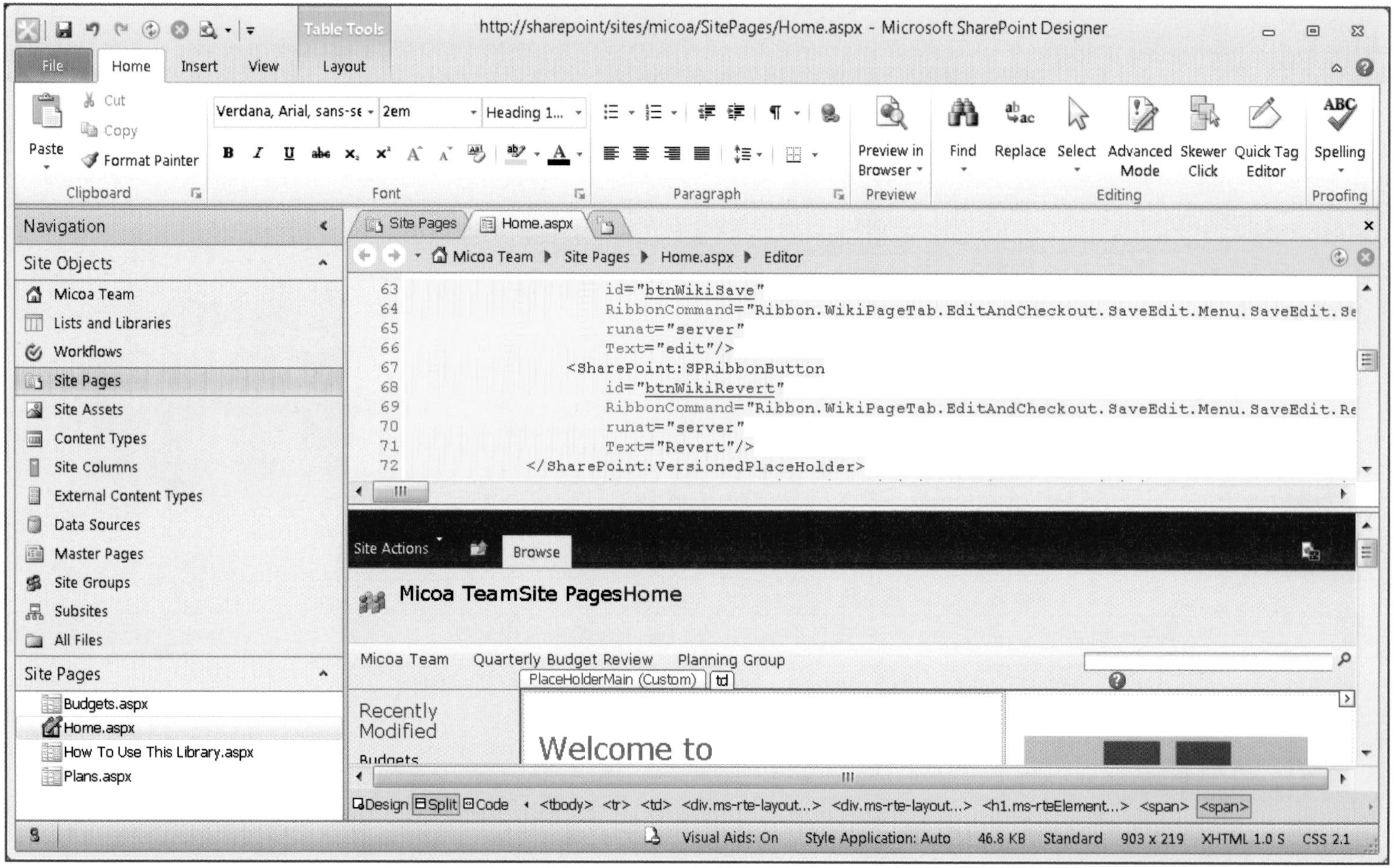

*Figure 8-11: **A page in SharePoint Designer's Split View lets you see part of a page in code and part the way it will look in a browser.***

Add Site Content

There are several ways to add or import elements, such as libraries and graphics, into your site. You could create a document library using SharePoint in a browser, but if you don't want site visitors to have access to your site files, you may want to add content to the site using SharePoint Designer.

1. In the Site Objects task pane, click **All Files** to open it.

2. Click the folder to which you want to import the image, such as the Images folder shown in Figure 8-12.

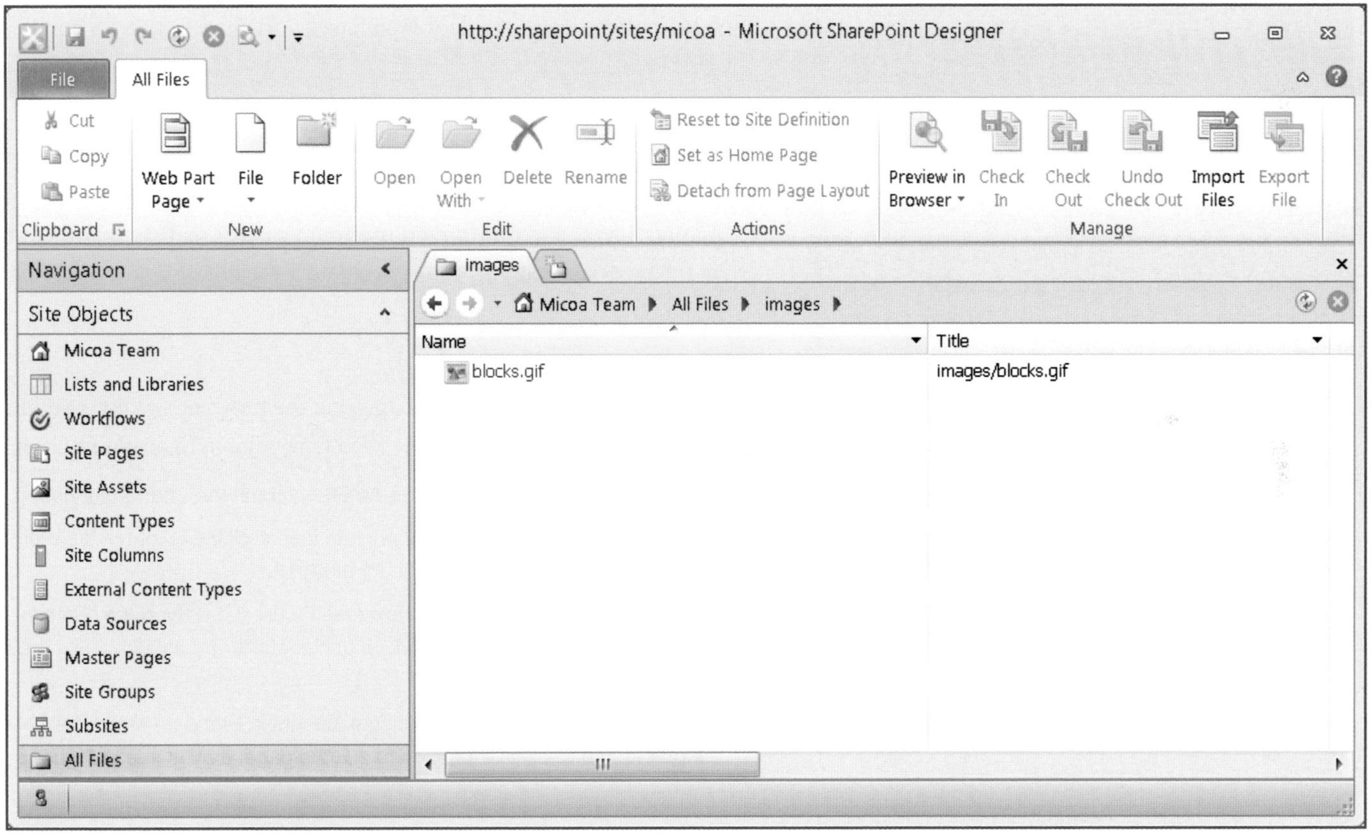

Figure 8-12: **You can import elements like graphics in SharePoint Designer and make the element files unavailable to site users.**

TIP

You can also click and drag files from Windows Explorer directly into a folder. To do so, follow steps 1 and 2 in "Add Site Content" and then drag your files from Windows Explorer into the desired folder.

QUICKSTEPS

MOVING AND COPYING FILES

A major reason that you may want to use SharePoint Designer is that it allows you to move documents from one library to another, and to copy files from one site to another.

MOVE FILES FROM ONE DOCUMENT LIBRARY TO ANOTHER

When content owners use a lot of folders, the content sometimes becomes deeply nested, resulting in frustration for those trying to find the content. If you want to reorganize content from one folder to another or from one document library to another, simply use the All Files task pane to drag, copy and paste, or cut and paste files. The All Files task pane works very much like Windows Explorer.

COPY FILES FROM ONE SITE TO ANOTHER

If you ever need to move or copy files from one site to another, SharePoint Designer makes it easy. Simply open the source site and the destination site each in SharePoint Designer; position the windows next to one another; and drag, copy and paste, or cut and paste files from the source site to the destination site.

3. On the SharePoint ribbon, click **Import Files**, click **Add File**, locate the file you want to import to the site, and then click **Open**.

4. Repeat step 3 until all of the files you want to import have been added, and then click **OK**. The file or files are imported to the site.

Start Customizing

Now that you know how to open your SharePoint site and open pages in your site, you can start customizing. In this section you will learn how to use SharePoint Designer to create a variety of new pages, add content to existing pages, customize the look of Web Parts, and get an introduction to editing workflows.

Create New Pages

There are many ways to create new pages in your site. As you learned in Chapter 3, you and authorized users can easily create and add content to pages via the browser. But you can also create a variety of pages with SharePoint Designer.

CREATE A NEW WEB PART PAGE

You can create new Web Part pages via the browser, as discussed in Chapter 3, or you can quickly create a new Web Part page in SharePoint Designer.

1. In SharePoint Designer, click the **All Files** tab on the SharePoint ribbon.

2. Click **Web Part Page** in the ribbon, and then click the layout of the Web Part page you would like to create, as shown in Figure 8-13.

3. In the New Web Part Page window (see Figure 8-14), type the name for the page, such as <u>Project Plan</u>, choose which document library should house the new page, and then click **OK**.

4. The new page opens in the Editing pane, but in Standard Mode. Click **Advanced Mode** on the SharePoint ribbon to edit the page, as you see in Figure 8-15.

Take extreme caution when working with files in SharePoint lists and libraries. The pages in the Forms folder for each list or library were created by the system when the Web Part was created, and if you delete or move them, bad things will happen. For example, in the Shared Documents document library, if you delete Upload.aspx, users will have no way to upload a document. So if you want to move or copy files to another location, do not move or copy the Forms folder.

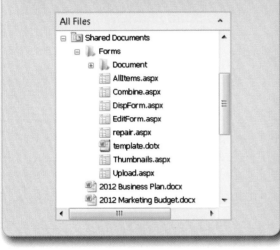

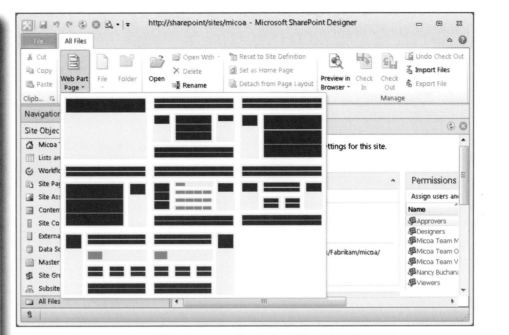

Figure 8-13: *You can create a Web Part page directly from SharePoint Designer.*

SharePoint 2010 stores new pages in the Site Pages document library by default.

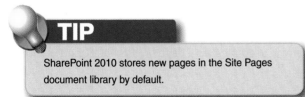

Figure 8-14: *Choose your page title and where you would like to store the page.*

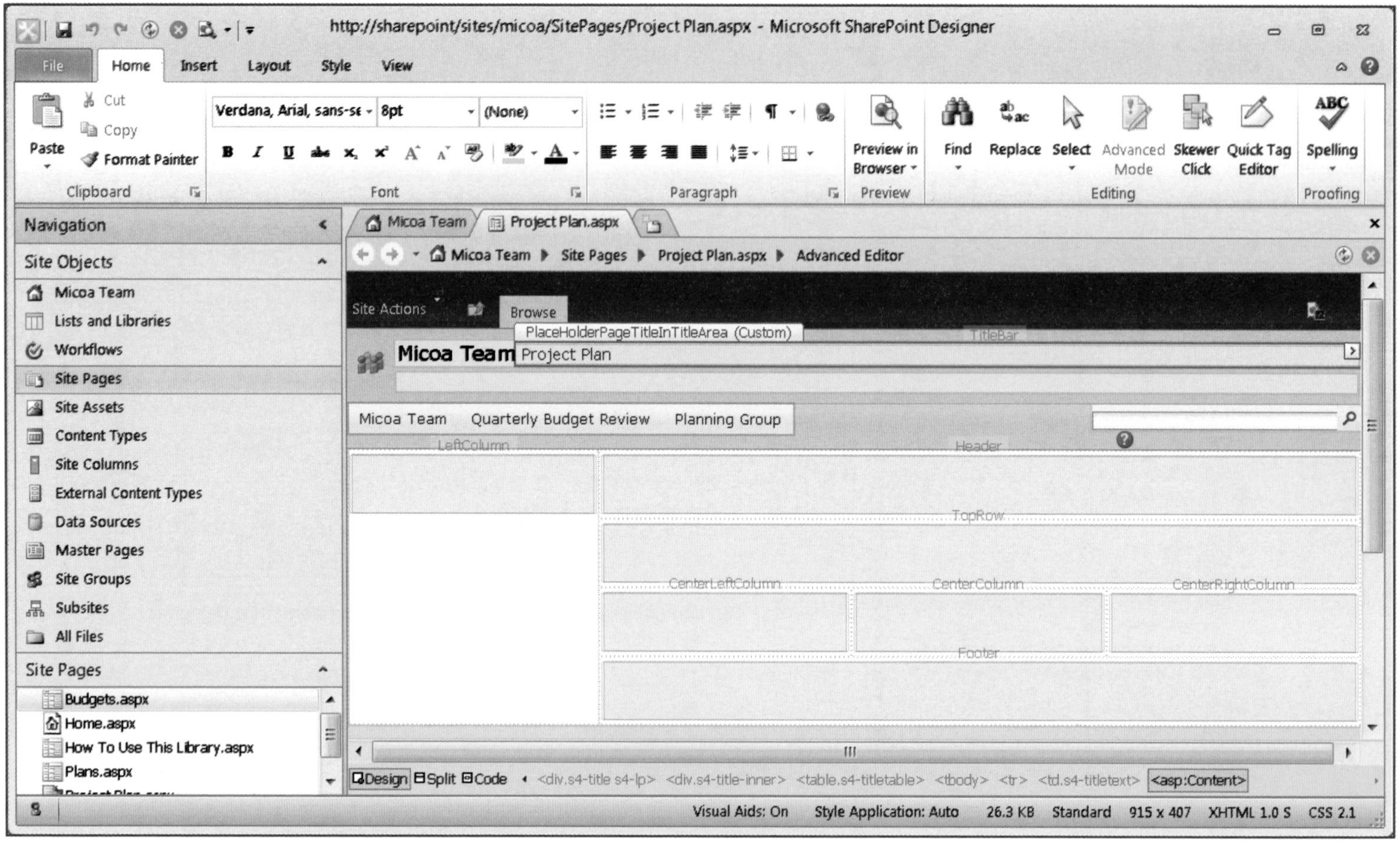

Figure 8-15: A Web Part page lets you select a layout and then creates a table to hold that layout.

CREATE A NEW BLANK PAGE

Sometimes you may want to create a simple blank page on the site. SharePoint Designer makes it easy.

1. Click **All Files** in the Site Objects task pane.

2. In the ribbon New group, click **File** and then click the type of page you would like to create, such as ASPX, which is the recommended file type, as shown in Figure 8-16.

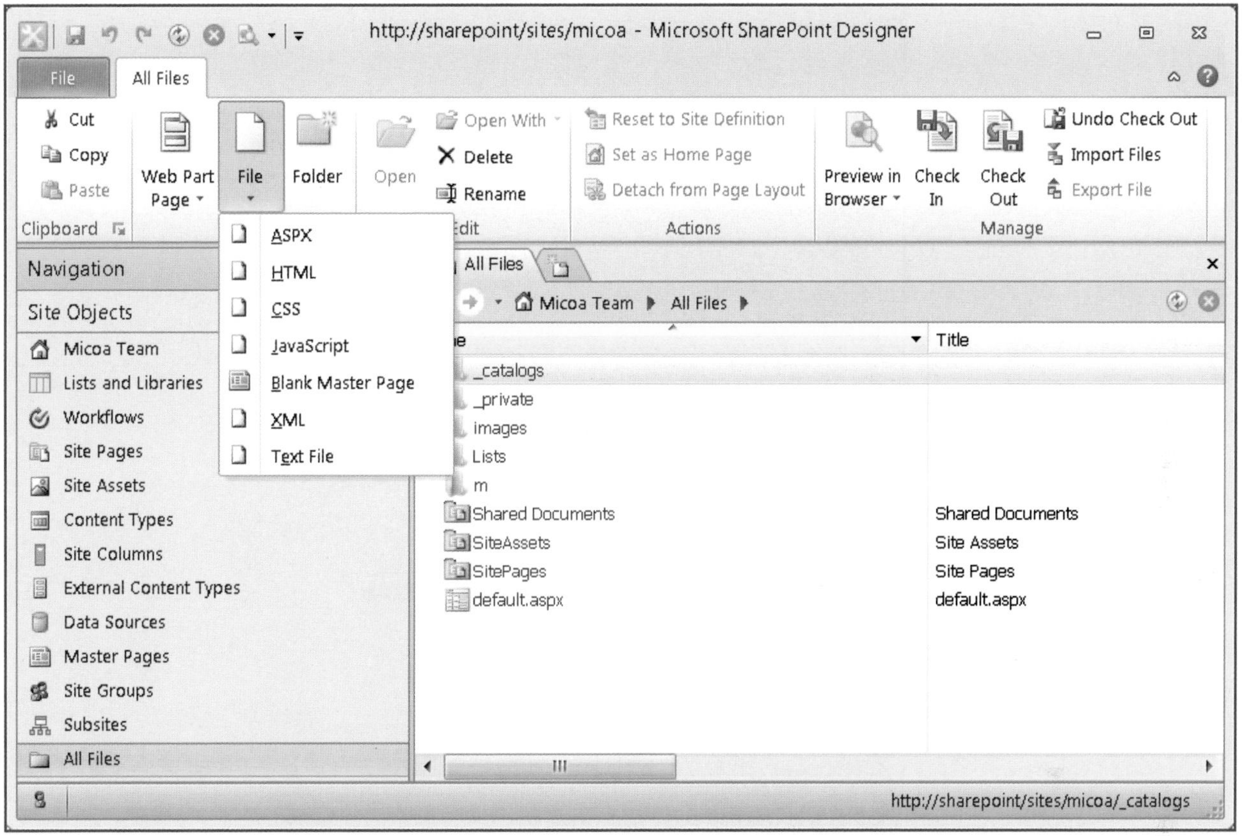

Figure 8-16: **Create a new ASPX or HTML page from the File option on the All Files tab of the SharePoint ribbon.**

3. The file is created as Untitled_1.aspx and placed in the root of the site, shown in Figure 8-17. Right-click the file, choose **Rename**, and then rename the file. This is also a good time to move the file (just drag it into the desired folder or document library) if desired.

4. If you are ready to edit the file, you can right-click it and then choose **Edit File In Advanced Mode**.

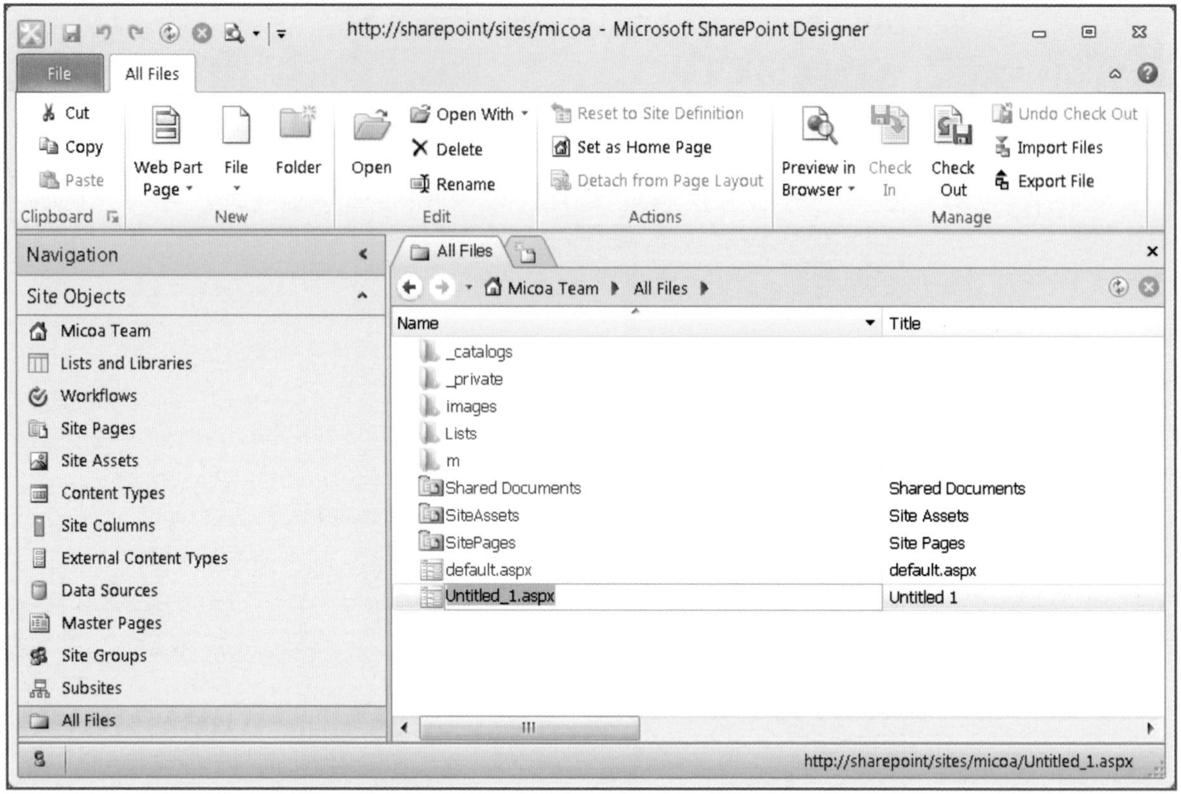

Figure 8-17: *The new page is created, but still needs to be named.*

CREATE A NEW PAGE FROM AN EXISTING PAGE

If you already have a page that contains a good percentage of the content you want on your new page, you can easily create a new page from it.

1. In the Site Objects task pane, open the document library or folder that contains the page you want to copy. For example, click **Site Pages** if you know that the page is located in the Site Pages document library.

2. Right-click the page you want to copy, and then click **New From Existing Page**, as shown in Figure 8-18.

3. The new page opens in the Editing pane as Untitled_1.aspx. Make your edits and then save the page.

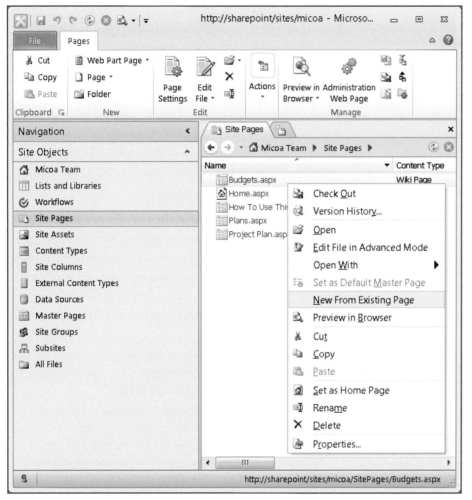

Figure 8-18: *It is easy to create a new page from an existing one.*

CREATE A NEW PAGE FROM A MASTER PAGE

Master pages control the structure of pages that are created on your site. You can see a list of the master pages available on your site by clicking **Master Pages** in the Site Objects task pane. The master pages available to you depend on the site template from which your site was created and your organization's implementation. For example, your organization might have its own master pages with their own unique names, or it may use the out-of-the-box master pages that were provided when your site was created. If you know which master page you want to create a page from, you can follow these steps to create the page.

1. Click **Master Pages** in the Site Objects task pane.

2. Right-click the master page from which you want to create your new page, and then click **New From Master Page**, as shown in Figure 8-19.

3. In the New Web Part Page dialog box, type the name for the page, such as Team Meetings, choose the document library in which to store the new page, and then click **OK**.

4. If you are told that the page is in Safe Mode, click **Yes**. This warning tells you that nothing can be edited unless you work in Advanced Mode.

At this point, the page has been created and can be viewed in the browser (it is "live" on the site) and opens in the Editing pane of SharePoint Designer for you to edit.

Add Content to Existing Pages

There are many tools in SharePoint Designer 2010 for adding text, images, behaviors, and positioning content. This section provides an overview of some of those tools you might want to use to edit content on existing pages in your SharePoint site.

POSITION CONTENT WITH TABLES

Many Web pages use tables to align or separate content. If you want to add text, images, or other content to an existing page with SharePoint Designer, first you might want to place existing content in a table and open new cells for your new content. This example steps through how you could insert a table at the top of the page for new text and images.

1. Open the page you want to edit in Advanced Mode in SharePoint Designer. For example, locate the file you want to edit in the Site Pages section of the Site Objects task pane, right-click it, and then choose **Edit File In Advanced Mode**.

2. If you click a Web Part in SharePoint Designer, it becomes highlighted in blue. You can then use the Quick Tag Selector at the bottom of the Editing pane to select the Web Part zone in which the Web Part resides (<WebPartPages:WebPartZone>), and then step further to the left on the Quick Tag Selector to highlight the <table> tag table that contains the Web Part zone. Once you have the <table> tag selected in the Quick Tag Selector, that table is highlighted in blue because it is selected (see Figure 8-20). Now you can press **HOME** on your keyboard to position your cursor above the table.

⬚Design ⊟Split ▣Code ◂ <td> <table> <tr> <td#_invisibleIfE...> <WebPartPages:WebPartZone#Header> ▸

3. On the Insert tab, click **Table** to insert a new table in which to place your new content.

Figure 8-19: *A master page acts like an organization's page template by providing the colors, fonts, layout, and possibly a logo that are the organization's standards.*

NOTE

Sometimes you want authorized site visitors to be able to add Web Parts to a page you author, and sometimes you don't. If you want them to be able to add Web Parts to a section of a page, insert a Web Part zone into that section (just click **Web Part Zone** on the Insert tab).

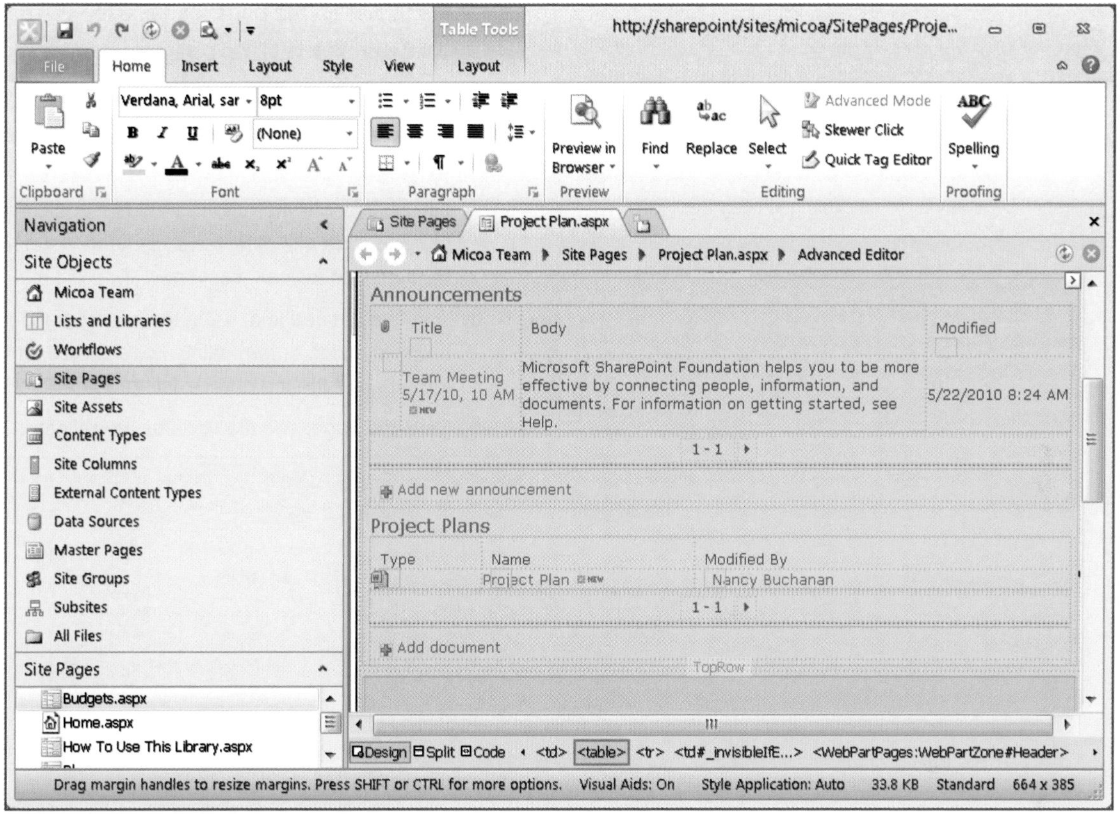

Figure 8-20: ***You can select and highlight elements on the page by selecting the element's tag in the Quick Tag Selector at the bottom of the Editing pane.***

> **TIP**
>
> If you are going to make substantial changes to a page, you might want to back it up before you add and save your changes. The easiest way to do this is copy and paste the file, and then rename the copy as "*page-name*-backup.aspx" or something like that (where *page-name* is the name of the existing page). That way, if you make a mistake, you can always replace your new page with the backed-up page.

POSITION CONTENT WITH <DIVS>

You can also choose to position content with layers instead of tables. To do so, follow steps 1 and 2 in "Position Content with Tables," but in step 3, click **Insert Layer** on the Layout tab. Once the new layer is created, you are ready to insert content such as text or images into it.

ADD TEXT

Not all of the content in your SharePoint site has to be in a Web Part. Sometimes you will have text that doesn't need to be edited in the browser, or sometimes you will have so much content on a page that you want to decrease the number

TIP

Traditionally, graphics files should go in the Images folder of your site, but technically speaking, they can be located at the root site or in another folder or in a document library instead. For example, if you want content owners to be able to edit graphics files or replace existing ones when they change without having to open the site in SharePoint Designer, you can place the graphics in a document library. On the other hand, if you don't want site visitors to be able to accidentally delete or change your site graphics, the graphics should probably go in the Images folder instead of in a document library.

of Web Parts so the page loads faster. Here is how you can add plain or formatted text to existing pages.

1. Open the page you want to edit in Advanced Mode in SharePoint Designer. For example, locate the file you want to edit in the Site Pages section of the Site Objects task pane, right-click it, and then choose **Edit File In Advanced Mode**.

2. Locate a place where you can safely add content in the page. For example, click in the new table cell or layer you created in the "Position Content with Tables" or "Position Content with <Divs>" section.

3. Type the desired text, using the formatting tools on the Home tab to change the text size, color, or formatting. For example, in Figure 8-21, text has been added and formatted at the top of an existing SharePoint page.

4. Save the page, and the updates are reflected when the page is viewed by a site visitor.

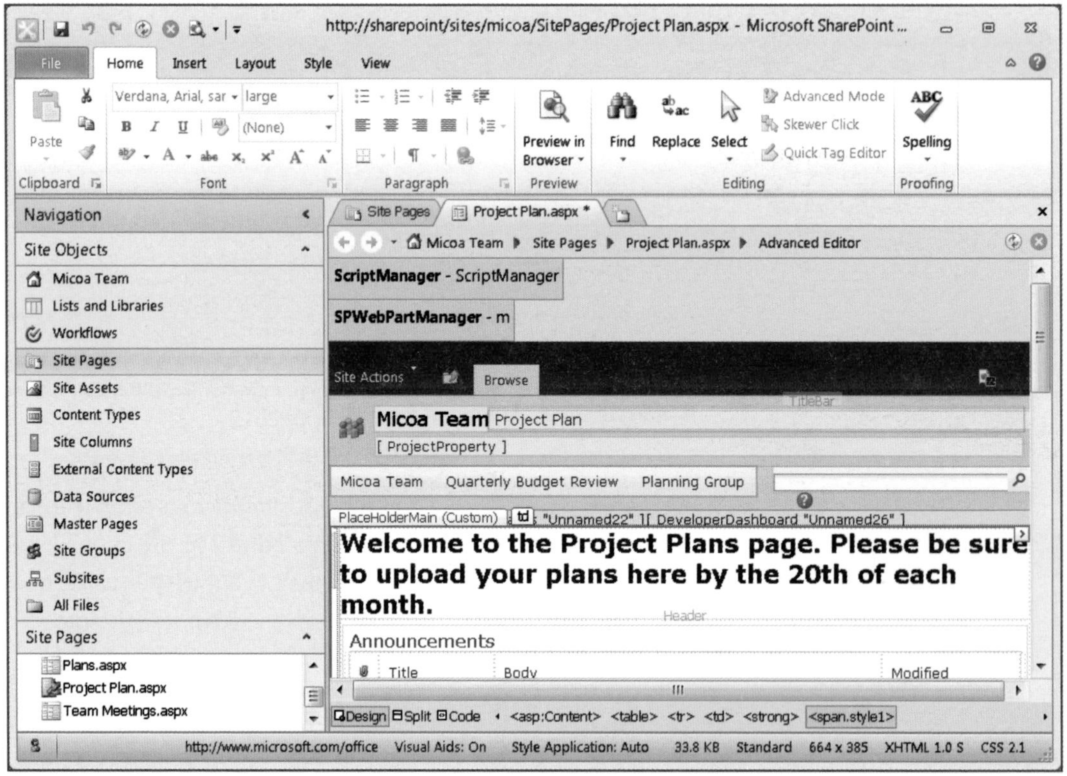

Figure 8-21: *SharePoint Designer allows you to add text and graphics virtually anywhere on a page.*

QUICKSTEPS

EMBELLISHING IMAGES WITH PICTURE TOOLS

SharePoint Designer 2010 comes with sophisticated tools to make it easy to manipulate images. Once the images have been added to a page with SharePoint Designer (see the "Add Images" section in this chapter), all you have to do is click the image and click the **Picture Tools I Format** tab on the SharePoint ribbon to open a range of image editing tools, as shown in Figure 8-22. Here are some of the most frequently used image-editing options:

- Effects like Bevel (shown on the graphic in Figure 8-22), Grayscale, and Wash Out give images an artistic look with very little work and no separate graphics editing tool.

- Crop images to remove all but the part of the image you want to appear on the page.

- Use the Link tool to turn the image into a button by adding a hyperlink to another page or e-mail address.

- Use the Hotspot tool to make individual sections of the image linked to a different webpage or e-mail address.

- Change the wrapping style to make surrounding text wrap around the image.

- Resize images in SharePoint Designer by clicking and dragging the corners, and when you save the page, SharePoint Designer asks you if you want to resample the image to look better (and decrease the file size if shrinking) or rename the image so that you do not disturb the original version.

ADD IMAGES

Like text, graphics or images can be added easily almost anywhere on a page.

1. Import the graphics file into your site (see the "Add Site Content" section earlier in this chapter to learn how).

2. Pin open the folder that contains the graphic you want to include on the page, such as the Images folder. To do so, click **All Files**, click the desired folder, and then click **Pin**. This keeps the Images folder open so you can work with it.

3. Open the page you want to edit in Advanced Mode in SharePoint Designer. For example, locate the file you want to edit in the Site Pages section of the Site Objects task pane, right-click it, and then choose **Edit File In Advanced Mode**.

4. Locate a place where you can safely add content in the page. For example, click in the new table cell or layer you created earlier.

5. Drag the graphic file from the Site Objects task pane to the desired location on the page.

6. In the Accessibility Properties window, type alternative text for the image in the Alternate Text box, and then click **OK**. It is important to include alternate text for all images on the site so that visually impaired visitors that use a site reader program can identify the graphics on the site.

7. The graphic file is now visible on the page, as shown in Figure 8-23. Click the graphic, and the Picture Tools appear on the SharePoint ribbon, ready for you to use to modify the image further.

8. Save the page to make your changes live.

ADD BEHAVIORS TO IMAGES

SharePoint Designer Behaviors are programming effects that you can add to layers, images, or text. For example, you can add a hover effect on the blocks

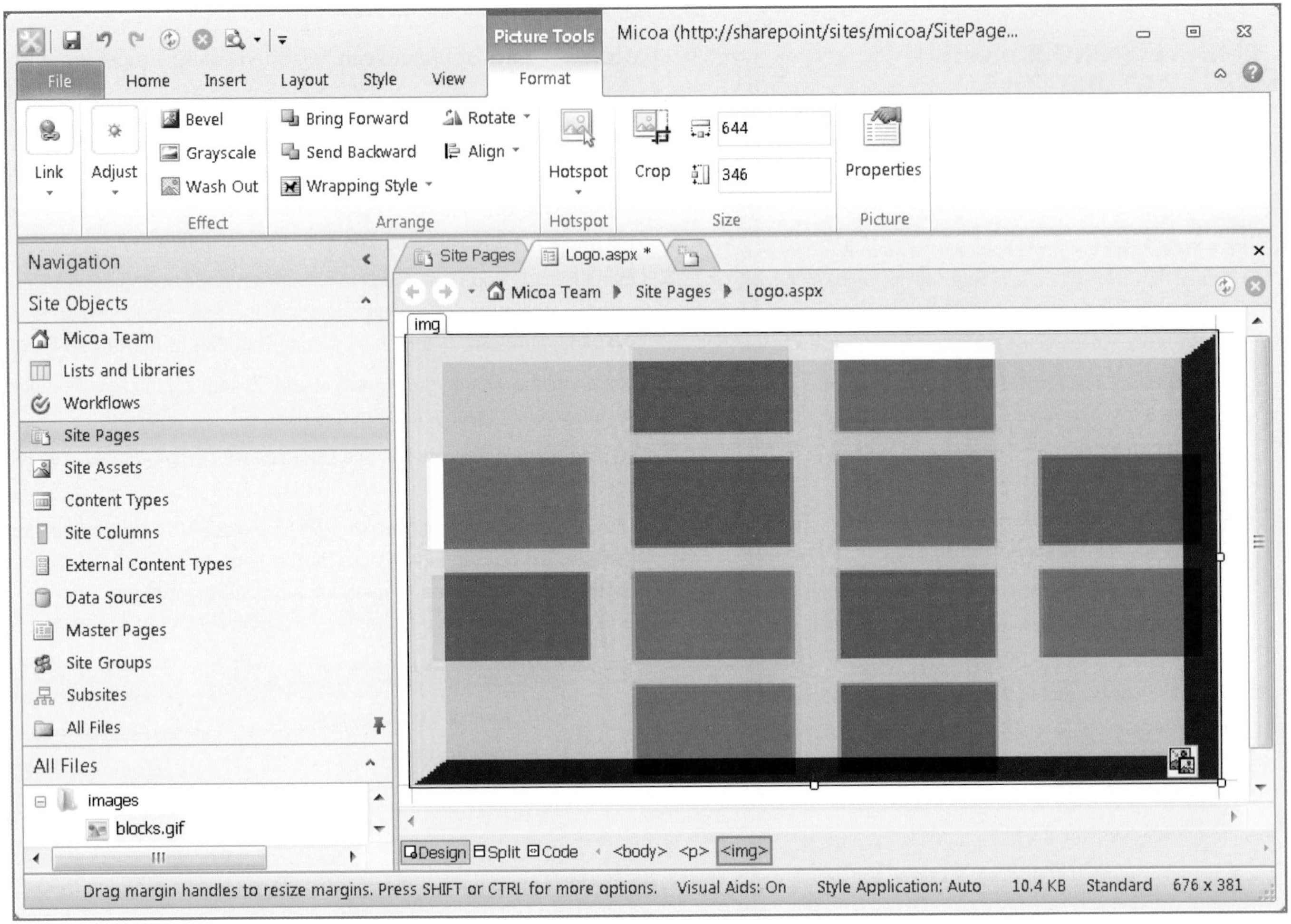

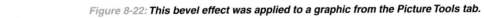

Figure 8-22: *This bevel effect was applied to a graphic from the Picture Tools tab.*

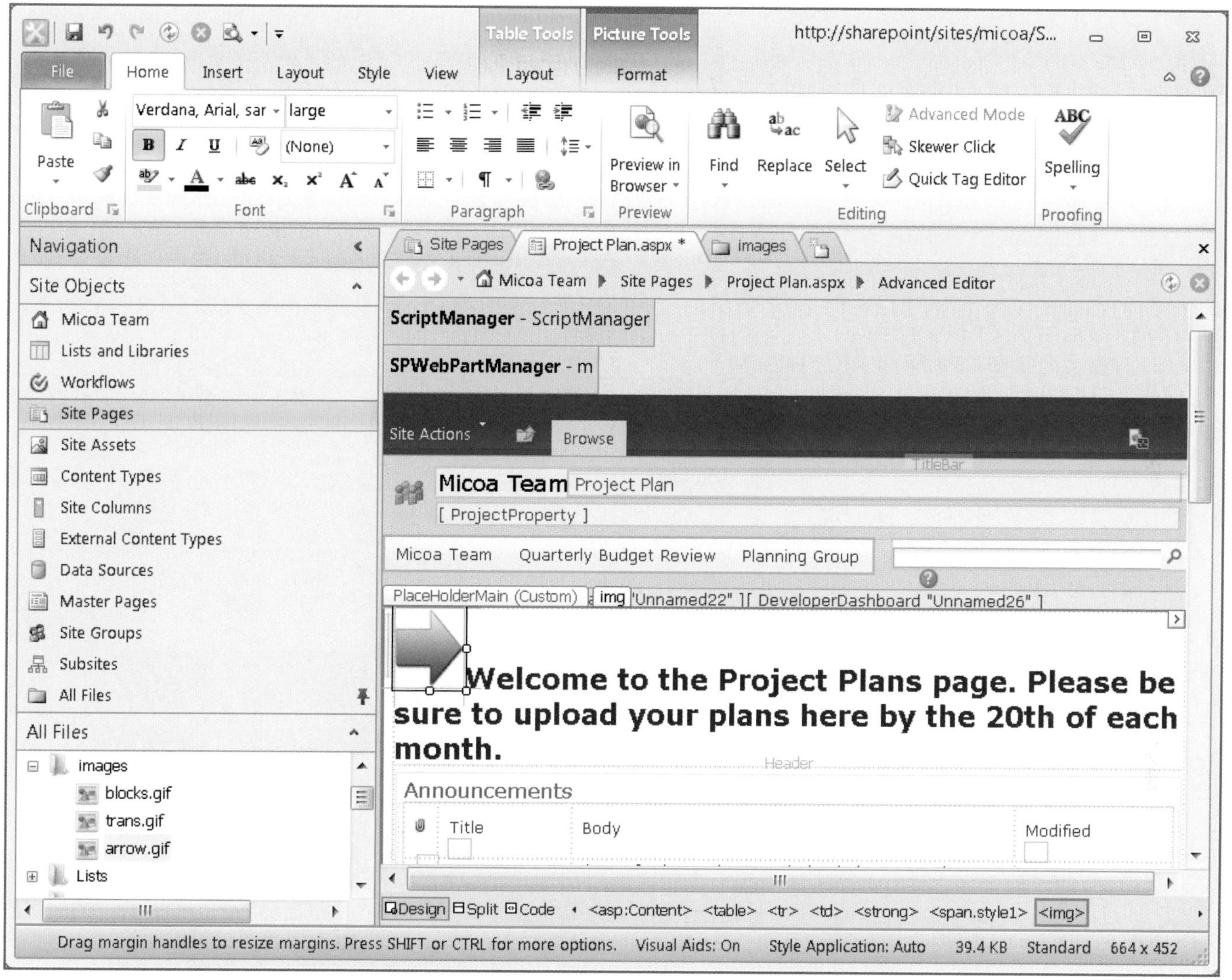

*Figure 8-23: **Graphics that add interest and convey information can be added easily to a page with SharePoint Designer.***

graphic shown in Figure 8-23 where the blocks image is replaced with another image, but only when the visitor's mouse is hovered over it.

1. Import the graphics file you will use as the swap image (the one displayed when the visitor hovers their mouse over the existing image) into your site (see the "Add Site Content" section in this chapter to learn how).

2. With the page that contains the image in it open in SharePoint Designer, open the Behaviors task pane by clicking the **Task Panes** option on the View tab and then clicking **Behaviors**. The Behaviors task pane opens to the right of the Editing pane.

3. Click **Insert** on the Behaviors task pane, shown in Figure 8-24, and then click **Swap Image**.

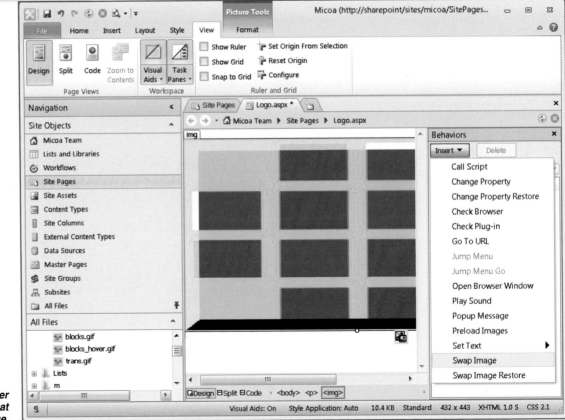

Figure 8-24: SharePoint Designer provides a number of behaviors that can be applied to objects on a page.

4. In the Swap Images dialog box, type the URL for the swap image in the Swap Image URL box (or click **Browse**, locate and then click the file, and then click **Open**). Make sure that the **Restore On Mouseout Event** option is selected, and then click **OK**.

Image Name	Original Image URL	Swap Image URL
Unnamed <img>	../images/blocks.gif	../images/blocks_hover.gif

Swap Image URL: ../images/blocks_hover.gif   Browse...

☑ Preload Images
☑ Restore on mouseout event   OK   Cancel

5. Save the page and then click **Preview In Browser** on the Quick Access toolbar to see the effect that happens when you hover your mouse over the image.

This example illustrates just one of the effects you can add using SharePoint Designer Behaviors.

Customize Web Parts in Pages

SharePoint sites can be customized in a myriad of ways from the browser. For example, you can change which fields are displayed, add Web Part titles, and revise the sort order without opening SharePoint Designer. However, there are times when you will be glad that you have SharePoint Designer to further refine how Web Parts display or behave. This section highlights some of the most common tasks.

SORT BY MORE THAN TWO ITEMS

In the browser you can change a view of a list or library to sort by up to two items. In SharePoint Designer, you can sort and group by more than two items.

1. In SharePoint Designer, open the page that contains the SharePoint list or library by which you want to sort more than two levels deep.

2. Click the Web Part for which you want to change the sort order. The List View Tools options open on the SharePoint ribbon, as shown in Figure 8-25.

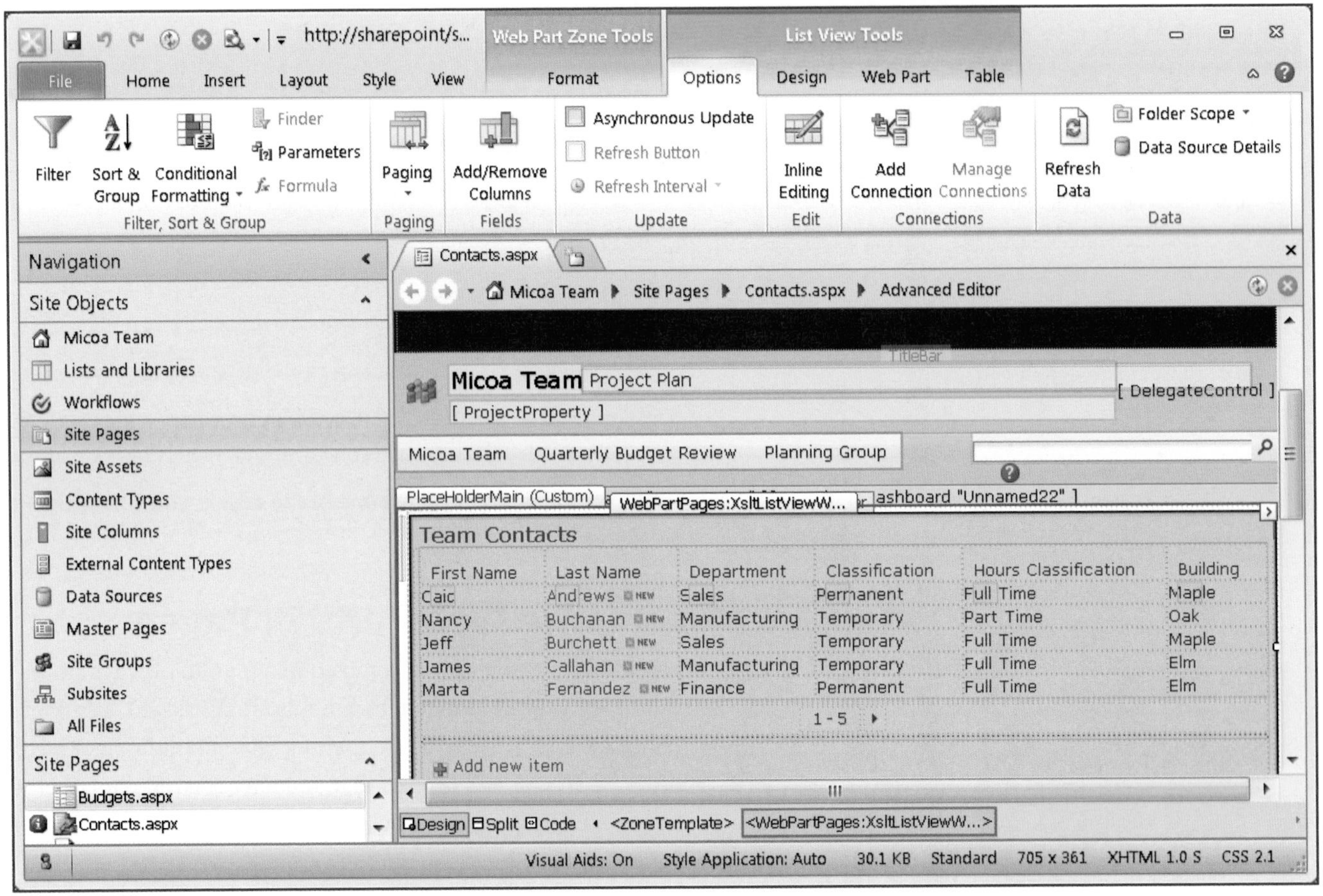

Figure 8-25: *The List View tabs provide a number of options for ordering, changing, editing, and formatting lists.*

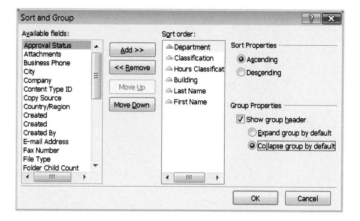

3. Click **Sort & Group** on the SharePoint ribbon.

4. In the Sort And Group dialog box, add and remove the fields on which to sort, and then click **OK**. Make sure that the sort properties (ascending or descending) are appropriate for each option. If you want the items to be grouped by a category, make sure that the Show Group Header option is selected for that item and that you have chosen whether to have category expanded or collapsed.

TIP

If you choose to group a list or library by a field, you probably don't need to display that field in the data displayed. Add or remove fields by clicking the Web Part and then clicking **Add/ Remove Columns** on the Options tab.

![Add/Remove Columns icon] Add/Remove Columns

5. Click **OK** and then save the page. Optionally, you can click **Preview In Browser** on the Quick Access toolbar to view the results, which are shown in Figure 8-26.

REMOVE CATEGORY FROM SORT GROUP DISPLAY

Figure 8-26 displays the results of a grouped and sorted list of contacts. If you wanted to remove the Department label (actually "Department:") from before each group, you couldn't do so from the browser. You can with SharePoint Designer, though.

1. Still in SharePoint Designer, in Advanced Mode and with the page that contains the grouped Web Part opened, click the label you want to remove, such as **Department:** as shown in Figure 8-27.

2. Press **DELETE** on your keyboard. Save the page, and when you preview it in the browser (press **F12**), you see the category label removed, as shown in Figure 8-28.

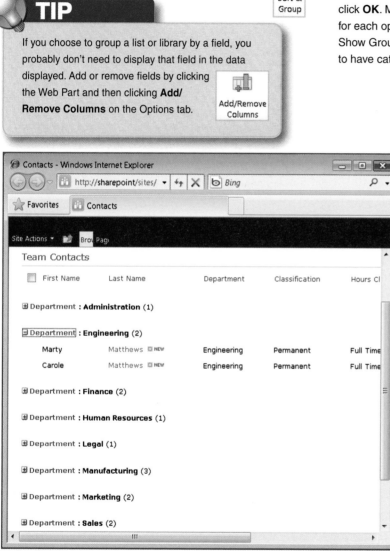

Figure 8-26: You can sort a list by multiple levels and then group it in a collapsed list by the header (department in the case shown here).

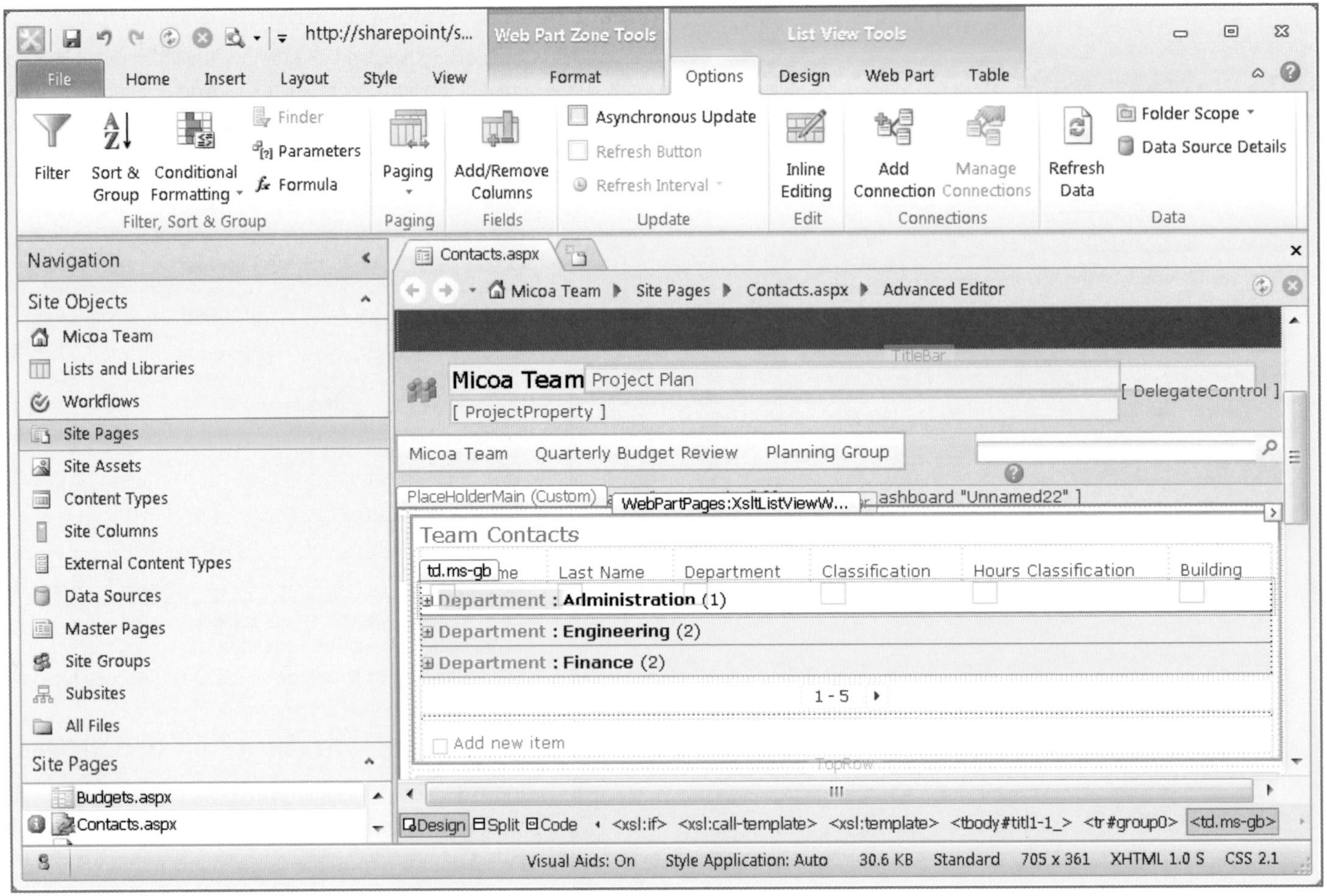

Figure 8-27: *In SharePoint Designer, you can remove a label by simply selecting and deleting it.*

CUSTOMIZE THE LOOK OF A WEB PART

SharePoint Designer 2010 allows you to precisely format the display of Web Parts by giving you access to the HyperText Markup Language (HTML) code that makes up their display. For example, when you open the Contacts list page

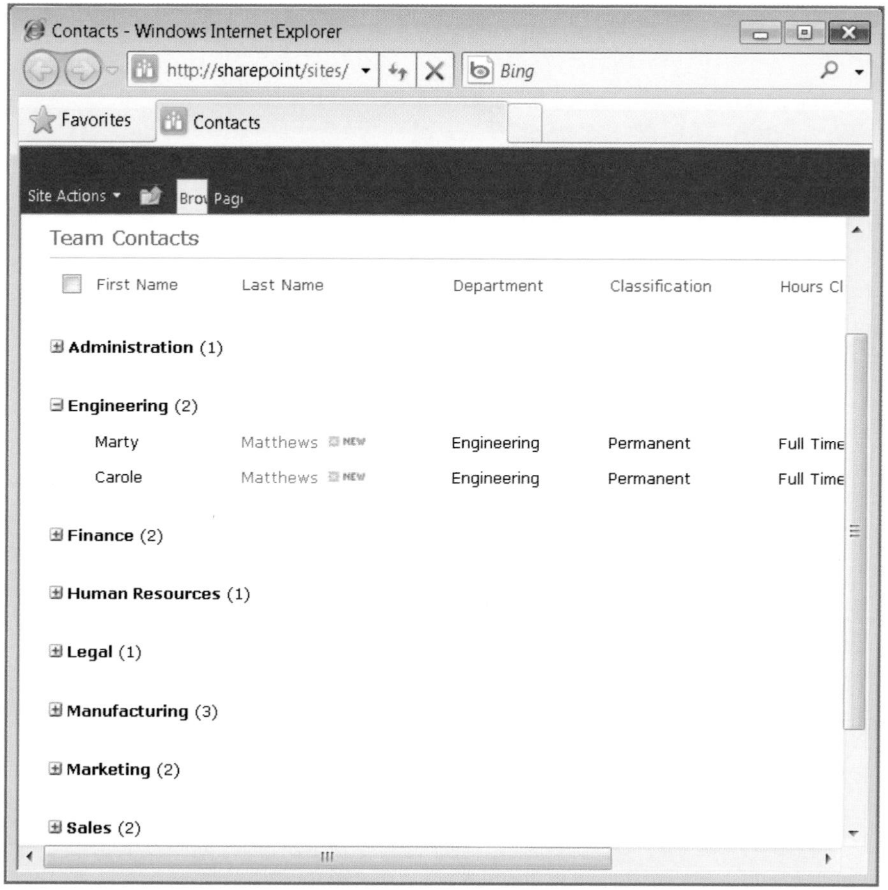

*Figure 8-28: **Removing a group label from group titles in a collapsed list is something you can only do in SharePoint Designer.***

in SharePoint Designer 2010, as shown in Figure 8-29, you can click a field or cell and use the Quick Tag Selector to find and edit the tags used to format the view.

For example, when you choose **Edit Tag** from the Quick Tag Selector options, the Quick Tag Editor opens and you can edit the HTML for that tag. In Figure 8-30 the HTML for the table cell has been changed to display big red text. When you make a change like this, it is immediate and applies to all of the other cells in that same column.

This is just one example of how you can use SharePoint Designer to edit the underlying HTML code that makes up the display of a Web Part. For more information about HTML code and how to use it, see *HTML, XHML, & CSS QuickSteps* by Guy Hart-Davis, published by McGraw-Hill/Professional.

DISPLAY DIFFERENT FORMATTING FOR DIFFERENT CONDITIONS

One of the most powerful aspects of SharePoint sites is that you can collect a lot of information from various sources and then display consolidated views on a webpage. This power is enhanced further when you set up rules to tell SharePoint to format the data differently depending on the values in a specific field—for example, a Sales Dashboard Web Part that collects a sales unit's goals and actual sales numbers for each region. Here is how to get SharePoint to automatically display a red light graphic if the region doesn't meet their sales goal and a green light if they do.

1. Import the graphics files you want to use as the green and red lights (see "Add Site Content" earlier in this chapter).

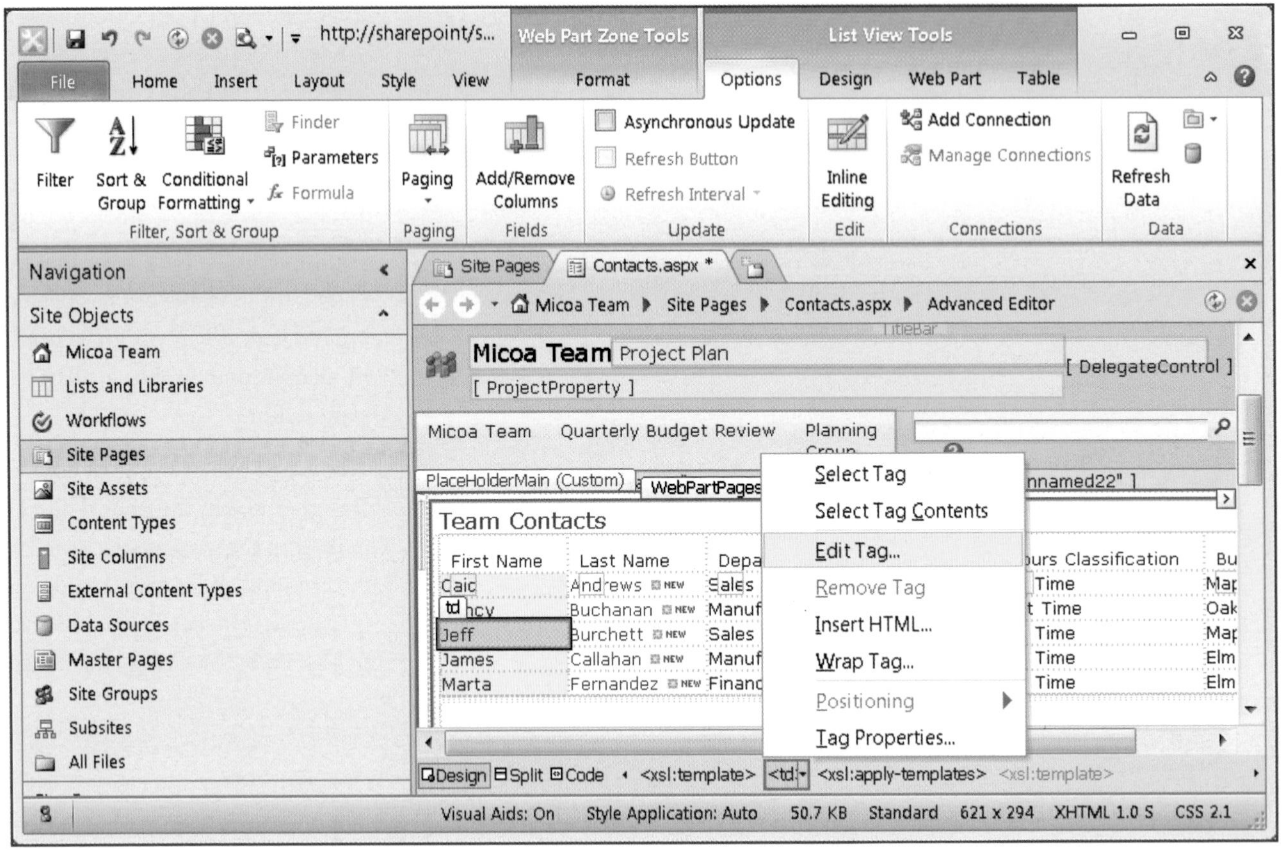

Figure 8-29: *You can use the Quick Tag Selector to edit a tag that makes up the formatting of a Web Part's display.*

2. Pin open the folder that contains the graphics you want to include on the dashboard, such as the Images folder. To do so, click **All Files**, click the desired folder, and then click **Pin**.

3. Still in SharePoint Designer, in Advanced Mode and with the page that contains the Web Part opened, click where you want to insert the graphics. For example, you could

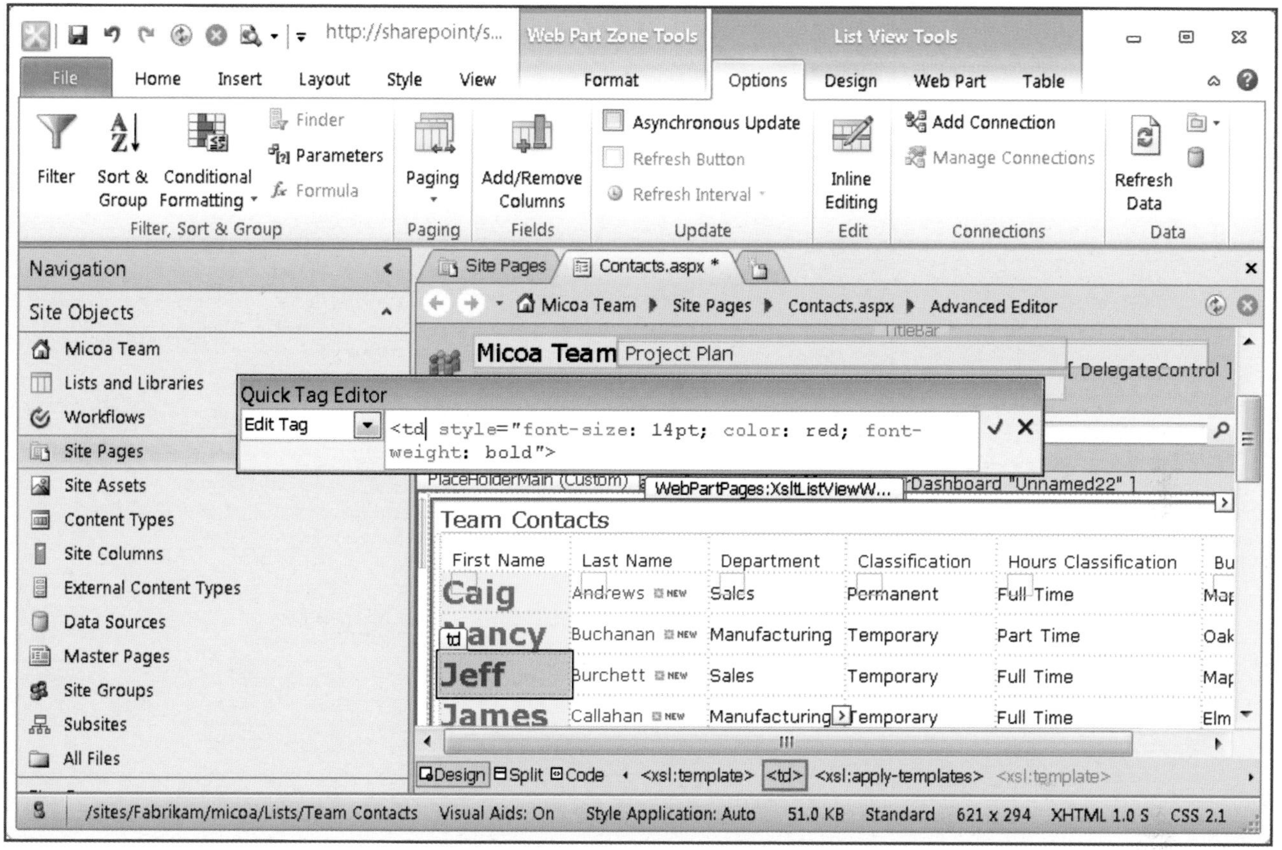

Figure 8-30: *The Quick Tag Editor can be used to edit the HTML code for a table cell.*

click the value in the Variance % column, as shown in Figure 8-31, and then press **END** to position your cursor to the right of that value.

4. Drag the red light image on the page where you want it. When asked for the Alternate text, type <u>Red</u>.

5. Drag the green light image on the page where you want it. When asked for the Alternate text, type <u>Green</u>. Now the page shows both red and green lights, as shown in Figure 8-32.

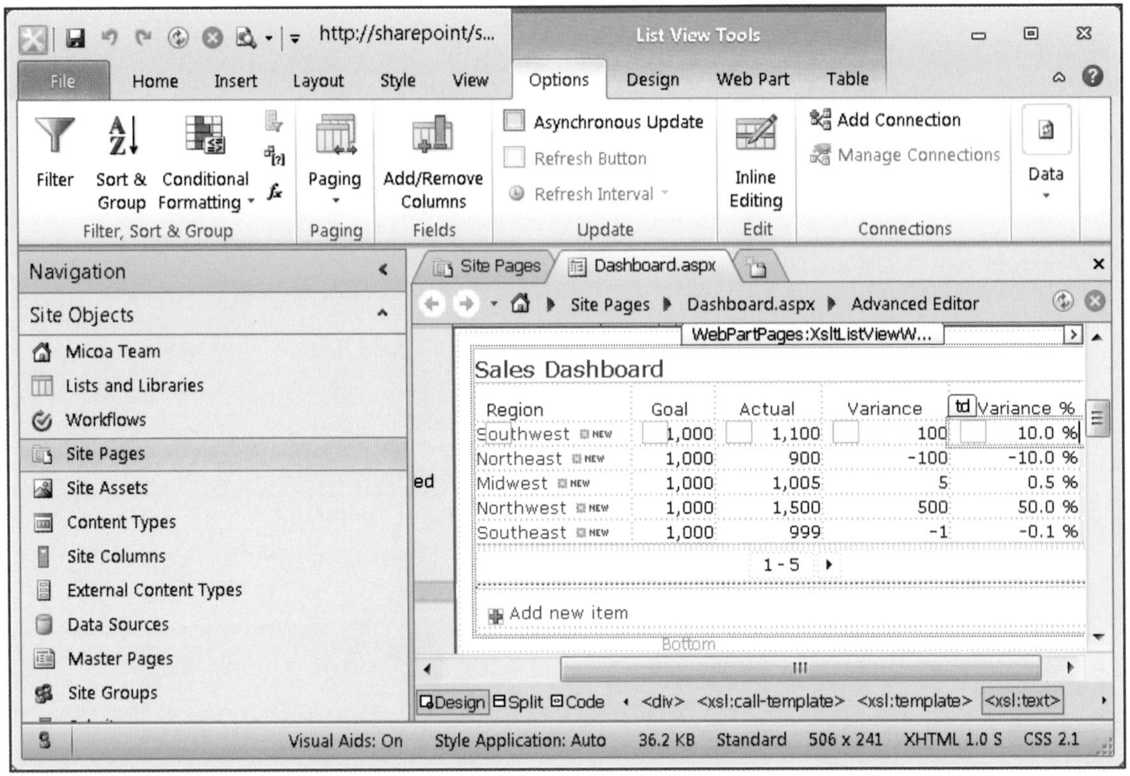

Figure 8-31: *Position your cursor where you plan to insert the graphics files.*

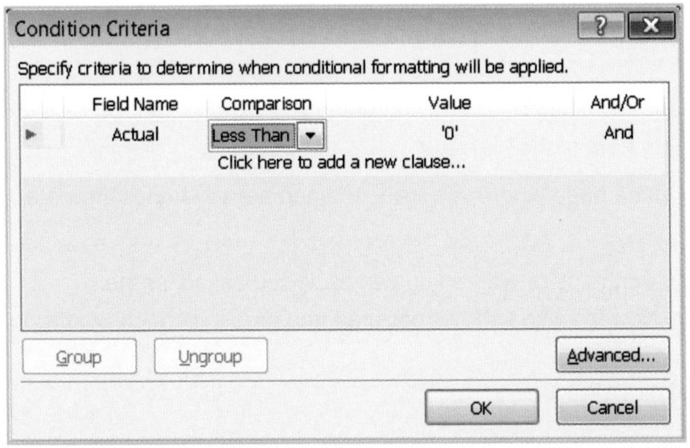

6. Right-click the red light, and choose **Conditional Formatting** (or click **Conditional Formatting** from the Task Panes option on the View tab). The Conditional Formatting task pane opens.

7. Click **Create** and then click **Show Content**.

8. Complete the Condition Criteria dialog box for the condition that must be true in order for this graphic file to appear. In our example, the Actual field must be less than 1000 for the red light to appear, and it must be greater than or equal to 1000 for the green light to appear. Then click **OK**.

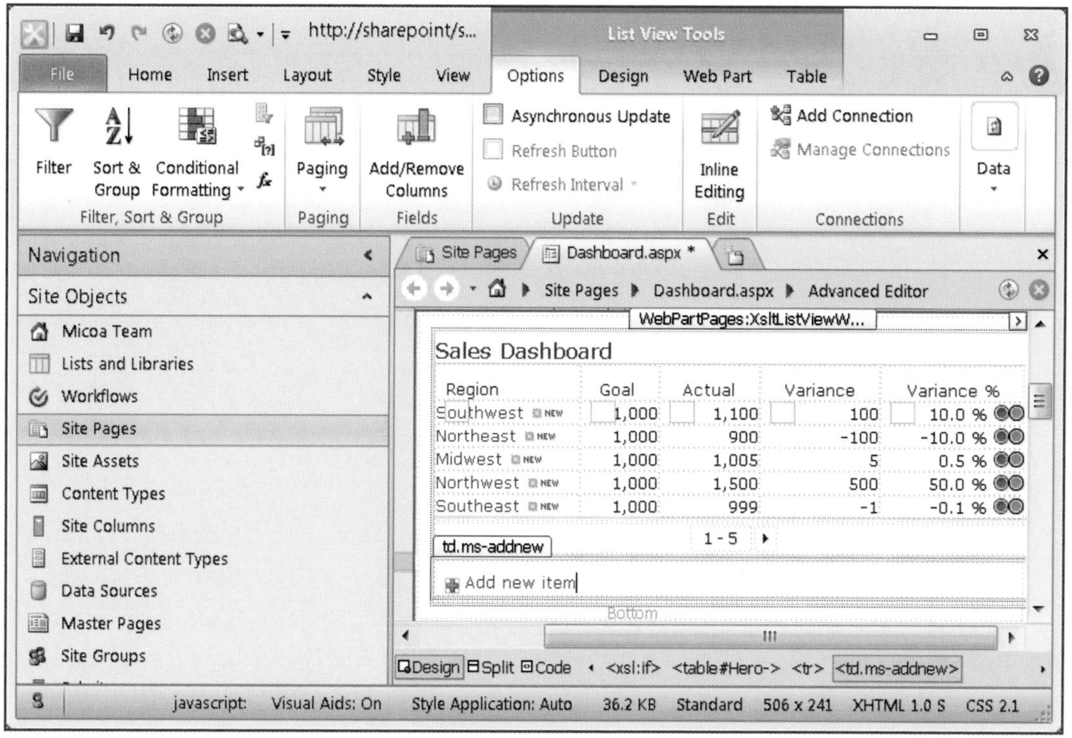

Figure 8-32: While it is being edited, the Dashboard displays both red and green lights.

QUICKFACTS

CHANGING WORKFLOW RULES

SharePoint sites have a powerful workflow engine built in that allows you to specify steps to take if you want to collect feedback about a document, approve a document, or sign off on a document. That's why SharePoint includes several out-of-the-box workflows, including ones for Feedback, Approval, and Signatures. You can also use SharePoint Designer to modify or create custom workflows. You access SharePoint Designer workflow customization tools in the Workflows option in the Site Objects task pane.

9. Repeat steps 6 through 8 for the green light graphic.

10. Save the pages and then preview it in the browser to see the effect (shown in Figure 8-33).

Change the Look of Your Site

The fastest way to change the look of your SharePoint site is to change the site theme. The theme determines site colors and font and formatting choices, as you saw in Chapter 1. The theme can be changed via the browser through the Site Settings area, or those same options can be accessed in SharePoint Designer

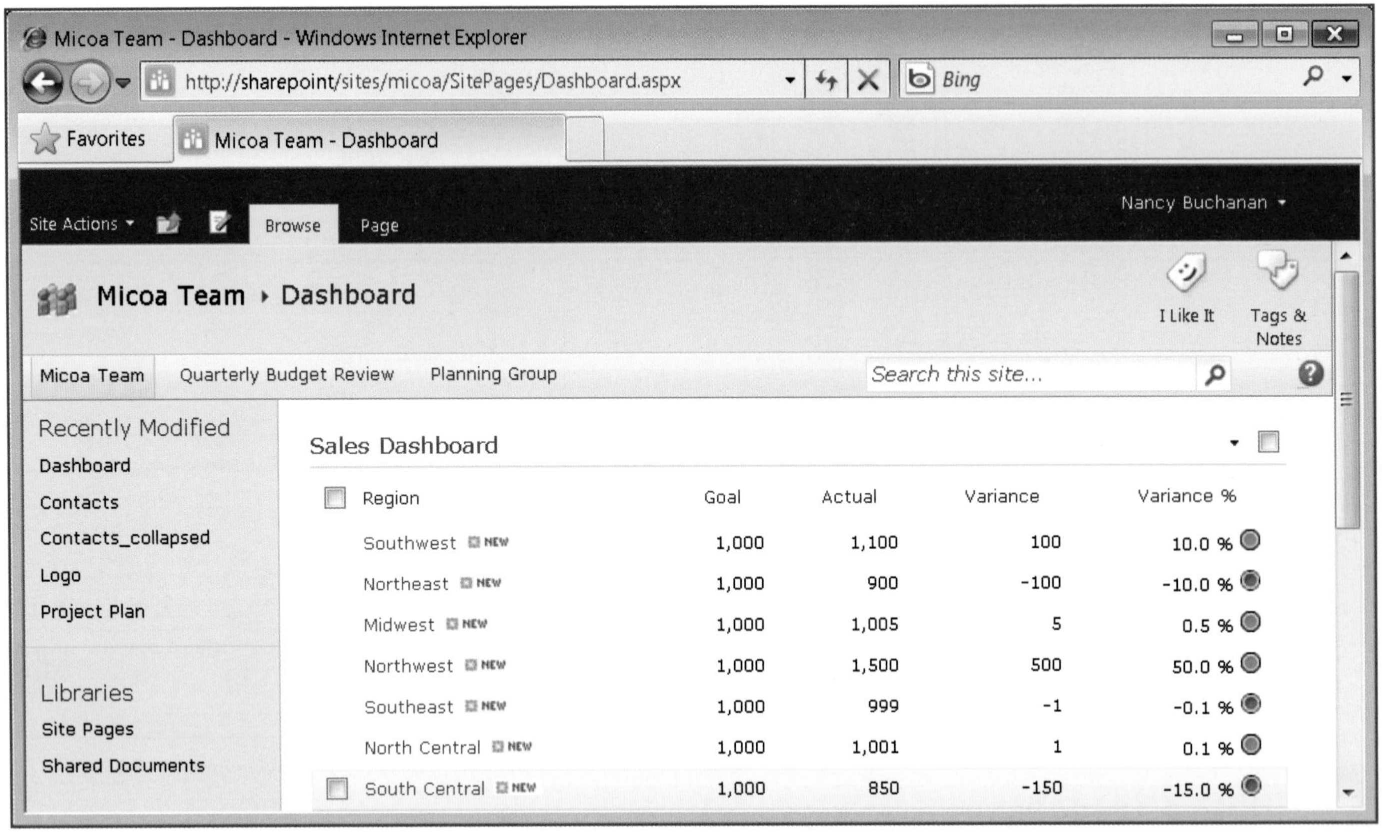

Figure 8-33: *The Sales Dashboard displaying automatic green and red lights depending on the value in the Actual column.*

by clicking the **Change Site Theme** option in the Customization section of the site information page shown in Figure 8-34.

Change Style Sheets

Each SharePoint site relies on one or more cascading style sheets (CSS) to tell it how to format hyperlinks, text, dialog boxes, drop-down menus, and more. CSS is an industry-standard set of formatting rules for Web sites and web applications.

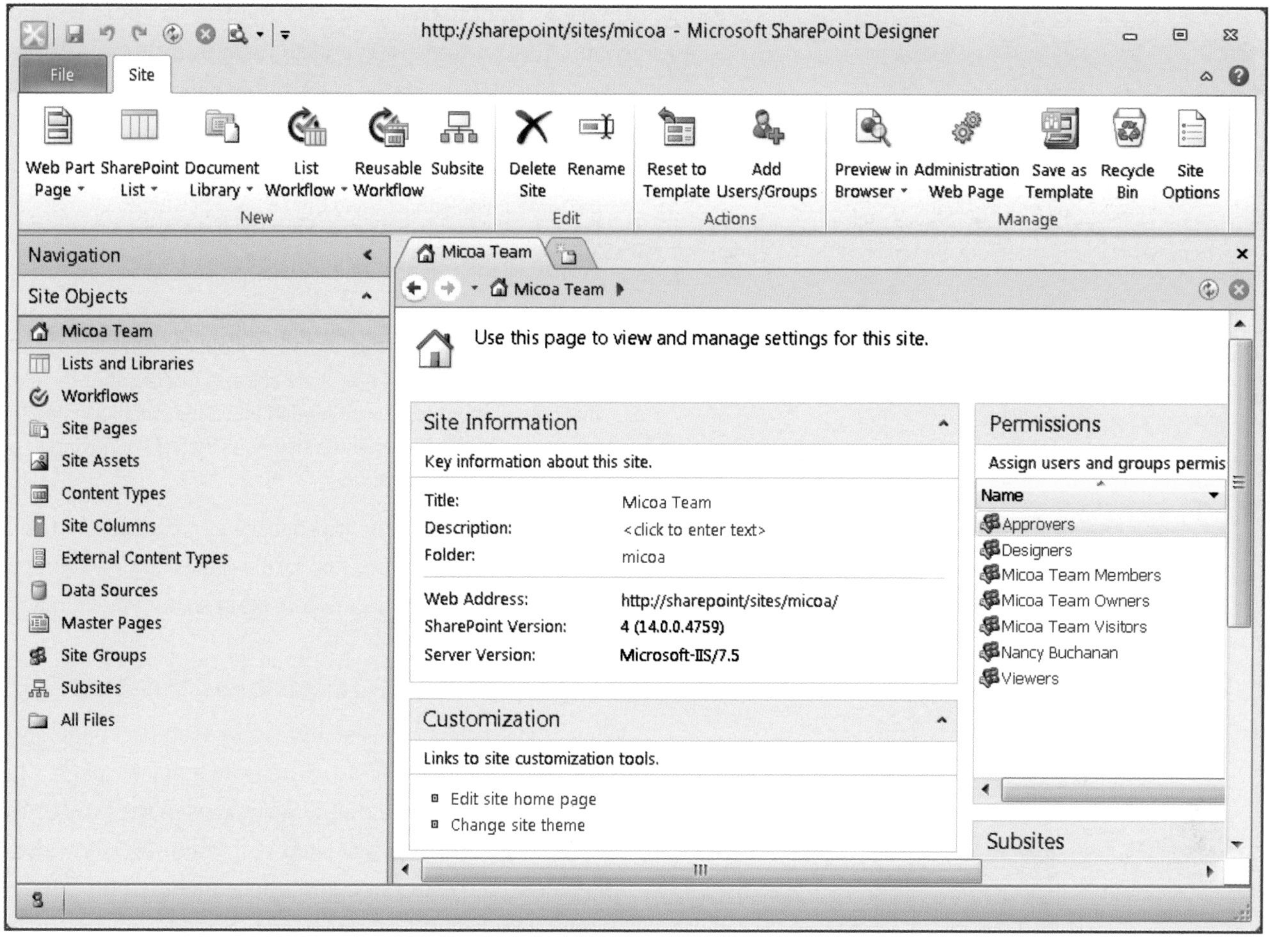

Figure 8-34: **The site theme can be changed in SharePoint Designer as well as in your browser.**

Because so many styles are defined in the style sheets used by SharePoint sites, and because a mistake in styles could drastically affect the ability to use the site, changing SharePoint site style sheets should be considered an advanced topic and should be done only by someone with expertise in web development, CSS, and SharePoint.

If you do want to change the styles used on your SharePoint site, there are two common ways to do so (you can learn more about CSS in *HTML, XHML, & CSS QuickSteps* by Guy Hart-Davis, published by McGraw-Hill/Professional):

- Create a new style sheet to supplement existing styles and then attach it to the site's master page(s). Because CSS rules tell SharePoint to process the last styles presented, you can just add the styles you want to change to your style sheet and make sure that your style sheet is attached after the default style sheet. Your style definitions will override the default style definitions used on the site.

- Copy the site's existing style sheet, attach it to the site's master page(s), and then make modifications to the copied version. As with the previous approach, you will need to make sure that your new style sheet is loaded after the site's default style sheet so that your custom styles are loaded last. This technique has the advantage of allowing you to search for styles and make edits instead of having to add new style definitions to a new style sheet.

If you use either of these approaches to create custom styles, be sure to test the effects on drop-down menus, forms pages, and system pages like the View All Site Content page. Styles are reused in many pages in a SharePoint site.

Change the Structure of Pages

When you create a new list, library, or Web Part page on a SharePoint site, the pages created take their structure from a master page. Master pages are page templates that not only define what goes in the header, left navigation, footer, and body areas of pages created with them, but they also include placeholders for content that could or could not be included on subsequent pages. For example, the default master page in SharePoint sites includes a page title placeholder that takes the page title you specify when you create a new Web Part page and places it in the breadcrumb area (see Figure 8-35).

Master pages in SharePoint sites are editable by authorized users, and can be found in the Master Pages section of the Site Objects task pane. Because master pages are so important to the function of SharePoint sites, you should take

CAUTION

The fact that master pages are editable doesn't mean that you should edit them. If you delete the page title area in the master page, for example, you might find that users get an "Unexpected Error" message on all of the pages in the site. The reason is that those pages are looking for where to place the site title information in the page, and without the placeholders in the master page, an error is shown.

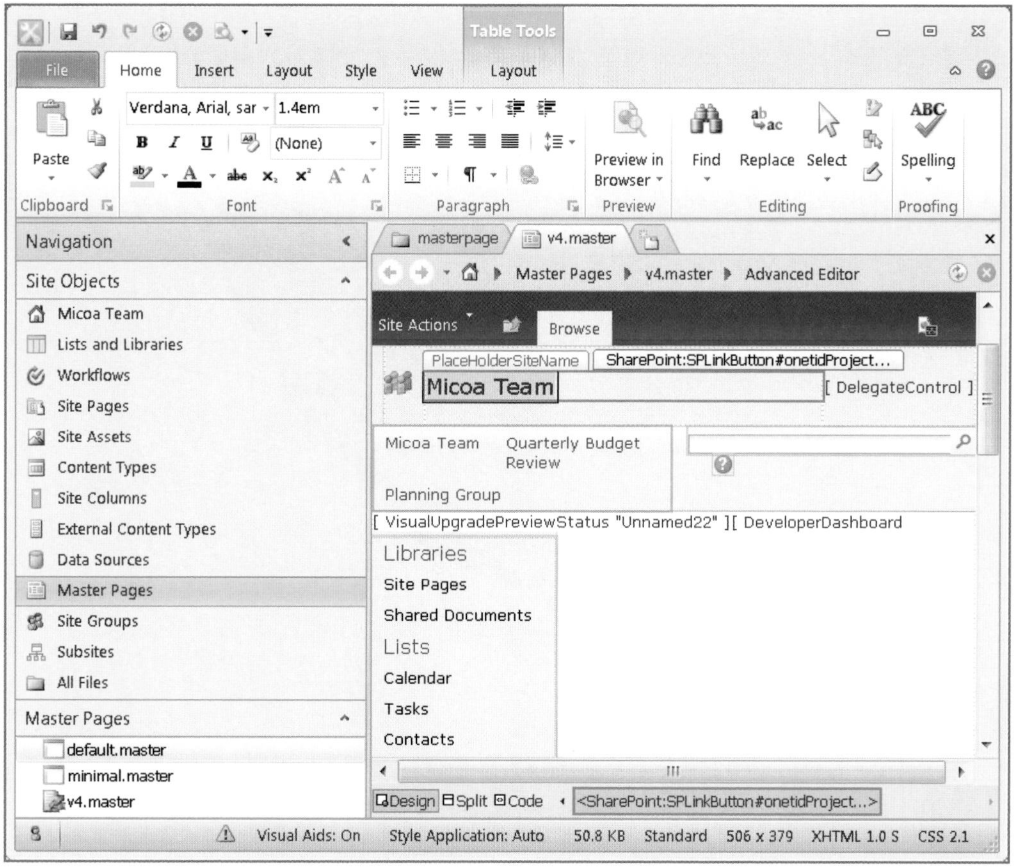

Figure 8-35: *The master page in a SharePoint site contains placeholders for various pieces of the page.*

extreme caution when editing them. Here are some tips to use should you decide to proceed:

- Try to accomplish the desired customizations via style sheet changes first before changing the site master pages. For example, instead of deleting the site logo in the master page, you could change the style for the site logo (titlelogo) to set display to "none." Therefore, the placeholder and code would still be in the master page, but no one would see the site logo because the style sheet tells it not to display.

- If you want to know what master page controls an existing page, open it in Code View in SharePoint Designer and search for code that contains "MasterPageFile=" such as "MasterPageFile="~masterurl/default. master"." This tells you that the master page you are looking for is called default.master.

- Never delete sections, especially if they contain placeholders. Move them or set them not to display in the style sheets, but don't delete them.

- It's a good idea to either create a new master page from an existing one and then apply it to test pages first, preview the test pages, and then if there are no problems deploy your custom master page to additional pages.

- Be sure to test how an edited master page works on downstream pages like the Web Analytics pages that are accessed via Site Settings. If you get an "Unexpected Error" message instead of the Web Analytics content, chances are that you have deleted a placeholder that the Web Analytics content requires.

Chapter 9
Working Offline with SharePoint Workspace

SharePoint Workspace is a separate Microsoft Office application that runs on your computer, not the server, and allows you to download and store on your computer a SharePoint site's content. This allows you to:

- **Access, view, edit, and search** SharePoint content while being offline, not connected to the SharePoint server, yet having available many of the SharePoint services and capabilities.

- **Automatically synchronize** the SharePoint content on your computer with the SharePoint content on the server the next time you connect with it. Changes made in your SharePoint workspace are replicated in the server, and changes made to the server files are replicated in your workspace.

- **Create shared workspaces** on your computer that you can use to collaborate with others, even if they do not have rights to your SharePoint site or even your corporate network.

- **Interact with SharePoint content** using the other Microsoft Office applications, including Outlook and InfoPath.

- **Work with SharePoint content** in an often faster, and possibly more comfortable, desktop environment.

- **Collaborate on files** that are too large to be uploaded to your SharePoint site.

TIP

SharePoint Workspace is available for use on a mobile phone running Office Mobile 2010. It lets you view and download SharePoint content while the phone is connected to your SharePoint server, then go offline, edit downloaded content, then go back online, synch with the server, save your changed content, and update the content you downloaded earlier.

NOTE

To use SharePoint Workspace, a SharePoint administrator must have enabled offline client availability in the SharePoint site collection.

In summary, SharePoint Workspace brings the capabilities of SharePoint to your desktop without having to be connected to a SharePoint server. SharePoint Workspace is most important to content creators who are responsible for generating and maintaining content, and who would find 24/7 access to their content beneficial.

SharePoint Workspace, previously called Microsoft Office Groove, is included in the Microsoft Office Professional Plus 2010 suite, and it can be purchased separately. In this chapter you'll see how to set up and use SharePoint Workspace to replicate much of what you do with SharePoint in a browser.

Initialize SharePoint Workspace

SharePoint Workspace is a stand-alone program that is part of the Microsoft Office suite. You need to establish how you want to start and run it, what you want to do with it, and the content you want to use.

Set Up SharePoint Workspace

There are two ways to create a SharePoint workspace. You can do it from the desktop by starting the SharePoint Workspace application, and you can do the same thing from your SharePoint site in the browser. Once started, you should consider how you want SharePoint Workspace configured so it will operate the way you want to work.

CREATE A SHAREPOINT WORKSPACE FROM THE DESKTOP

To start SharePoint Workspace from the desktop:

1. From Windows, open the **Start** menu, click **All Programs**, click **Microsoft Office**, and click **Microsoft SharePoint Workspace 2010**.

2. If this is the first time your computer has been used with SharePoint Workspace, you will be asked to establish a new account. Click **Create A New Account**, and click **Next**. If you weren't asked to create a new account, go to step 3. Type your user name and e-mail address, or your account configuration code and account configuration server, and click **Finish**.

3. The SharePoint Workspace Launchbar appears. Click **New**. A choice among two types of workspaces and a shared folder appear. See the "Comparing Workspaces" QuickFacts in this chapter.

4. Click **SharePoint Workspace** (we'll look at the other options later in this chapter) to open the New SharePoint Workspace dialog box. If requested, enter the URL for your SharePoint site and click **OK**.

5. In the Synch To SharePoint Workspace dialog box, click **Open Workspace**. The SharePoint Workspace window will open, as you can see in Figure 9-1.

CREATE A SHAREPOINT WORKSPACE FROM SHAREPOINT

You can decide that you want to work offline on SharePoint content using SharePoint Workspace from your browser.

1. With your SharePoint site open in your browser and displaying the site whose content you want to work with in SharePoint Workspace, click **Site Actions** and then click **Sync To SharePoint Workspace**.

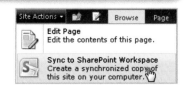

> **NOTE**
>
> Under certain circumstances, SharePoint Workspace may go ahead and automatically synchronize your desktop with the SharePoint server. In that case, you won't see the image shown in Figure 9-1. Instead you'll see your first list, Announcements in the example here, and the first item in the list will open.

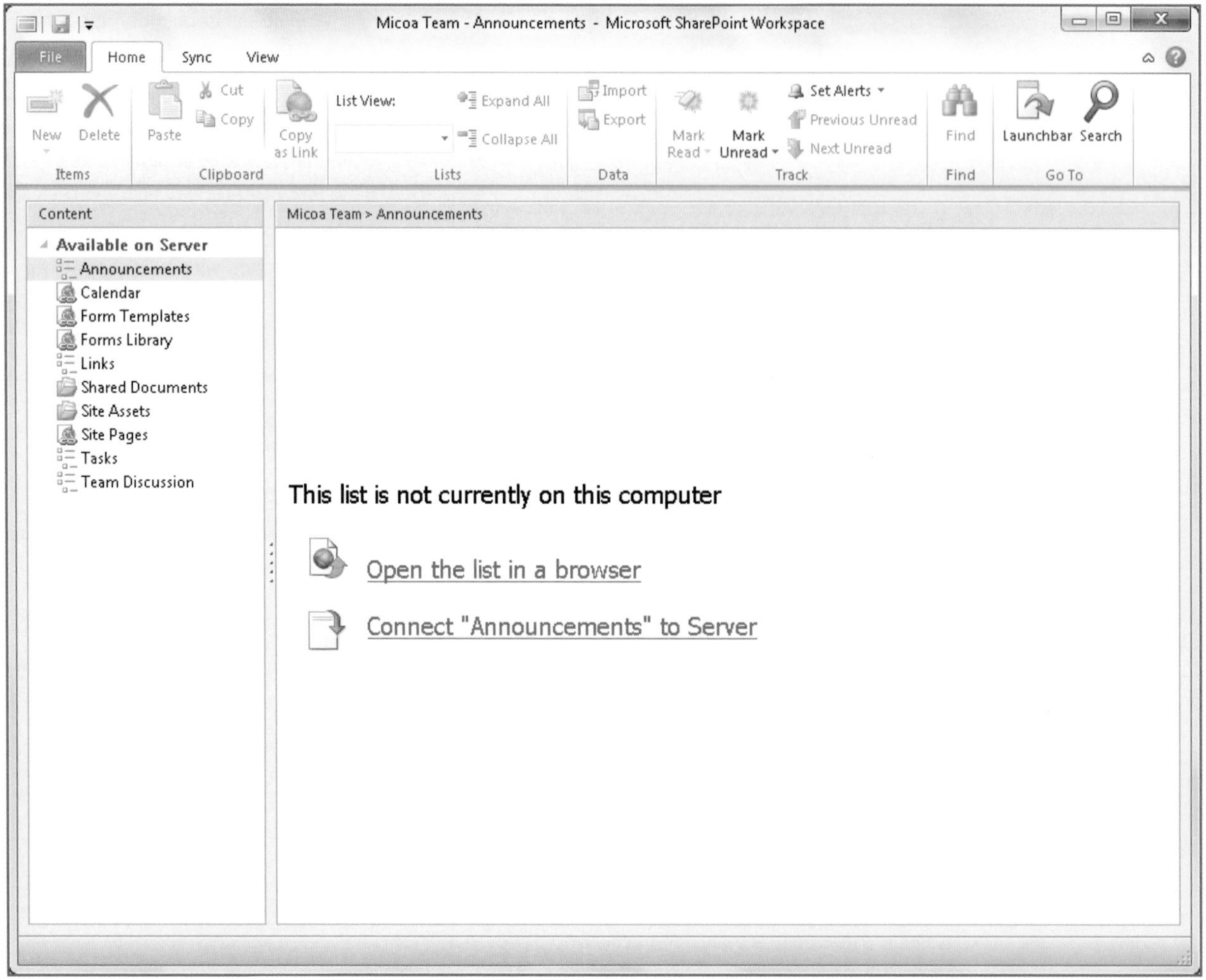

Figure 9-1: ***SharePoint Workspace brings files from your SharePoint server to your desktop and lets you work on them offline.***

NOTE

If you already synchronized your SharePoint site to your computer via SharePoint Workspace, the same workspace opens when you access it from the browser.

2. You may see a message saying that a website wants to launch Microsoft SharePoint Workspace. Click **Allow**. Alternatively or in addition, you may see a message asking if you want to synchronize your SharePoint site to your computer. Click **OK**.

   The SharePoint Workspace window will open, as you saw in Figure 9-1.

CONFIGURE SHAREPOINT WORKSPACE

Configuring SharePoint Workspace is similar to configuring other Office 2010 applications, and is done from the Backstage view.

1. With SharePoint Workspace open as you saw in Figure 9-1, click the **File** tab to open the Backstage view Info page shown in Figure 9-2 (if SharePoint Workspace automatically synchronized when you connected, you will have a Last Sync date and time and a different-looking thumbnail on the right).

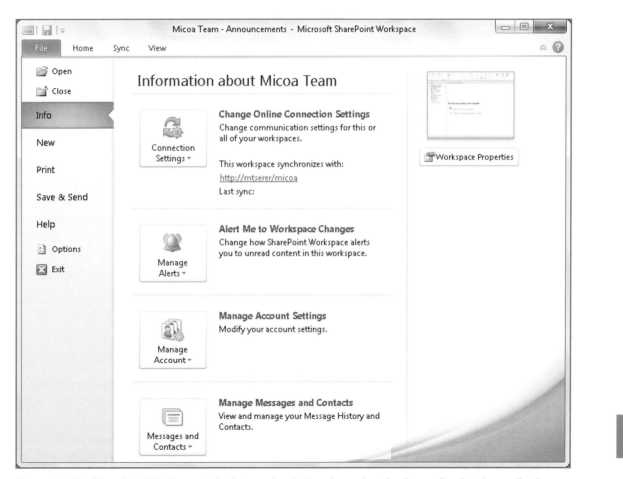

Figure 9-2: **The SharePoint Workspace's Backstage view is the primary location for configuring the application.**

2. Click **Connection Settings**. Here you can choose among the following actions:

> **Change Online Connection Settings**
> Change communication settings for this or all of your workspaces.
>
> Connection Settings ▾
>
> This workspace synchronizes with:
> ...icoa
> ...010 12:40 PM
>
> Pause Workspace
> Work Offline
> Communications Manager...

- **Pause Workspace** temporarily pauses the synchronization between SharePoint Workspace and the SharePoint server.

- **Work Offline** by disconnecting the connection between SharePoint Workspace and the SharePoint server.

- Open the **Communications Manager** to see the communications status of your workspaces and communication channels.

3. Click **Communications Manager** to open that dialog box. Here you can see the communications that are either in process or possible, pause or disconnect them, and review your network settings. When you are ready, click **OK**.

4. Click **File** again to return to the Backstage view, and then click **Manage Alerts**. You can click **Suppress Alerts** to prevent them from disturbing you, or you can click **Set Alerts** to set the level at which you will get an audio alert when there is unread content in a workspace. You can also choose and test the sound that will be used. When ready, click **OK**.

> **Alert Me to Workspace Changes**
> Change how SharePoint Workspace alerts you to unread content in this workspace.
>
> Manage Alerts ▾
>
> 🔔 Suppress Alerts
> 🔔 Set Alerts...

Communications Manager - Microsoft SharePoint Works...

Communicating ...   0 bytes   0 bytes

Activity	Status
☑ 📄 Instant Messages and Invitations	Idle
☑ ▢ Synchronizing Micoa Team	Idle

Work Offline   Pause All

Network Settings

OK

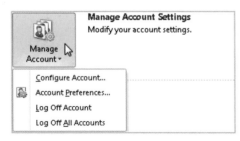

> **Manage Account Settings**
> Modify your account settings.
>
> Manage Account ▾
>
> Configure Account...
> 🔲 Account Preferences...
> Log Off Account
> Log Off All Accounts

5. Click **File** and click **Manage Account**. Click **Configure Account** to enter your account configuration code and account configuration server, if your organization uses them. Click **OK**.

6. Click **File** and click **Manage Account**. Click **Account Preferences** to review and possibly change a number of settings dealing with your account, security, alerts, options, and synchronization. When ready, click **OK**.

7. Click **File** and click **Manage Account**. Click **Log Off Account** or **Log Off All Accounts** to log off yourself or everybody connected to the current workspace and close the SharePoint Workspace application.

8. Click **File** and click **Messages And Contacts**. Click **Message History** to see a list of the messages you have sent and their content. Click **OK**.

9. Re-enter Backstage view, click **Messages And Contacts**, click **Message History**, and click **Contact Manager** to view a list of your contacts. Again, click **OK** when you are ready.

Initially Synchronize a SharePoint Workspace

When you initially create a workspace, you specify a SharePoint site that it is associated with and the SharePoint Workspace window displays the content of that site in the left column. Depending on whether the synchronization took place automatically, the content may still be only on the server and not exist yet in the workspace. To do that, you need to determine what content you want to work on and then bring that content down to your workspace and computer. This is the initial synchronization process. If synchronization took place automatically, you do not need to do the first four steps here.

1. In the SharePoint Workspace window in its initial state, as shown earlier in Figure 9-1, select one of the elements in the left column whose content you want to work with in SharePoint Workspace. It should be one of the lists, documents, or discussions, since some other content cannot be worked on in SharePoint Workspace (see the Note in this section).

2. Click **Connect "*content name*" To Server**. You'll see a message: "Initializing SharePoint Sync. This may take a few minutes." Then the element's content will appear in the right column.

QUICK**FACTS**

COMPARING WORKSPACES *(Continued)*

The major distinction between a SharePoint workspace and SharePoint in a browser is that a workspace is a single-user environment, allowing the user to access SharePoint content at any time from any place they have access to their computer, with or without connecting to the server.

USE GROOVE WORKSPACES

A Groove workspace is the construct of Microsoft Office Groove, the ancestor of SharePoint Workspace. Its primary purpose is to provide for collaboration on a collection of files that are not hosted on a SharePoint server. A Groove workspace does this using peer-to-peer networking, which can be accomplished when two or more computers are connected with a network and may or may not be online at the same time. Each computer serves as both a server and a client to the other computers in the network. Changes made on any computer are replicated on the other computers in real time, if the computers are connected. If the computers aren't connected, each computer is synchronized with the latest content when it is online again. Users must be given an invitation to join the collaboration, which provides good security.

With SharePoint Workspace 2010 you can use either Groove 2010 or Groove 2007. Groove 2007 workspaces are compatible with both Groove 2007 and SharePoint Workspace 2010. Groove 2010 workspaces are compatible with only SharePoint Workspace 2010.

A Groove workspace provides several tools for working with documents, calendars, discussions, and chatting. Also, the lists tool, when used with InfoPath, can create custom tools with a variety of input fields and layouts. A groove workspace should generally not be larger than 2GB to keep data transmission and synchronization manageable.

Continued . . .

3. Select the next element you want to work with, and repeat step 2.

4. When you have connected to all the elements that you want to access, select one of the elements. Its content will appear in the right column, as shown in Figure 9-3. Also you'll see a Welcome message saying you can double-click any document to open it.

Welcome to the SharePoint Workspace Documents Tool

You are now ready to download document contents to your workspace. Double-clicking on any document will download its contents.

OK

☐ Do not show this message again

5. Double-click a document to have it start its application and load, ready to work on, as you see in Figure 9-4.

6. When you are ready, close the document application, and return your focus to SharePoint Workspace.

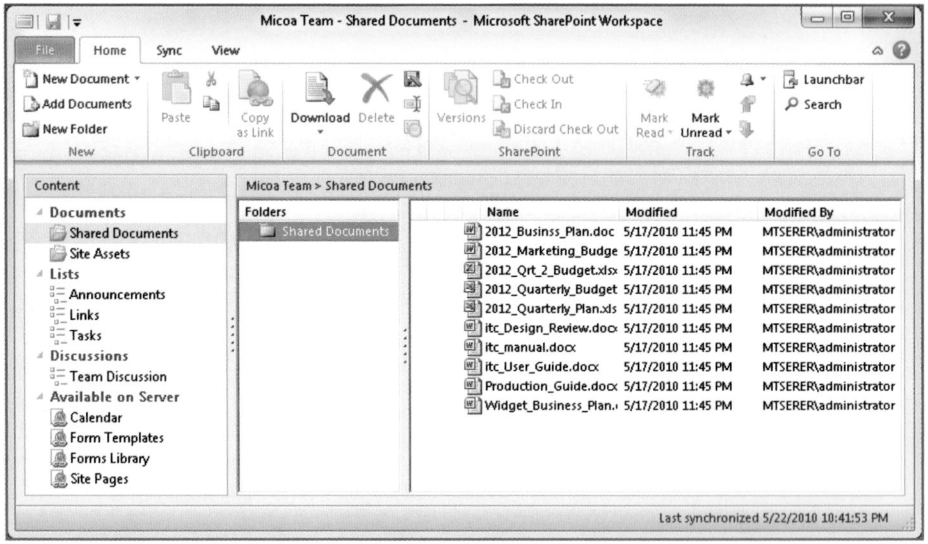

*Figure 9-3: **SharePoint Workspace displays your SharePoint content and lets you work with it.***

COMPARING WORKSPACES *(Continued)*

USE SHARED FOLDERS

A shared folder is a means of sharing content among a group of users using Groove peer-to-peer networking without needing to be online at the same time. It can, therefore, be considered a type of workspace that might also be useful to you if you use several computers. Like a Groove workspace, the shared folder requires users to have an invitation to share the workspace. It does not provide the tools that are available in a Groove workspace, but its content is synchronized with a SharePoint server when it is connected. Shared folders are a good way to synchronize only the files in a specific document library on a SharePoint site instead of synchronizing all files in a SharePoint site.

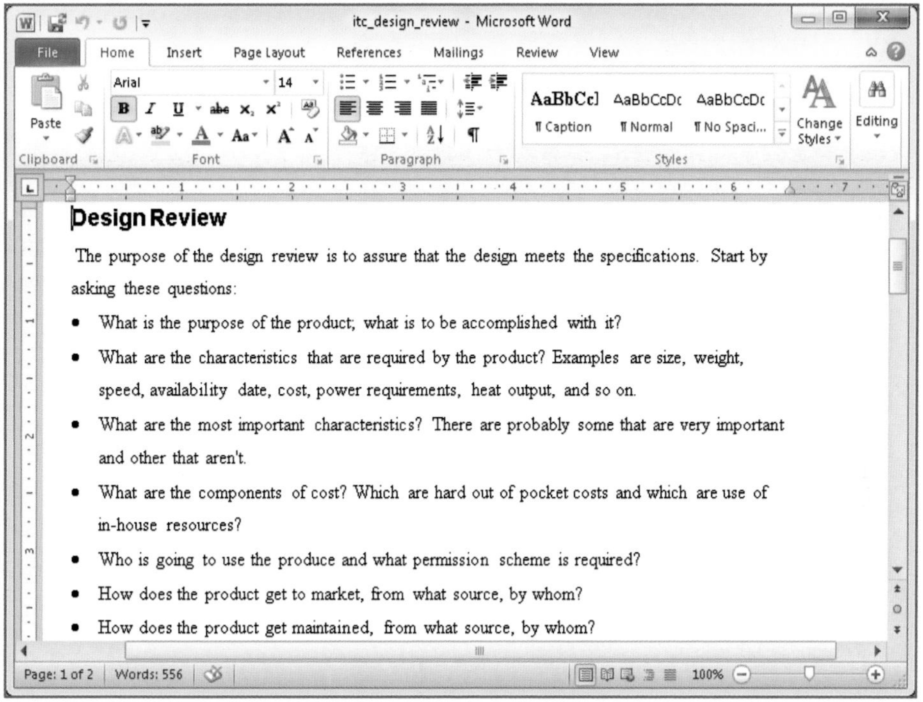

NOTE

Some types of SharePoint content cannot be worked on in SharePoint Workspace. This includes calendars, forms, site page lists, and meeting elements, such as agendas, attendee lists, and meeting objectives.

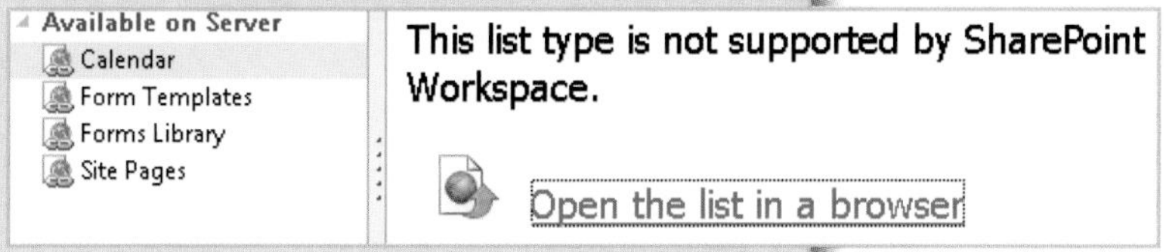

*Figure 9-4: **SharePoint Workspace opens the full applications, such as Word and Excel, and not the Web Apps, as SharePoint might.***

Use SharePoint Workspace

The intent of SharePoint Workspace is to replace SharePoint in a browser accessing files on a server, with an application running on your desktop, accessing files on your computer while not connected to the server. For many functions, SharePoint Workspace fulfils that objective, and for others it does not even try.

SYNCHRONIZING WITH SHAREPOINT WORKSPACE

After creating a new SharePoint workspace and downloading the SharePoint content you want to work with, changes to that content, both on your computer and on the server, are *synchronized* between the two computers. This is a two-way or bidirectional exchange such that the changes made to the SharePoint content in SharePoint Workspace on your computer are replicated in the SharePoint content on the SharePoint server, and changes made to the content on the SharePoint server are replicated in the content in your SharePoint workspace. To make this as efficient as possible, after the first download, only changes to the content are transferred. In Microsoft Office 2010 applications such as Word and Excel, the Save button in the Quick Launch toolbar changes in both look and function. A pair of circular arrows is added to the icon, and the button not only saves the file, but also updates it on the server.

When a SharePoint workspace is online, synchronization of all content takes place automatically, immediately for the changes you make in SharePoint Workspace and about every 10 minutes for changes made to the server. SharePoint Workspace tells you immediately when you go online if your content has been changed by telling you that you have unread content.

Besides the automatic capability, you can also do a manual synchronization at two levels:

- **To synchronize a single list or library**, click it in the Content pane on the left, open the **Sync** tab, click the **Sync** down arrow, and click **Sync Tool**. You'll see a message in the status bar on the progress of the synchronization.

Continued . . .

The SharePoint functions that SharePoint Workspace can do best include:

- Creating, editing, and updating the content in libraries and lists while either online or offline to a SharePoint server
- Sharing and collaboratively creating, editing, and updating the content in libraries and lists using a peer-to-peer network while either online or offline to a SharePoint server
- Providing a potentially faster, more familiar, and easier-to-use environment for working with SharePoint libraries and lists while either online or offline to a SharePoint server
- Maintaining synchronization with an online SharePoint site, keeping your SharePoint workspace up to date with the latest changes made on the server, and keeping the server up to date with the changes you have made in your SharePoint workspace

The SharePoint functions that SharePoint Workspace *cannot* handle include using:

- Calendar lists
- Site pages libraries
- Survey lists
- Form libraries
- Meeting lists and libraries

Save (Ctrl+S)

Save this document and refresh it with updates made by other authors.

❓ Press F1 for more help.

Documents	Folders	Name	Modified	Modified By
Shared Documents	Shared Documents	2012_Businss_Pla	5/17/2010 11:45	MTSERER\admini
Site Assets		2012_Marketing_	5/17/2010 11:45	MTSERER\admini
Lists		2012_Qrt_2_Budg	5/17/2010 11:45	MTSERER\admini
Announcements		2012_Quarterly_E	5/17/2010 11:45	MTSERER\admini
Links		2012_Quarterly_F	5/17/2010 11:45	MTSERER\admini
Tasks		itc_Design_Revie	5/17/2010 11:45	MTSERER\admini
Discussions		itc_manual.docx	5/17/2010 11:45	MTSERER\admini
Team Discussion		itc_User_Guide.d	5/17/2010 11:45	MTSERER\admini
Available on Server		Production_Guid	5/23/2010 5:10	MTSERER\admini
Calendar		This file is unread. Busines	5/17/2010 11:45	MTSERER\admini

To work with these functions, you must go online and use SharePoint in a browser.

Perform SharePoint Functions Offline

SharePoint Workspace gives you a number of ways to work with SharePoint content, both on- and offline. There are two windows in which to do this: the Launchbar and the full SharePoint Workspace window.

SYNCHRONIZING WITH SHAREPOINT WORKSPACE (Continued)

- **To synchronize all the content in a SharePoint workspace**, open the **Sync** tab, click the **Sync** down arrow, and click **Sync Workspace**.

You can change the synchronization settings in the Sync tab by clicking **Change Sync Settings**. If you are currently connected to the server, you will get an option to disconnect, which when selected gives you a warning asking if you really want to do that (when disconnected, the list or library is removed from the workspace but still available on the server and you simply have to reconnect to use it again). If you are currently disconnected, you get an option to reconnect.

USE THE LAUNCHBAR

Each site and subsite in SharePoint requires its own workspace in SharePoint Workspace. As a result, you can end up with a number of workspaces. The purpose of the Launchbar is to allow you to easily add, delete, and search workspaces, and navigate among them. For this reason, it opens when you initially start SharePoint Workspace, as you see in Figure 9-5, so you can select the workspace in which you want work.

1. Start SharePoint Workspace from your desktop, not from SharePoint in the browser. The Launchbar should open as shown in Figure 9-5.

2. **To add another workspace**, click **New**, click **SharePoint Workspace** (you'll learn how to use the other workspaces later in this chapter), type or paste the URL for the parent of the SharePoint site, and click **OK**. You'll see the site being synchronized to your workspace. When it is done, click **Close** to return to the Launchbar.

Figure 9-5: The Launchbar provides a "switching yard" for SharePoint workspaces.

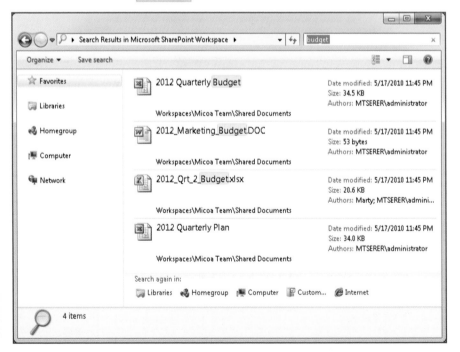

3. To delete a workspace, click the workspace to be deleted, and click **Delete** in the ribbon; or you can right-click the workspace, and click **Delete**. Note that you are only deleting the workspace from your computer and not affecting the site on the SharePoint server.

4. To search SharePoint Workspace, click **Search** in the Launchbar ribbon. A search window will open telling you it will be searching SharePoint Workspace. Type your search query in the search box in the upper-right corner (the magnifying glass). The results will appear in the same window, as you can see in Figure 9-6. Double-click an entry to open it. When you are done with the search, click **Close** in the window's upper-right corner.

5. To open a workspace, double-click it in the Launchbar. The full SharePoint Workspace window will open, as you saw in Figure 9-3 earlier in the chapter.

6. To return to the Launchbar, click **Launchbar** on the right of the ribbon. The Launchbar will appear, but the SharePoint Workspace window will stay on the screen.

NOTE

Any changes you make to the content of a SharePoint workspace, including additions, deletions, formatting, or other content changes, are replicated on the server SharePoint site, but if you delete the SharePoint workspace, it simply removes the workspace from the local computer and has no effect on the SharePoint server site.

NOTE

"Libraries" in SharePoint are called "Documents" in the SharePoint Workspace and in the Workspace window, the headings of "Documents," "Lists," and so on in the Content column are called "*tools*" in SharePoint Workspace.

Figure 9-6: SharePoint Workspace uses the standard Windows search to search its files.

WORK IN SHAREPOINT WORKSPACE

SharePoint Workspace lets you perform most of the functions you can perform on standard documents and lists with SharePoint in the browser, but do so offline on your own computer. These functions are either on the Home tab ribbon (see Figure 9-7) or in the context menu that is opened by right-clicking a document or list item. These differ depending on whether you have a library or

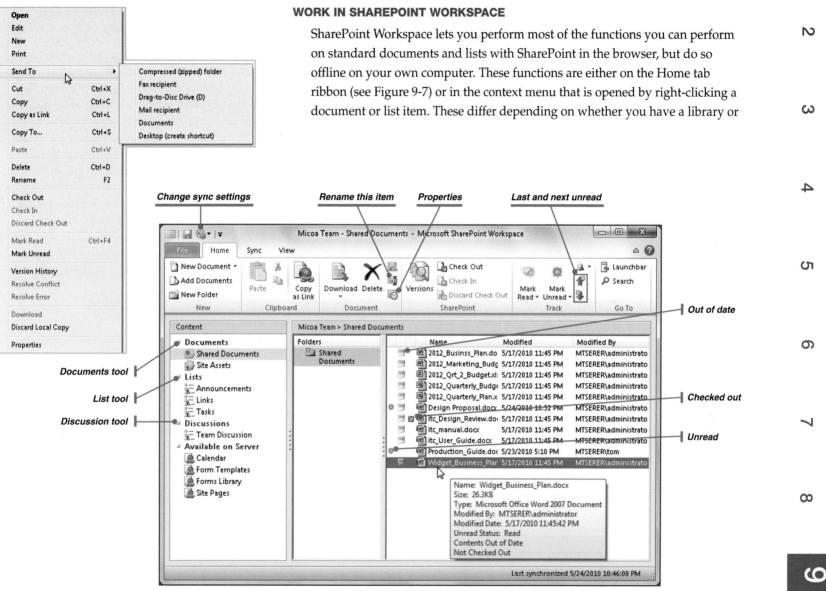

Figure 9-7: *SharePoint Workspace often provides more list and library features than are available in a browser.*

a list selected in the left column. For a document library, the functions that are available include:

- **New Document** opens Microsoft Word, allowing you to create a document. When you click **Save** or **Save As** and you are online, you will be taken automatically to your SharePoint workspace folder, where you can click **Save** to complete it (see Figure 9-8). If you are offline, you are taken to your personal Documents folder (for example, C:\Users\Marty\Documents, which is also shown as "My Documents" in the Navigation or left pane of Windows Explorer), where you can click **Save**. If you are online, you will see the new document appear in SharePoint Workspace's list of documents. If you are offline, you will not see the document in SharePoint Workspace, but if you click **Add Documents**, navigate to your Documents folder if needed, and double-click the document, it will be added to the document list in SharePoint Workspace and a "File Pending Upload" message will appear.

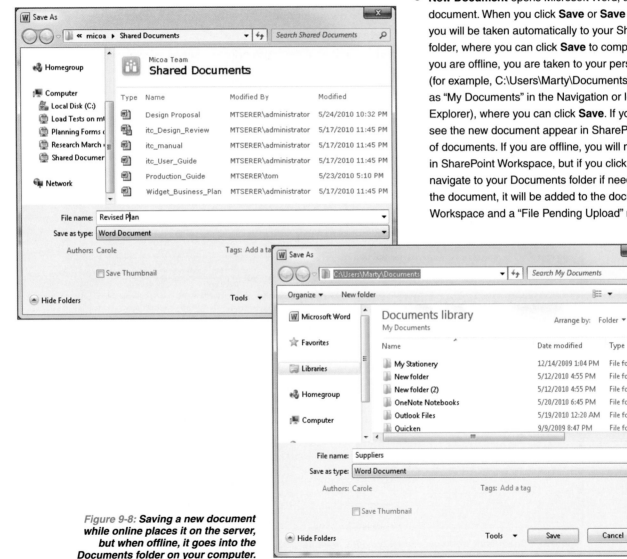

*Figure 9-8: **Saving a new document while online places it on the server, but when offline, it goes into the Documents folder on your computer.***

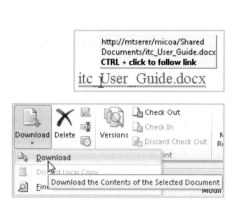

- **Add Documents** does that, as explained in the previous point. If you want to add several documents for a single folder, press and hold **CTRL** while selecting the documents you want; or select the first of a contiguous set of documents and press and hold **SHIFT** while clicking the last document.

- **Copy As Link** copies the document title with a link attached to it that points to the document on the SharePoint server. In this way you can add a link to a document or an e-mail message.

- **Download** requires you to be online, and allows you to download a document that hasn't been recently synchronized.

- **Delete** permanently removes a document from *both* your computer and the SharePoint server, although for the latter you must be connected to the server.

- **Save As** saves a separate copy of a document to your computer in any folder you would like.

- **Rename This Item** allows you to change the name of a document on *both* your computer and the SharePoint server, although for the latter you must be online.

- **Properties** and **Versions** display the respective dialog boxes, although for versions, you must be connected with the server.

- **Check Out** and **Check In** allows you, when online, to prevent others from editing a document while you have it. When you are done working on a document, you can check it in and thereby release your hold on it. You can also discard a checked-out copy to revert back to the copy that existed before it was checked out.

- **Mark Read** and **Mark Unread** allows you to change the read status of selected items or, by clicking the down arrow, change the read status of all items in the tool (for example "Documents" in Figure 9-8) or in the workspace.

- **Set Alerts** allows you to mark a tool or a workspace so you will be told about unread documents. You can set the level at which you are alerted from not displaying an alert to playing a selected sound.

- **Previous** and **Next Unread** lets you go directly from one unread message to another.

For lists, there are the following unique functions or actions:

- **New** opens a list form tailored to the type of list. Fill in the form, and click **Save & Close**.

- **List View** lets you select an existing view of the list.

- **Expand** or **Collapse All** applies to threaded lists with items nested within other items, and lets you see just the parent items (collapsed) or all items (expanded).

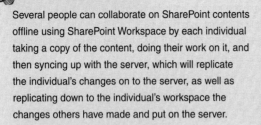

TIP

Several people can collaborate on SharePoint contents offline using SharePoint Workspace by each individual taking a copy of the content, doing their work on it, and then syncing up with the server, which will replicate the individual's changes on to the server, as well as replicating down to the individual's workspace the changes others have made and put on the server.

QUICKSTEPS

RESOLVING ERRORS

When SharePoint Workspace detects errors in a workspace, it lets you clearly know this, as you can see in Figure 9-9. To handle these errors:

1. Click the **Error Tools | Resolve** tab. What you see in the ribbon will depend on the error(s) that need to be resolved. In some circumstances, you'll get more information and guidance than in others. Review everything that is available.

2. When you are ready, click **Resolve Conflict Or Error**. What happens when you do that again depends on the error or conflict.

   - Under some circumstances, SharePoint Workspace will go about resolving the error on its own, and you need do nothing more.

   - In other circumstances, a dialog box will appear and ask for information. When you enter the information, SharePoint Workspace will fix the problem, and that will be all there is to it.

   - In yet other circumstances, a window will open, listing the errors and giving you an opportunity to fix them one by one.

Continued . . .

- **Import** or **Export** lets you save selected or all items in a list to an archive (Export), or bring back the items in an archive to an existing list (Import).

- **Find** searches for text you enter within a list.

Collaborate Using SharePoint Workspace

There are three ways to collaborate while using SharePoint Workspace:

- **With coauthoring** using SharePoint Workspace while online to the SharePoint server

- **With a Groove workspace** while online or offline to the SharePoint server, but with a peer-to-peer network connection

- **With a shared folder** while online or offline to the SharePoint server, but with a peer-to-peer network connection

Figure 9-9: SharePoint Workspace provides a lot of resources to resolve errors and conflicts.

UICKSTEPS

RESOLVING ERRORS *(Continued)*

3. Follow the instructions as they are presented to you. Once more, review all that is presented to you and then proceed. For example, here is a set of steps taken with a hypothetical error situation:

   a. Click **Actions** in the menu bar, and review the options. You might need to sign in or open the website, but look at the other options.

   b. The error is preventing uploading, so Upload All and Pause Upload are not viable options.

   c. Settings provide information about the operation of this window and don't help the situation.

   d. Click **Resolve** in the first error listed. The same menu as we saw under Actions appears. Click **Sign In** and do that. This resolves most of the problems. But on one we need to click Open. Word opens in Backstage view displaying the Info page and saying that this is an offline copy. Click **Convert To Server** and then click **Save**. That clears all of the errors.

4. When ready, close any remaining error-related dialog boxes and/or windows.

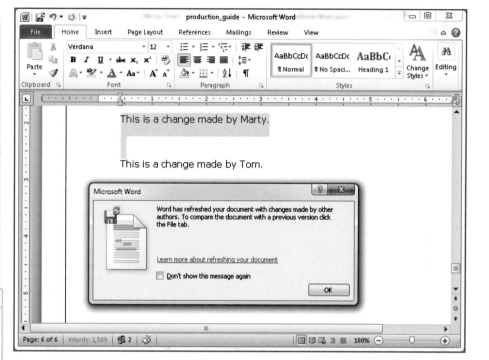

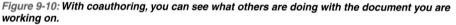

Figure 9-10: **With coauthoring, you can see what others are doing with the document you are working on.**

COLLABORATE WITH COAUTHORING

SharePoint Workspace provides for *coauthoring* in which several people can download and make changes to the same document at the same time. If the changes have been made offline, they will be merged into the content on the server with changes made by others. You are told that there are changes and they are highlighted (see Figure 9-10). If multiple people are online at the same time trying to make changes to the same document or list, the situation becomes more complex. This is handled as follows:

9

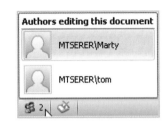

You are shown the other people online working on the document and what they are doing.

The second person to try to open the document sees a message that it is locked and therefore can be read-only, but they will be notified when the document is available.

When the second person eventually does open the document, they are told that they need to save it to see the changes the first person has made.

If two people try to change the same part of the same document, they are told that there is a conflict that needs to be resolved. Clicking **Resolve** opens a panel on the right in which you can accept or reject the change you made. You then need to save the document.

COLLABORATE USING GROOVE WORKSPACE

The Groove workspace is a carryover from the predecessor to SharePoint Workspace 2010, Microsoft Office Groove 2007. A Groove workspace provides online or offline, real-time collaboration with two or more people using a built-in peer-to-peer networking technology *without* the SharePoint server. This provides an obvious benefit in that you can now collaborate with people outside of your intranet by using peer-to-peer networking on the Internet (yes, it is reasonably secure, which is the best anybody can say about anything on the Internet).

NOTE

By default, Groove workspace is available for use in SharePoint Workspace, but there are options that an IT administrator can set that will prevent this. If you are having trouble using Groove workspace, see an IT administrator.

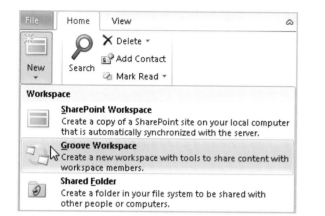

A Groove workspace provides a number of tools and benefits not found in a SharePoint workspace. Importantly these include working with calendars, meetings, and forms. People are invited to work in a Groove workspace, and once there, all online members instantly (more or less) see any changes or additions made in the workspace. Members can create, retrieve, edit, add to, organize, store, and delete content in the workspace. They also can "chat" and interact as if they were in a face-to-face meeting.

To create and use a Groove workspace:

1. Start SharePoint Workspace in one of the ways discussed earlier in the chapter. In the Launchbar that appears, click **New** and click **Groove Workspace**.

2. In the New Groove Workspace dialog box that appears, type a name for the new workspace, click the **Workspace Version** down arrow, and note that you have a choice between 2007 and 2010. Unless you need backward compatibility—for example, if a collaborator only has Groove 2007—it is recommended that you use 2010.

3. Click **Create**. A Groove workspace will appear in a SharePoint Workspace window, as shown in Figure 9-11. Notice two differences from the SharePoint Workspace windows shown earlier in this chapter: No SharePoint folders and files are displayed, and a list of members is shown in the lower-left area.

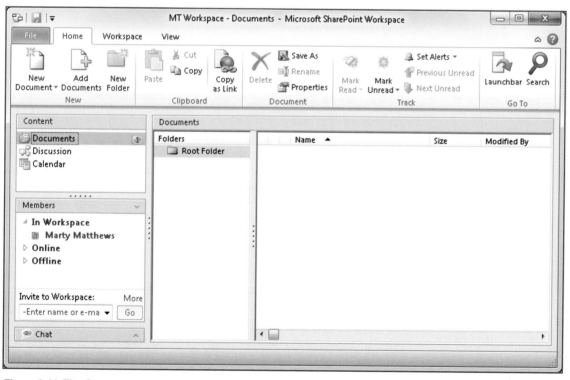

Figure 9-11: The Groove workspace provides for collaboration among invited members without the need to be connected to a server.

4. To add a new document, click that option in the Home tab ribbon. A list of all the documents that can be produced by the applications on your computer will appear.

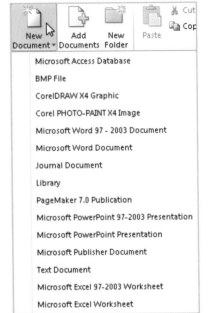

5. Click the one you want to use. Enter a name, click **OK**, and an entry will appear in the list of documents. To work on the document, double-click it. Its application will open so that you and others invited to the workspace can work on it. Save the document when you are done, and it will be sent to the other collaborators.

6. You can similarly add an existing document, including SharePoint documents, from your local computer and network (see the accompanying Tip).

7. To add other tools (Documents, Discussion, and Calendar are the default tools), right-click in the Content area, click **Add New Tool**, and click the tool you want to use.

8. To invite people to be a workspace member, click at the bottom of the Members area and enter a name, if it is in your Windows or Outlook contact list, or an e-mail address of the person you want to invite. Click **Go**. The Send Invitation dialog box will appear. Select the role of the invitee, enter a message if desired, and click **Invite**. The invitee must have SharePoint Workspace in order to participate, but the invitation contains an offer for downloading a free trial version of it. The invitation will open automatically when the invitee's SharePoint workspace loads, and the invitee can use a link in the message to join the Groove workspace.

9. When you have completed your work with the Groove workspace, you might want to send the members that are online a message that you are going to shut down by clicking the **Workspace** tab, clicking **Send Member Message**, typing your message, and clicking **Send**. Follow this by clicking **Cancel All Invitations**, confirming that you want to do that by clicking **Yes**. Finally, close SharePoint Workspace.

TIP

If you want to work on your SharePoint files in a Groove workspace, open SharePoint in your browser, and select and copy the address in the address bar. In the Groove workspace, click **Add Documents**, paste the address in the address bar, select the file you want, and click **Open**.

NOTE

The Lists tool can be used in conjunction with InfoPath to create forms to use in data collection and other purposes.

COLLABORATE USING SHARED FOLDERS

A shared folder is just that—a folder on your computer that has been shared—but in this case, you will use it loosely within SharePoint Workspace. You can create such a folder either in the SharePoint Workspace Launchbar or in Windows Explorer. Once created, it operates somewhat like a Groove workspace with some of the same tools. Most importantly, you can invite others to jointly store and work on files in the shared folder.

1. **To create a shared folder from SharePoint Workspace**, start SharePoint Workspace, in the Launchbar, click **New** and click **Shared Folder**. Enter a name for the folder, and click **Create**. Choose where you want to create the new folder, and click **OK**.

   –Or–

   To create a shared folder from Windows Explorer, open Windows Explorer, if desired, create a new folder, and right-click the folder you want to share. In the context menu that opens, click **Shared Folder Synchronization**, and then click **Start Synchronizing**. Click **Yes** to confirm that you want to synchronize.

Open
Open in new window

Share with ▸
Snagit ▸
Shared Folder Synchronization ▸ → Start synchronizing...
Restore previous versions → Learn more...

Scan for viruses

Include in library ▸
Adobe Drive CS4 ▸

Send to ▸

Cut
Copy

Create shortcut
Delete
Rename

Properties

Figure 9-12: *Shared folders can be used like any others while being shared with invited members across a network.*

2. In either case, the Windows Explorer will take on a new appearance, as you can see in Figure 9-12. Here you can invite people to use the shared folder and set other options as needed.

3. Use the shared folder as you would any other folder on your computer or the network. Create, store, and retrieve files with any application. Your collaborators will see the files in the folder just as you do and will be able to work on them just as you can.

SharePoint Workspace and the Groove workspace have many features and nuances that are outside of the scope of this book. It is strongly recommended that you explore these on your own by simply trying them out. You'll be surprised by what you find.

discussions (*Cont.*)
 handling, 149–152
 replying to, 48–50, 149
 settings, 150–152
 starting new topic, 50–51, 149
 threaded, 48, 50, 148, 149, 150
 using, 48–51
 views, 149–150
 vs. blogs, 149
Disposition Approval workflow, 11, 161
document libraries. *See also* libraries
 adding, 113–116
 considerations, 44, 217
 described, 117
 identifying, 212
 moving files between, 216
 templates, 117
Document library template, 117
document workspaces, 58
documents. *See also* items
 adding in Groove workspace, 262
 adding to folders, 257
 adding to libraries, 44
 alerts for, 136–137, 140–141, 257
 assigning workflows to, 162–165, 177
 checking in/out, 257
 copying, 216
 copying as links, 257
 creating in Word, 256
 deleting, 44, 257
 downloading, 257
 edit permission, 33
 editing, 45–46
 errors while saving, 187
 importing into sites, 215–216
 in libraries. *See* libraries
 marking as read, 257
 moving, 216

naming/renaming, 173, 257
navigating, 257
Office. *See* Office documents
offline use of, 252–258
opening in SharePoint, 32, 33
permissions, 33, 176, 177
precautions, 217
read status, 257
reviewing for approval, 11, 12, 161, 165–166
saving, 257
unread, 257
versions, 257
Documents tool, 255
Download function, 257

E

Edit Page button, 24, 25, 26
Edit page icon, 85
Editing Tools tabs, 25, 26
Editing View, 179
elements. *See also* items
 importing to sites, 215–216
 in layers, 29
 libraries/lists, 10
 navigating between, 209–211
 pages, 23–28
 in SharePoint, 10
 site hierarchy and, 29
e-mail, 190–196
 adding content via, 194–196
 attachments, 196
 receiving, 194–196
 sending forms, 201
 setting up, 190, 192–195
 in SharePoint, 190
e-mail alerts, 135–141. *See also* alerts
 for changed items, 193–194
 deleting, 141

described, 135
discussion notifications, 51, 149
for items/documents, 136–137, 140–141, 257
for lists/libraries, 136, 140–141, 196
managing, 140–141
multiple, 140–141
for searches, 137–140
setting up, 135–140, 192–194
types of, 135
errors
 resolving, 258–259
 "Unexpected Error" message, 240, 241
 while saving files, 187
events, 43, 188–190
Excel. *See also* Office
 collaborating with, 171–184
 Datasheet view, 98
 exporting to spreadsheets, 49
 PivotTables and, 170
 protected mode, 33
 tracking changes in, 181, 182–183
Excel spreadsheets, 49, 98, 170
Expand function, 257
Export function, 258
External list, 81
extranets, 14

F

favorites, 22, 192
files. *See* documents
Find function, 258
Firefox browser, 22. *See also* web browsers
folders
 adding documents to, 257
 shared, 249, 251, 258, 263–264
form libraries, 10, 117, 197–203
Form Library template, 117

forms, 196–203. *See also* InfoPath
    creating, 198–201
    e-mailing, 201
    filling out, 201–202
    libraries, 117
    merging information on, 203
    naming, 202
    new, 257
    previewing, 198, 199
    publishing, 200
    templates, 197, 198, 202, 203
Forms folder, 217
forums. *See* discussion boards

G

graphics. *See also* pictures
    importing into sites, 215–216
    including in discussions/blogs, 51
    libraries, 117
Groove workspaces, 249, 250, 258, 260–262, 263
Group Work Site template, 59, 73
groups. *See also* users
    adding groups to, 62, 64
    adding users to, 62, 64, 176, 208
    creating, 60, 63
    displaying members, 61
    modifying, 62
    permissions, 9, 60, 61–64, 104, 207
    removing, 62, 64
    removing users from, 62, 64
    security, 62
    settings, 62, 63–64
    specifying, 60–62
    types of, 61

H

Help icon, 24, 27
Home option, 26

Home page
    designating pages as, 22, 72
    navigating, 32–33
    overview, 23–28
horizontal navigation bar, 23–27, 32, 68–69, 70
HTML (HyperText Markup Language), 232–233, 235
HTML pages, 219
HyperText Markup Language. *See* HTML

I

Import function, 258
Import Spreadsheet list, 81
InfoPath, 196–203, 263. *See also* forms
InfoPath Designer, 196, 198, 201
information
    collaboration. *See* collaboration
    exchanging, 10
    managing, 12–13
    protecting, 8–9
    repository for, 4
    security, 13
    types of, 4
    validity of, 12, 96, 127, 202
inheritance, 9, 62, 63, 104, 176
Internet, 14
Internet Explorer, 2, 3, 21–22, 192. *See also* web
  browsers
intranets, 14
Issue Tracking list, 81
items. *See also* documents; elements
    alerts for, 136–137, 140–141
    assigning workflows to, 162–165
    deleting, 53
    importing/exporting, 258
    naming/renaming, 255
    permissions, 103
    read status, 257
    restoring, 53

L

Launchbar, 253–254
libraries, 109–134. *See also* document libraries
    adding multiple documents to, 123–124
    adding to pages, 113–116
    adding workflows to, 162–165, 176
    adding/deleting documents, 44
    alerts for, 136, 140–141, 196
    approvals, 130, 131
    basic, 113, 114
    columns, 127–129, 134
    connecting to from Outlook, 184–187
    considerations, 44, 110, 254
    creating, 117–118
    defining, 110–111
    deleting, 133
    described, 17, 44, 109
    elements, 10
    files in, 217
    form, 10, 117, 197–203
    importing into sites, 215–216
    layouts, 117, 118
    links, 123
    managing, 129–134
    modifying, 124–129
    modifying documents, 45–46, 123–124
    moving documents between, 216
    permissions, 133–134
    picture, 117
    preparing to add, 111–112
    purpose of, 110
    recent, 172
    report, 10
    saving documents to different location, 46
    saving Office documents to, 173
    sending e-mail to. *See* e-mail
    settings, 129–133
    slide, 117
    synchronizing, 252

searches
    for content, 32, 254, 258
    within lists, 258
    SharePoint Workspace, 254
security
    authentication, 8, 9, 61
    authorization, 9, 61
    information, 13
    passwords, 9, 22
    permissions. *See* permissions
security groups, 62
Server Foundation, 14
Set Alerts function, 257
shared folders, 249, 251, 258, 263–264
SharePoint
    authorization, 9, 61
    benefits of, 2, 12–13
    components, 13–20
    content in. *See* content
    elements in, 10
    exploring, 21–39
    features, 2–12
    Help, 24, 27
    layers, 13–14
    levels of changes, 4
    names connected with, 14
    opening documents in, 32, 33
    overview, 1–13
    starting Office documents in, 173–175
    using, 39–53
SharePoint Designer, 205–241
    adding site content, 215–216
    Advanced Mode, 212, 213, 216, 221–225
    customizing pages, 216–237
    getting started with, 208–216
    identifying authorized users, 206–208
    navigating between elements, 209–211
    opening pages in, 209–214
    overview, 205–208
    permissions, 207–208

Standard Mode, 212, 216
    starting, 209
    versions, 211
    views, 213–214
SharePoint elements. *See* elements
SharePoint Foundation, 15
SharePoint Home page. *See* Home page
SharePoint pages. *See* pages
SharePoint Server, 15, 196
SharePoint sites. *See* sites
SharePoint stack, 13–15
SharePoint suite of services, 13–14
SharePoint User Area, 14
SharePoint Workspace, 243–264. *See also* workspaces
    adding workflows to lists/libraries, 162–165
    Backstage view, 247, 248, 249, 259
    coauthoring, 258, 259–260
    collaborating via, 243, 258–264
    configuring, 247–249
    considerations, 244, 252
    creating new account, 244
    functions available in, 255–258
    Launchbar, 253–254
    offline functions, 252–258
    overview, 243–244
    resolving errors in, 258–259
    searching in, 254
    setting up, 244–249
    shared folders, 249, 251, 258, 263–264
    starting from browser, 245–246
    starting from desktop, 244–245
    synchronizing, 245, 246, 248, 249–253
    using, 251–264
    working offline, 243–264
SharePoint workspaces, 249–250
Site Actions menu, 24, 25, 85–86, 113
site administration, 65, 206
site assets library, 133
site groups, 207
Site Settings page, 59–69

sites. *See also* subsites
    accessing via URL, 21–22
    adding content to, 215–216
    adding to favorites, 22
    All Site Content, 28, 30, 51–52
    benefits of, 4
    blog, 10, 15, 141–147
    changing look of, 237–241
    creating, 58–59
    customizing. *See* customization
    description, 65
    elements in. *See* elements
    hierarchy, 29–32
    as information repository, 4
    location, 56
    navigating. *See* navigation
    opening in SharePoint Designer, 109
    overview, 15–16
    permissions. *See* permissions
    planning, 56–57
    searching for content in, 32, 254, 258
    style sheets, 238–240
    templates, 15–16, 22
    title, 65
    URLs for, 21–22, 109
    vs. websites, 2–3
    wiki, 27, 39
Slide Library templates, 117
slides, 117, 183–184, 185. *See also* PowerPoint
Split View, 213, 214
Standard page template, 111, 112
static lists, 11
style sheets, 238–240
subsite links, 24
subsites, 55–69. *See also* sites
    adding groups, 60–62
    adding users, 60–62
    collecting/analyzing statistics, 67, 68
    configuring, 59–69

considerations, 56
creating, 58–59
deleting, 66, 67
described, 55
location, 56
naming, 59
navigating to/from, 37–39
permissions, 56, 63–64
planning for, 56–57
resetting, 67
setting users/groups, 60–62
site hierarchy and, 31
templates, 56–60, 67
themes, 66
title/descriptions, 65
vs. pages, 56
Survey list, 81, 88–90
surveys, 152–158
analyzing, 49, 156–157
branching logic, 89, 154–155
creating, 153–155
described, 10, 46, 47, 152
managing, 157–158
opening, 47
responding to, 47–48, 155–156
results of, 48
settings, 153–158
using, 46–48
sync settings, 255

T

task lists, 35, 39, 41, 42, 162. *See also* tasks
tasks. *See also* task lists
adding, 39–40
changing, 41–42
deleting, 42
e-mail updates, 192, 195, 196
Tasks list, 35, 81

templates
blog, 141–142
calendars, 34
creating subsites, 58–59
forms, 197, 198, 202, 203
libraries, 110, 113–116, 117, 133
listed, 57, 117
lists, 16, 78, 79, 80–82, 85
pages, 70–71
provided by SharePoint, 52
sites, 15–16, 22
subsites, 56–60, 67
Web Part pages, 70, 71, 72, 111, 112
web parts, 70, 71
workflows, 11, 12, 163
Text Box list, 81
themes, 66
Things To Bring list, 81
threaded discussions, 48, 50, 148, 149, 150
threaded lists, 257
Three-State workflow, 11, 161, 162, 165
Title Bar Properties, 72
Top Link Bar, 65
Track Changes, 178, 180–184
Tree View, 65

U

"Unexpected Error" message, 240, 241
Uniform Resource Locators (URLs), 21–22, 109, 200, 209
unique, 176, 177
URLs (Uniform Resource Locators), 21–22, 109, 200, 209
user discussions. *See* discussions
User menu, 24, 25
user name, 9, 22
user surveys. *See* surveys

users. *See also* groups
adding to groups, 62, 64, 176, 208
adding to subsites, 60–62
authentication, 8, 61
permissions, 61, 63–64, 104, 176
removing from groups, 62, 64
setting, 60–62
SharePoint Designer, 206–208
workspace members, 262

V

validation, 12, 96, 127, 202
validation formulas, 202
versioning, 130, 131, 175, 176
Versions function, 257
views
discussion, 149–150
formats, 17–18
libraries, 125–127, 128
list, 93–99, 257
overview, 17–18
SharePoint Designer, 213–214
Visitors group, 61

W

Web Analytics, 67, 68
Web Apps, 173–174, 178–179
web browsers
Chrome, 22
considerations, 2
Firefox, 22
form completion, 201–202
Internet Explorer, 2, 3, 21–22, 192
navigating in, 31
starting SharePoint Workspace from, 245–246
support for, 22